A MARMAC GUIDE TO

FORT WORTH

· AND ·
ARLINGTON

A downtown view north on Main Street ends with the Tarrant County Courthouse, center. Take away the cars, Chase Texas Tower/City Center I building on your right, and the Renaissance Worthington Hotel, whose modernistic outline can be seen on the left, and you could be transported a hundred years back. Such is the ambiance of much of downtown. (Photo by Yves Gerem)

A MARMAC GUIDE TO

FORT WORTH

• AND •
ARLINGTON

By Yves Gerem

Assisted by Larisa Gerem

PELICAN PUBLISHING COMPANY
Gretna 2000

ISSN: 07368119
ISBN: 1-56554-429-3

To my sons Michael and Etienne, as well as my wife, Larisa

The Marmac Guidebook series was created by Marge McDonald of Atlanta, Georgia. As owner of a convention and sightseeing service in Atlanta for fourteen years, she learned from visitors and those relocating to Atlanta what information was important to them. She also served as president and CEO of the Georgia Hospitality and Travel Association for four years and in 1978 was named Woman of the Year in Travel by the Travel Industry Association of America.

Information in this guidebook is based on authoritative data available at the time of printing. Prices and hours of operation of businesses listed are subject to change without notice. Readers are asked to take this into account when consulting this guide.

Manufactured in Canada
Published by Pelican Publishing Company, Inc.
1000 Burmaster Street, Gretna, Louisiana 70053

CONTENTS

MAPS

KEY TO LETTER CODE

I	Inexpensive
M	Moderate
E	Expensive
CH	Entrance Charge
NCH	No Charge

FOREWORD

The Marmac guidebooks are designed for the resident and traveler who seek comprehensive information in an easy-to-use format and who have a zest for the best in each city and area mentioned in this national series.

We have chosen to include what we can recommend to you on the basis of our own research, experience, and judgment, as well as a few establishments (not necessarily the best) that are well-known locally or nationally.

We first escort you into the city, introducing you or reacquainting you as we relate the history and folklore that is indigenous to it. Next we assist you in *learning the ropes*—the essentials of the community, necessary matters of fact, transportation systems, lodging and restaurants, nightlife and theater. Then we point you toward various activities—sightseeing, museums and galleries, shopping, sports, and excursions into the heart of the city and its environs. And finally we salute the special needs of special people—the international traveler, senior citizens, the handicapped visitor, children, and students. New residents will discover a whole chapter of essential information just for them.

The Marmac guidebook can serve as your scout in a new territory among new people or as a new friend among local residents. You will find in this guide information that has not been gleaned from feel-good public relations tracts and is sometimes contrary to local myths.

While a few chapters, such as MATTERS OF FACT, LODGING, DINING, SIGHTS, VISUAL ARTS, and SHOPPING will be found in both Fort Worth and Arlington sections of this guide, please check the Fort Worth part if you don't see your subject listed in the Arlington section.

No fee or product was ever offered or accepted to include or name any establishment in this guide. Every effort was made not to be influenced in any way by anyone mentioned herein. Unless we felt that it would serve your interests, most inquiries were conducted anonymously in a manner most readers would do when seeking information.

Please write to us with your comments and suggestions at Pelican Publishing Company, P.O. Box 3110, Gretna, Louisiana 70054-3110. We will always be glad to hear from you.

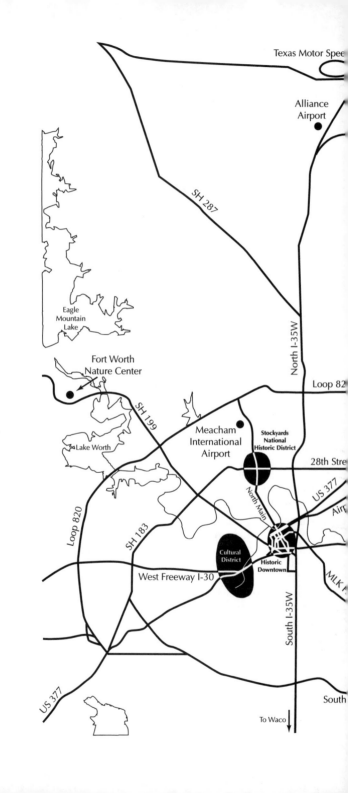

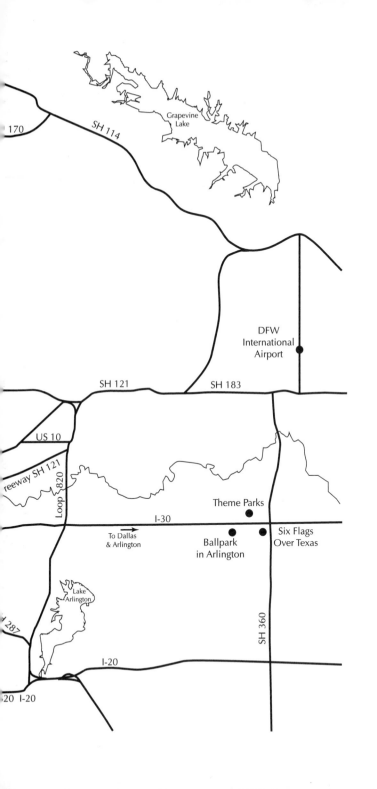

FORT WORTH PAST

Eager for settlers after winning its independence in 1836, the Congress of the Republic of Texas actually offered newcomers free land and to companies inducements to bring settlers to the new republic.

William Smalling Peters (d. 1866) of Louisville, Kentucky, organized Texas Emigration & Land Co., also known as the Peters Colony Co., in 1840 to speculate in Texas lands. Peters was an Englishman who arrived in Pittsburgh in 1820, but never became an American citizen. After he moved to Kentucky in 1829, he secured from the Congress the right to found a colony in north Texas. Although Peters himself never set foot in Texas, the Peters Company agreed to bring at least 300 families into this territory within three years. Each family that came received 640 acres of free land and each unmarried man was entitled to 320 acres, but they had to cultivate at least 15 acres for three years. In return, the Peters Company received an equal amount of land for its own use. The company sought settlers as far away as England, where it had its agents.

One of the first persons attracted by the Peters Company advertisements was **John Neely Bryan** (1810-1877), a young Tennessee lawyer of Scottish descent. Bryan lived for a while in Arkansas, where he traded with the Indians and learned their customs and language. During the summer of 1840, he made an exploring trip through north Texas, looking for a good place for a new trading post. The following year, he made a camp near today's downtown Dallas, on the east bank of the Trinity River. At that time, just a few other settlers were scattered in the area.

Six months earlier, on May 24, 1841, **Gen. Edward H. Tarrant** (1796-1858) headed a company of 69 Republic of Texas soldiers who expelled the last large group of Caddo Indians, about 1,000, living in the area. Tarrant's raid and burning of some 225 dwellings took place on Village Creek (then called Caddo Creek), which is now part of west Arlington. Tarrant's men killed a hundred Indians, mostly women and children unable to escape, as a warning against raids on the livestock owned by Anglo settlers. The sole casualty on the militia side was

11

Tarrant's aide, **Capt. John B. Denton** (1806-1841), an itinerant minister, lawyer, and part-time trooper for whom Denton County is named. A South Carolinian who served in the Battle of New Orleans with **Andrew Jackson** (1767-1845), the seventh president of the U.S., Tarrant died in Fort Belknap nearby.

In what was to become Dallas, Bryan was not well equipped for farming. His only plow was a forked tree branch, his harness for his Indian pony was made of strips of buffalo hide. Life was difficult then, but food was plentiful. Nacogdoches was the nearest town, more than 150 miles southeast, but there were no roads leading to the hamlet.

In 1846, the settlement of Dallas had only four families and two bachelors. Both housed in tiny log buildings, there was one store and the Dallas Tavern. The first hotel was still a year away. A trading post was established in 1845 at Cedar Springs, three miles north of Dallas.

Fort Worth was first settled on May 8, 1849, as an outpost along the Trinity River, but the river's flood sent the Second U.S. Dragoons to the top of the bluff in late July. **Maj. Ripley Allen Arnold** (1817-1853) founded this army post to protect settlers from attacks by Comanches and Kiowas. As to the exact location, the major relied on the advice from **Col. Middleton Tate Johnson** (1810-1866), who had already spent two years at Johnson Station, a fort-home three miles south of Arlington, where one hundred slaves tended his fields and ran his mills. The company camped at Cold Springs, near today's Tarrant County Courthouse, and on the following day, June 6, Major Arnold and Colonel Johnson selected the site for the future fort that happened to be on the property Johnson owned. In his correspondence at the time, Arnold asked that all his mail be forwarded to "Dallas, Dallas County, Texas, a town about 35 miles east of me."

The Fort Worth outpost was officially so named on November 14, 1849, after **Maj. Gen. William Jenkins Worth** (1794-1849), a commander of the Department of Texas and hero of the Mexican War. Worth never saw the fort or even knew it was named after him because he had died of cholera at San Antonio just a few weeks before. Arnold had served under Worth in the Florida and Mexico campaigns. In December, Tarrant County was created and named after General Tarrant. Although Army regulations forbade civilian businesses within a mile of the post, settlers were frequent visitors and the first store soon followed them.

In the summer of 1850, Arnold's wife and their four children arrived, bringing with them the first piano to Fort Worth. The Mississippi-born Arnold had graduated from West Point in 1838 and married the blue-eyed, brown-haired Catherine Bryant of Mississippi soon after. There was only one other woman living in the barracks at the time. Arnold's two younger children died shortly after their arrival at the post. In the fall of 1853, Arnold broke up an argument between the post surgeon and a drunken lieutenant at Fort Graham and had them arrested. Arnold and the surgeon engaged in a heated verbal exchange and drew pistols. The major missed twice and the surgeon shot him four times. His body was later reinterred in the southwestern part of Fort Worth's Pioneer's Rest Cemetery, in the 600 block of Samuels Street, near the graves of his children. General Tarrant is also buried here.

When soldiers abandoned the fort in September 1853 and pressed on westward to Fort Belknap, local settlers quickly moved into its empty but sturdy buildings and new settlers arrived. A competing merchant opened his store. By 1854, the settlement had its own school and two years later a post office. The school was started by **John Peter Smith** (1831-1901), a man knowledgeable in Greek and Latin who had walked most of the way from Kentucky to Fort Worth. The army stables were converted into Fort Worth's first hotel. A civilian physician arrived from Dallas to attend to a local resident and was so impressed that he stayed. A former lieutenant governor of Alabama built his plantation-style home nearby. The mail arrived on stagecoach operating between Dallas and Fort Belknap along the road that is still known as Belknap Street. Slave trade was booming and, according to one north Texas newspaper, black men were selling for up to $1,800 each, while black women fetched as much as $1,200.

In 1860, Fort Worth became the seat of Tarrant County, in part thanks to two barrels of free whiskey that swayed the vote four years before, when Fort Worth won over Birdville by seven votes. Nothing is left of the original fort on the bluffs overlooking the Trinity River, although it is known that it stood where the Old Tarrant County Courthouse, built of red granite in 1895, will be found today.

The abolitionist issue seemed to haunt everyone in 1860. "Two itinerant bricklayers from the North were found to be talking with Negroes in Tarrant County's small slave churches," writes Leonard Sanders in *How Fort Worth Became the Texasmost City*. Ned Purvis, himself a loyal slave, was forced to hide under a church floor during a meeting. He recounted that the two Yankees were advocating a slave uprising. "On September 13, 1860, (Anthony) Bewley and his companion, a Mr. Crawford, were hanged from Fort Worth's hanging tree." To warn other abolitionists, their bodies were left hanging until there was nothing left but their skeletons. **Abraham Lincoln** (1809-1865) was elected president two months later.

Secession carried Tarrant County by 27 votes out of 800 that were polled in 1861. Most Fort Worthians supported the Confederacy. As a result of the Civil War, Tarrant County's population dropped from about 6,000 to 1,000 and Fort Worth's to 250 settlers.

After the war, "Fort Worth, in essence, was a dry, dull, floundering frontier village—with neither a post office nor saloon—with no way to

go but up and no one to really show it the way," writes Caleb Pirtle in
Fort Worth: The Civilized West. But **Maj. K(hleber) M(iller) Van Zandt**
(1836-1930) changed all of that. "He rented a house and established a
mercantile store, even risked the shocking sum of $300 to purchase an
entire block of downtown Fort Worth." K. M. was the oldest son of
Isaac Van Zandt, congressman and Republic of Texas minister to the
United States.

Van Zandt, whose family came from Holland before the Revolution,
was born in Franklin County, Tennessee. He set out in a company of
four other young men for west Texas. As the distance they traveled
increased, the men accompanying him grew weary and lonely, as he
noted in his oral autobiography in 1929. "One by one they said, 'You
are going too far,' and they turned back. I rode on alone until I reached
Fort Worth, 180 miles from Marshall." Lincoln was shot four months
earlier.

He dictated to his daughter Alice that when he first saw Fort Worth
in the late afternoon in August 1865, he thought it was a sad and
gloomy picture. "The town had lost much of its former population due
to the War." With men, women, and children adding up to not more
than 250 people, "there were many more houses than there were people
to occupy them." Van Zandt, who remarried twice, was instrumental in
obtaining Fort Worth's first post office, cofounded the town's first newspaper, and led the effort that brought the first railroad to Fort Worth.

In the 1860s and 1870s, the Fort Worth settlers began trading with
the cowboys who drove cattle to markets in Kansas. It all started on a
large scale in the fall of 1865, when the Canadian-born **Capt. Ephraim
M. Daggett** drove a herd of cattle to Shreveport, where the longhorns
only brought six dollars a head above expenses. "With the market to
the east virtually closed," continues Sanders, "more than 200,000 Texas
longhorns were driven northward in 1866 in an effort to run the block-
ade imposed by Missouri against Texas fever, a tick-conveyed disease to
which Texas cattle were immune. Most of the traildrivers attempted to
go around Missouri by heading through eastern Kansas."

"The longhorn is the totem of Texas, its sacred beast, its quintes-
sential symbol," said a 1998 article in the *Dallas Morning News*. Thanks
to the longhorn, the cowboys who looked after them became this
nation's "most popular folk hero." The view the world has of Texas is
due to the longhorn. Some believe that no more than 4,000 longhorns
are left in the U.S. All of the other cattle breeds were created through
selective breeding. "The Texas longhorn is the result of natural selection and survival of the fittest."

In July 1867, "William [Buffalo Bill] Mathewson returned to Fort
Artbuckle [near today's Davis, Oklahoma] with two white youths he
had rescued from the Comanches," writes historian Sanders. "At the

fort he met a Texas traildriver who asked his advice on the best way to travel to Kansas with a herd of cattle." Buffalo Bill suggested the Chisholm Trail, so named after **Jesse Chisholm** (1806-1868), a half-breed Cherokee trader from Tennessee who drove his wagon and goods from Oklahoma to trading posts near Wichita, Kansas. Cattle drivers followed his wagon to Abilene and other Kansas towns and extended the route southward all the way to the Mexican border. In 1867, only 35,000 longhorns went to Kansas, notes author Pirtle. Two years later the number hit 350,000 and by 1871, 700,000 cattle were tramping the Kansas prairie, most driven by cowboys who feasted on Fort Worth beer and coffee. The lean times were over.

Early traildrivers were not impressed by Cowtown, which then was only a hamlet with a couple of stores and a blacksmith. But here was the last chance to buy provisions. Fort Worth was also the first town that these hardy men saw upon their return from Kansas, when they were just as desperate for a drink and a woman's company. Upon departure and on return they descended on saloons that never closed. One, Headlight Bar, encouraged patrons to ride and "get bar service in the saddle."

One local resident described the cowboy thus: "He enjoys a coarse, practical joke, or a smutty story; loves danger but abhors labor of the common kind; never tires of riding, never wants to walk, no matter how short the distance he desires to go. He would rather fight with pistols than pray; loves tobacco, liquor and women better than any other trinity. His life borders nearly upon that of an Indian." Many of the cowboys had been the sons of British businessmen, writes historian Pirtle. Others were outcasts, members of English nobility whose tainted deeds had stained their good British titles.

Pirtle observes that cowboys on the trail, generally, were young men, barely twenty years old and described by an older cattleman as "prematurely bowlegged, responsible, with a streak of hell in their hearts." By the time they were thirty, most were either broken or dead from too many long hours in the saddle. They worked from can till can't, from sun to sun, earning about thirty dollars a month and all the beans they could eat. When a cowboy rode alone, he carried between the folds of his yellow slicker a frying pan, some bacon, salt, coffee, flour, and a bottle of sourdough. "The cowboy firmly believed that God made some man large and some men small but that Colonel Colt, with his .45, made them all equal," adds Pirtle.

By the time the 1884 season came to an end, the Chisholm Trail was practically closed, according to Sanders. Established communities had moved the necessary open range for trail herds too far to the west. "Many ranchers were beginning to breed cattle that carried more beef, but they were not as well structured for walking as the longhorns. Ranchers were turning to rail shipments."

Between 1865 and 1868, the population of Fort Worth doubled and grew to 1,500 by 1872, when word spread that the railroad was coming to town. Already then, a Philadelphia writer noted that "the hotel accommodations at Fort Worth need to be greatly enlarged, but there are comfortable private dwellings, and the citizens are kind, courteous, and hospitable."

Dallas, which boasted a population of nearly 3,000, welcomed the first wood-burning locomotive by Houston & Texas Central Railway. It steamed into Dallas after a 15-hour voyage from Houston.

In 1872, president of the Texas & Pacific Railroad, Texas governor J. W. Throckmorton, and several capitalists from the East studied the suitability of Fort Worth as a rail stop. The railroad president told the city fathers bluntly that to have the tracks go through Cowtown, he wanted 320 acres of land south of town. Maj. K. M. Van Zandt, Col. T. J. Jennings, and Capt. Ephraim M. Daggett agreed to make it available within a few hours. The business in Fort Worth took off; it even included a photographer's atelier and an ice cream parlor.

Among the newly-arrived was also **Capt. Buckley B. Paddock** (1844-1922), a former scout for the Confederacy and editor of Fort Worth's first civic-minded newspaper. Born in Cleveland, Ohio, he studied law and was admitted to the Mississippi Bar, where he practiced until he moved to Texas in 1873. Paddock was mayor of Fort Worth from 1892 to 1900. It was he who originated the idea of the Tarantula Map, a drawing of Fort Worth as the center of future railroads leading off in several directions. The map was a promotional tool to attract other railroads.

In 1873, when Fort Worth measured 2,688 acres, **Dr. William P. Burts** (1827-1895) was elected as the first mayor. Born in Washington County, Tennessee, he completed medical school in Geneva, New York, and came to Fort Worth in 1858. And just when the town began sprouting feathers of self-confidence, a terrible financial panic and depression hit the country that fall. During the next four years, 18,000 businesses failed and a majority of the nation's railroads went into bankruptcy. By the end of 1873, the cattle markets in Kansas vanished. Railroad construction stopped thirty miles from Fort Worth, at Eagle Ford, as it did nationwide. "The decimation of Fort Worth left here about 1,000 people," wrote Paddock.

Major Van Zandt and several other civic leaders met with Texas & Pacific Railroad officials in Marshall and they agreed to continue building the railroad if the town would grade the bed for the rail line. Dallas and other towns were amused by the communal spirit and awaited a failure. Meanwhile, the Tarrant County Courthouse burned in March of 1876, resulting in "total destruction of the county records." By July of that year, "the residents of Fort Worth worked around the clock to bring the railroad the last few miles." The men had no time to build a proper trestle, so they just stacked up enough lumber and cross ties to span Sycamore Creek and kept going. Just before reaching the town, they dispensed with a roadbed and laid the tracks on a dirt road, weighing down the rails with rocks.

At 11:23 in the morning on July 19, 1876, the first train arrived in Cowtown. Amid celebrations, writes Leonard Sanders, "Some of the speakers were so carried away by the excitement that they made predictions that Fort Worth some day would have a population of 5,000 or more." From now on the cattle would be transported to Kansas without having to undertake a three-month trek north. By 1882, Fort Worth had direct rail connections to the north, south, east, and west. Thanks to the railroad, **Pres. Theodore Roosevelt** (1858-1919) visited Fort Worth in 1905, when 20,000 greeted him at the Texas & Pacific station downtown. Cattlemen **Burk Burnett** (1849-1922) and **William Tom Waggoner** (1852-1934) took him on a wolf hunt in Oklahoma Territory. Evans Hall opera house opened soon after the arrival of the railroad, with the Adah Richmond English Opera Troupe presenting an opera with forty singers and an orchestra a couple of years later.

By January 1877, more than a thousand persons lived in tents around Fort Worth. Tens of thousands heads of cattle awaited shipment north over the newly-built railroad. The charred Courthouse was torn down to make place for "a new and splendid edifice." Streetcars already served the length of Main Street and by the next spring there were gas lamps all over downtown. The 95-room Hotel Mansion opened in 1876 and was followed by the El Paso. One hotel claimed to have started a heretofore unheard of innovation—female waiters. The First National Bank was incorporated in 1877 and opened with $72,000 worth of deposits.

The Missouri-Kansas-Texas, the town's second railroad, came in mid-1880, followed by the Santa Fe Railroad a year and a half later; by 1900, nine railroads operated through Cowtown. Fort Worth became the railhead and passenger center for west Texas. Cowtown's population grew to 6,666 by 1880. By comparison, New York City's population exceeded one million and by 1882, when billiard parlors, tennis, electricity, and trolley cars were introduced, Dallas was the largest city in Texas.

Dr. Julian Feild, whose father had built the first gristmill, then served as the town's first postmaster; he had a telephone installed and claimed the number 1 as his own. Before the year 1882 was out, three dozen other subscribers also paid for the new contraption. *The New York Chronicle* noted, "The city is cosmopolitan. It has the rush and energy of a frontier town with strange contrasts of nationality. It smacks of Mexico and New York. Broadway and ranch brush against one another."

Following an outbreak of typhoid fever in 1881, and an epidemic of smallpox the following year, Fort Worth completed its first water system in 1883. That year, the first fire station also opened on Main Street at Eleventh. Fort Worth Opera House at Third and what is today Commerce Street also opened in 1883 and evolved into Greenwall's Opera House in 1900. Within five years, *The Merchant of Venice* and *Hamlet* were staged in Cowtown.

Over the years, gambling halls and saloons sprouted around the downtown intersection of Twelfth Street and Rusk (named for Gen. Thomas J. Rusk, hero of the Texas Revolution; renamed Commerce Street in 1917) to service the cowboys, buffalo hunters, and railroad men all in search of liquor, gambling, and women. Located roughly where the Fort Worth Convention Center stands today, it became known as Hell's Half Acre, "Fort Worth's marvelous shopping mall of sin." When the city council passed a series of ordinances against gambling and prostitution, the merchants felt the effects in their cash registers, so the regulations were suspended; bars, dance halls, and shooting galleries kept their doors open night and day. Drunken revelers raced "the length of the streets, emptying their pistols," annoyed respectable women, and picked fights with anyone in their way.

"The town's answer to this delicate problem was the 1876 election of Marshal Timothy Isaiah 'Long Hair Jim' Courtright, who was to have a long, stormy career as Fort Worth's most famous gunman," writes historian Leonard Sanders. Coming from an Illinois family that knew Abraham Lincoln, **Marshal Timothy Isaiah "Long Hair Jim" Courtright** served as a personal scout for the Civil War general **John Alexander Logan** (1826-1886). After the war, he was an Army scout for the Indian Wars with **"Wild Bill" Hickock** (1837-1876). He married an Arkansas girl somewhere around 1870 and they performed a shooting act with Wild West shows. When the couple came to Fort Worth, Betty Courtright, a crack shot, ran a shooting gallery in the 300 block of Main Street. Long Hair Jim, a six-foot-tall addicted gambler, was so popular in town that he occupied a house on Calhoun Street, between First and Weatherford. "Most merchants felt he should keep blood from flowing but not the liquor. He was urged not to arrest drunks until they spent all their money."

More than 120 years later, during the unveiling of the Visitors Center in the cultural district, the convention and visitors bureau chairman echoed a similar refrain when the *Fort Worth Star-Telegram* quoted him saying, "In Fort Worth, we've never met a visitor we didn't like as long as he or she spends some money here." The out-of-town visitors now spend more than $300 million in the city.

Marshal Courtright, disgusted by such politics, resigned and left to clean up a mining town in the New Mexico Territory. There, several killings were attributed to him. He was indicted for murder, escaped from jail, and eventually returned to Fort Worth, where he was appointed deputy marshal. He carried a $2,000 price on his head. In October 1884, he was arrested for a New Mexico murder but escaped and left for New York, Toronto, and Washington Territory. Two years later, Courtright returned to New Mexico and was acquitted on all charges. He came back to Cowtown and operated a detective agency until his fateful meeting with gambler Luke Short, on February 8, 1887. (For details of that incident, please see Jim Courtright-Luke Short Annual Shootout in the SIGHTS chapter.)

Meanwhile, the village of Arlington boomed after the railroad arrived and, by the 1890s, had its own college and a bank.

By the turn of the century, Hell's Half Acre grew from Thirteenth to Seventeenth streets, from Main to Jones, but was centered mostly along today's Commerce Street. It was here that **Butch Cassidy** could be often seen. Born as George Leroy Parker in Utah in 1866, he came under the influence of outlaw Mike Cassidy, who taught him how to handle guns. When George Parker left his father's ranch, he began calling himself George Cassidy and still later took the nickname Butch. While in Colorado, Butch Cassidy began robbing trains and banks and in 1894 was sentenced to five years in the Wyoming State Penitentiary for stealing thirty horses. Pardoned the following year by the governor, he left Wyoming and assembled a gang of outlaws, which became known as the Wild Bunch and in 1898 moved to Fannie Porter's house in Fort Worth's Hell's Half Acre. One of the gang was Harry Longbaugh, known as the **Sundance Kid,** after whom the central Fort Worth's Sundance Square was named.

During the winter of 1900-1901, a girl known as **Etta Place** came to work at Fannie Porter's and fell in love with the Sundance Kid. The Wild Bunch grew uneasy because it was being pursued by the renowned Pinkerton Detective Agency, which had been hired by the Union Pacific Railroad to put an end to their train robberies. Cassidy, the Sundance Kid, and Place took the train to New York, where Cassidy was to see the couple off for South America. He decided on his last robbery with the Wild Bunch, which took place in Wagner, Montana, on July 3, 1901. The gang attacked a Great Northern train that carried nonnegotiable currency from the U.S. Treasury. Since most of the notes were unsigned, the girls at Fannie Porter's helped with the signatures. A Dallas bank teller uncovered one of the notes and called Pinkerton; but it was too late because Butch Cassidy had already left for South America. Cassidy, the Sundance Kid, and Etta Place lived in Argentina for almost five years before Pinkerton's agency started tracking them down. After the Sundance Kid and Etta returned to the U.S. so that Etta could have surgery in Denver, her husband fled to South America and rejoined Cassidy. In 1911, the pair robbed a mule train in Bolivia and escaped with the payroll and a branded mule that was quickly recognized. Surrounded by the Bolivian cavalry, the Sundance Kid supposedly bled to death during the night and Cassidy killed himself with his last bullet before dawn.

The electric streetcar lines began operating in 1889 and changed the dating habits of Fort Worth men who would henceforth accompany ladies on streetcar rides on weekends. To provide entertainment in the spring, "when there were no places of amusement anywhere in the country," editor B. B. Paddock initiated the idea of a Fort Worth Spring Palace. "It was easily the most beautiful structure ever erected on earth," was Paddock's modest appraisal of the 225-by-375-foot structure, which was blanketed with Texas products. The $100,000 building, with a dome 150 feet in diameter, was supposedly surpassed in size only by the nation's Capitol. The governor of Nebraska opened the Spring Palace in May 1889. A year later, while 7,000 were in the building for a dress ball, the building burned to the ground in eleven minutes. **Al Hayne,** an engineer from Scotland who rescued several women and children, was the only casualty. (See Hayne Memorial entry in the SIGHTS chapter for more details.)

Starting in 1892, Mrs. D. B. Keeler formed a local public library association. The women worked six years to raise $12,000 toward a new library. When collection stalled, Mrs. Keeler wrote to the steel magnate **Andrew Carnegie** (1835-1919) and asked him to contribute the equivalent of "what a good cigar would cost." Carnegie responded with $50,000 and the library was built downtown in 1901, when Cowtown had 26,000 residents.

In 1896, writes historian Pirtle, rancher Charles McFarland stopped stockyard official Charles French and made a simple suggestion: "A show of fine stock sure would do a lot to develop our livestock industry," he said. French agreed. A year later, cattlemen staged their first livestock exposition in Fort Worth. Four exhibitors showed up. In 1906, according to Pirtle, the exposition left the oak trees (of Marine Creek) and moved up to the stock pens. Management decided folks should pay admission to see those blue-ribbon winners, and they did. Cattle was again king in the Cowtown economy.

"Efforts were made as early as 1876 to pack meat in Fort Worth and ship it by rail to Eastern markets," writes historian Sanders. Unfortunately, the methods used at that time weren't adequate enough for the meat to arrive in satisfactory condition. "But by the late 1880's, Fort Worth civic leaders knew that a major industry was needed to replace the dwindling income from trail herds." In 1902, Swift and Armour built plants that by 1909 processed 1.2 million cattle and

870,000 hogs annually. The city's population shot from 26,688 in 1900 to 73,312 in 1910.

The first cars arrived in Fort Worth in 1903 and soon became a nuisance that had to be regulated; the following year, the city council required their registration and the speed limit was set at ten miles per hour. In August of that year, one Colonel Peterson, who drove a $2,600 car, set the speed record between Fort Worth and Dallas, making the 33-mile distance in one hour and a half—the time it can take you today if the traffic conditions conspire against you. What is believed to have been the most devastating fire in Cowtown's history took place in the spring of 1909, when it burned 17 square blocks and destroyed more than 280 buildings around Main and Lancaster streets. It was started by children playing with matches.

After oil was discovered on the Stringer Ranch near Electra, Texas, "Farmers, in debt for breakfast, were millionaires by dinner time." Fort Worth's population went through the roof and grew to 106,472 in 1920, helped in no small measure by an expanding aviation industry.

In 1917, an Army commission came to Fort Worth to consider sites for a large training camp and settled on an area in Arlington Heights, on the city's west side—Camp Bowie—which was to house 35,000 men. More than 100,000 men in all trained at Camp Bowie, although some fell ill from a measles epidemic and then a few months later from Spanish influenza. Hell's Half Acre was in business again.

The 2,000-acre Camp Bowie was bounded by University Drive on the east, Lake Como on the west, West Vickery Boulevard on the south and White Settlement Road on the north. The popular roadway that today slices through the northern portion of the former camp and is known as Camp Bowie Boulevard starts at the intersection of University Boulevard, Bailey Avenue, and Seventh Street—near the Amon Carter Museum—and ends at the Weatherford traffic circle at Alta Mere Drive, or State Highway 183. A 2.25-mile brick section of Camp Bowie—stretching from Boland to Prevost streets—was first laid in the 1920s and current residents of west Fort Worth made it plain they want the bricks to remain.

Around 1921, the Fort Worth civic booster **Amon Carter** (1879-1955), publisher of the *Fort Worth Star-Telegram*, began tinkering with the novelty called radio. Carter was the kind of fellow who would start his speeches by shouting, "Texas forever!" A friend told him that radio was destined to kill off newspapers so Carter, according to witnesses, said to his circulation manager, "If this radio thing is going to be a menace to newspapers, maybe we'd better own the menace." The manager invested in a homemade rig and the Star-Telegram was on the air, although the reception was poor and transmission supposedly illegal.

Then commerce secretary, **Herbert Hoover** (1874-1964), who was later the thirty-first president of the U.S., licensed the station with the call letters WBAP, meaning We Bring A Program, and it began its transmission on May 2, 1922. Cattleman W. T. Waggoner lived two miles away and heard the signal loud and clear. Five years later—when Charles Lindbergh flew into town—Fort Worth Airport was dedicated as Meacham Field, named after the former mayor, and by 1962 it became one of the busiest executive airports in the nation.

The times were booming and Fort Worth, like the rest of the nation, thought it would last forever. "When the W.I. Cook Memorial Hospital was completed in 1929," writes historian Pirtle, "its reception room dazzled with travertine marble walls from Italy inlaid with 18-carat gold." It took the stock market crash of October 1929 to convince the town to the contrary, while unemployment in the industrialized world quadrupled to 21 million in the next six months.

But the Cowtown czar Amon Carter would not acknowledge the coming depression. In a front page editorial in his daily he said the Great Depression was nothing more than a "ridiculous spectacle brought on by idle gossip, unfounded rumors, and a state of hysteria." Some townspeople must have been skeptical, for more than a thousand mobbed Fort Worth's First National Bank, the city's second-largest (with deposits of $24 million and only one million on hand) on the morning of February 18, 1930. Were it not for the assurances from the ailing Carter, who "crawled out of a sick bed," it surely would have gone belly up, like Fort Worth's Texas National Bank, which had failed two weeks earlier. By 6:30 in the evening, the mob calmed down and chomped on free sandwiches and hot dogs that Carter provided.

Within the next two months, the 93-year-old civic leader, banker, and "extremely devout" K. M. Van Zandt died. On the day of his funeral, schools, businesses, and city and county offices were closed. Three years later, the Stockyards "were on the brink of collapse" and "400,000 head of cattle were shot to avoid the cost of transporting them to slaughtering plants," according to Pirtle. By 1932, Fort Worth suffered a $2.6-million budget deficit because of delinquent taxes. Soup lines were not uncommon.

The Texas Legislature in 1934 sanctioned creation of a commission to choose a site for a centennial fair. No one had any idea where the exposition might end up until the candy salesman and former Dallas mayor **Robert L. Thornton** (1880-1964) gathered other influential businessmen and brought it to Dallas, even though the city had nothing like San Antonio's Alamo or the battlefield at San Jacinto, near Houston. A Fort Worth representative noted tartly that holding a "Centennial Celebration at Dallas, is like celebrating Washington's Birthday at Buckingham Palace." In fact, Dallas did not even exist a hundred years earlier. During his presentation, Thornton assured the 21 commission officials that a centennial fair will be held, "whether the State of Texas or the government of the U.S. contribute one cent" or none.

By September 1935, says author Kenneth Ragsdale in his 1987 history of the Texas Centennial Exposition, Dallas launched one of the largest peacetime construction programs in the state's history. In ten months a 185-acre State Fair of Texas complex was transformed into a twenty-five-million-dollar world's fair. More than 6.3 million people attended the Centennial Exposition.

But the Fort Worth promoter Amon Carter felt that Cowtown must not be outdone and convinced his cronies that an unofficial Fort Worth Frontier Centennial Exposition, also to celebrate the state's freedom from Mexico, was just what Texas needed. He hired New York showman Billy Rose, at $100,000 for one hundred days, to put on the greatest extravaganza Fort Worth had ever seen "and teach those dudes over there [in Dallas] where the West really begins." Rose offered the Ethiopian emperor Haile Selassie $100,000 to appear with his lions. Hoping to sell lots of tickets, he engaged Sally Rand, a Quaker nude dancer. This exposition focused around the newly-built Casa Manana, the world's largest open-air theater that could seat more than 3,800. During the square dancing, the caller would chant:

"Hurry, girl, and don't get lazy,
Big fat hogs and lots of gravy,
Star-Telegram, full of news,
Grab that gal with the high-top shoes."

But in spite of all the hoopla and Rose's promise to "bring five million visitors down here," the Fort Worth Frontier Fair, "an Amon Carter production from start to finish," was a financial flop and only 986,000 showed up, mostly to be titillated by the sensuous music and the Quaker girl who really did not show that much flesh after all.

While Hitler overran much of Europe, the city of Fort Worth purchased 526 acres of land and in 1942 donated it to the U.S. Army for a bomber plant site. In less than three years, the 35,000 Convair plant employees built 3,000 bombers and transport planes. It eventually became General Dynamics and today Lockheed Martin makes F-16 fighter jets there. Next to it, the Army constructed the Fort Worth Army Airfield Pilot Training Facility, which in 1948 was renamed Carswell Air Force Base and is now known as Naval Air Station Fort Worth Joint Reserve Base. **Maj. Horace Carswell** (1916-1944) was a Fort Worth aviator killed in action as he returned from the South China Sea. While he sank a Japanese cruiser, his plane sustained direct hits. Carswell remained at the controls of his crippled bomber until his men could bail out, then crashed into a mountain. Crews were also trained to fly the B-24s at Carswell. Years later, General Dynamics built the F-111, a plane that could fly three times the speed of sound, next door to Carswell. During the Vietnam War, Bell helicopters were assembled in Fort Worth. Since the 1940s, more military aircraft have been built in Cowtown than in any other American city, according to former Speaker of the House of Representatives, Jim Wright of Fort Worth.

In mid-June 1955, Fort Worth's greatest champion, the "ebullient, gracious, intractable, articulate, pompous, argumentative, egotistical, phenomenal, mesmerizing, dictatorial" Amon Carter, went into a coma. Fort Worth journalist Jerry Flemmons also labeled him "kind, magnanimous, overwhelmingly generous, and altruistic one minute, petty, greedy, spiteful, and selfish the next." On June 19, Father's Day, the "outrageously profane" Amon briefly awoke to ask, "Am I still here?" then lapsed again into unconsciousness, according to the 33-year *Star-Telegram* veteran Jerry Flemmons. He died four days later.

Carter's was the largest funeral in Fort Worth history. Fifteen thousand people came to pay their respects. "Services were at four o'clock because the cowboy said he wanted to be buried in the late afternoon, near sundown," writes Flemmons. Downtown merchants closed their doors for the day and flags were stationed at half-mast. Amon, the neurotic perfectionist, was gone. "No Caesar ever thumped his Rome as energetically as Amon peddled Fort Worth."

But probably the saddest day in modern Metroplex history is November 22, 1963. Ironically, the dugout of **John Neely Bryan** (1810-1877), the founder of Dallas, was at the spot where, 122 years later, **John F. Kennedy** (b. 1917) was assassinated.

Air Force One landed at Carswell Airforce Base at 11:07 p.m. on November 21. "A large crowd, estimated in the thousands, had waited near the runway for more than four hours," noted the *Fort Worth Star-Telegram*. Kennedy spent his last night at what was then known as Hotel Texas. He was the first sitting president to visit Fort Worth since 1936, when **Franklin D. Roosevelt** (1882-1945), the thirty-second president, rode in an open touring car down Main Street. Also part of his entourage were Texas governor **John Connally**, who died in 1993 at age 75, and his wife Nellie, who was 81 years old in 2000; the Connallys had lived in Fort Worth during the 1950s and early 1960s.

The following morning, on November 22, Kennedy was honored at a breakfast here for 2,000 business leaders and apologized for his wife's tardiness, saying, "She is busy organizing herself. It takes her longer because she is prettier than the rest of us." Later, Kennedy made a quick speech in the hotel's parking lot, while standing amid light drizzle on the flatbed of a truck, with Vice-President **Lyndon B. Johnson** (1908-1973) and Governor Connally looking on. From there, Kennedy flew to Love Field airport and, following a motorcade down Dallas's Main Street, was assassinated just past noon.

Before leaving for Washington, D.C., Vice-President Lyndon B. Johnson was sworn in as the next president. A 24-year-old New Orleans-born employee of the Texas School Book Depository, **Lee Harvey Oswald** (1939-1963), was arrested and charged with the murder. Oswald attended Ridglea West Elementary and Arlington Heights High School, both in Fort Worth. In its 1964 report, the investigative Warren Commission reached the conclusion that Oswald acted on his own, although many conspiracy theories have arisen ever since. Two days later, and forever on record in front of TV cameras, Oswald was fatally shot in the basement of the police station in downtown Dallas by Dallas nightclub owner **Jack Ruby.** Ruby was convicted of Oswald's murder the following March, but in 1967 he died from cancer at Parkland Hospital in Dallas while awaiting retrial. Oswald is buried at Rosehill Cemetery in east Fort Worth, just north of Lake Arlington.

Fort Worth grew by 10 percent during the 1960s, while its suburbs, boasting even stronger commercial activity, expanded by 90 percent. The city had "more than 3,500 retail stores and accounted for almost a quarter of all retail sales in Texas." By 1970, Fort Worth numbered some 390,000, while the suburbs had 280,000.

According to Texas A & M professors, Victoria and Walter Buenger, in their 1998 history of Leonard Brothers Department Store, "Race differences increasingly divided city from suburb." In Fort Worth, there was one black for every seven citizens, while in the suburbs the ratio of whites to blacks was fifty to one.

By 1950, blacks made up 15 percent of the city's population. While the Buengers note that the story of Fort Worth's integration remains untold, they do point out that city leaders have testified and newspaper articles suggest that desegregation began earlier and was not as strife-ridden as in most other Southern cities. In 1961, a group of Freedom Riders stopped in Fort Worth on their way from Los Angeles to Jackson, Mississippi, and found many restaurants as well as the bus station already desegregated. "Schools would take longer to integrate, but Jim Crow vanished from most aspects of everyday life before passage of the landmark civil rights laws of the mid-1960's."

By 1963, all of Fort Worth's restaurants, hotels, department stores, theaters, and churches were open to all regardless of race.

"Since 1927, Fort Worth and Dallas both had dreamed of possessing a great international airport," notes historian Pirtle. He writes that the two cities "could not get together, and neither city would step back and offer its support to the other" until 1964, when the Civil Aeronautics Board ordered both to bury their hatchet and select a site to serve the two cities. Dallas-Fort Worth International Airport, which was three times the size of Kennedy Airport in New York, was inaugurated on September 22, 1973, and touted as the world's largest. Country singer Willie Nelson sang at its dedication.

The Metroplex economy was booming, and, after its premiere in 1978, so was the televised fantasy about Dallas, where a make-believe television *Dallas* family ruled amid deception, treachery, and infidelity. In an episode televised in 1980, a record 80 million Americans tuned in to see who shot J. R. Ewing, the show's chief protagonist, a fictional, fraudulent Dallas businessman. Fort Worth native Larry Hagman played J. R. Ewing with some conviction. The soap opera ended 13 years later as the second longest-running television fluff ever, and the 1991 Metroplex economy too was in trouble well before the series ended.

According to historian Darwin Payne, "the awesome development and construction boom in the Dallas area in the late 70's and early 80's was fueled at first by profits from skyrocketing oil prices, always handy for Texans, and then carried further after deregulatory policies of the Reagan administration permitted savings and loan institutions to build up their deposits overnight by offering extra-high dividends." Rather than finance homes, the banks and thrifts, whose deposits were insured by the government, backed some of the most outlandish schemes. Exorbitant loans were approved on inflated appraisals, but when the economy cooled down, millions of dollars worth of loans ended in default. A savings and loan collapse, centered in Dallas, took place "at a cost to taxpayers estimated as much as $300 billion for the thrifts alone," says Payne. In the late 1990s NationsBank merged into Bank of America. Fort Worth, amazingly, eluded most of this madness; only one bank failed during the bust.

From 1991 to 1995, Kay Granger served as the first female mayor of Fort Worth. Daughter of a teacher and a highway patrolman, she received her degree from Texas Wesleyan University and was a city councilwoman from 1989 to 1991. Granger is the first Republican woman to serve in the U.S. House of Representatives from Texas.

After the 1991 Defense Department's cancellation of the A-12 attack plane, which was in the development stage at General Dynamics, 3,500 local employees were immediately laid off. Unemployment peaked at 7.2 percent the next year. By the close of 1999, it dropped back down to under 3 percent.

In 1964, Fort Worth was selected by the National Civic League as an All-America City, an honor it received again in 1993, thus fueling the competition between the Cowtown and Big D, just like in the days of Amon Carter. Carter would probably be beside himself with pride if still alive. In 1995, again under Kay Granger's administration, Cowtown received an award from the National League of Cities for its innovative redevelopment programs.

While the mayors of the two cities dueled over expansion of flights at Dallas's Love Field airport in 1997, the Dallas mayor attended a black-tie dinner banquet in Big D, sponsored by a gay and lesbian civil rights organization, and reportedly asked the audience:

"What do you get when you cross LSD with a cow patty?"

"A trip to Fort Worth," went his answer.

There was a bit of tension over the insult for a week in Fort Worth, but in the end a Cowtown city councilman dispatched a letter to Dallas inviting the mayor, together with his wife "and the couple of your choice for an evening in Fort Worth. It is apparent that you have not spent any quality time in Fort Worth, at least not that you can recall. . . . We know you have been under a lot of stress lately. . . . You need a night away from all those problems facing Dallas."

A Fort Worth posse of four cowboys rode in on horseback into town and to Dallas City Hall a couple of days later bearing the invitation. It said the mayor was to be picked up in a longhorn-trimmed limousine and taken to the Fort Worth's Reata restaurant. A horse-drawn tour of downtown and the Stockyards was proposed and included a show at Caravan of Dreams nightclub.

The Dallas mayor accepted.

FORT WORTH TODAY

Fort Worth has a population of about 500,000, making it the 27th or 28th most populous American city and the sixth largest in Texas. It measures 301.6 square miles. The city's median age is 32 years and per capita income just shy of $20,000. Slightly over one-quarter of all residents have a college degree. In 1998, about 318,000 of the Cowtown's residents were whites, 109,000 African-Americans, and 95,000 Hispanics. Those under 18 years of age numbered 132,000 and residents over 65 years 68,000.

Exports from the Fort Worth-Arlington area, ranking 43rd in the nation, as defined by the Commerce Department, grew to just over $3 billion in 1997. Dallas was in 15th place with exports valued at $8.64 billion.

Fort Worth metro cities, in a descending population order, include Arlington, North Richland Hills, Bedford, Euless, Hurst, Haltom City, Grapevine, Watauga, Mansfield, Benbrook, Keller, and Colleyville.

Fort Worth has 202 parks measuring 9,720 acres. There are 35 fire stations, 21 recreation centers, 15 hospitals, 13 libraries, 12 museums, and five municipal golf courses.

Everything here is just a bit bigger and better, or so the Fort Worth natives would have you believe. Incidentally, finding such natives in these parts is becoming increasingly difficult due to continuous migrations.

Texas is still one of the friendliest states anywhere and Fort Worthians are no exception. It is one of the few remaining larger American cities where complete strangers will still greet you with "Howdy" on the street. Texans, although clannish, will go out of their way to make you feel welcome, whether you are visiting from England, California, or Canada.

Dallas may have gained notoriety because of the Kennedy assassination, but the debut of the television soap opera *Dallas* in 1978, began a worldwide infatuation with a city that only exists in imagination and a mythical, greedy, devious, rich American oil baron and rancher who fascinated viewers from Austria to Russia. Tourists flocked to Dallas like never before, only to discover that the real Dallas is much less glamorous and Fort Worth is also worth seeing. Many actually prefer it over the Big D.

"Fort Worth—Where the West Begins" is the phrase that has been around since the civic booster Amon Carter adopted the city, and it still applies today. It's not the Wild West of yesteryear, but the West that has its roots in ranching and agriculture. If Dallas is a noisy, bragging child, Fort Worth is a thoughtfully quiet relative, patiently tolerating the other's loud outbursts. But it really has not been that long since the cattle drives took place through downtown Fort Worth and oil gushed west of it, so Cowtown, too, is somewhat rough at the edges. The myth of the West flourishes in Cowtown, particularly in the Stockyards district. Were it not for cowboys and cattle, there would be no Stockyards. The stockyards are still here, but they are now better known as the Stockyards Station, where leather wallets count for more than leather whips.

Fifteen minutes after arriving in Cowtown, it will not surprise you to find out that almost a million people come to Will Rogers Memorial Center every January for the 100-plus-year-old Southwestern Exposition and Livestock Show, where auctions, exhibitions, and rodeo competitions take place. But did you know that Fort Worth's Kimbell Art Museum had the sixth most attended art exhibit in the western world? Monet's Mediterranean art attracted 338,000 visitors, just behind a 20th-century art exhibit in Berlin, but ahead of a Viennese art exhibition in Amsterdam. Considered one of the best small art museums in the United States, it is almost across the street from the Modern Art Museum of Fort Worth, which was chartered in 1892.

The Dallas and Fort Worth metropolitan area is often referred to as the Metroplex—a term made up by an advertising copywriter in 1971—which includes a dozen smaller but fast-growing cities that surround them both from all sides. The Metroplex covers 100 miles, going as far north as Denton, which is less than 40 miles from the Oklahoma border, and has a population of more than four million. Dallas accounts for a quarter of that.

Towns like Colleyville, Euless, Keller, Mansfield, Saginaw, and Southlake grew from four to 14 percent between 1997 and 1998 alone. Flower Mound, a town on the northern Tarrant County border and north of D/FW Airport, grew from 15,527 in 1990 to 40,000 in 1998, when the town council voted unanimously to stop issuing building permits for nine months. The Texas Supreme Court has ruled that cities have the right to protect their residents from the ill effects of urbanization and to control the rate and character of community growth.

Fort Worth is Dallas's big brother, divided in the north by the Dallas-Fort Worth International Airport. And, like among most siblings, there is a perennial squabbling between the Cowtown and Big D and bragging on both sides seems the order of the day.

The three areas that make up Fort Worth's triangle of interest to residents and tourists are downtown, the cultural district 1.5 miles to the west of it, and Stockyards two miles north of downtown on Main Street.

Downtown Fort Worth is located roughly within Interstate 30—which connects it with Dallas—Henderson Street on the west, Belknap Street on the north, and perhaps as far east as Elm Street. It could take you two days on horseback and mule-drawn wagon to get from here to the D/FW airport, but by car you might manage it in one hour. Changes of time have given downtown Fort Worth contrasts rich in history, fanciful tales of the Old West, and highrises of glass and steel.

"Downtown Fort Worth," declared *Texas Monthly*, "has become Texas' liveliest urban environment." With the streets packed with people on the weekends and full of activity during the week, "Fort Worth, the place you used to pass through on the way to somewhere else—Where the West Begins—is now a destination unto itself."

As one of the Bass brothers told the magazine, Fort Worth, due to its size and scale, is big enough for a real downtown, but it's still small enough to be manageable. The Bass family is one of the world's richest families, whose fortune was started by their great-uncle Sid Richardson, who left the four brothers $2.8 million each.

Three hundred million public dollars have been invested in downtown Fort Worth over the past twenty years, while the private investments amounted to $800 million over the same period. Fort Worth has an operating budget of about $550 million and more than 5,000 employees.

"Urban planners hail Fort Worth as proof that no downtown is beyond rescue," noted the *New York Times*, adding that the city's "success has inspired open envy especially in Dallas, a city long used to regarding its smaller neighbor as laughably mired in stockyard muck."

"While the praise is plentiful, a few critics surface now and then," says the *Fort Worth Star-Telegram*, quoting a University of Texas at Arlington professor who specializes in planning and who called downtown's a "nostalgia architecture," then continued pointedly: "Why not set up a design ordinance by the city of Fort Worth that all buildings be designed by David Schwartz?" The professor referred to the Washington architect who designed the Sundance West apartments, the AMC Palace Theater block, the Bass Performance Hall, and the Central Library facade on Third Street.

Fort Worth and Toluca, the capital of the state of Mexico, located about an hour's busride southwest of Mexico City, linked their towns as

Sister Cities in 1998. Fort Worth's other Sister Cities are Bandung in Indonesia, Budapest in Hungary, Nagaoka in Japan, Reggio Emilia in Italy, and Trier in Germany.

In 1999, Fort Worth celebrated the 150th anniversary of the city's founding as a frontier fort. Those who have taken to liking the downtown Cowtown almost wish that the place would stop growing and forever remain somewhere between a city and a town. Fort Worth grew almost 10 percent between 1990 and 1998, and Arlington a full 17 percent.

Climate and Dress

July and August are the hottest months. Out-of-towners sometimes underestimate the Texas heat and end up being treated for heat exhaustion or severe sunburn. If you enjoy the heat come in the summer, but don't forget comfortable cotton clothing, a hat, and a sun blocker, or you will end up with a sunburn. The sun here is so intense that if you are exposed to it for a prolonged period of time and your body is not conditioned for it, you risk developing skin cancer.

Beyond those two extreme summer months, a visit during almost any month would be acceptable, for temperatures seldom drop below freezing. January is usually the coldest month and May is the rainiest. Here are the Metroplex's *average* precipitation and temperatures. D/FW Airport is the official area's recording station so these apply to both Dallas and Fort Worth.

	Inches of Rainfall	Fahrenheit Temperatures	Celsius Temperatures
January	1.83	56-35	13-2
February	2.18	59-38	15-3
March	2.77	68-46	20-8
April	3.50	75-55	24-13
May	4.88	83-63	28-17
June	2.98	91-71	33-23
July	2.31	95-74	35-24
August	2.21	95-74	35-24
September	3.39	88-67	31-19
October	3.52	79-57	26-14
November	2.29	67-46	19-8
December	1.84	58-37	14-3

Since 1953, when official tornado tabulations began, and through 1996, there have been more than 5,800 tornadoes in Texas, causing 458 deaths.

The worst flood in Fort Worth's history began on May 16, 1949, when a foot of rain fell on the city, and is known by locals as the Big One. The downpour brought the Trinity River up to the second-story windows of the Montgomery Ward's department store, which opened its eight-story retail and marketing operation on West Seventh Street in 1928. About 12 inches of rain fell in eight hours and in some areas water was 12 feet deep. The flooding took the lives of ten people and 13,000 were left homeless.

Temperatures exceed 90 degrees on about 96 days of the year and fall below freezing 63 days of the year. The average relative humidity at noon is 57 percent. Winds average eleven miles an hour and are predominantly from the south.

The hottest day in Fort Worth was June 26 and 27 of 1980, when the temperature reached 113 degrees Fahrenheit and six people died from the heat. That year saw 69 days of 100-degree or higher temperatures. The Cowtown's coldest day was February 12, 1899, when the temperature plunged to minus eight degrees Fahrenheit.

Two Internet sites for you to check on the Metroplex weather and the forecast for the days ahead include: www.kxas.com, which is the NBC affiliate KXAS-TV, Channel 5, in Fort Worth, and www.wfaa.com, the ABC affiliate WFAA-TV, Channel 8, in Dallas.

When you come to visit, be sure to wear comfortable clothes. Unless you go to a formal business gathering, to an expensive restaurant for dinner, or to a cultural event, like the opera or symphony, be comfortable.

At the height of summer, shorts are worn by many. Whatever you decide to wear, you're better off if it's cotton because the heat and humidity will take their toll if your clothes cannot breathe. Except for a period between November and February, you will seldom need anything warmer than a sweater and jacket, but a raincoat might be appreciated at times.

A word about air-conditioning. The Metroplex uses more of it than are the entire state budgets of some developing countries. Grapevine Mills mall spends more than $200,000 a month on air-conditioning in the summer, the Dallas-Fort Worth International Airport (see individual entries) almost twice as much a month. Air-conditioning is a badge of Texas lifestyle. It is so cold in some offices at the height of the summer that some workers are blue and have to turn on their portable heaters, while others strut around in complete comfort. A breakdown in one's air-conditioning is tantamount to a national crisis. Texans went without air-conditioning until about fifty years ago, but it is just as unthinkable to be without it today as it is asking for drinking water without ice in a restaurant.

MATTERS OF FACT

Here is a list of telephone numbers (with some addresses) that you might need whether you visit Fort Worth once, are a new resident, or have lived in the city for years.

Some of these and other numbers of interest to you might also be listed in chapters THE INTERNATIONAL VISITOR, NEW RESIDENTS, TRANSPORTATION, etc.

Adoptions—Gladney Center, 2300 Hemphill St., (817) 922-6000.
Airports—Alliance Airport, (817) 890-1000.
    Fort Worth Meacham Airport, (817) 871-5400.
    Dallas-Fort Worth International, (972) 574-8888.
Alcohol and Drug Abuse—Al-Anon-Alateen Information Service, (817) 336-2492; Alcoholics Anonymous, (817) 332-3533; Drug Treatment Center, (817) 336-5454; Tarrant County Council on Alcoholism & Drug Abuse, (817) 332-6329; Teen Challenge, (817) 336-8191; Texas Alcoholic Beverage Commission, (817) 451-9466.
Ambulance—911 for emergencies, (817) 922-3150 for non-emergency calls.
American Automobile Association—
    Emergency Road Service, (800) 222-4357 or (817) 370-2503. Office located at 5431 South Hulen St.
American Cancer Society—3301 West Freeway, (817) 737-9990.
American Express Travel Agency—(817) 738-5441 or 820-0000.
American Heart Association—2401 Scott Ave., (817) 315-5000.
American Red Cross—(817) 335-9137; 24-hour emergency number, (817) 924-4231.
Amtrak—(817) 332-2931, General Information.
Animals—Animal Control/Dog Licensing, (817) 871-7290; Humane Society of North Texas, (817) 332-5367; Metroport Humane Society, (817) 491-9499.
Apartment Association of Tarrant County—(817) 284-11231, Complaints.

Area Codes—Mostly 817. (See also Telephone and Telegrams in THE INTERNATIONAL VISITOR chapter.)

Attorney—District Attorney, (817) 884-1400.

Automobile License—See the NEW RESIDENTS chapter.

Automobile Registration & Title—See the NEW RESIDENTS chapter.

Baby-Sitting—See Child Care Facilities in the NEW RESIDENTS chapter.

Better Business Bureau—1612 Summit Ave., (817) 332-7585.

Billy Bob's—2520 Rodeo Plaza, Stockyards, (817) 589-1711.

Botanic Garden—(817) 871-7686 or 871-7689. (See also the SIGHTS chapter.)

Bus Service—(817) 215-8600; to D/FW Airport, (817) 334-0092.

Business Assistance Center—100 East 15th St., Suite 400, (817) 871-6001.

Caravan of Dreams—312 Houston St., (817) 429-4000.

Carelink Physician Referral Service—3609-A West Seventh St., (817) 735-3627.

Casa Manana—3101 West Lancaster Ave., (817) 332-9319.

Chambers of Commerce—See the NEW RESIDENTS chapter.

Children's Medical Center Hospital—(817) 332-3116.

Children's Services—Advocacy, Inc., (800) 252-9108; Child Find/Missing Children, (800) 426-5678; Child Support Services, (800) 252-8014; Children with a Disability/TEA, (800) 252-9668; Day Care Information Hotline, (800) 862-5252; Suicide Prevention Service, (817) 927-5544; Texas Runaway Hotline, (888) 580-4357.

City Hall—1000 Throckmorton St. at West Tenth, (817) 871-8900.
Fire Department, (817) 871-6800.
City Manager's Office, (817) 871-6111.
Mayor's Office, (817) 871-6117.

City of—Bedford, (817) 952-2100; Benbrook, (817) 249-3000; Burleson, (817) 295-1113; Colleyville, (817) 577-7575; Crowley, (817) 297-2201; Dalworthington Gardens, (817) 274-7368; Edgecliff, (817) 293-4313; Euless, (817) 685-1400; Everman, (817) 293-0525; Forest Hill, (817) 568-3000; Haltom City, (817) 834-7341; Haslet, (817) 439-5931; Hurst, (817) 788-7000; Keller, (817) 431-1517; Kennedale, (817) 478-5416; Lake Worth, (817) 237-1211; Lakeside, (817) 237-1234; Mansfield, (817) 473-9371; North Richland Hills, (817) 581-5500; Pantego, (817) 274-1381; Richland Hills, (817) 595-6635; River Oaks, (817) 626-5421; Saginaw, (817) 232-4640; Sansom Park, (817) 626-1921; Watauga, (817) 281-8047; Westlake, (817) 430-0941; Westover Hills, (817) 737-3127; Westworth Village, (817) 738-3673; White Settlement, (817) 246-4971.

Climate—see Climate and Dress in FORT WORTH TODAY chapter.

Code Compliance Division—(817) 871-6320.

Community Service Organizations—American Civil Liberties Union, (817) 534-6883; Big Brothers-Big Sisters of Tarrant County, (817) 877-4277; Dispute Resolution Services of Tarrant County, (817) 877-4554; Goodwill Industries, (817) 332-7866; League of Women Voters of Tarrant County, (817) 336-1333; Parents Without Partners, (817) 560-8242; Salvation Army, (817) 332-2495; Tarrant County Community Churches, (817) 922-9446.

Consumer Protection—Attorney General, (800) 252-8011 or (800) 337-3928; Better Business Bureau, (817) 332-7585; Consumer Product Safety Commission in Dallas, (214) 767-0841; County District Attorney, (817) 884-1400; Federal Trade Commission in Dallas, (214) 979-0213; Food and Drug Administration, (817) 334-5218; Securities and Exchange Commission, (817) 978-3821; Texas Department of Insurance Consumer Complaints, (800) 252-3439.

Convention and Visitors Center—Fort Worth Convention & Visitors Bureau, 415 Throckmorton St., (800) 433-5747 or (817) 336-8791; Fort Worth Convention Center, (817) 884-2222.

Counseling and Guidance Services—Baptist Marriage and Family Counseling Center, (817) 921-8790; First United Methodist Counseling Service, (817) 924-8521; Gamblers Helpline, (800) 742-0443; Jewish Family Services, (817) 294-2660; Parenting Center, (817) 332-6348; Planned Parenthood of North Texas, (817) 332-7966; Pregnancy Control, Inc., (817) 335-6641; Right to Life of Tarrant County, (817) 338-0591; Survivors of Suicide, Inc., (817) 654-5343; Tarrant County MHMR, (817) 335-3022; Widowed Persons Service, (817) 551-2922.

Courts—City of Fort Worth, Traffic Fines, (817) 871-6700; Tarrant County Civil & Criminal Courts, (817) 884-1111.

Cowtown Coliseum Rodeo—121 East Exchange Ave., (817) 625-1025.

Crime Stoppers Hotline—(800) 252-3432 or (817) 469-8477.

Crisis Services—Child/Elderly Abuse Hotline, (800) 252-5400; Missing Persons Clearinghouse, (800) 346-3243; Parents Anonymous/Texas Parent Heartline, (800) 554-2323; Rape Crisis Center, (800) 886-7273 or (817) 927-2737; Suicide Prevention Service, (817) 927-5544.

Customs Service—at D/FW International Airport, (972) 574-574-2132 at Terminal B; (972) 574-2131 at Terminal A; (972) 574-2010 at Terminal E.

Day Care Association of Fort Worth—(817) 831-9893.

Dentists Referral—(800) DENTIST (336-8478) or (800) DOCTORS (362-8677).

Disabled Programs—Adult Abuse Hotline, (800) 252-5400; Association for Retarded Citizens, (817) 877-1474; Cerebral Palsy of Tarrant County, (817) 332-7171; Tarrant County Association for the Blind, (817) 332-3341; Texas Department of Human Services, (817) 625-2161.

Doctor—Dial 911 for emergencies. (See also the NEW RESIDENTS chapter.)

Doctors Referral—(800) DOCTORS (362-8677) or (800) DENTIST (336-8478).

Driver's License—(817) 284-1490 for general information.

Emergencies—911.

Environmental Protection Agency—(800) 887-6063, U.S. Government agency.

Equal Employment Opportunity Commission—Dallas District, (214) 655-3355, U.S. Government agency.

Events Line—(817) 332-2000.

Export Assistance Center/Commerce Dept.—Fort Worth International Center, 711 Houston St., (817) 212-2673; Fax, 978-0178.

Federal Bureau of Investigation—(817) 336-7135 or (214) 720-2200 in Dallas, U.S. Government agency.

Family and Children Services—Child Abuse Hotline, (800) 252-5400 or (817) 649-5500; Child Study Center, (817) 336-8611; Crisis Intervention, (817) 570-7985; Family Service, (817) 927-8884; Lena Pope Home, (817) 731-8681; Suicide Prevention Service, (817) 927-5544; Texas Runaway Hotline, (888) 580-4357.

Federal Information Center—(800) 688-9889; TDD Hearing Impaired, (800) 326-2996.

Fire—911 for emergencies, (817) 922-3000 for non-emergencies.

Food and Drug Administration—(817) 334-5218, U.S. Government agency.

Fort Worth Independent School District—Administrative Offices, 100 North University Dr., (817) 871-2000.

Fort Worth Mayor—1000 Throckmorton St., (817) 871-6118.

Fort Worth Star-Telegram—(817) 390-7400; Classified advertising, (817) 332-3333; Editorial, (817) 390-7411. (See also Press, Radio, and TV in the NEW RESIDENTS chapter.)

Fort Worth Symphony—(817) 921-2676.

Fort Worth Zoo—(817) 871-7050.

Garbage Pickup—See Public Services in the NEW RESIDENTS chapter.

Golf Courses—See the SPORTS chapter.

Health Services—Alcohol/Drug Abuse Hotline, (800) 832-9623; Alzheimer's Information Referral, (800) 523-2007; Alzheimer's Program, (800) 242-3399; American Diabetes Association, (800)

252-8233; Arthritis Foundation, (817) 926-7733; Assistance for the Blind, (800) 252-5204; Cancer Care Services of Tarrant County, (817) 921-0653; Carter Blood Center, (817) 335-4935; Community Health Foundation of Tarrant County, (817) 871-7394; Infectious Diseases, (800) 252-8239; Lion's Organ & Eye Bank, (817) 921-2996; Insurance Board/Consumer Complaints, (800) 252-3439; Mental Health Association, (817) 335-5405; Muscular Dystrophy Association, (817) 338-1024; Multiple Sclerosis Society, (817) 877-1222; National Pesticide Telecommunications Network, (800) 858-7378; Parkinson's Support Group of Tarrant County, (817) 275-1909; Planned Parenthood of North Texas, (817) 332-7966; Public Health Department, (817) 871-7200; Texas Library for the Blind/Talking Book Program, (800) 252-9605.

Hospital Emergencies—Call 911. (See also Hospital Emergencies in THE INTERNATIONAL VISITOR chapter.)

Hospitals—See the NEW RESIDENTS chapter.

Immunization Clinic—(817) 871-7250.

Immigration and Naturalization Service—(214) 655-5384 in Dallas, U.S. Government agency.

Internal Revenue Service—Federal tax forms, (800) 829-3676; Federal tax information, (800) 829-1040; TDD Assistance for the Deaf, (800) 829-4059.

International Center—711 Houston St., (817) 212-2666.

John Peter Smith Hospital—1500 South Main St., (817) 921-3431.

Kimbell Art Museum—3333 Camp Bowie Blvd., (817) 332-8451.

Lawyer Referral—(800) 252-9690.

Legal Services—Child Support Enforcement, (800) 252-3515; Legal Line Hotline, second and fourth Thursdays, 6-8 p.m., (817) 335-1239; West Texas Legal Services, (817) 336-3943.

Library—Central Library, 300 Taylor St., (817) 871-7701. (See also the SIGHTS chapter.)

License Plates—(817) 884-1100.

Local Laws—You must be at least 21 years old to drink in public places in Texas. Liquor stores are open 10 a.m.-9 p.m., and are closed Sundays and some holidays. No alcoholic beverages can lawfully be sold before noon. If driving while intoxicated, you may be subject to a mandatory jail sentence.

Marriage License—Tarrant County Courthouse, (817) 884-1195.

Mesquite Championship Rodeo—I-635 at Military Pkwy. Exit, (214) 222-BULL.

Modern Art Museum of Fort Worth—1309 Montgomery St., (817) 738-9215.

Municipal Court—1000 Throckmorton St.; Parking tickets, (817) 871-6742; Ticket information, (817) 871-6700.

NAACP—1063 Evans Ave., (817) 332-8919.

National Response Center for Toxic Chemicals—(800) 424-8802.

National Weather Service—Metro, (214) 787-1111.

National Youth Crisis Hotline—(800) 448-4663.

Narcotics—Drug Enforcement Administration, (817) 978-3455; State Narcotics Service, (817) 284-1490. After 5 p.m., Saturdays, Sundays, and holidays, (817) 284-0591.

Newspapers—See Press, Radio, and TV in the NEW RESIDENTS chapter.

Oil Information Library—1401 West Fifth St., (817) 332-4977.

Passports—Information, (817) 317-3634, or (817) 884-2520.

Peace Corps—(214) 767-5435 in Dallas, American Volunteer Corps Serving Abroad.

Pharmacies—Eckerd Drug Stores open 24 hours:
2706 Jacksboro Hwy. at Long Avenue, (817) 626-8255.
Hwy. 80 West at Las Vegas Trail, (817) 560-0130.
Woodmont Plaza Mall, McCart Ave. at Altamesa Blvd., (817) 294-7373.
1201 North Beach at East Belknap St., (817) 834-6369.

Poison Center—(800) POISON-1 or (800) 441-0040.

Police—Emergency, 911; Non-emergency, (817) 335-4222. Accident Reports, (817) 877-8005; Auto Theft, (817) 877-8249; Detectives, (817) 877-8303; Drug Hotline, (817) 922-3224; Missing Persons, (817) 877-8046; Narcotics, (817) 921-1500; Sexual Assaults, (817) 877-8317; Traffic Citations Information, (817) 871-6700. (For suburban police and fire non-emergency departments, see THE INTERNATIONAL VISITOR chapter.)

Postal Service— Consumer Affairs, (817) 317-3623.
Downtown Station, (817) 334-2975, Mon.-Fri., 7:30 a.m.-7 p.m.
Express Mail, (817) 317-3616.
Passports, (817) 317-3634.
Zip Code Information, (972) 647-2996, Weekdays 8 a.m.-5 p.m.

Property Appraisal—Tarrant County Appraisal District, (817) 284-0024.

Public Health—Animal Control, (817) 871-7290; Immunizations, (817) 871-7217; Information, (817) 871-7200; International Travel Clinic, (817) 871-7360.

Public Safety/Highway Emergencies Only—(800) 525-5555.

Presbyterian Hospital Ask-a-Nurse Service—(214) 891-4000.

Radio Stations—See Press, Radio, and TV in the NEW RESIDENTS chapter.

Road Conditions—(800) 452-9292.

Senior Citizens Services—Adult Abuse Hotline, (800) 252-5400; Area Agency on Aging, Information & Assistance, (817) 258-8100;

Senior Citizens Nutrition Program, (800) 635-4116; United Way First Call, (817) 258-0100; Housing Options for Seniors, (817) 258-8100; Senior Citizens Services of Tarrant County, (817) 338-4433; Social Security Administration, (800) 772-1213; Texas Department of Human Services, (817) 625-2161.

The Sixth Floor Kennedy Museum—Elm and Houston St., Dallas, (214) 653-6666.

Social Security Administration—819 Taylor St., Room 1A07, (800) 772-1213.

Social Services—Fair Housing, (800) 669-9777; Governor's Crime Victim Clearinghouse, (800) 252-3423; Income Assistance, AFDC & Food Stamps, (800) 252-9330; Literacy, (800) 441-7323; Mothers Against Drunk Driving/MADD, (800) 382-6233; Parents Without Partners, (817) 275-5262; Tarrant Council on Alcoholism & Drug Abuse, (817) 332-6329; Texas Crime Stoppers, (800) 252-8477; Texas Department of Aging, (800) 252-9240; United Way of Tarrant County, (817) 258-8000; The Women's Center of Tarrant County, (817) 927-4040.

Southfork Ranch—3700 Hogge, Parker, (800) 989-7800 or (972) 442-7800.

SPCA of Texas—(214) 651-9611.

State Fair of Texas—Fair Park, Dallas, (214) 565-9931.

Stockyards Museum—131 East Exchange Ave., (817) 625-5082.

Suicide Prevention Service—(817) 927-5544.

The "T"—(817) 215-8600.

Tarrant County—Sheriff: 911 for emergencies, (817) 884-1212 for non-emergencies.

Tarrant County Public Health Dept.—1800 University Dr., (817) 871-7248.

Taxes—Change of Address, (817) 284-4063.
City/County Property Taxes, (817) 884-1100.
Homestead Exemption Application, (817) 284-4063.

Telephone Directory Assistance—411.

Telephone Operator—0.

Teletypewriter Service for the Deaf—(817) 332-1445.

Television Stations—See Press, Radio, and TV in the NEW RESIDENTS chapter.

Tennis Reservations—See the SPORTS chapter.

Texas Department of Public Safety—(817) 284-1490. After-hours/emergencies, (214) 226-5230; Regional Office in Garland, (972) 274-8251.

Texas Department of Transportation—24-hour road conditions, (214) 374-4100.

Texas Highway Patrol—(817) 284-1490.

Texas Rangers—350 Interstate 30 West, Garland, (214) 861-2000.
Texas Stadium—2401 East Airport Fwy., Irving, (214) 438-7676.
Texas State Travel Guide/Free—(800) 888-8839.
Time and Temperature—844-4444/6611.
Time Zone—Central, on Daylight Savings Time, April-October.
Traffic Laws—Seat belts and infant and child safety seats are required
   by law. You may turn right on red. Consuming alcoholic beverages
   while driving is illegal.
Traffic Citations—(817) 871-6700.
Transportation—City bus service, (817) 871-6200.
   Fort Worth Trolley, (817) 626-5995.
   Fort Worth Transportation Authority, (817) 215-8600.
   Van service to D/FW Airport, (817) 334-0092.
U.S. Marshall Service—(817) 334-3161, U.S. Government agency.
United Way—(817) 878-0100.
Utilities—GTE Southwest, (800) 483-4400.
   Problems with utility companies, (817) 871-6798.
   Southwestern Bell Phone Repair, (800) 246-8464 or (817) 464-
   7928.
   TXU Electric, (972) 791-2888 or (800) 242-9113.
   TXU Gas, (800) 817-8090 or (817) 921-6400.
   Water department, (817) 871-8210 or (817) 871-8300.
Van Cliburn International Piano Competition—(817) 738-6536.
Visitor Information Centers—415 Throckmorton St., (800) 433-5747
   or (817) 336-8791.
   East Exchange Ave. in the Stockyards, (817) 624-4741.
   Fort Worth Museum of Science & History, (817) 732-1631.
   Sid Richardson Collection of Western Art, (817) 332-6554.
   Will Rogers Memorial Center, (817) 882-8588.
Voter Registration—(800) 252-8683; County Election Administrator,
   (817) 884-1115.
Weather—National Weather Service Forecast, (214) 787-1111;
   Recreation-Travelers Weather Recording, (214) 787-1701; Other
   weather information, weekdays 8 am-4 pm, (817) 429-2631.
Western Union Telegrams and Money Transfer—(800) 325-6000.
Will Rogers Memorial Center—One Amon Carter Square.
   Business Office, (817) 871-8150.
   Rodeo Ticket Office, (817) 877-2420.
   Stock Show Office, (817) 877-2400.
   Visitors Center, (817) 882-8588.
Women's Services—Rape Crisis Center, (817) 927-2737; Women's
   Center of Tarrant County, (817) 927-4000; Women's Heaven of
   Tarrant County, (817) 535-6464; Women's Shelter, (817) 460-5566.
Yellow Cab Co.—(817) 534-5555.

Youth Organizations—Boy Scouts of America, (817) 738-5491; Camp Fire Boys & Girls, (817) 831-2111; Emergency Youth Shelter, (817) 877-4663; Girl Scouts-Circle T Council, (817) 737-7272; YMCA, (817) 332-3281; YWCA, (817) 332-6191.

Zoo—(817) 871-7050. Also see the SIGHTS chapter.

TRANSPORTATION

Air

Chances are that you will be coming to Cowtown through the Dallas-Fort Worth International Airport, which is located halfway between the two cities and was one of the largest and most advanced facilities when it opened in 1974. It was built at a cost of about $750 million, with its tenant airlines investing another $2 billion in improvements since then.

"Though the beginnings of D/FW Airport go back to the 1960's, the amassing of that much real estate and technology would today be beyond the democratic capabilities of even Dallas and Fort Worth," wrote historian A. C. Greene in 1984, while writing about the former Dallas mayor Erik Jonsson. No other person in the history of the city could have called for and received support from all of the local, state, and federal government agencies affected. "Thus, D/FW Airport is probably the final monument to Dallas' famous (or infamous) oligarchy, because the decision to build it, to operate it in conjunction with Fort Worth and the method of operation through an independent board came only because there was unity in the views of those who made the decisions—and unity in their acceptance of Jonsson as a man every participant trusted." If the undertaking had not worked, the result would have been an "irreversible regional disaster."

Dallas-Fort Worth International Airport, (972) 574-8888; Airport Assistance Center, (972) 574-4420; Ground Transportation, (972) 574-5878; Visitor Information, (972) 574-3694; Lost & Found, (972) 574-4454; Emergency Car Service, (817) 283-2121; Emergency Medical Service, 911 or (972) 574-4454; Non-Emergency Police & Fire, (972) 574-4454; TDD for Hearing-Impaired, (972) 574-5555; Western Union, (972) 574-4420; Internet www.dfwairport.com.

Federal agencies serving D/FW Airport: USDA/APHIS, Plant Protection & Quarantine, (972) 574-2166; Veterinary Services, (972)

885-7850. Department of Interior, Fish and Wildlife Service, (972) 574-3254. Drug Enforcement Administration: Airport Narcotic Task Force, (972) 574-2111; Dallas, (214) 767-7151; Fort Worth, (817) 334-3455. Immigration & Naturalization Service, (972) 574-2187. Federal Aviation Administration, (972) 453-4200. U.S. Customs Service, (972) 574-2170. U.S. Postal Service, (972) 574-2687; Express Service, (972) 574-2685.

You can enter the airport from the south on State Highway 183, also known as Airport Freeway. From the north, enter on Highway 114, 121, or Interstate 635, also known as Lyndon B. Johnson Freeway. All exits are to your left.

The airport's main road, International Parkway, runs the length of the airport, from north to south. When departing the airport, the parkway connects directly to major freeways serving the Metroplex. Downtown Fort Worth and Dallas are about 17.5 miles from the airport, or one hour's drive, possibly longer, depending on the time of day.

Covering 28.1 square miles, with seven runways and the eighth under construction, the airport is larger than the island of Manhattan in New York City. Four heavy jets can land simultaneously in good weather, and three heavy jets can land using cockpit instruments in bad weather. D/FW is now the fifth busiest airport in the nation in the number of passengers carried and third in the number of takeoffs and landings. There are more than 2,300 passenger takeoffs and landings daily with 160 destinations worldwide serving 57 million passengers every year. Terminals include some 150 aircraft boarding gates. The D/FW area is also the headquarters for 14 Fortune 500 companies. Some 42,000 people—more than the equivalent of the entire population of the town of Grapevine—work at the airport.

In 2000, the airport started a multibillion-dollar expansion, overhauling the airport's existing terminals, building new concourses and terminals, a new people-moving rail system linking the terminals, and replacing the quarter-century-old tram in use now, as well as skywalks-crossing roads, automated baggage movers, and rerouting roads, all of which will double the airport's capacity.

All baggage claim areas are located on the arrival level. Ground transportation services, other than taxicabs, depart from the lower level and arrive on the upper roadway. International Parkway runs through the center of the airport; all terminal buildings, parking facilities, rental car lots, and the airport hotels are accessible from this road.

About 2,500 of the airport's 18,000 acres were officially designated in 1979 as a foreign trade zone—as lying outside of U.S. Customs territory—by the U.S. Commerce Department. The zone allows business activity to occur under the same rules as would apply if the activity were performed outside the U.S. For more details, call (972) 574-3121.

Airlines Serving the Metroplex ────────

You are within a three-hour flight of any city in the continental U.S. D/FW Airport is served by two dozen airlines, connecting Fort Worth with more than 150 U.S. destinations and several international cities. Among the foreign countries with direct service are Canada, Mexico, Germany, the United Kingdom, and Japan.

Airline	Terminal and Gate(s)	Reservations
Aeromexico/ Air Tran	Terminal E, Gates 2, 37-38	(800) 237-6639
Aero California	Terminal A, Gates 21-28	(800) 237-6225
AirTran Airways	Terminal E, Gate 2	(800) 247-8726
America West Airlines	Terminal B, Gate 16	(800) 235-9292
American Airlines	Terminal A, Gates 6-39 Terminal C, Gates 2-39	(800) 433-7300 Locally (214) 267-1151
American Eagle/ Simmons	Terminal A, Gates 1-5, LL	(800) 433-7300 Locally (214) 267-1151
American Trans Air	Terminal B, Gate 12	(800) 225-2995
Atlantic Southeast	Terminal E, Gates 22-26	(800) 282-3424 Locally (214) 630-3200 or (817) 336-8341
Big Sky	Terminal E, Gate 30	(800) 237-7788
British Airways	Terminal B, Gate 33	(800) 247-9297
Canadian Airlines International	Terminal A, Gate 20	(800) 426-7000
China Air Lines	Terminal A, Gates 16-39	(800) 227-5118
Continental Airlines	Terminal B, Gates 12-16	(800) 525-0280 Locally (972) 263-0523
Delta Airlines	Terminal E, Gates 7-38	Dom. (800) 221-1212 Intl. (800) 241-4141 Locally (214) 630-3200 or (817) 336-8341

There are two children's play areas at D/FW: American Airlines' is in Terminal C and Delta's is in Terminal E.

Foreign Currency Exchange

You can exchange foreign currencies at these Thomas Cook airport locations, which also sell dollar-denominated traveler's checks that you can use to pay for lodging, meals, and while shopping:

Terminal A: Gates 28 and 35, open 7 am-7 pm; (972) 574-4686.
Terminal B: Gates 31 and 36, open 9 am-5 pm; (972) 574-3878.
Terminal E: Gate 13, open 9 am-5 pm; (972) 574-2814.

There is a 24-hour foreign currency exchange machine located in terminal A, near gate 35, dispensing U.S. dollars in exchange for 20 different currencies. The automated currency machine, owned by Thomas Cook, features a multilingual touch screen and has a $300 transaction limit.

American Express at Ridgmar Town Square, 6952 Ridgmar Meadow Rd.; (817) 738-5441, located one block north of Ridgmar Mall (see entry) is practically the only other Fort Worth facility that exchanges foreign currencies. It is open Mon-Fri 10 am-6 pm and also issues traveler's checks and airline tickets.

Fort Worth Meacham Airport, Hwy. 287 at Interstate 820, (817) 871-5400; Internet www.meacham.com, is located in northwest Fort Worth, a few minutes north of the Stockyards, west of Interstate 35 and south of Interstate 820 Northwest.

Built in 1925 under the name of Fort Worth Airport, it changed its name to Meacham two years later to honor a former mayor of Fort Worth, Henry Clay Meacham. Meacham and Fort Worth czar Amon Carter were for years as thick as thieves, but fell out for publicly unknown reasons. Meacham's store stopped advertising in Carter's *Star-Telegram*, depriving the owner of $100,000 annually. Until 1947, the airport was referred to in the paper generically as the Municipal Airport, until Carter "suddenly—and with considerable irony—married Minnie Meacham Smith, second daughter of his old foe."

In 1925, aviator Charles Lindbergh circled the 170-acre open field three times in his *Spirit of St. Louis* before landing. In a parade down North Main Street, 30,000 school children greeted Lindbergh, who spent the night at Hotel Texas, now Radisson Plaza (see entry), downtown. Central Airlines was in 1949 the first commercial airline to fly out of Meacham Field, in part with the financial backing from actor James Stewart. Humphrey Bogart and Amelia Earhart were among the countless celebrities that also landed here. It also was the airport that in 1928 boasted Texas' first interstate passenger flight, and the following year witnessed the world's first air-to-air refueling. Meacham has been relegated mostly to corporate aircraft during the last decade. There is no taxi service at Meacham, but car rentals are available.

Inside the two large aluminum hangars, past the terminal building and Sandpiper Airport Inn, at 400 North Main Street, there is the **Vintage Flying Museum,** located at 505 Northwest 38th Street. It is open Saturdays 10 am-5 pm, Sundays noon-5 pm. CH. Only group tours can be scheduled weekdays. A B-17 reconnaissance aircraft, nicknamed Chuckie, built by Lockheed-Vega in 1944, is on display here, as are a Stearman 1920s biplane and Texas Air Command 1950s fighter jet. Restoration of other aircraft also takes place here. A gift shop sells souvenirs.

Alliance Airport, (817) 890-1000 or (817) 837-1000, is a 418-acre industrial airport surrounded by an 8,300-acre industrial park in far north Fort Worth, west of Interstate 35 West.

Alliance is managed for the city of Fort Worth by developer Ross Perot, Jr., son of the former presidential candidate, who amassed billions with the Electronic Data Service, which he sold to General Motors. Ross Perot, Jr., has also built the new downtown Dallas sports arena.

The airport opened in 1989 at a cost of $200 million and is intended for manufacturers and companies that need easy access to planes shuttling in parts and supplies as an alternative to the D/FW Airport. The development has 12.5 million square feet of warehouse and industrial space and claims more than 60 corporate clients.

The man who rallied public officials to annex nearly 5,620 acres that included Alliance Airport is the Chicago-born and longest-serving former mayor of Fort Worth, Bob Bolen (b. 1926), whose 6-foot-2-inch bronze statue is on display near the base of the airport's control tower. It was created in 1999 by artist Sandi Clark of Loveland, Colorado. A former toy, bicycle, and greeting-card salesman, Bolen joined the City Council in 1979 and served as mayor from 1981 to 1991. To qualify for Federal Aviation development funds, the city accepted donations of Perot's land for the airport, worth several million dollars, and used it to meet federal requirements for local matching funds.

Nearby, Intel Corporation was to build a 530-acre, 1.5-billion-dollar manufacturing facility scheduled for completion in 2003. Although the company had already spent $70 million in land acquisition and initial construction, it decided against building here and went to a Phoenix suburb, where tax breaks are more favorable. Texas, despite its business-friendly climate, is being passed over for other large projects because the state does not alleviate the high property and franchise taxes imposed on captial-intensive projects, such as Intel's. Property taxes in the state are among the highest in the country. City and county governments can abate some of that, but about 65 percent of it is paid to school districts.

Fort Worth Spinks Airport, (817) 447-8304, Internet www.ftw texas.com/spinks, is located 14 miles south of downtown, east of Interstate 35 West and south of Interstate 20. Situated on 822 acres, it was completed in 1988 and named after aviation pioneer Maurice Hunter "Pappy" Spinks. Spinks, which accommodates the excess small aircraft traffic from D/FW and Meacham airports, is municipally owned and operated.

Ground Services To and From D/FW Airport

The D/FW airport is serviced by the city-owned bus service, private tour companies, rental car agencies, and taxicabs. Information boards located near baggage claim areas inside all terminals have details about courtesy vehicles that serve more than 50 Metroplex hotels and motels. Well over 100 limousine services provide transportation to and from the airport.

Public bus service from and to Fort Worth is available at least hourly by the Fort Worth Transit Authority, or the "T." Fares cost up to $8 each way, payable by credit card, traveler's check, or cash. Loading and unloading of passengers takes place on the lower level of each terminal. Service to and from the Renaissance Worthington Hotel, Radisson Plaza, and other hotels is also available by the "T." For details, call (817) 334-0092.

The Airporter Park and Ride Service, e-mail: Airporter@the-T.com, from or to downtown costs $10 per person or $5 for senior citizens. The downtown Airporter Park and Ride lot is located at 1000 East Weatherford Street. You can board daily from 5 am to midnight at all major downtown hotels.

If going to or coming from the D/FW Airport, you can also call one of the shuttle services: **Classic Shuttle,** (214) 841-1900 in Dallas or (817) 222-2000 in Fort Worth; **Super Shuttle,** (817) 329-2000 or (800) 258-3826 if calling outside the city; or **TBS Shuttle,** (214) 361-7637 or (817) 267-5150. The cost to or from the D/FW Airport to downtown Dallas or to Fort Worth is less than one-half that of taxi, but you will likely spend more time waiting for the van to make its way through the stops before picking you up.

Taxi

Taking a taxi, as you already know, is expensive and only a sensible alternative if you use it sparingly. You will find taxis in front of better hotels. It is preferable to call for a taxi on the phone than trying to hail one on the street. Never get inside a taxi that already has more than one person, the driver.

If you go from D/FW Airport to downtown Fort Worth and the Stockyards (see entry), or the other way around, the taxi cost is about $35. The fare to downtown Dallas is about the same. The fare to Arlington is under $20. Please note that the airport taxi service is available on the upper level of each terminal for arriving passengers and on the lower level for those being discharged. For more information about taxi fare regulations or to complain, call the city of Dallas Department of Transportation at (214) 670-3161.

While there are almost two thousand taxis operated by more than a dozen companies in Dallas, Fort Worth only has two taxi franchises, **Yellow Cab** and **Checker Cab** with 500 taxis, both owned by a married couple and having a reputation for somewhat spotty service. Call for a taxi at least one hour before you need it.

Taxi companies authorized to service the Dallas/Fort Worth airport include:

Allied Taxi Service	(214) 654-4444
Big Tex Taxi Corporation	(214) 350-4590
Checker Cab Company (Fort Worth)	(817) 318-8088
Choice Cabs	(972) 222-2000
City Taxicab Company	(214) 902-7020
Cowboy Cab Company	(214) 428-0202
Eagle Cab Company	(214) 421-7788
Executive Taxi	(972) 554-1212
Golden Cab Company	(972) 484-4848
King Cab Company	(972) 241-3337
Ranger Taxi Company	(214) 421-9999
Republic Taxi Company	(214) 902-7077
State Taxicab Company	(214) 630-9595
Taxi Dallas	(214) 821-8294
Terminal Taxi Corporation	(214) 350-4445
West End Cab Company	(214) 902-7000
Yellow Cab (Fort Worth)	(817) 534-5555

Small Airplanes and Helicopters ————

Sightseeing tours of Fort Worth, Arlington, and Dallas, or any other Metroplex area of your choice, are available from a small plane or a helicopter.

Alamo Aviation, (817) 472-8307, is situated at Arlington Airport. For upwards of $120 for up to five passengers, you can enjoy the sight of downtown Cowtown and Arlington, as well as The Ballpark, Six Flags, and downtown Dallas for 30 minutes.

Lone Star, Inc., (972) 931-1051, fax 931-7073, is located at 4505 Claire Chennault in Addison. It provides helicopter sightseeing tours for two or four passengers, starting at about $200 per hour.

Sky Helicopters of Garland, (214) 349-7000, and **Zebra Air** of Dallas, (214) 358-7200, provide helicopter tours of various Metroplex locations, starting at $200 for 30 minutes.

Starlight Flights, (817) 588-1817, will also be found at Addison Airport. Their tours include practically any area of the Metroplex and start at about $120 for 30 minutes.

Automobile

Without an automobile in the Metroplex today, you might well feel like the Fort Worth founder Maj. Ripley Allen Arnold of the U.S. Army when he arrived from San Antonio in 1849.

You are just as good as done for without a car. Yes, you can travel by public transportation, but both Fort Worth and Dallas are so spread out—measuring together about 700 square miles—it might take you a year to explore it by public transport. But seriously, you only have four choices: walking, buses, rail, or private automobile.

Walking in Fort Worth is fine within the neighborhoods, such as downtown, in the historic Stockyards, and the arts district if the weather is all right and you do so during the day. Practically the only sensible way to get through the rest of the city is by bus or automobile.

Fort Worth is almost entirely encircled by Loop 820 and Interstate 20, which runs southeast toward Dallas.

The major north-south thoroughfare is Interstate 35, which runs from the Mexican border through San Antonio, Austin, and on to Oklahoma. Highway I-35 East runs through Dallas and I-35 West (also known as North or South Freeway) through Fort Worth. In the north the two meet at Denton, in the south near Hillsboro, about 75 miles from Dallas.

These are among the worst traffic areas in Fort Worth and Arlington:

• The downtown Fort Worth Mixmaster interchange connecting I-30 and I-35W, where reconstruction has been going on since 1996.

• Northeast Loop 820, between I-35W and the Airport Freeway/Loop 820 interchange, where traffic is congested most of the day.

• Rufe Snow Drive, at Northeast Loop 820. Traffic on southbound Rufe Snow is particularly congested in the morning.

• Texas 360 through the Union Pacific Railroad overpass in east Arlington. The freeway narrows to three lanes in each direction, resulting in a bottleneck for northbound traffic in the morning and southbound traffic in the evening.

• Interstate 20, between Matlock Road in Arlington and Spur 408 near Grand Prairie.

To check on road conditions, visit the *Dallas Morning News'* Internet site at www.dallasnews.com/index/traffic.htm, or the Texas Department of Transportation site at www.dot.state.tx.us/hcr/roads.htm.

Bus

Greyhound Bus Lines has a terminal in downtown Fort Worth, at 901 Commerce St., across the street from the Fort Worth Cnvention Center and Radisson Plaza Hotel (see entries), (800) 231-2222, Spanish speakers call (800) 531-5332.

Its terminal in Arlington is located at 2075 East Division St., (817) 461-5337, in the middle of nowhere; there is no eating or drinking place in sight but for a hamburger joint, several minutes away.

The Greyhound bus station in Dallas is located at 205 South Lamar and Commerce streets, (214) 655-7082.

All Metroplex bus stations and Greyhound buses have limited facilities for handicapped and elderly passengers. The 1,000 disabled riders that use Greyhound monthly should call 48 hours ahead to be lifted onto buses, although the Dallas-based bus company has only about two dozen buses with lifts.

Rail

Passenger rail service is available at **Fort Worth Union/Santa Fe Depot** (see entry) via **Amtrak,** at 15th and Jones streets downtown, (800) USA-RAIL or (817) 332-2931. When the Trinity Railway Express commuter line connects Fort Worth with Dallas in the year 2000, a new station will be built for both a couple of blocks away.

You can take the Texas Eagle, an Amtrak train from Fort Worth to Austin and San Antonio, daily. The coach fare to San Antonio is $53-$98 per person.

Going north, the same service is available to Little Rock, St. Louis, and Chicago. The coach fare to Chicago is $168-$298 per person, the sleeper $474-$796 per person. Most of the trains in either direction include freight cars to defray some of the cost.

Daily Amtrak passenger train service between Fort Worth and Oklahoma City—with stops in Gainesville, Texas, and Ardmore, Oklahoma—began in the spring of 1999.

AROUND FORT WORTH

Public Transportation—Buses

For schedules and information about Fort Worth's public transportation, where bus service is operated by the "T," please call (817) 215-8600, Internet www.the-T.com/index.html. **The T Customer Service Center** is located at 808 Houston and West Eighth streets, next to the historic W.T. Waggoner Building (see entry). The customer service center is open Mon-Fri 7 am-6 pm, Sat 8 am-2 pm.

Bus rides downtown are free roughly within Henderson, Jones, Belknap, and Lancaster streets. Outside that zone the cost is one dollar each way, 50 cents for students and children ages 5-15, the same as for seniors and disabled persons with a valid identification card. Transfers, valid for up to two hours, are free. Monthly passes are $30. If you pay cash, be sure to have exact change because the bus operator cannot make change.

There is bus service from downtown to the cultural district and the Stockyards. The bus line #2 starts from Throckmorton Street downtown, goes west on Camp Bowie to all museums, and continues on all the way to Ridgmar Mall and back. If you do not mind the time it takes, you can also go by bus to Hulen Mall (see individual entries), perhaps the best of all Fort Worth shopping centers. You will again start out on line #2 on Throckmorton, then change to bus route #25 at Hulen Street.

Bus line #1 also starts at Throckmorton downtown and goes northward on North Main Street, continuing on Ellis, and right to the edge of the Stockyards. If you get off across the street from Hotel Texas, you will be within easy walking distance of this historic district. To return downtown, go to the opposite side of the street. Going south, line #1 ends at Fort Worth Town Center Mall (see individual entries).

There is also an expanded door-to-door bus service known as the **Rider Request,** which blends by-request only with the fixed-route service. It operates in pockets across the city, such as southeast Fort Worth, the Town Center Mall area, Altamesa Boulevard, Northside Drive and Samuels Avenue, and the cities of Richland Hills and Lake Worth. Rider Request must be booked 24 hours in advance by calling (817) 390-7684. There is no bus service from downtown to the Alliance Airport.

Lost and found articles may be located by calling (817) 215-8600, Mon-Fri 6 am-8 pm, weekends 8 am-5 pm.

The Fort Worth Trolley

An old-fashioned trolley service is available between downtown, the historic Stockyards (see entry), and cultural district, roughly 10:20 am-6:20 pm. The trolley makes regularly scheduled stops about every half hour at the Stockyards, the Renaissance Worthington, Clarion, Ramada, Radisson hotels, and at the Visitors Center, all downtown, at Omni Theatre in the cultural district, and Joe T. Garcia's Tex-Mex restaurant, on the southern edge of the Stockyards. The ticket booth is located across the street from the Stockyards' Visitors Center, on East Exchange Avenue. Tourists can purchase all-day trolley passes for $8.

A nine-mile $35-million fixed-rail trolley system connecting downtown, cultural, and historic districts is also being considered. It would run from Exchange Avenue, going south on North Main Street, through downtown along Houston and Commerce streets, and continue west along West Seventh Street and Camp Bowie Boulevard.

DART (Dallas Area Rapid Transit) Electric Rail Service

Since 1997, a ten-mile DART commuter rail line, known as **Trinity Railway Express,** linking downtown Dallas Union Station, Medical Center, Market Center, and south Irving is utilizing diesel cars seating up to 96 riders with upholstered seats and climate control. Trinity Railway is a joint project between DART and the Fort Worth Transit Authority.

The line, continuing on to Hurst and Richland Hills, was extended to downtown Fort Worth in the year 2000, and will continue to Dallas-Fort Worth International Airport in 2005. The Trinity Express trains on this line will get you from south Irving to Dallas in 20 minutes. They run Mon-Sat 6 am-11:35 pm.

Car Rental

But the public transportation does not add up to much when you consider that Dallas and Fort Worth alone measure some 700 square miles. And visitors to the Metroplex are not likely to stand on the street corners for a bus that might transport them only part of the way to their final destination.

Fort Worth residents, like those in Dallas, have their own answer for this—their automobiles. In spite of nerve-wracking traffic tie-ups and the scorching heat during the summer, they refuse to use public transportation. It is a Texas badge of independence and no accident that most cars you see on public byways carry only one passenger. Fort

Worth residents enjoy the freedom a car provides; it will be many years before they change their habits, if ever.

Renting a car is often the preferred option of a visitor to the region.

If the expense of renting an economy car for upward of $50 a day is acceptable to you, there is no alternative to having an automobile in the Metroplex, although parking can be expensive, time-consuming, and sometimes difficult to find.

Upon your arrival at the Dallas-Fort Worth international airport, the rental company's shuttle bus can pick you up and bring you to the rental office. A $150-million rental car facility opened on a 150-acre site near the airport's south shuttle parking lot in 2000. A 40-vehicle fleet of buses operated by the airport and the car companies take customers to the two-story facility located on the airport's southeast corner, off State Highway 183, in Euless. Avis, Budget, Hertz, and National are located here and together with seven other companies, offer 5,000 cars under one roof. Access to the facility is outside the airport's tollbooth area and customers can leave the airport and re-enter the rental center without leaving to go through the booths.

You cannot pay cash for your rental car, unless you have made prior arrangements at home. Most rental agencies require that you be at least 25 years old and some will check your driving history. Make sure that you have sufficient insurance coverage. Return your vehicle with a full tank of gas or you might be charged as much as $4 a gallon to fill it up.

Car rentals are subject to a ten percent sales tax and if you pick up your vehicle at the D/FW airport there is another eight percent surcharge.

Among the major car rental companies with branches in the Metroplex:

D/FW Rental Phone

Advantage Rent-a Car	(800) 777-5500	(972) 257-1032
Alamo Rent-a-Car	(800) 327-9633	(972) 621-0236
Avis Rent-a-Car	(800) 331-1212	(972) 574-4130
Budget Rent-a-Car	(800) 527-0700	(972) 574-2115
Dollar Rent-a-Car	(800) 800-4000	(972) 929-8888
Enterprise Rent-a-Car	(800) 325-8007	(972) 986-0205
Hertz Rent-a-Car	(800) 654-3131	(972) 453-0370
National Rent-a-Car	(800) 227-7368	(972) 574-3400
Thrifty Rent-a-Car	(800) 367-2277	(972) 929-1234

Distances from Fort Worth
to Other Cities

If you should drive from Fort Worth to the cities below, here are the distances in miles, kilometers, driving time, and flight time:

Cities	Miles	Kms	Drive Time	Flying
Amarillo	340	547	6 hours	1 hour
Austin	190	305	3½ hours	50 minutes
Corpus Christi	372	599	7½ hours	1½ hours
Dallas	33	59	½ hour	———
El Paso	608	978	11½ hours	1½ hours
Houston	270	434	5½ hours	1 hour
San Antonio	270	434	5½ hours	1 hour
Texarkana	216	347	4 hours	1 hour

Private Car

When driving in Fort Worth and Arlington, you will encounter these roads with colloquial as well as official names:

South Freeway—Interstate 35 West between I-30 and the Tarrant County line in the south. It is known as **North Freeway** north of Interstate 30.

East Freeway—Interstate 30, running from southern Dallas to southern Fort Worth. It becomes **West Freeway** at Interstate 35 West, creating a giant cross southeast of downtown Fort Worth.

Southwest Loop 820—Interstate 20, roughly from Benbrook to Arlington. It changes its name as it winds around Fort Worth.

Airport Freeway—State Highway 183 from State Highway 114 to the south entrance of D/FW airport.

Collins Street, running through Arlington roughly between Interstate 20 and Airport Freeway, is also known as FM 157.

Watson Road, parallel with Collins Street and forming the eastern border of Arlington, is also referred to as State Highway 360.

To check on the condition of Texas interstate highways, U.S. highways, state highways, and other roads, go to the state's Internet site www.texas.gov.

The city of Fort Worth installed 2,000 programmable electronic parking meters in 1999. The hourly rate goes up to 75 cents downtown, but less than what you would pay in Dallas or Houston. In addition to coins, the meters also accept debit cards.

Tours

There are only two formal tours available in Fort Worth. The one downtown is given by Bill Campbell, an enterprising Fort Worth resident who enjoys showing tourists the Cowtown highlights. His pager and voice mail is (817) 327-1178, his e-mail address is dwcjr@swbell.net. The tour starts in the morning at the Radisson Plaza Hotel and ends at the Renaissance Worthington Hotel (see individual entries) about an hour later.

In the Stockyards historic district, you can sign up for an hourly walking tour of the area at the Visitors Center, next to the Stockyards Station and across the street from the Cowtown Coliseum (see individual entries).

There are no tours available of Arlington, except for the Texas Rangers' Ballpark.

Walking

Walking is a fine alternative in these neighborhoods, provided the weather is all right and you do so during the day:

Downtown, particularly the Sundance Square area, is as safe as you will get. Fort Worth residents might advise you not to walk alone after dark south of Ninth Street, even around the Fort Worth Convention Center or Fort Worth Water Gardens. If you stay at Care-A-Lot-Inn, Radisson Plaza, Park Central Hotel, and particularly Ramada Plaza Hotel downtown, be especially careful at night (see individual entries in the LODGING chapter).

You should have no problems walking through Sundance Square, day or night. The city and the Basses, who own large tracts of the Square, have gone out of the way to make the 12-block area between Fifth and Second on both sides of Main Street safer than most American downtowns. Sundance Square, in addition to the regular city police, is also patrolled by more than 100 private security officers on bicycles, horseback, and even skates.

The **Stockyards** historic district is safe by day and in the evening, while there are other people about. This includes mostly the east-west Exchange Avenue and a couple of blocks north and south on North Main Street only. Avoid all other areas at night, unless you are in the company of others.

The **Cultural District,** while notable for its many museums, such as the Kimbell, Modern, and Amon Carter, does not lend itself to walking, at least not in the summer. If the weather is agreeable, you could walk from one museum to the next, but that's about it; there are streets in the cultural district that do not even have sidewalks. The *Fort Worth Star-Telegram* reported in early 2000 that the city council considered requiring sidewalks in all new residential and commercial developments—"an excellent idea that's long overdue," opined the daily.

A downtown walking tour is included in the SELF-GUIDED CITY TOURS chapter.

LODGING

According to the Fort Worth Convention & Visitors Bureau, the city claims some 90 lodgings with about 7,500 hotel rooms, 2,200 of them downtown. The county, unfortunately, has the lowest percentage of full-service hotels among the major Texas markets. Only 29 percent of all lodgings are full-service hotels, compared with 50 percent in Dallas and 40 percent in San Antonio. About one-third of all Tarrant County hotels have limited service only.

The Bureau estimates that more than six million out-of-town travelers visit Cowtown, with an "economic impact of $1.7 billion."

All hotels below are listed as located downtown or elsewhere, then grouped into one of these approximate price categories:

I   Inexpensive, up to $50 for a single room
M   Moderate, $50-$100 for a single room
E   Expensive, more than $100 for a single room

Classifications are based on the regular daily rates, although many hotels offer special weekend and holiday deals. Ask also whether you qualify for a business, government, or another discount rate. Many hotels offer complimentary breakfast. Check-in time is usually between 11 am and 3 pm, check-out time between 11 am and 1 pm.

All hotels accept major credit cards, most take dollar-denominated traveler's checks, but none will accept foreign currencies as payment. You can exchange foreign currencies at Dallas-Fort Worth International Airport or Ridgmar Mall (see entries), which is located in southwest Fort Worth.

Fort Worth hotel-room tax is 15 percent, six percent of which is returned to the state. Of the remaining nine percent, seven percent is earmarked to promote local culture and tourism. Since 1998, an additional two percent on the bed tax has raised money earmarked for renovation of the Fort Worth Convention Center (see entry). Fort Worth sales tax is 8.25 percent and is added to most goods and services, including meals.

Toll-free 800 telephone numbers are included, where available, so you can call these hotels free of charge from anywhere in the U.S. to make reservations.

Some Fort Worth hotels will let you make local telephone calls— meaning inside area code 817—free of charge, while others might charge for them. Ask if this expense is of concern to you. You will always pay long distance rates—to Dallas and the other way around— unless there is a metro number available. Sometimes you pay whatever the traffic will bear. Always ask about long-distance charges before you make the calls.

Other amenities available are noted with these abbreviations:

C tells there is a concierge available on the premises.

CF designation means that there is no charge for children who occupy the same room as the adult that accompanies them. The minimum age limit varies.

CM indicates cable television and movies are available in your room.

FT means that the hotel provides free shuttle to and from the airport, or complimentary transportation within a few miles, such as to the nearest shopping center, or both.

HC indicates there are health club facilities available, although sometimes there may be a charge for the use of equipment.

HR will alert you to hotels that provide rooms for the handicapped and which are handicapped-accessible.

MF indicates that meeting facilities are available.

PA designation is included if pets are allowed.

PT abbreviation indicates the hotel is near public transportation, such as city bus route.

RS tells that room service is available.

DOWNTOWN
FORT WORTH HOTELS

CARE-A-LOT INN, 1111 West Lancaster Ave. at Henderson St.; (800) 952-3011 or (817) 338-0215, Fax 338-2539. M. Has 114 rooms and suites priced at $60-$120 a night. Located west of downtown on the way to the cultural district and museums, such as Kimbell, Modern and Amon Carter, or attractions like Will Rogers Coliseum and Casa Manana (see individual entries).

Amenities: Restaurant & cocktail lounge, complimentary in-room coffee, guest laundry, gift shop, swimming pool. Also CF, CM, HC, HR, MF, RS.

An independent family-owned six-story hotel that provides complimentary transportation within a two-mile radius, which includes all of downtown and the cultural district, but not the Stockyards (see entry) historic district, which is about three miles north of here.

CLARION HOTEL, 600 Commerce St. between Fifth and Sixth streets; (800) CLARION or (817) 332-6900, Fax 877-5440. M. Has 297 rooms on 13 floors, some non-smoking, priced at $80-$100 a night. Located in the central business district, diagonally across the street from the Bass Performance Hall on the edge of Sundance Square (see entries). Across East Fifth Street is Mexican Inn Cafe; across Commerce, Larry North Fitness Studio, which hotel guests can use free of charge.

Amenities: Safe-deposit boxes; restaurant & lobby lounge; business center with computer, copier, and fax; business-class rooms with desks, dataports, and speakerphones; coffeemakers with complimentary coffee; ice machines; laundry service; covered parking. Also CM, HC, HR, MF, PT, RS.

Back-to-back against Courtyard by Marriott, Clarion has a fairly large lobby filled with books, mostly Reader's Digest Condensed Books. A coffee shop and bar blend with the lobby that has plenty of sofas and easy chairs.

COURTYARD BY MARRIOTT, 601 Main at East Fifth St.; (800) 321-2211. It has 203 rooms and suites. Weekday rates range from $105 to $140 a night, on weekends from $60 to $90. Located on the edge of Sundance Square downtown, about a block southwest from the Bass Performance Hall (see individual entries). Guests can walk to most downtown sights and restaurants, day or night, thanks to the impressive security in the area. Corner Bakery restaurant is on the premises; Chili's Bar & Grill and Picchi-Pacchi are across the street; Tex-Mex Mi Cocina is a half-block north. Larry North Fitness Studio is across Commerce Street.

Amenities: No restaurant on the premises, indoor swimming pool, valet parking. Also C, CF, CM, FT, HC, HR, MF, PA, PT.

Originally known as the Blackstone Hotel (see entry in SIGHTS chapter), this 22-story Art Deco hotel initially opened a couple of weeks before the stock market crash of 1929, when rooms started at $2.50 a night. "Radio receiving sets are included, so that entertainment from distant places can be had by any guest," noted a flyer at the time. It was designed by the firm that also drafted the Rice Hotel in Houston, the Galvez Hotel in Galveston, and the St. Anthony Hotel in San

Antonio. In its heyday the Blackstone welcomed such luminaries as
Presidents Herbert Hoover and Richard Nixon. From 1952 to 1962, it
was known as the Hilton and has had several owners since then.

The Blackstone closed in 1982 and was gutted 16 years later to make
space for the Courtyard by Marriott, while the 1950s-era annex was
turned into a parking garage. Tax abatements obtained from the city
insured that the building's exterior was preserved down to the terra-
cotta detail. The compromise between the hotel's interior designer and
Marriott resulted in a hostelry having the chain's living-room-like
relaxed atmosphere, as well as a few distinctly Art Deco touches. The
lobby is understated. A section of the original stairway can be seen
upon entering on you right and next to it is a laser printer port.

Amon Carter, founder of the *Fort Worth Star-Telegram,* was one of
the first guests to check in at the Blackstone; in 1999, his daughter
Ruth Carter Stevenson was the ceremonial first guest.

PARK CENTRAL HOTEL, 1010 Houston at Ninth St.; (817)
336-2011 or (800) 848-PARK, Fax 336-0623, Internet www.parkcen-
tralhotel.com. M. Has 120 smoking and non-smoking rooms and suites
priced at $65-$225. A 60-year-old hotel showing its age located next to
the Fort Worth Convention Center and Flatiron Building downtown.
Radisson Plaza Hotel, City Hall, and Del Frisco's Double Eagle steakhouse are also nearby (see individual entries).

Amenities: American & Mexican cuisine restaurant, Jazz & blues
club with entertainment in the building, second-floor outdoor patio,
coin-operated washers & dryers, ice & beverage machines. Also CF,
CM, HC, MF, PT, RS.

The Sundance Square, with its new Bass Performing Hall is just a
few blocks to the north. The cultural district, with the Kimbell,
Modern, and Amon Carter museums is 1.5 miles to the west,
Stockyards historic district two miles northwest of here (see individual
entries).

RADISSON PLAZA, 815 Main at East Eighth St.; (800) 333-3333
or (817) 870-2100, Fax 882-1300, Internet www.radisson.com. E. Has
517 rooms and suites starting at $150 and going to $1,200 for a 2,500-
square-foot two-bedroom suite. Located downtown, across General
Worth Square from the Fort Worth Convention Center, and a few
blocks south of the Sundance Square (see individual entries). With
61,200 square feet of meeting space and the largest room accommodating 1,300 persons, this is one of the largest convention facilities in
Tarrant County.

Amenities: Two restaurants & cocktail lounge, heated rooftop
swimming pool with whirlpool and exercise room, gift shop. Also C,
CF, CM, HC, HR, MF, PT, RS.

Before being renamed Radisson in 1991, this was a Hyatt Regency Hotel. But most in the Metroplex know this as the Hotel Texas, where John F. Kennedy spent his last night. The following morning, on November 22, 1963, Kennedy was honored at a breakfast here for 2,000 business leaders. He made a quick public speech in the hotel's parking lot, while standing amid faint drizzle on the flatbed of a truck, with Vice-President Lyndon B. Johnson and Governor John Connally looking on. From there, Kennedy flew to Dallas's Love Field airport and, following a motorcade down Main Street, was assassinated just past noon.

The 15-story red-brick hotel was designed by the prolific Fort Worth architectural firm of Sanguinet and Staats. It was built in 1921 by a group of local leaders after the oil boom of 1917 and establishment of Camp Bowie and for many years it served as the showplace of Fort Worth. Boxer Jack Dempsey and film idol Rudolf Valentino were among its many prominent guests. "Ken Maynard, the celluloid cowboy, smartly rode his horse through the lobby of the hotel, eased into an elevator and came galloping out on the 14th floor," observes Caleb Pirtle in his Fort Worth history.

"The Kennedys drew no joy from Suite 850," at the Hotel Texas, according to Jim Bishop's 1968 book, *The Day Kennedy Was Shot*. "The management had redecorated and painted the three rooms, but, when the President arrived shortly after midnight, he and Mrs. Kennedy had looked the place over with little appreciation. The suite had been selected by the Secret Service because, as it stood in an elbow of the corridor, it was the easiest to protect." The suite has long since been demolished and several photos on display on the mezzanine are perhaps the only reminder of JFK's visit.

In 1967, Sheraton added a 230-room annex with a walkway to the addition over Commerce Street. In 1980, Hotel Texas was reconstructed into a Hyatt Regency, with an atrium, five-story skylight, and a 26-foot cascading waterfall.

Radisson Plaza, the largest Fort Worth hotel, is connected by skywalk to the 40-story glass and steel Continental Plaza (see entry), now also known as the Union Pacific Plaza, which was erected in 1982 and houses the Petroleum Club.

RAMADA PLAZA HOTEL, 1701 Commerce and East Fifteenth streets; (800) 2-RAMADA or (817) 335-7000, Fax 335-3333, Internet www.ramadaplaza.com, E-mail ramada@flash.net. E. Has 434 rooms and suites in two towers priced at $139-$450 a night. Located southeast of downtown, just north of Interstate 30, a couple of blocks from the Fort Worth Convention Center and across the street from the Fort Worth Water Gardens (see individual entries).

Amenities: Two restaurants & cocktail lounge, executive level for

business travelers, indoor heated swimming pool, hair dryers, coffeemakers, free parking. Also C, CF, CM, HC, HR, MF, PA, RS.

Fort Worth's third largest hotel, dumpy and crawling with groups
and conventioneers. It is owned by the Indonesian Pudjiadi family.
Some rooms have a good view of downtown from the upper floors.
Indonesian cuisine Bali Grill & Seafood, also owned by the hotel's
owners, a sports bar next to it, and a coffee shop, are all part of this
Ramada. In 2000, a $5-million renovation to its lobby, meeting spaces,
restaurants, guest rooms, and fitness facilities was begun.

While the area is safe during the day, we advise individual guests
against walking around at night.

RENAISSANCE WORTHINGTON HOTEL, 200 Main and
Second streets; (800) 433-5677 or (817) 870-1000, Fax 338-9176,
Internet www.worthingtonhotel.com. E. Has 504 rooms and suites
priced at $185-$750 a night. The Van Cliburn Suite goes for $1,000 a
night and includes a piano he plays when staying here, as well as photos of him and past Van Cliburn International Piano Competition winners. Located downtown on the northern end of the 12-block
Sundance Square (see entry), with some two dozen restaurants and bars
within walking distance. The hotel spans three city blocks and has one
of the half-dozen largest meeting facilities in Tarrant County. Neiman
Marcus offers complimentary shuttle service to and from the hotel.

The Stockyards, perhaps the city's best-known historical landmark,
which was a destination for cattle drives, is located about two miles north
of the hotel; the Kimbell, Modern, and Amon Carter museums (see individual entries) are situated in the cultural district 1.5 miles west of here.

Amenities: Two restaurants & cocktail lounge, two rooftop tennis
courts, indoor swimming pool. Also C, CF, CM, HC, HR, MF, PA, PT,
RS. The music that you hear on the phone when on hold, by the way,
is played by Cliburn.

Conceived by the Fort Worth billionaire Sid Richardson Bass,
designed by architect Paul Rudolph and built in 1981 as the
Americana, the 12-story polygon-shaped Worthington is the second
largest and the most luxurious city hotel. Until now independently
owned and locally operated, it gets four stars from the *Mobil Guide* and
four diamonds from the American Automobile Association.
Cosmopolitan, spacious, and comfortable, with elegant decor and
mahogany furniture, including desks and armoires, the Worthington
was renovated in 1995. A three-level underground parking garage is
also available. The hostelry was bought by Marriott in 1999, when it
became part of its full-service Renaissance group. Marriott operates
nearly 1,900 properties worldwide under 11 nameplates, including
more than 50 in the Renaissance chain.

Reflections (see entry in DINING chapter) is the more formal of the two Worthington restaurants and one of the most elegant eateries in Cowtown. The Star of Texas Grill serves traditional Texas cuisine, while the Bridge offers a "luscious buffet of more than 100 culinary delights," during Sunday brunch 10 am-2 pm. The lobby bar is suspended above the lobby. Check out The Real Deal at the Star of Texas: if you want to see a movie downtown during the weekend and eat at the Star before that, just call 882-1793 before noon on Friday and your tickets, along with an express menu, will be waiting for you.

In front of the Worthington, on the corner of Houston and West Second streets, you will see a sidewalk plaque where Fort Worth's first telephone exchange was founded in 1881; it initially served 40 customers and employed three persons.

A block from the hotel is a 155,000-square-foot discount mall at the Fort Worth Outlet Square (see entry), once named Tandy Center, which also houses a skating rink. You will find outlets for many well-known clothing manufacturers and other brands. Several informal restaurants are housed inside, including the well-known Sonny Bryan's Smokehouse.

OTHER FORT WORTH HOTELS

Roughly two dozen hotels are located inside or within about three miles, or ten minutes, of the Dallas-Fort Worth International Airport terminals. There are an additional 52 hotels in Irving, farther east.

Outside the central business district, budget travelers may also want to consider Motel 6, a French-owned chain based in Dallas, with 780 units nationwide and a dozen in and around Fort Worth. An average room still costs under $40 a night and includes a telephone, color television, and fax machine access. There are no meeting rooms, suites, or floors for business travelers at Motel 6, and the only discount is 10 percent off for members of the American Association of Retired Persons.

AMERICAN AIRLINES TRAINING & CONFERENCE CENTER, 4501 State Hwy. 360 South; (817) 956-1000, Fax 967-4867, Internet www.amrcorp.com/amrtg, E-mail aatcc@tg.amrcorp.com. E. Has 299 guest rooms and suites. Located on 30 wooded acres about three miles south of the Dallas-Fort Worth International Airport (see entry). From the airport, take the south exit and the Highway 360/Arlington exit, which bears to the right. From Fort Worth, take Interstate 20 East to Dallas, then Highway 360 North to Trinity Boulevard/FAA Road exit.

The training and conference center is "designed to encourage learning and professional growth without distraction, by providing comfortable surroundings, state-of-the-art facilities, and personal conveniences, all under one roof." There are 75 training, conference, and executive board rooms, accommodating up to 300 persons, some computer-equipped.

Amenities: Restaurants & cocktail lounge, business center, alarm clocks & coffeemakers, outdoor swimming pool & sand volleyball court, game room, hair salon, gift shop. Also CM, FT, HC, HR.

Single-occupancy rates in 1999 started at $220 a night and included room, breakfast, lunch, and dinner; meeting space; fitness facilities; and service charges.

American Airlines C.R. Smith Museum (see entry), chronicling the history of commercial aviation, is within walking distance.

AMERISUITES/HULEN MALL, 5900 Cityview Blvd. at Bryant Irvin Rd.; (800) 833-1516 or (817) 361-9797, Fax 361-9444. E. Has 128 suites priced at $100-$130 a night. Located in southwest Fort Worth, south of Southwest Loop 820, and one mile west of Hulen Mall (see entry), Fort Worth's largest shopping center.

Amenities: Business center, complimentary breakfast & newspaper, heated outdoor swimming pool, refrigerator & microwave, voicemail & dataport phones, laundry & valet service, iron & ironing board. Also CF, CM, HC, HR, MF.

There are several restaurants and a sports bar within walking distance. Hulen Mall has department stores like Dillard's and a hundred other shops and restaurants. Texas Christian University is four miles away, downtown business district 12 miles, and Stockyards historic district about 17 miles (see individual entries).

BEST WESTERN/WEST, 7301 West Fwy. at State Hwy. 183; (800) 528-1234 or (817) 560-0060, Fax 244-3047. M. Has 118 rooms and suites priced at $50-$95 a night. Located in west Fort Worth, south of Interstate 30 (also known as West Freeway), between Ridgmar Mall and North Z Boaz Park & Golf Course. The cultural district, with the Kimbell, Modern, and Amon Carter art museums, is about seven minutes east of here (see individual entries).

Amenities: Cocktail lounge, outdoor swimming pool, fax service, complimentary Continental breakfast, 24-hour coffee & tea service, coin laundry. Also CF, CM, MF, PA, PT.

There is a Bally Total Fitness health club located adjacent to Ridgmar Mall, at 6833 Green Oaks Rd. Golf facilities are available at North Z Boaz Golf Course, south of here. Neiman Marcus, Dillard's, and J.C. Penney's are located at the mall.

COMFORT INN/WEST, 8345 West Fwy. at Las Vegas Trail; (800) 228-5150 or (817) 244-9446, Fax 560-0801. M. Has 55 single or double rooms, some for non-smokers, priced upward of $55 a night. Located in west Fort Worth, about six miles west from downtown, south of Interstate 30 (also known as West Freeway) and east of Jim Wright Freeway (also known as Loop 820). Ridgmar Mall (see entry), which has several restaurants and Dillard's and Neiman Marcus department stores, is a couple of miles east of the hotel.

Amenities: Complimentary Continental breakfast, free local calls, outdoor swimming pool, coffeemakers and computer connections in all rooms, fax machine and copier on the premises, laundry facilities, free parking. Also CF, CM, HR, MF, PA.

A handsome hostelry that has no restaurant, but there are eating facilities nearby. The YMCA health club is located three blocks away, the city bus route behind the inn. It has a small practice putting range and a basketball goal.

Another Comfort Inn, with 99 rooms, is located in east Fort Worth at 2425 Scott Avenue, at Interstate 30 and Beach St.; (817) 535-2591.

A Comfort Inn Suites, with 45 suites, is situated in south Fort Worth at 6504 South Freeway (also known as I-30 West) and Altamesa Blvd.; (817) 568-9500.

COURTYARD BY MARRIOTT, 3150 Riverfront Dr. at South University Dr.; (800) 321-2211 or (817) 335-1300, Fax 336-6926. M. Has 130 rooms and suites priced at $105-$140 a night. Located in southwest Fort Worth, south of Interstate 30 (also known as West Freeway), north of the Trinity River, and west of Forest Park.

University Park Village shopping center is within walking distance from the hotel, but the Fort Worth Zoo and the Log Cabin Village are probably too far on foot. Texas Christian University is about half a mile away, Fort Worth Botanic Garden is within two miles (see individual entries).

Amenities: Breakfast cafe & casual lounge, lobby fax service, outdoor swimming pool, in-room coffee & tea service, complimentary newspaper, guest laundry. Also CF, CM, HC, HR, MF, PT.

In addition to Hoffbrau Steaks, there are several other restaurants in the shopping center, as well as on the other side of South University Drive.

GREEN OAKS PARK, 6901 West Fwy.; (800) 433-2174 or (817) 738-7311, Fax 737-4486, E-mail greenoak@onramp.net. M. Has 133 rooms and suites priced at $70-$110. Located in west Fort Worth at West Freeway (also known as Interstate 30), between State Highway 183 and Green Oaks Road. The hotel stands between the Ridgmar Mall (see entry) in the north and North Z Boaz Park & Golf Course.

New Orleans Nights restaurant and bar is on Calmont Avenue behind the hotel.

Amenities: Restaurant & cocktail lounge, airline desk & car rental counter, two outdoor swimming pools, gift shop, golf course nearby. Also CF, CM, HC, HR, MF, PA, RS.

FAIRFIELD INN, 3701 Northeast Loop 820; (800) 228-2800 or (817) 232-5700, Fax 232-5547, Internet www.marriott.com/fairfield-inn. M. Has 106 smoking and non-smoking rooms and suites priced at $65-$80 a night. Located in north Fort Worth, east of Interstate 35 West, also known as North Freeway. Exit on North Beach Street and stay on frontage road.

Amenities: Twenty-two suites feature spa, refrigerator & microwave, complimentary breakfast, indoor swimming pool, free local phone calls, same-day dry cleaning service.

Luby's Cafeteria is within walking distance. North East Mall and North Hills Mall are located on both sides of Northeast Loop 820 and State Highway 183, also known as Airport Freeway. Stockyards (see individual entries) historic district is about four miles southwest of here, downtown another mile south.

Another Fairfield Inn, with 81 rooms, is located in southwest Fort Worth, at 1505 South University Dr., (817) 335-2000, a mile from the Fort Worth Zoo (see entry). There are several restaurants within walking distance.

HAMPTON INN MEACHAM, 4681 Gemini Place at Meacham Blvd.; (800) 270-8307 or (817) 625-5327, Fax 625-7727. M. Has 66 smoking and non-smoking rooms priced at about $75. Located in a business park about four miles north of downtown Fort Worth and half a mile south of Loop 820 at Interstate 35 West, also known as North Freeway. A Cracker Barrel restaurant is nearby.

Amenities: Complimentary breakfast buffet, refrigerators in all rooms, swimming pool, dataport phones, fax & copy service, hair dryers, coffeemakers, washer & dryer. Also CF, CM, HR, MF.

Another Hampton Inn is located in west Fort Worth at 2700 Cherry Lane, south of Interstate 30; (800) HAMPTON or (817) 560-4180.

HARVEY HOTEL D/FW AIRPORT, 4545 West John W. Carpenter Fwy., Irving; (800) 922-9222 or (972) 929-4500, Fax 929-0733. E. Has 506 rooms and suites, some non-smoking or for the handicapped. Located east of D/FW International Airport (see entry), on Carpenter Freeway (also known as State Highway 114), and Esters Boulevard. Situated across Carpenter Freeway from Harvey Suites D/FW (see below).

Amenities: 34 meeting rooms, cocktail lounge, free parking, foreign language capabilities, indoor & outdoor swimming pools. Also CM, FT, HC, PA, RS.

The largest hotel in Irving, where 56 hotels—ten of them, like Harvey, luxury hostelries—with 8,600 rooms, were located in 1998.

Benton's Grill, open daily for breakfast, lunch, and dinner 5:30-10 pm, is a little-known hotel restaurant that serves good Southwestern cuisine. Scoops is an informal 1950s-style cafe open daily 11 am-midnight.

HARVEY SUITES D/FW AIRPORT, 4550 West John W. Carpenter Fwy., Irving; (800) 922-9222 or (972) 929-4499, Fax 929-0774. E. Has 164 suites, some non-smoking, and two for handicapped. Located on Carpenter Freeway (or State Highway 114) at Esters Boulevard, east of D/FW International Airport (see entry).

Amenities: Free parking, outdoor swimming pool, kitchenettes, complimentary breakfast. Also C, FT, HC, HR, MF, PA.

A business all-suite hotel, with no room service or restaurant on the premises, but has a lobby bar and shares two restaurants with Harvey Hotel D/FW Airport, across Carpenter Freeway (see above).

HOLIDAY INN D/FW AIRPORT NORTH, 4441 State Hwy. 114 West, Irving; (972) 929-8181, Fax 929-7302. M. Has 282 rooms, some for non-smokers, and five suites. Located on State Highway 114 (also known as West John W. Carpenter Freeway) at Esters Boulevard, east of Dallas-Fort Worth International Airport (see entry) and about seven miles from Holiday Inn D/FW Airport South (see below).

Amenities: Safe-deposit boxes, business center, restaurant & cocktail lounge, complimentary morning coffee, free parking, airline desk, foreign language capabilities, outdoor swimming pool, coin-operated laundry on premises, coffeemakers & hair dryers. Also CM, FT, HC, HR, MF, PA.

Situated about 25 miles from downtown Fort Worth. A 24-hour Denny's restaurant is within walking distance.

HOLIDAY INN D/FW AIRPORT SOUTH, 4440 West Airport Fwy., Irving; (800) 360-2242 or (972) 399-1010, Fax 790-8545. M. Has 409 rooms, seven of them suites, 301 non-smoking, six wheelchair-accessible. Located on State Highway 183 (also known as Airport Freeway), between Esters Boulevard and Valley View Lane, south of the D/FW International Airport (see entry).

Amenities: Safe-deposit boxes, two restaurants, indoor & outdoor swimming pools, free parking, children under 12 eat free from special menu, dry cleaning & laundry service available Mon-Sat, coin-operated washer & dryer, gift shop, travel agency, and ATM. Also CF, CM, FT, HC, MF.

Built in 1967, this hotel was upgraded in 1996 to include voicemail, coffeemakers, ironing boards, and hair dryers. Holidome Indoor Recreation Center in the atrium is open 9 am-10 pm and features pool tables, miniature golf, table tennis, and electronic games. There is a Kids Korner play area for children under the age of 10 years.

A notable Southwestern-cuisine restaurant, Circle Spur Grill is open daily for breakfast, lunch, and dinner 5-10 pm. Bennigan's restaurant is next door and Red Lobster across West Airport Freeway.

HOLIDAY INN NORTH, 2540 Meacham Blvd. at Interstate 35 West; (800) HOLIDAY or (817) 625-9911, Fax 625-5132. M. Has 247 rooms and suites on six floors priced at $90-$200 a night. Non-smoking rooms are available. Located five miles north from downtown Fort Worth at exit 56A, adjacent to an industrial park. Except for a McDonald's fast-food restaurant across the street, there are no eating or entertainment facilities within walking distance.

Amenities: Safe-deposit boxes, two full-size restaurants—one a steakhouse—and a cocktail lounge, gift shop, indoor swimming pool, sauna & whirlpool, clock radios, computer dataports & desks, laundry facilities, irons & hair dryers, complimentary parking. Also C, CF CM, HC, HR, MF, RS.

Holiday Inn Central, with 185 rooms, is located on a four-acre hilltop in east Fort Worth, two miles from downtown, at 2000 Beach St. and Interstate 30; (817) 534-4801. It has 16,300 square feet of meeting space and the largest room can accommodate 300 persons.

HOLIDAY INN SOUTH, 100 East Altamesa Blvd. at Interstate 35 West; (800) HOLIDAY or (817) 293-3088, Fax 551-5877, Internet www.holiday-inn.com/hotels/ftwso. M. Has 247 smoking and non-smoking rooms with double and king-size beds on six floors, priced at $85-$185 a night. Suites are equipped with Jacuzzi. Located in a business park seven miles south of downtown Fort Worth, at the southeast crossing of Southwest Loop 820 (known here as Interstate 20) and South Freeway, also known as Interstate 35 West.

Amenities: Safe-deposit boxes, restaurant & sports bar, indoor swimming pool, sauna & whirlpool, laundry facilities, gift shop, iron & ironing board, free parking. Also CF, CM, HC, HR, MF, PA, RS.

The Rig Steakhouse, with live country and Western music, is located nearby; Hulen Mall (see entry) is about four miles northwest of here.

HOTEL TEXAS, 2415 Ellis at West Exchange avenues; (800) 866-6660 or (817) 624-2224, Fax 624-7177, Internet www.fortworthians.com/hotel. M. Has 20 smoking and non-smoking rooms with queen-size beds priced at $50-$110 a night. One room has a king-size bed with Jacuzzi. Located in the historic Stockyards district, two miles north of downtown. Within walking distance of White Elephant Saloon, Billy Bob's honky-tonk, Cowtown Coliseum, Stockyards Station, and many eating and drinking establishments (see individual entries).

Amenities: Safe-deposit boxes, security cameras at front & back doors, free parking, complimentary coffee. Also CF, MF, PT.

Formerly known as the Exchange Hotel, the two-story Hotel Texas was built in 1939. It is owned by Steve Murrin, a former Fort Worth councilman and an unofficial mayor of the Stockyards. Its light-yellow, hollow tile and brick trim has been preserved, while the interior was renovated. Not exactly the place for you if you tend to be loud or are bothered by hearing others, but perfect for would-be cowboys who just come in at night to recharge for another day of sightseeing. Only registered guests are allowed inside the hotel after midnight.

Hotel Texas, Stockyards Hotel, and Miss Molly's bed and breakfast are the only lodging houses in the Stockyards district (see individual entries).

HYATT REGENCY D/FW, International Pkwy., D/FW Airport; (800) 233-1234 or (972) 453-1234, Fax 615-6825/456-8668, Internet www.hyatt.com. E. Has 1,369 soundproofed rooms and suites, some non-smoking, or for the disabled, priced at $185-$1,100 a night; has 850 employees. Located inside the D/FW International Airport (see entry). With 130,000 square feet of meeting space, this is among the half-dozen largest convention facilities in Tarrant County.

Amenities: Free parking, 82 meeting rooms, airline desk, foreign language capabilities. Also C, CM, FT, HC, HR, RS.

Hyatt Regency D/FW, supposedly the world's largest airport hotel, consists of two separate towers that have the third largest number of hotel rooms in the Metroplex, after Dallas's Adam's Mark and Wyndham Anatole hotels:

The **West Tower,** with 550 rooms, was constructed in 1972 and has a swimming pool. Its only eating facility is SOS Diner, which serves lunch and dinner.

The **East Tower,** having 815 rooms, was built in 1980. It houses three restaurants: Papaya's, serving Southwestern and Tex-Mex cuisine for lunch and dinner, is also popular for its set-price weekend seafood buffet, featuring lobster, swordfish, stuffed crab, and salmon. Papaya's is both for smokers and non-smokers and wheelchair-accessible. If dining here, validate your parking ticket and you will leave the airport free of charge.

For smokers only there is also Mr. G's, serving steaks and seafood Mon-Fri 6-10 pm. For non-smokers only is Il Nonos, an Italian-cuisine restaurant open Mon-Sat, also 6-10 pm.

The Hyatt's two 18-hole golf courses, seven tennis courts, and ten racquetball facilities are located at Bear Creek, off State Highway 360 and Mid-Cities Boulevard, about five miles south of the airport.

LA QUINTA NORTH, 4700 North Fwy.; (800) NU-ROOMS or (817) 222-2888, Fax 222-2229, Internet www.laquinta.com. M. Has

133 rooms and suites priced at $95-$140. Located in north Fort Worth at Interstate 35 West (also known as North Freeway) and Meacham Boulevard. Meacham International Airport is four miles west of here, downtown Fort Worth about five miles south.

Amenities: Complimentary breakfast, heated outdoor swimming pool, jogging trail, some rooms with microwaves & refrigerators, in-room coffeemakers, laundry facilities, dry cleaning service. Also CF, CM, HC, HR, MF, PA.

Cracker Barrel is the sole restaurant within walking distance. You will need a car or taxi to get around. Fossil Creek Golf Course is two miles away.

Other La Quintas with similar amenities are located at 1450 West Airport Fwy. in Bedford, at 17920 Bedford-Euless Rd. in North Richland Hills, at 4900 Bryant Irvin Rd. in southwest Fort Worth, and at 7888 Interstate 30 West in White Settlement.

MARRIOTT D/FW AIRPORT, 8440 Freeport Pkwy., Irving; (972) 929-8800, Fax 929-6501. E. Has 770 rooms and suites, some non-smoking and for handicapped. Located at the crossroads of John W. Carpenter Freeway West (also known as State Highway 114) and Freeport Parkway, east of D/FW International Airport (see entry). It is one of almost two dozen hotels located within about three miles of the airport. The hotel has completed a $40-million expansion.

Amenities: Safe-deposit boxes, 24 meeting rooms, free parking, 24-hour complimentary airport shuttle, indoor & outdoor swimming pools, iron & ironing board, valet & laundry service. Also C, CM, HC, HR, PA, RS.

A deluxe hotel located near the north entrance of the D/FW Airport and close to the Las Colinas Urban Center. The second largest Irving hotel in 1998. Marriott's Business Center—open Mon-Thu 7 am-6 pm, Fri 7 am-3 pm—provides typing, faxing, photocopying, and desktop publishing services.

JW's Steakhouse, open Mon-Sat 6-10:30 pm, serves dinner in luxurious surroundings. Marriott Cafe is a more casual setting for breakfast, lunch, and dinner. Pitcher's Tavern is a sports bar with games and satellite television.

Golf and tennis facilities are available nearby.

RAMADA INN MIDTOWN, 1401 South University Dr. at Rosedale St.; (800) 228-2828 or (817) 336-9311, Fax 877-3023. M. Has 182 rooms—no suites—priced at about $75 a night. Located in southwest Fort Worth, south of Interstate 30, also known as West Freeway. The Fort Worth Botanic Garden is located half a mile north of here, just across I-30, the Fort Worth Zoo and Log Cabin Village are a mile south in Forest Park. Within walking distance of a couple of restaurants. The cultural district, with attractions such as the Kimbell Art Museum or Casa Manana are about a mile north from here.

Amenities: Restaurant & sports bar, hospitality suite, outdoor swimming pool, free parking, self-service laundry. Also CF, CM, HC, HR, MF, PA, PT, RS.

RESIDENCE INN BY MARRIOTT/FOSSIL CREEK, 5801 Sandshell Dr.; (800) 331-3131 or (817) 439-1300, Fax 439-3329. *E.* Has 114 suites priced at $100-$150 a night. Located in north Fort Worth, east of Interstate 35 West (also known here as North Freeway) and north of Northeast Loop 820. Adjacent to Fossil Creek Golf Course and two blocks from a UA Cinema. North Hills Mall, a few miles southeast from the hotel, has several restaurants and department stores, such as Foley's and Mervyn's.

Amenities: One- or two-bedroom suites with kitchens & microwaves, complimentary Continental breakfast, sports court with basketball, volleyball & paddle tennis, heated outdoor pool, grocery shopping service, dry cleaning & laundry facility, housekeeping service, free parking, complimentary newspaper, coffee & popcorn. Also CF, CM, HC, HR, MF, PA with a $100 non-refundable fee.

A handsome lodging house that caters to long-term guests. There is no restaurant on the premises, but Chili's and J. Christens Grill & Bar steakhouse are nearby. Social hour is Mon-Thu 5:30-7 pm.

RESIDENCE INN BY MARRIOTT/RIVER PLAZA, 1701 South University Dr. at Interstate 30; (800) 331-3131 or (817) 870-1011, Fax 877-5500. *E.* Has 120 studio and 930-square-foot penthouse smoking and non-smoking suites, many with fireplaces, priced at $110-$150 a night. Located in southwest Fort Worth along the Trinity River and south of I-30, also known as West Freeway. University Village shopping center is across the street and has several restaurants, while the much larger Hulen Mall is several miles southwest of here. Texas Christian University, Botanic Garden, Fort Worth Zoo, and the cultural district, with the Kimbell, Modern, and Amon Carter museums are all located within a mile.

Amenities: Complimentary breakfast & newspaper, sport & tennis court, heated outdoor swimming pool, complimentary van service & grocery shopping service within 10 miles, kitchens with microwaves & coffeemakers, 24-hour coin-operated guest laundry & one-day dry cleaning service, free parking. Also CF, CM, FT, HC, HR, MF, PA, PT, RS.

Consists of several rustic buildings, facing inward, with a tiny lobby and small breakfast area.

STOCKYARDS HOTEL, 109 East Exchange Ave. at North Main St.; (800) 423-8471 or (817) 625-6427, Fax 624-2571. *E.* Has 52 rooms and suites priced at $105-$275 a night. Located in a 1906 brick building in the heart of the Stockyards historic district (see entry), with all the Stockyards restaurants, saloons, and other attractions within an easy walking distance.

The hotel owes its existence to Armour and Swift meat-packing plants, which began operating in 1902 and created a need for Stock Yards Club Saloon that in 1904 included furnished rooms above it. The hotel was built in 1907 by Col. Thomas Marion Thannisch (1853-1935) of the Confederate Army and was enlarged to its current size in 1913, when the saloon was demolished. Thannisch's watch and bankbook are on display in the lobby vitrine.

The hotel's name was changed six times and by 1981, when it was closed down by the health department "for numerous code violations," it offered rooms for $5 a night with a bath down the hall. Modern-day brigands Bonnie Parker and Clyde Barrow, who terrorized bankers during the Depression, hid out at this hotel in 1933 while being chased by the law; they checked into Room 305, which overlooks Main and Exchange and provides a good lookout point. One of Bonnie's guns, along with papers of authenticity, is displayed at the hotel. Thannisch's heirs sold the property in 1982, when the new owners restored the building as an exclusive hotel that opened in 1984. The lobby is filled with old furnishings, there is a Western-style registration desk, and if you look out of the lobby windows, you can easily imagine you are in the Old West.

Rooms are furnished with Western memorabilia, such as horsehide seats, and are decorated in Western, Indian, Mountain Man, and Victorian style.

Amenities: Coffeemakers, hair dryers, irons & ironing boards. Also CF, CM, MF, PA, RS.

There is the Hunter Brothers' H3 Ranch steakhouse next door (see the DINING chapter). If you want another authentic taste of Cowtown, stop at the adjacent Booger Red's Saloon, which has saddles instead of stools at the bar. It was named after a well-known bronc rider Samuel "Booger Red" Privett (1864-1924), whose flaming red hair gave him away. The name stuck after a homemade explosive blew up in his face at age 13; as he was being carried to the hospital a friend supposedly exclaimed, "Gee, Red sure is all boogered up." He performed with Buffalo Bill's Wild West Show and supposedly rode as many as 40,000 bucking horses in his entire career—86 in one day in 1915 in San Francisco. His wife claimed that his last ride, at age 60, took place at the 1924 Fat Stock Show in Fort Worth, or what is now known as the Southwestern Exposition and Livestock Show (see entry). The saloon has been in business since 1907.

ALTERNATE LODGING

Bed and Breakfasts

Staying in a hotel is one thing, but living like a Texan is another. Consider a bed and breakfast, Texas style—chances are you will like it. The rates are about the same as those at a mid-priced hotel, but that's where most comparisons end.

You will stay with hosts who want to have you in their home and will be proud to share with you some of that Texas hospitality. You can stay for one night or a month.

Among the Fort Worth bed and breakfast choices:

AZALEA PLANTATION, 1400 Robinwood Dr.; (800) 68-RELAX or (817) 838-5882, Internet www.ftworthians.com/azalea. E. Has only four rooms priced $100-$150 a night, including breakfast. Located in northeast Fort Worth, three blocks west of Haltom City (once called Birdville), in a "stately plantation-style home reminiscent of Tara, nestled among almost two acres of majestic oaks, magnolias and azaleas."

This historic home was built in 1948 (when an upscale Philco Radio-Phonograph Console sold for $389.95 downtown) by W. J. Browning, a prominent Fort Worth builder, and was enjoyed by his own family for 22 years. All rooms have private baths, two have whirlpool tubs; terrycloth robes are provided.

BED & BREAKFAST AT THE RANCH, 8275 Wagly Roberson Rd.; (888) 593-0352 or (817) 232-5522, Internet www.fortworthi-ans.com/branch. M. Has only four rooms priced $85-$125 a night, including breakfast buffet on weekends, Continental breakfast on weekdays. No pets. Smoking is allowed in the smokehouse. Located one mile north of the town of Saginaw. From Interstate 35 West, take N.E. Loop 820 heading west. Take the Saginaw-North Main exit #13 and go north four miles to Bailey Boswell Road, then turn right and follow that road for one mile.

"Originally built in the early 1900s, this house was once the ranch headquarters for several thousand acres where cattle were raised," say hosts, Scott and Cheryl Stewart. "From the moment you step into our Ranch House on 20 glorious acres, you will feel the warmth and rugged personality of your surroundings. A large living room with a stone fire-place is yours to enjoy. Board games, television, or a book from the library area are also available."

"Col. K. M. van Zandt's very own ball and claw bathtub is yours for soaking" in the Hideaway Room on the second floor. "Brands, some of which have been in the family for 100 years, are on display" in the Lazy B Ranch Room, where there are also antiques that date back to before the Civil War.

ETTA'S PLACE, 200 West Third St.; (817) 654-0267, Fax 878-2560, Internet caravanofdreams.com. *E.* Has ten rooms, priced at $125-$185 a night for doubles, including a four-course breakfast. Brunch is served Sat-Sun 10 am-noon, but non-guests must reserve 24 hours ahead. Visitors must ring a bell to enter, then take an elevator upstairs. Located around the corner from the Caravan of Dreams night club on Sundance Square (see individual entries) downtown in a restored seven-story brownstone.

Downtown's only B&B is named after the Sundance Kid's girlfriend, Etta Place, who returned from Argentina in 1906 to have her appendix removed. Outlaws Butch Cassidy and his sidekick Sundance Kid were mowed down in a dusty Bolivian village, while Etta's whereabouts were unknown. Soon after the bandits' death, a woman known as Eunice Gray began operating the Waco Hotel in the area, at 110 East 15th Street, and held it until a fire killed her and destroyed it in 1962. The 77-year-old Eunice Gray was believed to have been Etta Place.

The *Fort Worth Star-Telegram* calls it "an oasis of charm in the heart of thriving downtown," but "expensive." The ten rooms on the second floor are individually decorated with Texas antiques. Not many know that from Etta's, you have direct access to the Caravan's Grotto Bar without exiting the B&B.

MISS MOLLY'S, 109½ West Exchange Ave., (800) 996-6559 or (817) 626-1522, Fax 625-2723, Internet www.missmollys.com. *M.* Has eight rooms priced at $95-$175 a night, including breakfast. Located in the historic Stockyards, on the second floor of a 1910 building with a steep flight of stairs, above what is now the Star Cafe. Billy Bob's, Cowtown Coliseum, Livestock Exchange Building & Museum, and other attractions are all within walking distance.

"The floors creak and groan just like at grandma's house," says the *Fort Worth Star-Telegram.* "The decor is turn-of-the-century Western, with heavy doses of Victorian froufrou." Free parking, but no smoking on the premises.

This was originally a prim rooming house, which in the 1940s became a bordello named the Gayette Hotel. Seven rooms are modeled after the original hotel—the bathrooms with iron tubs, pull-chain toilets, and pedestal sinks are down the hall—the eighth room, named Miss Josie's, was the madam's quarters, where you could rent the girls along with the rooms, and has Victorian decor and the only private bathroom.

Miss Molly's, Hotel Texas, and the Stockyards Hotel are the only lodging houses in the Stockyards district (see individual entries).

THE TEXAS WHITE HOUSE, 1417 Eighth Ave. at Magnolia; (800) 279-6491 or (817) 923-3597, Fax 923-0410. E. Has three rooms priced at $105 a night and $85 for each additional night, including breakfast. Located near All Saints Episcopal Hospital (see entry), about five miles southwest of downtown. Forest Park is farther southwest from here.

This 1910 home is a historical landmark decorated in a simple country style. The first floor offers a parlor, living room with fireplace, formal dining room, and half bath. "I guarantee a stay to be comfortable, relaxing and enjoyable," promises hostess Jamie McMains, who will, upon request, provide even a feather bed. No children or pets are accepted.

Ruth Wilson, who has managed **Bed & Breakfast Texas Style** since 1982, runs a bed and breakfast service, providing rooms throughout Texas. Call her Mon-Fri 8:30 am-4:30 pm CST at (800) 899-4538 from anywhere in the U.S., or (972) 298-8586 in Dallas to make reservations. She suggests that you contact her a couple of weeks in advance, perhaps by fax, at (214) 298-7118, with your instructions as to when you will arrive and how long you plan to stay. You will need to make a deposit equal to one night's accommodations by a credit card and can pay the balance to your hosts or prepay the entire bill on your credit card.

Apartments

If you need more space and privacy than you would get at a hotel and can stay for several months, you can probably save money by considering an apartment as the alternative to high-priced lodgings.

Perhaps the best known apartment complex in Fort Worth is **Sundance West,** (817) 339-7777, a luxury apartment house at 333 Throckmorton Street, around the corner from the Caravan of Dreams night club and across the street from the Fort Worth Outlet Square (see individual entries). Overlooking Sundance Square, it offers 59 units, beginning on the sixth floor, as well as retail establishments on the ground. It opened in 1992.

There are one-, two-, and three bedroom apartments with 38 floor plans available at Sundance West, ranging from 605 to 2,268 square feet, priced at more than $1 a square foot. The eleventh and twelfth floors contain nine penthouse apartments with Jacuzzis and fireplaces. Some of the units have terraces, walk-in closets, frost-free refrigerators, built-in microwaves, and ceiling fans. Underground parking comes with restricted access and there is 24-hour concierge service. Prices go up to $3,300 a month.

Although some of Sundance West units are the "home of downtown gentry and four-figure monthly rents," even the Basses, among other tenants, according to news reports, have had to deal with the embarrassment that "several of the units have suffered significant water damage" in the past.

There is a waiting list at Sundance West, as is at the historic **Electric Building,** at 410 West Seventh Street, (817) 877-0433, next to the Fort Worth Star-Telegram Building (see individual entries in the SIGHTS chapter). But the one notable difference is that the service at the Electric Building is sorely lacking. It is practically impossible to speak to anyone and you will be lucky just to get a fax of what is available.

The Electric Building, located diagonally across from Burnett Park, with Matisse's sculptures, contains 106 one- and two-bedroom apartments, priced at about $1 a square foot, or up to about $1,500 a month. Deposit is $350-$500; deposit for a cat $500, of which $150 is nonrefundable. One parking "stall" is included with each unit. There is no concierge on the premises.

Also managed by Sundance West are the 59 loft-style apartments at **Sanger Lofts,** also in Sundance Square. They are located in the Sanger Brothers Building, 222 West Fourth, between Houston and Throckmorton streets, diagonally across from Bank One Tower and next to the Modern at Sundance Square Annex (see individual entries).

The 54 one-bedroom units and five penthouses on the sixth floor range from 840 to 1,532 square feet with hardwood floors, frost-free refrigerators, walk-in closets, 24-hour laundry facilities, reserved underground parking, and concierge service. Prices range from $1,000 to $2,200 a month.

Southwest of downtown and east of Forest Park, at 2306 Park Place Blvd., (817) 926-2306, is located **The Forest Park,** a high-rise apartment building with twelve floors and three homes on each floor. When opened in 1927, it was "considered one of the finest buildings in town," according to the authors of a 1998 history of Leonard Brothers Department Store; its founder lived here for a while with his wife. The one-, two-, and three-bedroom apartments measure from 1,015 to 1,610 square feet. Deposit is one month's rental. They sport hardwood floors, microwaves, dishwashers, washers and dryers, covered parking, and, if you are lucky, a view of Forest Park and the Fort Worth Zoo (see individual entries).

Several other apartment complexes are available around downtown, including:

Firestone Apartments, 1001 West Seventh and Henderson streets in upper west Fort Worth, (817) 654-2888, where 350 apartments rent for $750-$1,700. This was originally a 1930 Firestone Service Center. "There's no Starbucks in the area," says the *Fort Worth Star-Telegram.* "Neither is there a grocery store." There is a basketball half-court and fitness room with showers, as well as a swimming pool. Includes a business center with conference rooms and copier.

Houston Place Lofts, 910 Houston, between East Eighth and Ninth streets, claims 300 units priced $975-$2,150 a month.

The Reserve, a project of the Dallas billionaire Trammell Crow, at 1000 Henderson St., also in upper west Fort Worth, (817) 332-1670, where 194 units go for $775-$1,650. Has a small fitness room and business center with conference room. Also a small heated swimming pool and spa, and laundry facilities.

The Gates of Seventh Street Station, a project still farther west from downtown—across from what was in 1928 a $2-million Montgomery Ward operation at 2601 West Seventh Street—with 189 apartments renting for $875-$1,700. Has gated entry, a lounge, club room, and business center open 24 hours a day. Also outdoor swimming pool and a separate hot tub. Units with a view of the pool are an additional $50 a month. Some of the apartments are wheelchair-accessible.

Hillside Apartments, with 172 units, and **The Cotton Depot,** with 220, all of which rent for $700-$1,400, both located at Crump and East Fourth streets, on the eastern edge of downtown.

Remington Place, 1000 West Belknap Street—the first downtown residences for sale in recent history—consists of 18 townhomes built by Perry Homes, starting at $248,000.

The company that we found helpful in locating an apartment in Fort Worth or Arlington was **Texas Apartment Locators,** (800) 930-7346 or (817) 633-2300. **Apartment Hunters** in Bedford, (817) 545-4868, also does a good job.

See also the TARRANT COUNTY REAL ESTATE chapter.

DINING

There are more than five hundred restaurants in Fort Worth. While here, you can treat yourself not only to the usual fare you will find in other cities, but also to excellent barbecue, chili, Mexican food, and superb steaks—all foods that Texas is famous for.

In 1997, the city adopted an ordinance under which Fort Worth restaurants had until the year 2000 to ban smoking from their premises or install air-purification systems. Restaurants with fewer than 50 seats are exempt from this regulation. The ordinance is similar to measures that regulate smoking in public places in Arlington, Carrollton, and Plano.

Of the 1,087 restaurants, snack bars, and delis in the city, 563 have declared no-smoking areas at the beginning of 2000.

Reviews of the restaurants below include select snippets of local media reviews. None of the establishments knew when the reviewers visited. No gratuity or service was ever given or offered to influence any review. Brunches are noted under individual entries.

For more opinions on these and other restaurants, see also the *Fort Worth Star-Telegram's* Friday's Star Time, *Dallas Morning News's* Guide, free weeklies *FW Weekly* and *Dallas Observer, D Magazine, Texas Monthly,* and *Zagat's* yearly booklet surveys. Check also the Internet site www.fortworth.com.

All restaurants are grouped into one of these three price categories:

I   Inexpensive (up to $10 per person)
M   Moderate ($10-$25 per person)
E   Expensive (more than $25 per person)

While meals in the moderate and expensive categories could include an appetizer, entree, dessert, or non-alcoholic beverage, the prices do not factor in alcoholic beverages or gratuities.

Credit cards are so widely accepted that we single out only a few establishments that do not take any of them. Fort Worth residents usually tip 10-15 percent, depending on the level of service, but almost never less than a dollar.

And, finally, be aware that none of the Metroplex cities has ordinance regulating valets. Established valet companies must live up to certain standards, but to save money, many restaurants use their own staff to park cars. "Such valets are often inexperienced," says *The Met* weekly, "and because of the lack of regulation may freely operate with either minimal insurance coverage or no coverage at all."

RESTAURANTS BY AREA

Downtown/Sundance Square ————————

8.0, Eclectic
Angeluna, New American
Cabo Mix-Mex Grill, Mexican tropical seafood
Chili's Grill & Bar, Cafe
Coffee Haus, Cafe
Del Frisco's Double Eagle, Steaks
Ellington's Southern Table, American
Flying Saucer, Pub
The Grape Escape, Wine bar
La Madeleine French Bakery & Cafe
Mexican Inn Cafe, Mexican
Mi Cocina, Mexican
Parthenon, Greek
Picchi-Pacchi, Italian
Pizzeria Uno, Italian
Randall's Cafe & Wine Bar
Razzoo's Cajun Cafe
Reata, Southwestern
Reflections, New American
Riscky's Bar-B-Q, Barbecue
Rodeo Steakhouse, Steaks
Surf Club USA/The Brew Co., American
Terry's Grill, Barbecue
Tommy's Hamburgers

Stockyards ————————————————————

Cattlemen's Steak House
Hunter Brothers' H3 Ranch, Steaks
Joe T. Garcia's Mexican Dishes

Los Vaqueros, Mexican
Old Spaghetti Warehouse, Italian
Riscky Rita, Mexican

Cultural District

The Back Porch, Home cooking
Dos Gringos Cantina, Tex-Mex
La Familia, Mexican
Michaels, Contemporary ranch
Sardines, Italian

Other Areas

Angelo's, Barbecue
Aventino's, Italian
The Balcony at Ridglea, Continental
Benito's, Mexican
Bistro Louise, New American
Blue Mesa, Southwestern
Cafe Aspen, New American
Celebration, Home cooking
Edelweiss, German
Hoffbrau Steaks
Isabella's Italian Bistro
Kincaid's, Hamburgers
La Piazza, Italian
Lucile's Bistro, New American
Maharaja, Indian
Ol' South Pancake House, American
The Original, Mexican
The Railhead Smokehouse, Barbecue
Ruffino's, Italian
Saint-Emilion, French
Uncle Julio, Mexican
Venecia, Italian
Water Street Seafood

RESTAURANTS BY CUISINE

American

Ellington's Southern Table, 301 Main and East Second streets; (817) 336-4129. M. Open daily, 11 am-11 pm. Wheelchair-accessible.

Located downtown in Sundance Square, two blocks from the Tarrant County Courthouse, and next to La Madeleine French Bakery & Cafe. An unlucky location, for restaurants seem to come and go on this corner. Until you look at the menu, you cannot tell that Ellington's is a "home cooking" establishment.

Clad in dark wood, Ellington's was opened by the owners of Mi Cocina three blocks south of here. It serves popular Southern dishes, such as liver and onions and pork chops, although similar dishes are priced at about $3 less at lunch.

St. Louis-style ribs are $17, the same as Southern-fried shrimp or fried oysters. An 8-ounce tenderloin is about the most expensive dish at $20. Chances are you will like the chicken and dumplings in a ceramic crock or the chicken pot pie. All entrees are served with two vegetables. Meals for children 12 and under are $5 each. Has a full bar and respectable wine list.

The Grape Escape, 500 Commerce St.; (817) 336-9463. M. Open Mon-Thu 11 am-11 pm, Fri-Sat 11 am-midnight. Located in Sundance Square downtown, across the street from the Bass Performance Hall, Flying Saucer pub, and Barnes & Noble Booksellers (see individual entries).

One of only a handful of wine bars in north Texas. The owner, Michael Baudouin, picked up the idea in the late 1970s when he lived in Paris. "Simply one of the best wine bars in the country," says the *Dallas Observer*, "with a well-executed tasting protocol and constantly shifting wine selections that make experimenting and learning about wine fun." *D Magazine*, "looking for the place where the service, food, and atmosphere combine to create a singular sensation," selected this as one of only five new Metroplex restaurants in 1998, and noted that "Grape Escape is trying (one more time) to take the tension out of wine pretension."

Yes, there are some 80 wines by the half-glass, glass, or bottle. A flight (sampler) offers a variety of three to five one-and-a-half-ounce servings that are served on a paper place mat that numbers the glasses in recommended drinking order. This is also a wine retail outlet. Light food offerings include cheese, pâté, olives, and carpaccio, but there are also six-inch pizzas. Among the desserts, you can sample crème brulée, apple- and almond cream-filled pastry, or fresh strawberries marinated in cabernet sauvignon.

Surf Club USA and The Brew Co., 425 Commerce St.; (817) 335-5400. M. Open Mon-Fri 4 pm-2 am, Sat-Sun 7 pm-2 am. The Brew is open Tue-Sat only, 9 pm-2 am. Wheelchair-accessible. Has a bar and a separate smoking section. Happy hour daily until 9 pm. Has large-screen TV sets and billiards. Located downtown on Sundance Square, across the street from the Flying Saucer pub and in the windowless basement of the Barnes & Noble Booksellers building, across the street from the Bass Performance Hall (see individual entries). A three-dimensional Statue of Liberty is affixed to the building's exterior. An ATM is located near the entrance.

Formerly known as The Great American Steakhouse, now Tuesdays include a $500 Bikini Contest. Wednesday is Ladies' Night. Thursday is 1980s Music Night.

The Surf Club appetizers for two include spicy buffalo wings, fried clam strips, and chicken quesadillas, at $5 each. The Brew offers cheeseburgers, grilled chicken sandwiches, ribeye cheesesteak sandwiches, and chicken tenders at $5 each, or Cajun popcorn shrimp for $7.

Barbecue

"Texas boasts a fast-growing population of 2,100-plus barbecue establishments that collect over $500 million a year," said *Time* magazine in 1998. "The state hosts over 200 separate barbecue competitions, more than the rest of the nation combined."

Angelo's, 2533 White Settlement Rd. at Vacek St.; (817) 332-0357. I. Open daily, except Sunday, 11 am-10 pm. Cash only. It accommodates 300. Located in a cavernous, rustic building filled with stuffed moose, deer, and buffalo, northwest of downtown and northeast of the museum district.

Angelo George opened a bar with four tables on St. Patrick's Day in 1958. "It started out as a beer joint," says Skeet George. "The barbecue was introduced later, only as a side item. My dad put pepper on the barbecue to make it hotter to sell more beer." The restaurant is now considered one of the best barbecue establishments in Fort Worth. When Joseph Heller, author of *Catch-22*, lectured at Texas Christian University (see entry) in the early 1980s, he insisted on eating at Angelo's.

Angelo's was also one of only three Metroplex barbecue restaurants that made the list of 50 best barbecue eateries in Texas; five staffers from *Texas Monthly* magazine ate at 245 establishments in 1997 and judged the top three to be located in Lockhart, Taylor, and Plano. "We enjoyed tender, marbled hickory-smoked brisket (a little salty); pork ribs that were crusty outside and tender within; and an exemplary quarter-chicken: pink, smoky, juicy meat protected by a lightly browned, supple skin; slaw, potato salad, and ranch-style beans did not excite," they wrote about Angelo's in their review.

One thousand Metroplex residents, volunteering their opinions for the New York-based *Zagat Survey*, rated Angelo's one of the most popular barbecue joints. The *Fort Worth Star-Telegram* gives it five stars for "no-frills saloon atmosphere" and four for "sensational meaty pork ribs."

Angelo's beef, pork ribs, ham, and sausage plates—each one under $10 and served with beans and potato salad—are finger-licking good. One-half plates are also available, along with the whole, one-half, or one-quarter chicken baskets. All these meats are also served as Texas-style sandwiches that you can wash down with ten- or 18-ounce frosted steins of beer on tap.

Angelo George died in 1997 at age 71 of complications following heart surgery.

The Railhead Smokehouse, 2900 Montgomery and Lovell streets; (817) 738-9808. *I.* Open Mon-Sat 11 am-9 pm. Located one block south of West Freeway (also known as Interstate 30), southwest of Will Rogers Coliseum, Amon Carter, Modern, and Kimbell Art Museums (see individual entries).

The building's facade consists of an old country porch not far from the railroad yards. Inside, you will find vinyl chairs and lawn furniture, while the walls are covered with mementos. The bar divides the two dining areas that many Texans consider heaven when it comes to sliced beef and pork ribs. This is one of the best and most popular barbecue joints in Fort Worth and a place where even the Basses, the Fort Worth family of billionaires, come now and then to reacquaint themselves with their Texas roots. Metroplex residents, voting for the New York-based *Zagat Survey*, rate it one of the most popular barbecue restaurants. The *Fort Worth Star-Telegram* gave it five stars for "large, meaty, not-too-greasy pork ribs and tender beef brisket, sliced into thick planks. Both bear excellent smoke flavor." The readers of the *FW Weekly* named it the "best barbecue restaurant."

Whether a one-time tourist or a regular, proceed carefully because you might get hooked on this stuff. Sliced beef, sausage, ham, or ribs sandwich, none is over $5. Sandwich plates with beans and potato salad are even lower, dinners less than $10. You can have an 18-ounce mug of beer for a couple of bucks, soft drinks and tea for half that, with unlimited refills. Even when back in Manchester, England (if that's where you call home), you will still remember the tangy smell of this smokehouse barbecue.

Riscky's Bar-B-Q, 300 Main at East Second St.; (817) 877-3306. *M.* Open Mon-Thu 11 am-10 pm, Fri-Sat 11 am-midnight, Sun noon-11 pm. Happy hour Mon-Fri 3-7 pm, live entertainment nightly. Located downtown, a couple of blocks south of the Tarrant County Courthouse, across Main from La Madeleine French Bakery & Cafe, and diagonally across from the Renaissance Worthington Hotel (see individual entries).

After the railroad came to Fort Worth in 1876, this block was the entertainment center for adventurers arriving with the trail herds. The first regularly established theater, The Adelphi, was also started here in

1876. Later, it reopened as Theater Comique, which was succeeded by My Theater in 1880, exactly where Riscky's stands today. "Orchestras paraded daily to attract crowds and a tight-rope walker performed over the street," says a plaque on the Weber Building housing the restaurant. The original White Elephant Saloon, now in the historic Stockyards (see individual entries), was also located on this block.

In 1912, a 16-year-old Marcilia Bunkervich married Joe Riscky, both being immigrants from Poland. Joe had saved $400 from his salary of $9 a week at Armour Packing Co., but spent it all on their wedding. They opened a grocery store in 1927. Today, the tradition is continued by their grandson Jim Riscky, who has restaurants scattered all over the town. This large Western-style eatery has a bar and a small patio in the back. Bison heads and other game are displayed in the front room with exposed rafters. The *Fort Worth Star-Telegram* calls it "crowded, loud."

Baskets for the "lighter appetite" include beef brisket sandwiches, pork spare ribs, one-half smoked chicken, and smoked catfish fillet. There are also platters for larger appetites and Riscky's promises that "You won't walk away hungry!" All-You-Can-Eat beef ribs are under $10.

Other Riscky's barbecue joints are located at 2314 Azle Ave., west of the Stockyards, and North Richland Hills, a town whose roots extend back to 1807. The Azle Avenue location is the original Riscky's, which goes back to 1927 and where meat is smoked for all other Riscky's restaurants. The *Fort Worth Star-Telegram* gave this location four stars for "lean and meaty" pork ribs and "tender and not too lean" brisket.

Sonny Bryan's Smokehouse, Lower level of the Fort Worth Outlet Square, 150 Throckmorton St.; (817) 878-2424. I. Open Mon-Thu 10 am-8 pm, Fri-Sat 10 am-9 pm, Sun noon-6 pm. Located on the northwestern corner of Sundance Square downtown, across Throckmorton from the Renaissance Worthington Hotel and across Taylor Street from the Fort Worth Central Public Library (see individual entries).

In 1910 Elijah Bryan moved his family from Tennessee to Dallas. His son, William Jennings Bryan, opened his own restaurant in nearby Oak Cliff in 1935. Sonny Jennings Bryan left his father's kitchen in 1957 and opened his own place the following year. And the rest is history, as they say.

Unlike this Fort Worth Outlet Square (see entry) location, Sonny Bryan's restaurants are typically Texan, simple, and rugged. Be prepared for the barbecue sauce to splatter over your blouse or tie. There are smoked meat sandwiches and plates of every description available.

"The ribs, one of the two most frequently ordered dishes here, are at least one reason that Sonny Bryan's eateries have been listed by People Magazine in the American Top 10 Best Barbecue Spots," says the *Fort Worth Star-Telegram* about Sonny's Grapevine location, at 332 South Park Blvd.; (817) 424-5978.

Terry's Grill, 902 Houston at West Eighth St.; (817) 334-0820. *I.* Open for lunch Mon-Fri 11 am-3 pm. Cash only. Located downtown, next to The Blarney Stone Pub. Established in 1928, it claims to be the oldest downtown restaurant. Has a simple, old-fashioned interior.

The specialty of the house is barbecue with apple sauce, smoked daily. Also serves chicken fried steak, sliced barbecue beef, barbecue sausage, and barbecue hamburgers.

Cafes

Chili's Grill & Bar, 515 Main at Fifth St.; (817) 885-8680. M. Open Mon-Thu 11 am-10:30 pm, Fri-Sat 11 am-midnight, Sun 11 am-10 pm. Located on the edge of Sundance Square, across the street from Courtyard By Marriott and Clarion hotels.

A standard American cafe. You can start with chili or soup of the day. Steaks run from $10 to $14 and include vegetables and mashed potatoes (but you can substitute any side). Half a dozen salads are on the menu, too. Try grilled chicken pasta or blackened catfish. There are pitas stuffed with your choice of filling. Burgers and sandwiches are also available.

Coffee Haus, 404 Houston at West Third St.; (817) 336-5282. *I.* Open Mon-Thu 8 am-midnight, Fri-Sat 8 am-1 am, Sun 10 am-midnight. Located on Sundance Square, diagonally from Billy Miner's Saloon and next to Milan Gallery. On the other end of the block is The Modern Museum at Sundance Square Annex (see individual entries).

If you have an hour to kill, this may just be the spot to do it at. Sitting at a table on the sidewalk, you can watch the world go by and see the Haas's *Chisholm Trail* mural across Houston Street and the Bass Performance Hall two blocks away (see individual entries).

Various beverages could be had, although "its watery coffee isn't worth the effort," notes the *Dallas Morning News*. Bagels, pastries, and breads are also available. A few sandwiches and desserts just might do the trick while you sightsee along Sundance Square but want to sit down for half an hour.

Cajun

Razzoo's Cajun Cafe, 318 Main at Third St.; (817) 338-2866. M. Open Sun-Thu 11 am-11 pm, Fri-Sat 11 am-2 am. Located downtown in the historic Sundance Square in the Western Union Building, which was designed by Fort Worth architect and engineer James B. Davies, Sr., and constructed in 1931. It stands across the street from Knights of Pythias Hall. On the other side of this block is Billy Miner's Saloon (see individual entries).

"Loud, friendly, crowded," calls the *Fort Worth Star-Telegram* and it is; you can sometimes hear the music a block away. An authentic Cajun-Creole establishment serving jambalaya, crawfish, and grilled gator tail. The menu looks very much like the restaurant, a helter-skelter of dishes, from Cajun "soup o' life" to Big Ernie's Nightmare Seafood Platteroux for four, costing about $40. Among the Cajun plates, you will find real shrimp Creole, hickory-grilled fish hollandaise, stuffed shrimp skillet, and Cajun étouffée with crawfish tails.

Another Fort Worth Razzoo location is at 4700 Bryant Irving Rd.

Chinese

Szechuan, 5712 Locke Ave. at Camp Bowie Blvd.; (817) 738-7300. M. Open Sun-Thu 11 am-10 pm, Fri-Sat 11 am-11 pm. Located in southwest Fort Worth, on the southwest corner of Interstate 30 and Horne Street, across the street from Dunkin' Donuts and behind Seven-Eleven.

"Encyclopedic menu is consistently excellent; also offers friendly service and understated, classy atmosphere," says the *Dallas Morning News*, while the *Fort Worth Star-Telegram* notes the restaurant is a "perennial favorite both for spicy Sichuan entrees and elegant setting; try the moo-shu pork, the shrimp-fried rice and the eggrolls." Readers of the *Star-Telegram* voted it the "best" Asian restaurant in Tarrant County.

There are 22 poultry dishes, several of them hot and spicy, in addition to several pork and some 15 beef entrees, almost 150 in all. The costliest seafood dishes are lobster Cantonese and lobster with hot ginger sauce, followed by sesame shrimp and countless other shrimp dishes. The readers of *FW Weekly* named it the "best chinese restaurant."

Another Szechuan location is at 4750 Bryant Irving at Interstate 20.

Contemporary Ranch

Michaels, 3413 West Seventh St.; (817) 877-3413. M. Open for lunch Mon-Fri 11 am-2:30 pm, for dinner Mon-Sat 5:30-10 pm, bar Sat until 11 pm. Ancho Chile Bar is next door. Wheelchair-accessible. Has a smoking area. Casual brunch on Sundays. Located between Montgomery Street and University Drive, about two miles west of downtown and a couple of blocks north of Kimbell Art Museum. The Back Porch restaurant (see individual entries) is also nearby.

Bare concrete floors, exposed ceilings, and white walls with Andy Warhol silk-screen prints of Buffalo Bill and John Wayne, as well as works by local artist Matt Clark, define this contemporary restaurant influenced by Mediterranean flavors. Metroplex residents, volunteering their opinions for the New York-based *Zagat Survey*, rated Michael's one of the most popular Southwestern-cuisine restaurants.

Small plates include shrimp cocktail, ranch goat cheese tart, orange jalapeno quail, and ranch shrimp. There is a large array of salads, from Michael's tumbleweed to grilled chicken Caesar. The daily features include soup, pizza, daily pasta, the chef's entree, or fish. Among the ranch classics, which include vegetables, you can choose from chicken fried steak, baked crab cakes, tortellini, pork tenderloin, steak, or lamb chops. Pan-seared beef tenderloin medallions with an ancho chile-bourbon sauce is one of the costlier entrees. Other plates, which also include vegetables, span from the oven-roasted chicken to coal-roasted salmon, from New York strip sirloin to peppered strip steak.

"Our meal was more than satisfying," says FW Weekly, "and the bill was less than the tab for our review meal at a chain Mexican joint."

Continental

The Balcony at Ridglea, 6100 Camp Bowie Blvd.; (817) 731-3719. E. Open for lunch Mon-Fri 11:30 am-2 pm, for dinner Mon-Thu 6-10 pm, Fri-Sat 6-10:30 pm, Sunday brunch. Located above La Madeleine French Bakery & Cafe and around the corner from the Italian Aventino's, between Westridge and Winthrop avenues, north of the Ridglea Golf Course. Cafe Aspen is situated across the street, at 6103 Camp Bowie. (See individual entries for more details.) A block from here, at 6025 Camp Bowie, is the laser light show Ridglea Theater, which originally opened in 1950.

Owned and run since 1973 by a couple—one of whom was the chef; they sold it to a partnership that includes the owner of the Ridglea Village shopping center in 1997. One of the best restaurants, even if some consider it a dinosaur from another age fit for little old ladies. "Continental dishes keep strictly to tradition," says the Fort Worth Star-Telegram, which also singles out the "attentive service that doesn't fawn." After its renovation in 1998, the daily called it "Fort Worth's last old-fashioned, traditional fine-dining restaurant."

Appetizers include escargots Swiss-style and crab meat Lorenzo. There are salads, like shrimp on ice, and soups, like vichyssoise or cold Spanish soup. From the French kitchen, you can order the $50 roasted rack of lamb for two or the veal Neptune for one. Other French entrees include medallions of beef, beef tenderloin, pepper beef Oriental, sliced beef Stroganoff, and broiled chicken breast. There is also the chateaubriand for two, at $44, or New York-cut sirloin for two, at $42. Ribeye steak and broiled lamb chops are also on the menu. Among the seafood selections, you will find orange roughy, shrimp, fresh fillet of sole, and broiled lobster. You can also enjoy fillet of trout or frog legs. Amaretto cheesecake and Black Forest cake are two among the desserts.

"Unfortunately," notes *Texas Monthly*, "the prime pepper steak was a real disappointment—undersized, overcooked, and tough."

In 2000, The Balcony added a variety of chops to its menu and began serving midnight breakfast, from 11:30 pm to 12:30 am, in an effort to attract younger diners.

Eclectic

8.0, 111 East Third and Commerce streets; (817) 336-0880. M. Open Mon for lunch and dinner 11 am-midnight, Tue-Sun 11 am-2 am. Wheelchair-accessible. Located in Sundance Square downtown and on the same block as the 1901 Knights of Pythias Castle Hall, which now houses Haltom's Jewelry store. The restaurant is located in the Knights of Pythias Club Building, an addition constructed in 1920.

A restaurant and "the original art bar" with a shaded outdoor seating area situated diagonally across the street from Barnes & Noble Booksellers and next to Casa on the Square theatre (see individual entries). Interiors are decorated "thanks to the wonderful, zany genius of these dedicated artists": Carol Benson, Dan Blagg, Ed and Linda Blackburn, Ann Ekstrom, J. T. Grant, East Texan Bill Haveron, Cindy Holt, Nancy Lamb, Jim Woodson, and Shannon Wynne. "This place would be just another dump without them," says the menu. A waitress explained that the restaurant's name, 8.0, stands for "eight partners, zero experience." *FW Weekly* readers named it the "best place to pretend you're somebody important," as well as the "best place to meet someone of opposite sex."

The food is all right and reasonably priced, but the service a bit slow. The lunch plates include grilled or blackened chicken or 6-ounce New York strip steak, and several vegetarian dishes. There are burgers and sandwiches. The most expensive entree is the grilled salmon pasta primavera, followed by grilled snapper, poached salmon, and grilled or fried fish tacos. "No trip to 8.0 would be complete without the Pangburn chocolate sundae served in a huge martini glass," says the *Fort Worth Star-Telegram*. "It's so good, it'll make you wanna slap your mama."

Randall's Cafe & Wine Bar, 907 Houston, between West Eighth and Ninth streets; (817) 336-2253. M. Open Tue-Fir 11 am-10 pm, Sat 5:30-10 pm. Located downtown, a block north of the Fort Worth Convention Center, across the street from The Blarney Stone Pub, and next door to the well-known Peters Bros. Hats (see individual entries).

"Cozy, quiet and intimate," is how the *Dallas Morning News* describes Randall's, adding that "the charming little bakery-turned-restaurant has a stellar gourmet menu, an excellent wine list and a romantic ambience." The *Fort Worth Star-Telegram* notes that "this lovely, intimate bistro, with exposed brick walls, antique furnishings and low lighting, has matured into a fine restaurant reminiscent of San Francisco or Greenwich Village."

However, what most patrons think of when Randall's name comes up in conversation are the 60 kinds of cheesecake "to die for," as the *Dallas Observer* noted on one occasion and rated three of them "exceptional without exception" on another. Entrees include fish, hen, steak, and pasta. Randall's wine list sports more than 15 wines by the glass.

Branding Iron Grill, 911 Houston St.; (817) 332-5153, is located next to Randall's. The *Dallas Morning News* calls this a spot "where you can grab a quick meal for about $5 and thoroughly enjoy the experience."

Sundance Market & Deli, 353 Throckmorton and West Third streets; (817) 335-3354. I. Open Mon-Thu 7 am-9 pm, Fri 7 am-11 pm, Sat 8 am-11 pm, Sun 9 am-3 pm. Wheelchair-accessible. No smoking. Live music Friday nights. Located downtown in Sundance Square, across the street from the Fort Worth Outlet Square shopping center and a block from the Renaissance Worthington Hotel (see individual entries).

"It's a market and a deli, but also a coffeehouse, a bakery and a restaurant serving blue-plate specials and gourmet salads cafeteria-style in the heart of downtown's Sundance Square. Whew!" says the *Dallas Morning News*. Has a good variety of salads and sandwiches. Blue-plate daily specials could include meat loaf, chicken and dumplings, or taco salad. Desserts are made from scratch.

French

La Madeleine French Bakery & Cafe, 305 East Main and Second streets; (817) 332-6099. M. Open Sun-Thu 7 am-8 pm, Fri-Sat 7 am-11 pm. Wheelchair-accessible. Smoking on patio only. Located downtown on the edge of the refurbished Sundance Square, two blocks south of the Tarrant County Courthouse and next door to Sid Richardson Collection of Western Art and the 1901 Knights of Pythias Castle Hall (see individual entries).

This three-story building was constructed in 1908 as a saloon with guest rooms on the top floors of what was once known as the 50-room Savoy and later Plaza Hotel. Owned by Winfield Scott, who made a fortune in the cattle business, this place was popular with cattlemen marketing their herds at the Stockyards (see entry). It is one of the best remaining examples in Fort Worth of a small cattle-era hotel.

La Madeleine founder Patrick Esquerre arrived in Dallas in 1982 and opened his first bakery on the edge of the Southern Methodist University campus the following year. Some 65 La Madeleine cafes now operate in several states, but the founder, who once said, "Food is not just something you feed your body with. It's a way of life," has sold out his share and only time will tell whether La Madeleine can maintain the quality of its food and its atmosphere.

There are few spots in the Metroplex where food will taste as good and the prices will be as low, provided you do not mind cafeteria-style self-service. La Madeleine has built its reputation with the salads, pastas, and soups that are as delicious as those you will find in France. Caffeine addicts will appreciate unlimited cups of several varieties of coffee and tea. At the bakery counter you can buy baguettes, croissants, or any of several breads. The desserts are fresh and scrumptious. A friendly cafe where you will consistently get your money's worth. The readers of FW Weekly named it the "best bakery."

Another Madeleine is located at 6140 Camp Bowie Blvd., at North Bryant Irvin, beneath The Balcony at Ridglea restaurant (see entry). Its Arlington location is at 2101 North Collins St., two blocks north of Interstate 30.

Saint-Emilion, 3617 West Seventh and Montgomery streets; (817) 737-2781. E. Open for dinner daily 6-10 pm. Located north of the cultural district and west of University Drive.

Named after the area from which the French-born owner Bernard Tronche, "owner of one of the sexiest French accents around," comes from. The readers of Gourmet magazine voted it among the four most popular restaurants in the Metroplex. "The brick-walled country French atmosphere is charming and the food is mostly terrific," declares a D Magazine restaurant reviewer, while the Fort Worth Star-Telegram notes: "Impressively crafted country French creations including duck, lamb and numerous unusual fresh fish flown daily from Boston." Texas Monthly reviewers sampled halibut cheeks encrusted with almonds in lemon butter sauce and bone-in pork ribeye and declared that "both were superb and we swore we'd order the spectacularly presented Maine lobster next time."

The staff of FW Weekly named it the "best restaurant" in Fort Worth, explaining that although the restaurant is expensive, it's worth it: "Excellent country French food and the kind of service most restaurants don't even know how to give. Save your dollars and go there." They recommended the roasted duck.

The wine list features vintages from the Saint-Emilion region of France.

German

Edelweiss, 3801-A Southwest Blvd. at Weatherford Traffic Circle; (817) 738-5934. M. Open Tue-Thu 5-10:30 pm, Fri-Sat 5-11 pm, closed Sundays and Mondays. Oompah band and dancing. Located in southwest Fort Worth, west of Ridgmar Mall and north of Hulen Mall (see individual entries).

"Dances, folk singing and hearty German dishes," says the *Dallas Morning News*. Roasted or boiled ham shank is the costliest meat dish, followed by smoked pork ribs, Hungarian-style veal goulash, center-cut pork loins, beef tenderloin tips, and filet of turkey breast, filled with ham and Swiss cheese. Deep-fried shrimp and skewers of grilled shrimp are two among the seafood entrees. If your midsection can handle it, there are also desserts, like apple strudel and chocolate candy cake. It also has a full-service bar.

That "oddly beautiful—almost unearthly—sound" you might hear comes from the Wiesbaden-born 40-year Fort Worth female resident who took 15 years to learn how to play a saw with a violin bow. "It comes from the old mining days when German cities were only villages," she told the *Fort Worth Star-Telegram*. Although the villagers loved music, they couldn't take musical instruments with them to the mines. They learned to make music with the tools.

Greek

Parthenon, 401 North Henderson St.; (817) 810-0800. M. Open Mon-Sat 11 am-9 pm. Handicapped-accessible, no smoking. Located on the northern edge of downtown, two blocks north of Belknap St.

Owned by the Katzianis brothers from Cyprus, Parthenon has two dining rooms, big windows, and a pleasant setting. Gus Katzianis, one of the owners, assures his patrons that his Greek food is authentic. He says that while he wears the chef's hat, it is his mother "looking over my shoulder to make sure I'm getting it right."

"All the Greek standards are here, done exceptionally well," says the *Dallas Morning News*. Appetizers, salads, Greek entrees, seafood, gyros, it's all here, in addition to Greek desserts, like baklava, with "just the right amount of sweetened syrup in the filling, which kept it from being brick-like," says *FW Weekly*, while *Texas Monthly* "found an outstanding leg of lamb and grilled swordfish, both served with a Greek salad." Beer and Greek wine are also available.

Hamburgers

"What the croissant is to France, what goulash is to Hungary, the hamburger is to Texas," notes the *New York Times*. "It's a symbol, a necessity and a triumph, a part of the cultural patrimony so tightly woven into the fabric of Texas life that Texans themselves do not even remark on it until they are presented with the gray-tinged, underfurnished, suspiciously geometric hamburger that the rest of America lives with."

Texas asserts it created the hamburger during the 1880s. There is a historical marker in Athens, about 60 miles southeast of Dallas, that marks the spot where Fletcher Davis, a local cafe owner, first served fried patties between two slices of bread.

Kincaid's, 4901 Camp Bowie Blvd. at Eldridge St.; (817) 732-2881. M. Open Mon-Sat 11 am-6 pm. Cash only. Located west of downtown and southwest of the cultural district, across the street from Papa John's Pizza and next to Showdown Saloon.

Spacious, ugly, noisy, friendly, without personality, and famous. Formerly a grocery store, but now sugar, jello, pickles, and garbage bags, all for sale under the stand-up counters, look tacky. It started out as a meat market in 1946, when the city was one-third the size of today's Fort Worth. O. R. Gentry, a meat cutter at the store since 1947, bought Kincaid's in 1967 and began making hamburgers on a grill in the back room to sell to regular customers and use up excess meat ground fresh daily. At first, up to 50 burgers were sold daily, mostly to customers in the neighborhood. As business evolved, some of the grocery items were removed, shelves were cut down to counter-top heights, and wooden doors were placed on top to make space for customers to eat. *Texas Monthly* chose Kincaid's as the "best burger in Texas."

The first Saturday after it was chosen "best burger" in the U.S. by a panel of food critics who samples burgers at 400 joints nationwide in 1982, Kincaid's sold 3,300 burgers.

Kincaid's burgers are big and tasty, but cost $3 for a half-pound patty. Check the walls for Kincaid's history. The menu is brief and simple, consisting mostly of burgers, hot dogs, and side dishes. You can eat at one of the several large communal tables, such as you will find at La Madeleine French Bakery & Cafe (see entry), or at the stand-up counters that are merely a cheap decoration these days. There are rowdy kids everywhere on Saturdays. You will find lots of magazines to read.

"The actual truth is that a Kincaid's hamburger is too big to get your mouth around and too good not to try," says *D Magazine*.

Tommy's Hamburgers, 400 Houston at West Third St., (817) 625-6654. *I.* Open Sun-Thu 11 am-9 pm, Fri-Sat 11 am-10 pm. Live jazz on weekends. Located in Sundance Square downtown across from Etta's Place B&B and Caravan of Dreams Club and diagonally across from Billy Miner's Saloon, which also has good burgers.

"Great burgers, barbecue, sandwiches from a local legend," says the *Fort Worth Star-Telegram*. "We sunk our teeth into a juicy mushroom Swiss burger and found burger nirvana," raves the *Dallas Morning News* reviewer about Tommy's Sundance Square location. "The half-pound beef patty was lean, perfectly grilled and oozing with melted cheese and grilled mushrooms." Tommy's burgers taste particularly well when washed down with a draft beer. There are sandwiches, salads, and desserts. Dinners include the chicken fried steak, catfish dinner, and chicken fingers. *FW Weekly* readers named it the city's "best hamburger" joint. Tommy's was founded in 1983 in a Lake Worth convenience store and has three other locations, including one at 3431 West Seventh St.

Home Cooking

The Back Porch, 3400 Camp Bowie Blvd. at Boland St.; (817) 332-1422. M. Open for lunch and early dinner Mon-Sun 11 am-9 pm. Located across the brick-paved Camp Bowie from Kimbell Art Museum and a few doors east of Sardine's Italian eatery (see individual listings). Jack Bryant's *Horse Thief* bronze is across Boland Street (see the VISUAL ARTS chapter).

Already in 1984, in her guide *Short Trips In and Around Dallas,* author Laura Trim noted that "one of the pleasures of visiting the museums in Fort Worth is the opportunity to amble across the street to the Back Porch for homemade ice cream in numerous flavors or to the Next Door Cafe for a luscious buffet of cold salads and desserts where you pay for your meal by the ounce. Sandwiches and soups are also offered here, as well as homemade cakes and pies." Also on the menu are homemade pizzas.

But it is those three dozen kinds of ice cream—including banana pudding and strawberry pecan—that you will not forget for weeks, even months, whether your waist can handle them or not.

The Back Porch at 2500 West Berry St., in southwest Fort Worth, near Texas Christian University (see entry), (817) 923-0841, has different owners, but similar menu and just as many varieties of ice cream.

Celebration, 4600 Dexter Ave., on the corner of Camp Bowie Blvd. and Hulen St.; (817) 731-6272. M. Open for lunch Mon-Fri 11 am-2:30 pm; dinner Mon-Thu 5-9 pm, Fri 5-10 pm, Sat 11 am-10 pm, Sun 11 am-9 pm. Wheelchair-accessible. Located in west Fort Worth, near the cultural district.

A sister restaurant of a Dallas eatery that occupies an entire former ice house. More than ten years old, it is spacious and has a relaxed, informal feel to it. You can eat in one of the several rooms, at the bar and, after you are done, digest your food on the porch, while you watch the traffic go by on the brick-paved Camp Bowie.

The *Fort Worth Star-Telegram* raves over its "vegetables, such as divine mashed potatoes, pinto beans, steamed broccoli, spinach or squash casserole." "Seconds of entrees are offered free, but who has room?" asks the *Star-Telegram*, whose staff voted Celebration the "best" family dining spot in Tarrant County. Beef entrees include grilled tenderloin, pot roast, meat loaf, and chicken fried steak. There is fresh broiled salmon, shrimp, or fried catfish. Among the ten poultry dishes, you will find barbecued chicken and grilled chicken Dijon. Lemon bars, chocolate-dipped strawberries, and cream de menthe squares are just three of the desserts.

Luby's Cafeteria, 251 University Dr., between Seventh St. and White Settlement Rd.; (817) 870-9875. M. Open for lunch Mon-Fri 10:45 am-2:30 pm, for dinner 4:15-8 pm, Sat-Sun all day. Located in west Fort Worth, about one-and-a-half blocks from the Greenwood Cemetery, where the publisher Amon Carter, a Cowtown icon, is buried, along with the former Fort Worth mayor Henry Clay Meacham.

Cafeterias are a Southern as well as Texas institution, particularly for those eligible for an AARP membership card. But they are disliked by some affluent singles. "I'd rather have my feet cut off than eat in a cafeteria," one professional in his thirties who likes to be seen in fashionable eateries was quoted by local press. Cafeterias are popular for their variety, speed, and low prices. Many, like Luby's, serve dinner as early as 4:15 pm.

There are more than 200 Luby's cafeterias in the U.S. and about 30 of them in the Metroplex. Their premises are clean and attractive, the food is fresh and decent, and the personnel friendly. Patrons over 40 years of age seem to predominate. There are daily specials and several other entrees, from fish to chicken to beef. "Luby's Cafeteria has everything a good cafeteria should," says the *Fort Worth Star-Telegram*, "a great selection, fresh food, large servings and, of course, dessert."

There are several other Luby's locations in Fort Worth and Arlington, including the one at Hulen Mall (see entry), 4800 South Hulen St., in Fort Worth.

Ol' South Pancake House, 1509 South University Dr.; (817) 336-0311. I. Open 24 hours daily. Located just south of Interstate 30 (also known as West Freeway), north of the Log Cabin Village and the Fort Worth Zoo, and across the street from the University Park Village shopping center. (See individual entries for more details.)

Huge and plain, Ol' South opened in 1962 and is still going strong; the readers of *Fort Worth Star-Telegram* voted it the "best" late-night spot in Tarrant County. Even actor Eddie Murphy, singer George Strait, and Van Cliburn are said to have eaten here. "Ol' South has become the most popular late-night study hall for many TCU students," says *Fort Worth, Texas,* magazine.

But the service occasionally runs out of gas when an order gets lost. We could also do without all the paid advertising on the menu. The 20 kinds of pancakes and a dozen ways with waffles may be great, but we were not impressed by the basic eggs-and-sausage breakfast on plastic plates, with plastic spoons and forks. Also serves sandwiches, burgers, and desserts. The decaffeinated coffee is awful and weak every time we stop by, but the service is passable. To our way of thinking, this place could only appear great when one is inebriated and has no place else to go.

Another Ol' South Pancake House is located at 5148 East Belknap St.

Indian

Maharaja, 6308 Hulen Bend Blvd.; (817) 949-2475. M. Open for lunch Mon-Fri 11 am-2 pm, for dinner Sun-Thu 5:30-10 pm, Fri-Sat 5:30-10:30 pm. Located in southwest Fort Worth, west of Interstate 35 West, and a couple miles south of Hulen Mall (see entry).

"Adventuresome fare includes meats and breads from a tandoor oven," says the *Dallas Morning News*. The readers of the *Fort Worth Star-Telegram* and *FW Weekly* named it the best Indian restaurant.

Italian

Aventino's Ristorante, 3206 Winthrop Ave. at Camp Bowie Blvd.; (817) 731-0711. M. Open for lunch Mon-Fri 11 am-2 pm, dinner Mon-Thu 5-10 pm, Fri-Sat 5-11 pm. Located in southwest Fort Worth, on the edge of the cultural district, in the Ridglea Village mall, around the corner from La Madeleine French Bakery & Cafe and The Balcony at Ridglea. The "quietly elegant" New American cuisine Cafe Aspen, where live jazz can be heard on weekends, is located across Camp Bowie.

There are soups, salads, meat, and cheese appetizers. Spaghetti, rigattoni, tortellini, ziti, fettuccini, and gnochi de patate pastas are available with half a dozen sauces, some as baked pastas. There are several veal entrees, including à la Francese, à la Milanese, and à la Florentina, as well as chicken dishes, all served with bread and salad. Several seafood dishes are also available, some priced on the day of your order.

Tiramisu, cappuccino pie, and cheesecake are among the desserts. Cappuccino and expresso could also be had.

Isabella's Italian Bistro, 4255 Camp Bowie Blvd., at Tremont Ave.; (817) 732-9595. M. Open for lunch Mon-Fri 11 am-3 pm and for dinner Mon-Thu 5-10 pm, Fri 5-11 pm, Sat 11 am-11 pm. Happy hour at the bar Mon-Fri 3-7 pm. Wheelchair-accessible. Has a separate smoking section. Located in west Fort Worth, not far from the cultural district—if you have your own transportation, that is—and a couple of blocks west of the Veterans Memorial Park, headquarters of the 36th Division, U.S. Army, from 1917 to 1919.

"This charming location on the bricks of Camp Bowie has been home to many restaurants, but this one, with mainstream Italian cuisine, seems to have gotten it right; patio dining is lovely in nice weather," says the *Fort Worth Star-Telegram*.

A handsome Italian eatery whose tables are clad in white linen and a dining room overlooks Camp Bowie. One of the co-owners once owned an Italian restaurant in New York's Gramercy Park. There is a nice assortment of fish, with the costliest entree being linguini with clams, scallops, shrimp, calamari, and mussels. It is followed by several chicken, veal, and beef dishes, including grilled ribeye with porcini mushroom brandy sauce. Pastas include baked lasagna and veal cannelloni.

La Piazza, 1600 South University Dr.; (817) 334-0000. E. Open for lunch daily 11:30 am-2 pm, for dinner Sun-Thu 5:30-10 pm, Fri-Sat 5:30-11 pm. Located in the University Park Village shopping center, just south of West Freeway (also known as Interstate 30), next to several other restaurants in the mall.

Metroplex residents, voting their opinions for the New York-based *Zagat Survey,* rated La Piazza one of the most popular Italian-cuisine restaurants in Fort Worth. "You'll forget you're in a shopping center in this richly appointed nook, with upscale Italian cuisine, upscale wines, upscale patrons," says the *Fort Worth Star-Telegram.*

La Piazza seems to have mostly an older clientele from the days when it was located in Sundance Square (see entry). You will find the usual array of appetizers, soups, and salads, such as calamari, clam chowder soup, mozzarella, and tomato soup. La Piazza would not be an Italian restaurant if you could not find at least half a dozen pastas on its menu. You can also choose from entrees like beef tenderloin, chicken, veal, and fish. To conclude your meal, try the tiramisu, the traditional Italian dessert.

The food is good and the service satisfactory, but the management strikes one as pompous. They refused to fax the menu even after we made reservations to dine there. Pianist Van Cliburn is just one of the celebrities to have dined here.

Old Spaghetti Warehouse, 600 East Exchange Ave.; (817) 625-4171. M. Open Sun-Thu 11 am-10 pm, Fri-Sat 11 am-11 pm. Located on a hill overlooking the Stockyards historic district (see entry). This once Swift & Co. office building, from which the company's meatpacking operations were overseen, was built in 1902. The two-and-a-half-story brick building has a two-story wooden porch that wraps around three sides of the building and is supported by Tuscan columns. Swift closed its plant in 1971 and this structure was vacant for five years before being renovated for use as a Spaghetti Warehouse, when a rear section was also added.

"The building is the most complete and important structure remaining in the Swift and Company complex," says Carol Roark, author of *Fort Worth's Legendary Landmarks.* It seats at least 200 and has an adjacent bar, which was brought from Colorado. You can dine inside an old Dallas streetcar without wheels. The glass-topped elevator on display once carried Prime Minister Churchill and General Eisenhower to the British War Office. The Golden Goddess statue, which supposedly brought good luck to oil traders, came from the now-demolished Westbrook Hotel (see entry, 400 Block of Main and Third Streets in the SIGHTS chapter). The Old Spaghetti Warehouse is friendly, busy, and noisy when full.

"Standard pasta dishes in family-friendly setting," describes *FW Weekly*. Starters include mozzarella cheese sticks and toasted ravioli. There are more than half a dozen spaghetti dishes, of course. Combination platters include lasagna, spaghetti, and chicken fettucini. Shrimp Alfredo, chicken tettrazini, ravioli, cannelloni, and fettucini Alfredo dishes are also available, with wines by the glass or the bottle.

Old Spaghetti Warehouse in south Arlington is located at 1255 West Interstate 20, at The Parks at Arlington Mall (see entry).

Picchi-Pacchi, 512 Main at West Fifth St.; (817) 870-2222. *I.* Open Mon-Thu 11 am-3 pm, Fri-Sat 11 am-10 pm, closed Sunday. Located in the Sinclair Building, on the edge of Sundance Square downtown (see individual entries).

"Upscale Italian fast food," says the *Fort Worth Star-Telegram* about this simple two-level eatery with self-service. Lasagna, spaghetti, fettucine, tortellini, mannicotti, and cannelloni are the pastas served, in addition to pizza by the slice, sandwiches, and salads.

Pizzeria Uno, 300 Houston at West Second St.; (817) 885-8667. *M.* Open for lunch and dinner 11 am-11 pm, Fri-Sat 11 am-1 am. Located next to AMC Sundance 11 cinema, across the street from the Renaissance Worthington Hotel. Also across from Cabo Mix-Mex Grill, a restaurant that serves Mexican tropical seafood (see individual entries).

"All pizza chains should be this good," declares the *Fort Worth Star-Telegram*. There are appetizers, salads, soups, sandwiches, burgers, and, of course, deep-dish and thin-crust pizzas. The menu lists 13 deep-dish pizzas, from eggplant and artichoke to steak and cheese. Pastas include fettucine Alfredo and broccoli, and chicken fettucine.

Another Uno restaurant is located at 1301 North Collins St. in Arlington.

Ruffino's, 2455 Forest Park Blvd. and Park Hill Dr.; (817) 923-0522. *M.* Open Mon-Thu 11 am-10 pm, Fri-Sat 11 am-11 pm, closed Mondays. Wheelchair-accessible. Located southwest of downtown, on the edge of Forest Park, where Fort Worth Zoo and the Log Cabin Village (see individual entries) will also be found.

The brothers Franco and Robert Albanese serve veal, chicken, beef, and pasta to the Berkley/Park Hill/Texas Christian University neighborhoods. The *Fort Worth Star-Telegram* labels the restaurant "dim, intimate and clubby. Ruffino's would be a fine place to take a person on a third date." Although situated in a small barren strip shopping center, the brothers claim theirs is "*the* place to propose marriage."

There are almost 20 pastas on the dinner menu, the costliest being frutti di mare, which comes with shrimp, scallops, mussels, and clams over linguini. Grilled tuna, shrimp, and salmon are listed among the fish entrees. You can choose from among half a dozen chicken dishes. The beef and veal entrees are the most expensive, particularly filets sofisticata with shrimp, and beef wrapped in prosciutto.

"Ruffino's rich two-inch morsel [of tiramisu] was somewhere between sinful and heavenly," noted the *Star-Telegram*.

Sardine's Ristorante Italiano, 3410 Camp Bowie Blvd.; (817) 332-9937. M. Open for dinner Mon-Thu 5-11:30 pm, Fri-Sat 5 pm-12:30 am, Sun 3-11:30 pm. Live jazz pianist Tue-Fri and a combo Sat-Mon, starting at 7 pm. Located across Camp Bowie from the Kimbell Art Museum, near Amon Carter, and Modern Art Museums (see individual entries). The front dining room, with antiques and old photographs, has a view of the brick-paved Camp Bowie Boulevard and there is an outdoor patio. The readers of *FW Weekly* named it the "best Italian restaurant."

An authentic, but also casual and romantic candle-lit restaurant that has been owned by the Salvatore Matarese family of Naples for more than twenty years. Several salads, such as Caesar's, are just one of the antipasti you can start your meal with; others could include mushrooms with escargot or fresh squid dipped in beer. Sardine's has one of the largest pasta menus around, some twenty-five, including spaghetti, lasagna, linguini, manicotti, fettuccine Alfredo, cannelloni, tortellini, and ravioli. The most expensive entree is chicken and scampi; other main dishes available are veal piccata, parmigiana cutlet, beef tenderloin, broiled baby lamb chops, chicken, and scampi. Tiramisu, Amaretto cheesecake, and cappuccino pie are some among the desserts.

Venecia Ristorante, 3702 Altamesa Blvd.; (817) 370-7603. M. Open for lunch Sun-Fri 11 am-2:30 pm, for dinner daily 5-10 pm. Wheelchair-accessible, no smoking. Located in southwest Fort Worth, about three miles southeast of Hulen Mall (see entry), in a strip shopping center.

Venecia, which opened in 1997, "is cozy and casual, with tile floors and paintings by local artists," says the *Dallas Morning News*, whose restaurant reviewer thought that "best by far was the colorful linguine del golfo, a plate brimming with fresh mussels and clams still in the shell, shrimp, juicy sea scallops and some of the most tender calamari rings we've ever had."

Aside from some twenty pastas—including linguine puttana, named for ladies of the night—you have a choice of several veal and chicken entrees, and seafood specials, which, in addition to linguine del golfo, include Dover sole amandine, priced on the day of the purchase. The costliest dishes are half a dozen steaks, such as bistecca Diana. You will have several choices of wine by the glass. Tiramisu and Amaretto cheesecake are two among the desserts.

Mediterranean

Bistro Louise, 2900 South Hulen St. at Oak Park Ln., (817) 922-9244. E. Open for lunch Mon-Sat 11 am-2 pm, for dinner Mon-Thu 6-9 pm, Fri-Sat 6-10 pm. Tapas from 5 pm. Saturday brunch 11 am-2 pm. Located at Stonegate Commons shopping center, west of the Texas Christian University and east of the Trinity River. The infamous former Cullen Davis Mansion (see individual entries), owned by a Fort Worth multimillionaire—who was acquitted of wounding his estranged wife and killing her lover and her 12-year-old daughter from a previous marriage—and which until 1998 housed various restaurants, is situated nearby.

A native of Monroe, Louisiana, who has lived in Fort Worth for thirty years, the European-trained Louise Lamensdorf managed the French Apron School of Cooking in Fort Worth until 1990. She opened this bistro "with a Mediterranean attitude" in 1996, after dreaming of starting one for fifteen years. Some consider her one of the best cooks in the city and the *Dallas Observer* characterizes this as "one of the best places to eat in Fort Worth." The *D Magazine* restaurant reviewer confessed to having driven forty miles just "to re-experience this bistro's tea-smoked duck," one of the menu entrees that takes three days to prepare. "I'll walk if I have to" to come again, concluded the reviewer.

Among the soups you can pick from Southwestern corn chowder or Creole lobster gumbo. Appetizers include the Japanese macadamia shrimp, risotto and zucchini pancake, and smoked salmon ravioli. Try a plate of French cheeses for two, whether as an appetizer or dessert. There are salads as varied as Oriental spinach, Southwestern Caesar, and Belgian endive. Seafood dishes include pan-seared Chilean sea bass, potato-crusted salmon, Idaho ruby red trout, and grilled salmon. Malaysian curry pasta, pecan fried chicken, and North Carolina quail could be the choices among the fowl entrees. The most expensive meat dishes are pan-seared venison and beef tenderloin. Bread is baked on the premises. Your weight allowing you such a luxury, consider Louise's cheesecake for dessert.

Mexican

Benito's, 1450 West Magnolia Ave.; (817) 332-8633. M. Open for lunch and dinner Sun-Thu 11 am-9 pm, Fri 11 am-2 am, Sat 10 am-2 pm. Located in south Fort Worth, roughly between Eighth Avenue and Hemphill Street.

While the giant fig tree just inside its front door is occasionally spruced up, the food seldom changes and has earned Benito's many accolades. "So traditional it doesn't serve chips and salsa," says the *Fort Worth Star-Telegram*, whose staff also voted it the "best" late-night spot in Tarrant County. Among the entrees, you will find poblano peppers stuffed with white cheese or beef, beef or chicken fajitas, beef steak cooked in Mexican style, and Milanesa, a pan-fried steak Mexican style. There are also about a dozen combination meals, with enchiladas, fajitas, and tacos. Broiled red snapper and rainbow trout are two among the fish dishes. A good selection of beers and wines is also available.

Another well-regarded restaurant on this avenue is the **Paris Coffee Shop,** at 700 West Magnolia, which, says *Texas Monthly*, "is so popular it's hard to tell the late-breakfast folks from the early-lunch crowd."

Cabo Mix-Mex Grill, 115 West Second at Houston St.; (817) 336-8646. M. Open Sun-Wed 11 am-10 pm, Thu-Sat 11 am-1 am. Has a smoking area. Wheelchair-accessible. Located on the edge of Sundance Square downtown, across from the Renaissance Worthington Hotel (see individual entries).

The food is a spicy blend of South and Central American flavors with the influence of Yucatan and Southwestern spices.

Owned by the same people who gave you Lucille's Stateside Bistro on Camp Bowie Boulevard and H3 Ranch in the Stockyards Hotel, the 4,500-square-foot Cabo opened in 1998. According to *FW Weekly*, "You get trendy ingredients for your money, if that carries weight with you. That shrimp salad, for instance, is covered in crunchy 'sticks,' which isn't necessarily what one wants in a salad."

Spicy shrimp tacos, chargrilled yellowfin tuna sandwiches, and shrimp quesadillas are some among the worthwhile choices at the restaurant named for the Pacific coastal resort Cabo San Lucas.

A *Fort Worth Star-Telegram* food reviewer complains that coming in on a Friday night is a "big mistake, unless you like watching drunken guys waving cigars and slobbering over the server who should be bringing you a drink by now"; but then he adds, "we liked the food so much on that Friday, we went back on an afternoon the next week to make sure it was still that good."

Dos Gringos Cantina, 1015 North University Dr. at Darnell St.; (817) 338-1286/9393. M. Open for lunch and dinner Sun-Thu 11 am-9 pm, Fri-Sat 11 am-midnight. Has a bar. Happy hour 4-7 pm. Located in the cultural district, one block north of Casa Manana and Will Rogers Memorial Center, also near the Kimbell, Amon Carter, and Modern art museums (see individual entries).

Appetizers run from nachos and quesadillas to flautitas and fajitas. There are taco salads and fajita sandwiches. From the grill, try the grilled chicken, fajita steak, or fresh bacon-wrapped shrimp. Beef, chicken, pork, and marinated shrimp and grilled fajitas are specialties of the house. There are also the mariachi platter, steak à la Tampiquena, and fajadillas. Healthy Gringo plates include pollo de Acapulco, camarones brochette, and the Southwest salad.

Joe T. Garcia's Mexican Dishes, 2201 North Commerce at Northeast Twenty-Second St., two blocks east of North Main St.; (817) 626-4356, 429-5166, or 624-0266. M. Open for lunch and dinner Mon-Thu 11 am-2:30 pm and 5-10 pm, Fri-Sat 11 am-11 pm, Sun 11 am-10 pm. Cash only. No reservations. Wheelchair-accessible. Located on the north side of Fort Worth and on the southern edge of the Stockyards historic district (see entry). Has a huge patio and dining areas around a swimming pool.

An enormously popular Tex-Mex restaurant that is more than any other associated with Cowtown. The Garcia family has been serving meals here since 1935, when Joe T. and Jessie started a small cafe with six tables. They both grew up in the small town of Yurecuaro, Mexico. Joe was 16 when he arrived in 1914. He immediately went to work for meat packer Armour and Co. and stayed for twenty years, although he and his uncle started a grocery store in 1919. Publisher Amon Carter "liked to entertain out-of-town guests there," writes J'Nell Pate in her North Fort Worth history, adding that "up until 1970, the restaurant did not even give checks with the meal. At the cash register the customer simply told what he had eaten and paid for it."

The restaurant now seats well over 1,200 and 13 family members work here. Ronald Reagan and Bill Clinton stopped by while governors; presidential candidate and Dallas businessman Ross Perot and broadcaster Dan Rather's egos were also too big to eat anonymously. "Tommy gun in hand, Bonnie and Clyde dropped by for a bite in the early 1930's," says *Fort Worth, Texas,* magazine. The Garcias are wealthy now and have bought up surrounding properties and expanded the restaurant, but in many ways theirs still has the same homey atmosphere as it always did.

Fort Worth Star-Telegram readers and food critics voted it one of the best of its kind. It also received the 1998 James Beard Foundation Award as one of America's "best grass-roots restaurants." The basic meal includes beans with nachos, cheese enchiladas, tacos, Spanish rice, guacamole, and tortillas. Beef and chicken fajitas, chicken flautas, and chicken rellenos are served all day. The *Fort Worth Star-Telegram* claims it serves one of the best margaritas. Breakfast could be had Sat-Sun 11 am-3 pm.

La Familia, 2720 West Seventh St.; (817) 870-2002. *I.* Open for lunch Mon-Wed 11 am-3 pm, for lunch and dinner Thu-Sat 11 am-9 pm, for breakfast and lunch Sun 8 am-3 pm. Wheelchair-accessible, no smoking. Located west of downtown, between University Drive and Carroll Street, on the eastern edge of the museum district.

"In a city that can't seem to get enough Mexican restaurants, La Familia is a new entry that stands out from the pack," wrote the *Dallas Morning News* reviewer in 1997, a few months after the restaurant opened. "Fresh, flavorful Mexican food (no plates swimming in grease here), efficient and friendly service," seems the rule. There are half a dozen cheese, beans, beef, and chicken nachos as appetizers. You will find two dozen enchiladas and tacos, served in every conceivable combination, in addition to chicken and beef flautas, and breast of chicken, all served with rice and beans in a casual setting. The readers of *FW Weekly* named it the "best Tex-Mex restaurant" in the city.

Saturdays and Sundays, try a La Familia's breakfast, such as eggs scrambled with crisp bacon, with pepper and onions, or with sausage.

Los Vaqueros, 2629 North Main St.; (817) 624-1511. *I.* Open for lunch and dinner Mon-Thu 11 am-10 pm, Fri-Sat 11 am-11 pm, Sun 11 am-9 pm. Located in a restored 1915 meat-packing house in the Stockyards historic district, about a block from Billy Bob's Texas, "world's largest honky-tonk" (see individual entries).

A sprawling eatery owned by the Cisneros family that could seat as many as 500, including a peaceful, green patio on the ground floor behind the building. Vaqueros specialties include the eight-ounce charbroiled Steak Ranchers blanketed with Monterey Jack cheese, Mexican pepper steak, tacos al carbon (grilled strips of marinated tenderloin wrapped in hot flour tortillas), carne asada (sliced tenderloin), pescado Vera Cruz (filet of grilled fish), and beef, chicken, and shrimp fajitas. There are half a dozen cheese, beef, chicken, spinach, and mushroom enchiladas, in addition to other traditional dinners, such as Los Vaqueros (toasted meat taco, tortilla with chile con queso, enchilada, and tamale).

Mexican Inn Cafe, 516 Commerce at East Fifth St.; (817) 332-2772). *I.* Open for lunch Mon-Fri 11 am-3 pm. Other locations serve dinner Sun-Thu until 9 pm, Fri-Sat until 10 pm. Located downtown near the Bass Performance Hall (see entry).

Open since 1930, this cafe stopped serving dinner years ago. There is a large mural painted on the wall inside. Original owner died in 1973. "They still make those puffy, homemade Frito-style chips, served with good salsa and old-fashioned Tex-Mex platters in one of Fort Worth's original Mexican-food eateries," says the *Fort Worth Star-Telegram*. Cheese enchiladas, beef chalupas, beef tacos, and chicken are the mainstays of the menu.

Other Mexican Inn Cafes are located at 1625 Eighth Ave., 612 North Henderson St., 2700 East Lancaster Ave., and 5716 Camp Bowie Blvd., about which the *Star-Telegram* noted at another time: "The food is neither innovative nor surprising—probably a key to the restaurant's longevity in a town where Mexican food is tops on the comfort register. In fact, this Mexican food could be served anywhere in the country and be met with recognition."

Mi Cocina, 509 Main, between Fourth and Fifth streets in Sundance Square; (817) 654-4466. M. Open for lunch and dinner Sun-Thu 11 am-10 pm, Fri-Sat 11 am-11 pm. Located downtown in the Wells Fargo five-story building, across the street from the historic Burk Burnett Building (see entry). There is an ATM next door. The Arts Council of Fort Worth, an umbrella fund-raising organization established in 1963, is also located in this building.

A surprisingly contemporary setting for a down-to-earth Tex-Mex eatery. Has a dark interior and sports a courtyard. One of the six Metroplex restaurants where lunch specials could be had Mon-Fri 11 am-4 pm. "The Cocina platter could easily feed four people as an appetizer or two for a meal," noted the *FW Weekly* reviewer, adding, "We thought both the beef taco and enchilada were very salty, a real disappointment for Tex-Mex taste buds." The costliest à la carte entrees are various kinds of shrimp dishes, followed by enchiladas, tacos, and tamales. It was here that President Clinton tasted spinach enchiladas, one of his favorite foods.

The Original, 4713 Camp Bowie Blvd. and Bryce Ave.; (817) 738-6226. I. Open Sun-Thu 11 am-9 pm, Fri-Sat 11 am-10 pm, closed Mondays. Located in west Fort Worth, across the street from Lucile's bistro and a few blocks east of the famed Kincaid's hamburger joint (see individual entries).

Established in 1930 and owned by the Pineda family, this is one of the oldest Mexican restaurants in the city. There is an array of dinner plates, from steak and marinated shrimp to broccoli and shrimp enchiladas. You can enjoy chicken and meat nachos and bean and cheese burritos to your heart's content. Appetizers include flautitas and quesadillas. Tacos and fajitas are also listed in several combinations, as are several chicken dishes.

Riscky Rita, 140 East Exchange Ave.; (817) 626-8700. M. Open Sun-Thu 11 am-10 pm, Fri-Sat 11 am-midnight. Happy hour 3-7 pm Mon-Fri. Located on the edge of the Stockyards Station, on the bottom of the hill where the Old Spaghetti Warehouse stands in the historic Stockyards district (see individual listings).

You can eat inside or on the climate-controlled patio. Grilled and Tex-Mex dishes are available. The *Dallas Morning News* says that "plenty of food, tequila and beer seems to be the draw. The atmosphere is Tex-Mex kitsch." An all-you-can-eat lunch buffet is available Mon-Fri 11 am-2 pm for about $5 per person. All-you-can-eat fajitas, beef, or chicken is under $10. A la carte dishes include shrimp, ribs, chicken, various enchiladas, and other Mexican plates. Serves good margaritas. Burgers and a menu for children under 12 years of age are also available.

Uncle Julio's, 5301 Camp Bowie Blvd., (817) 377-2777. M. Open for lunch and dinner Sun-Thu 11 am-10:30 pm, Fri-Sat 11 am-11:30 pm. Sunday brunch is held 11 am-3 pm. Located in southwest Fort Worth, on the brick-paved Camp Bowie and northeast side of West Freeway, also known as Interstate 30.

Has a "comfortably disheveled" look, nice patio, and good Tex-Mex food, along with noisy atmosphere. Monthly *D Magazine* once picked Uncle Julio's as one of the 15 best Mexican restaurants in the Metroplex.

Start with nachos or tamales and progress to enchiladas and tacos. There are several Tia Maria's chicken, cheese, and beef enchilada platters. You will enjoy a variety of fajitas, perhaps even the $15 mesquite-grilled frog legs. The most expensive is the shrimp platter with grilled chicken or beef fajitas. "Plan to come very hungry, or you're going to end up taking food home. Portions are generous, as well as delicious," says *D Magazine*, and the place can get crowded. A children's menu is available. Also serves a decent breakfast.

New American

Angeluna, 215 East Fourth St.; (817) 334-0080. M. Open for lunch Mon-Fri 11:30 am-2:30 pm, Sat-Sun noon-3 pm; for dinner Sun-Thu 5:30-10 pm, Fri-Sat 5:30-11 pm. Complimentary valet parking at dinner. Smoking at the bar only. Located on Sundance Square downtown, across the street from the Bass Performance Hall and around the corner from the Barnes & Noble Booksellers (see individual entries). "A livery stable on the present-day Angeluna site served the passing cattle drives, but when stallions gave way to sedans, garages and tire shops sprang up in what is now the Bass Performance Hall," according to the *Fort Worth Star-Telegram*.

"American, Oriental and European flavors are married in ambitious dishes; sip martinis and people-watch the expense-account crowd and social set," notes the *Star-Telegram*. "The food somewhat redeems the jackhammer decibel levels. Don't miss Joe's Shrimp Paesano-lightly breaded jumbo prawns sauteed in vodka-lemon butter," advises *D Magazine*. The readers of *FW Weekly* rated it as the city's "best restaurant."

There are plenty of starters, salads, and pizzas in Angel Moon, as the name would translate from Italian, although the food seems to be "more about food style than taste," according to the *Dallas Observer*. Among pastas and noodles, you can try cavatelli with pecan oysters or Thai rice noodles. The costliest dish is hickory-grilled angus ribeye steak, followed, in descending order of price, by black-and-blue ahi tuna, veal short ribs, seared salmon, pork tenderloin, roasted basil shrimp, pan-roasted chicken, and lamb shank. It has more desserts than your midriff can accommodate and a large wine, beer, brandy, vodka, and tequila list.

Cafe Aspen, 6103 Camp Bowie Blvd.; (817) 738-0838. E. Open for lunch Mon-Sat 11 am-2 pm, for dinner Mon-Thu 6-9 pm, Fri-Sat 6-10 pm. Live jazz on weekends. Located in southwest Fort Worth, on the edge of the cultural district, across Camp Bowie from Aventino's, The Balcony at Ridglea, and La Madeleine French Bakery & Cafe (see individual listings).

"Long a favorite among Fort Worth's fine food fans," notes the *Fort Worth Star-Telegram*, adding, "and yeah, the service is unfailingly polite, whether you're a table of pearl-draped septuagenarians or a twosome or recent college grads." The cafe has other fans. "The marvelous rack of lamb with a coating of Dijon mustard and herbs—accompanied by wild mushrooms, scalloped potatoes, and grilled vegetables—left our friend murmuring accolades," declares *Texas Monthly*, while another reviewer describes the eatery as "quietly elegant, almost spare room." You can start your dinner with an Aspen Greek salad or a Caesar's. The costliest dinner entrees are the 14-ounce bone-in ribeye and classic veal picatta, followed by bone-in veal chop, chili-crusted tuna, grilled beef tenderloin, grilled Atlantic salmon, Sicilian trout, and chicken Florentine.

Nearby, at 6115 Camp Bowie, is a Starbucks cafe, "a cool place to see the culturally elite and get wired on caffeine," according to the *Star-Telegram*. Three blocks from Cafe Aspen, at 6471 Camp Bowie, you will find Fat Albert's, which the readers and staff of the *Star-Telegram* voted as the "best" pool hall in Tarrant County.

Lucile's Stateside Bistro, 4700 Camp Bowie Blvd. near Hulen St.; (817) 738-4761. M. Open Mon-Thu 11:30 am-10 pm, Fri 11:30 am-11 pm, Sat 9 am-11 pm, Sun 9 am-10 pm. Breakfast is served Sat-Sun 9 am-2 pm. Located in west Fort Worth, not far from the cultural district, and a couple of blocks east of the renowned Kincaid's hamburger joint. Behind the bistro is the Connell Baptist Church, across Camp Bowie The Original, a Mexican cafe (see individual listings).

"Cozy neighborhood bistro," the *Fort Worth Star-Telegram* calls it. The paper's readers and staff claim it serves the best martinis. A sixteen-ounce cut of prime rib is the costliest entree, followed by the ten-ounce bacon-wrapped tenderloin, 14-ounce-ribeye, and 12-ounce center-cut sirloin. The price of live Main lobster, according to the menu, is "based on lobster's disposition."

Maryland crab cakes, chicken cacciatore, wood-roasted half chicken, rainbow trout, crawfish etouffee, and fried butterfly shrimp are "Lucile's Favorites," served with Caesar's or house salad. There are wood-roasted pizzas, burgers, sandwiches, soups, and salads. Among desserts, you will find "to die for" chocolate cake and New York-style cheesecake.

Reflections, 200 Main at Second St.; (817) 882-1765. E. Open for dinner Mon-Sat 5-10 pm, closed Sundays. Reservations are suggested. Although jacket and tie are not mandatory for men, they are recommended. Located on the mezzanine level of the Renaissance Worthington Hotel downtown, overlooking the historic Sundance Square. The Caravan of Dreams (see individual listings) jazz and blues venue with a rooftop bar is a block away.

To some romantic, to others elegant, but to most one of the classiest and priciest restaurants in Fort Worth, with water fountains and piano music piped in nightly from the lobby. *Mobil Guide* gives it a four-star rating, AAA four diamonds. "The most elegantly attired people come here to eat the most artistically presented haute cuisine," claims the *Fort Worth Star-Telegram*. The first sign of such class may start on the telephone; if you are put on hold, you will hear the sounds of Fort Worth's adoptive son, Van Cliburn, playing the Tchaikovsky with which he won the first international piano competition in Moscow in 1958 and whose recording became the first classical album to sell more than a million copies.

Appetizers include peppered Texas ostrich loin, wild mushroom and pheasant sausage, sauteed snails, New York-state foie gras, pecan-crusted sea scallops, and Russian beluga caviar. Lobster bisque and smoked corn are two among the soups. Traditional Caesar's and baby spinach leaves are some of the salad choices. The most expensive dish is Colorado rack of lamb Dijonnaise. Entrees could include the Gulf snapper, grilled beef tenderloin, Washington state sturgeon, sauteed veal chop, rack of lamb, or assorted shellfish. Steak and lobster entrees are priced when reservations are made. The least expensive meal is the $20 "vegetarian arrangement." Desserts are luscious and include chocolate cheesecake terrine, cinnamon crème brulée with fresh berries, and strawberries flambé with ice cream. If you are willing to spend about $100 a shot, you can also enjoy the 75-year-old Remy Martin Louis XIII cordial.

You can also try out the Chef's Table for four in the alcove and watch your culinary virtuoso prepare your meal next to the kitchen. A four-course meal will set you back $40 per person and five courses $50, excluding wine.

The $30 fixed-price Sunday brunch, served 10:30 am-2:30 pm, is a feast for your palate, your eyes, and your nose.

Pubs

The Flying Saucer, 111 East Fourth, between Commerce and Main streets; (817) 336-7468/7470. M. Open Mon-Wed 11 am-midnight, Thu-Sat 11 am-2 am, Sun noon-midnight. Live entertainment Fri-Sun. Has a covered brick patio. Located downtown on Sundance Square, diagonally across from the Bass Performance Hall, also across the street from the Barnes & Noble Booksellers and Surf Club USA and The Brew Co. This brick, sandstone, and iron Land Title Building, was designed by Haggart & Sanguinet and built in 1889.

"A beer guzzler's dream come true—or should that be a nightmare?" asks the *Fort Worth Star-Telegram*. It boasts well over one hundred lagers and pales, ambers and browns, porters, stouts, and dark beers that range in price from $2 to $11. Food is tailored to make you drink more beer and includes sausage and cheese plates for from two to six, as well as sausages, cheeses, quesadillas, Texas chili, wursts, and wurst plates. Among the "gourmet" sandwiches, there are turkey, apple chicken salad, reuben, and hot ham and cheese.

Mustard on our pastrami sandwich was so hot it brought tears to our eyes and smoke from our nose, but did nothing to our taste buds. The German Spaten Premium beer was much too warm for the middle of the summer, which was the reason that we came in in the first place.

Another Flying Saucer is located at Lincoln Square in Arlington. Unlike the Cowtown location, it serves a full lunch and dinner menu of sandwiches and bratwurst.

Seafood

Riscky's Catch, 140 East Exchange Ave.; (817) 625-1070. M. Open Mon-Wed & Sun 11 am-9 pm, Thu 11 am-11 pm, Fri-Sat 11 am-midnight. Lunch specials are served 11 am-3 pm Mon-Fri. Happy hour is 3-7 pm Mon-Fri. Live entertainment Wed-Fri, starting at 7:30 pm. Located in the Stockyard Station in the historic Stockyards district, next to several other restaurants (see individual entries).

"The renowned Riscky's empire turns its attention to seafood, serving up fried catfish and the trimmings in a prime Stockyards location next to the Tarantula train tracks," says the *Fort Worth Star-Telegram* about still another Riscky restaurant in Cowtown, this one inaugurated in 1996. Aside from fried and smoked catfish, you will also find platters of fried oysters, crab cake, clam strips, shrimp, and grilled and stuffed red snapper. The most expensive dish is Alaskan snow crab legs with corn and potatoes. There are also appetizers, sandwiches, burgers, soups, salads, and kids' meals.

Water Street Seafood, 1540 South University Dr.; (817) 877-3474. M. Open Sun-Thu 11 am-10 pm, Fri-Sat 11 am-11 pm. Located in the

University Park Village shopping center, southwest of downtown, across University Drive from Fairfield Inn and Residence Inn, as well as next door to Blue Mesa Grill (see individual listings).

Water Street Seafood Co. is based in Corpus Christi and also has similar restaurants in Austin, Houston, and San Antonio. "Fresh is the emphasis in this airy (and arty) dining room," says the *Fort Worth Star-Telegram*, whose staff voted it the "best" seafood restaurant in Tarrant County. The fish can be ordered sauteed, blackened, broiled, or fried. The house specialties include tenderloin, steak and shrimp, brandy mushroom trout, shrimp enchiladas, and crawfish chicken. There are deep-fried dishes, like shrimp and oysters, and large Gulf shrimp. Several salads and sandwiches are on the menu, as are the starters, such as seafood gumbo, calamari, and crawfish tails.

"Water Street won't knock your sea socks off. But if you take it for what it is—a casual place to get a fresh, often tasty plate of food—you'll be in for more than a few pleasant surprises," says the *Dallas Observer*, while the readers of *FW Weekly* named it "the best seafood restaurant."

Southwestern

Blue Mesa, 1600 South University Dr.; (817) 332-MESA. M. Open for lunch and dinner Mon-Thu 11 am-10 pm, Fri-Sat 11 am-11 pm, Sun 10 am-10 pm. Reasonably-priced Sunday brunch. Located in the University Park Village shopping center, southwest of downtown, and next door to Water Street Seafood (see individual entries).

"This purveyor of Southwestern-style Mexican food has improved ten-fold since its opening" in 1996, said *FW Weekly* in 1998. The costliest item on the menu is the beef tenderloin on adobo-Madeira sauce with a blue crab and shrimp cake, followed in a descending order of prices by Tex-Mex grill, seafood mixed grill, Blue Mesa fajitas, red chile-crusted salmon, and citrus chicken. Pastas include grilled Navajo chicken on fettucine and salmon on spinach fettucine. There are appetizers, like blue corn nachos, quesadillas, soups, and salads. For dessert, try Jack Daniels chocolate pecan pie or chocolate mousse taco. Serves good margaritas. The readers of *FW Weekly* named it the "best tequila bar" and as having the "best happy hour" in the city.

Reata, 500 Throckmorton and West Fifth streets, (817) 336-1009. E. Open for lunch daily 11 am-2:30 pm, for dinner Mon-Thu 5:30-10 pm, Fri-Sat 5:30-10:30 pm, Sun 5-10:30 pm. Wheelchair-accessible. No smoking. Features Tequila & Cigar Bar and the Vodka Bar, open daily until midnight. Located in Sundance Square downtown, near The Modern Museum at Sundance Square Annex.

The 14,000-square-foot Reata, named after the ranch in the 1956 film *Giant* (with James Dean, Elizabeth Taylor, and Rock Hudson), sits atop the 35th floor (normally a suspect sign for a restaurant) of the Bank One Tower and has the most spectacular 360-degree view of Fort Worth that you can hope to get anywhere. Floor-to-ceiling windows afford you the view of what was once the Chisholm Trail, the legendary trade route, as well as the Tarrant County Courthouse and the Stockyards (see individual entries), where America's beef production was concentrated at the turn of the century.

The New York-based *Zagat Survey* rates Reata one of the most popular Southwestern-cuisine restaurants in the Metroplex. *Dallas Observer* weekly voted it as capable of fixing you the best steak in Cowtown, adding "its pepper steak makes it worth the nosebleed elevator trip" to the top floor. Seven hundred diners are served on a typical weekend night and emphasis is on the cowboy cuisine: big steaks and the spicy Mexican dishes.

Lunches include fried chicken salad, meat loaf, beef tamales with jalapeno, chicken-fried steak, and the mesquite-grilled ribeye steak. Jalapeno soup, bacon-wrapped shrimp, East Texas crawfish, and South Texas venison ribs are a few among the dinner starters. The costliest dinner entree is the pan-seared pepper-crusted tenderloin. Other choices include rotisserie chicken, pork and red chili enchiladas, mesquite-grilled Texas T-bone steaks, penne pasta, barbecue shrimp enchiladas, and fish of the day. "A hefty, perfectly cooked T-bone (your waiter will insist on cutting it open to make sure it is perfectly cooked) makes you rejoice in your carnivorousness," says an *Observer* review, "and is accompanied by a rich enchilada filled with herb-flecked cacciotta. For once," concludes the reviewer, "a restaurant where the food is about flavor, not fashion." Biscuit pudding and Texas pecan pie are two among the desserts.

The original Reata (Spanish for "rope") opened on Highway 118 North in Alpine (pop. 5,600), 500 miles west of Fort Worth, in 1995. Five years later Reata opened on Rodeo Drive in Beverly Hills, California, where diners go wild over Texas cowboy cuisine and cowboy hats in the gift shop sold out before the restaurant opened.

Steaks

Cattlemen's Steak House, 2458 North Main St. at East Exchange Ave.; (817) 624-3945, Internet www.cattlemenssteakhouse.com. E. Open Mon-Thu 11 am-10:30 pm, Fri-Sat 11 am-11 pm, Sun 1 to 9 pm. Happy hour 3-6 pm Mon-Fri. Located about two miles north of downtown, in the Stockyards, not far from Billy Bob's Texas (see individual entries), the world's largest "honky-tonk," featuring country music entertainment.

Considering that in Texas parlance the West begins at Fort Worth, there are not as many quality steakhouses in Cowtown as there are in Big D to the east. Cattlemen's, established in 1947, is one of the best and quite popular with the tourists who flock to the Stockyards, as well as with locals in cowboy attire. "It's the real thing," says *D Magazine*. The three dining rooms have a 1950s atmosphere and friendly service. Private dining rooms accommodate up to 200 diners.

The most expensive cut is the 24-ounce Cattlemen's porterhouse steak, followed by the 18-ounce Texas strip sirloin, and 18-ounce bone-in ribeye steaks. Other cuts on the menu include the 13-ounce K.C. strip sirloin, 16-ounce Texas T-bone, nine-ounce Rose O'Texas tenderloin, 11-ounce spicy pepper steak, and filet mignon. If you want to tell your friends back home that you tried the real Texas stuff, sample the barbecued spare ribs or southern fried chicken, both among the chef's recommendations. There is also the steak and lobster tail, shrimp and steak, rock lobster tail, and Idaho rainbow trout. After entrees like these, all of which come with a baked potato or french-fried potatoes and salad, few can add a dessert, but if you can, try a homemade pie or cheesecake. Children under the age of 12 can have a six-ounce sirloin steak, chicken fried steak, or barbecued spare ribs at reduced prices. A large selection of wines, by the glass or bottle, is available.

Del Frisco's Double Eagle, 812 Main at West 8th St.; (817) 877-3999. *E.* Open Mon-Thu 5-10 pm, Fri-Sat 5-11 pm. Valet parking. Reservations are suggested. Located downtown, across Main Street from Radisson Plaza Hotel, a block from the Fort Worth Convention Center and southeast of the Sundance Square (see individual entries). The original building erected here in 1890 was the Hurley, Fort Worth's first high-rise named after a saloon keeper who owned it. There was a bathhouse in the basement, where men would get a shave and gamble at cards. A fire destroyed the building in 1934, but it was rebuilt in 1940.

This 250-seat steakhouse, housed in a nicely restored building that previously served as a clothing store, opened in 1996. The downstairs dining room is paneled in mahogany and adjacent to a bar; there is also a second-floor dining area.

This is one of the top steakhouses in the Metroplex, according to a *Gourmet* magazine readers' poll. It is also one of the highest grossing restaurants in Tarrant County. Its owners bought the 1998 grand champion steer at the Southwestern Exposition and Livestock Show (see entry) for $75,000. Del Frisco's serves prime beef that is first wet-aged and then dry-aged for a total of 21 days and cooked in an upright broiler at 1,800 degrees. Be prepared to spend $50-$70 per person, excluding wine.

The costliest steak is the 24-ounce prime porterhouse, at $30. The 12-ounce filet mignon, 16-ounce prime strip, and the Santa Fe peppercorn steak are other choices. Lobster, which will be priced at the time of your order, and several varieties of veal are also on the menu. Vegetables are priced separately. There are appetizers, salads, and soups.

Hunter Brothers' H3 Ranch, 105 East Exchange Ave. at North Main St.; (817) 624-1246. M. Open for lunch and dinner Mon-Thu & Sun 11 am-11 pm, Fri-Sat 11 am-2 am. Breakfast served Sat-Sun 9 am-2 pm. Has a smoking section. Located next door to the Stockyards Hotel—which is owned by the same company—on the northeast corner of Exchange Avenue and North Main Street in the historic Stockyards district. Adjacent to the hotel is also Booger's Red Saloon with its bar stools that are topped with saddles. The White Elephant Saloon is across the street (see individual entries).

In 1873, brothers Robert, William, and David Hunter founded Hunter & Evans, a livestock commission company with offices in Fort Worth, Kansas City, and East St. Louis. Eleven years later, the brothers owned and leased eleven million acres of land and 386,000 head of cattle, including three ranches under the H3 brand. Descendant Robert Hunter McLean opened this steakhouse 125 years later. Heavy tables and the wide-planked wooden floors give it a rugged look. Depending on when you come, an entire suckling pig may be spinning in an open rotisserie.

Steaks, pork ribs, chicken-fried steaks with cream gravy, suckling pig (at $13 a plate), and several seafood dishes could be had. The tender, flavorful, 9-ounce tenderloin arrived exactly as ordered, a medium-rare. The reviewer from the *Fort Worth Star-Telegram* was disappointed with the lunchtime order of roast suckling pig. "Instead of the rosy, pulled pork that we were expecting, thick slices of pale meat were topped with an odd whitish gravy. The offering was as off-putting to the eye as it was to the palate." Says *FW Weekly:* "Of note at H3, though, was the excellent quality of service."

Hoffbrau Steaks, 1712 South University Dr.; (817) 870-1952. M. Open for lunch and dinner Sun-Thu 11 am-10 pm, Fri-Sat 11 am-11 pm. Located in southwest Fort Worth, south of Interstate 30 (also known as West Freeway), and near the Trinity River. University Park Village shopping center is nearby, as are the Fort Worth Zoo and the Log Cabin Village (see individual entries).

"Here's the place to wear shorts and T-shirts to feast on steaks panfried in butter, juicy chicken blanketed in cheese and mushrooms and grilled quail," says the *Fort Worth Star-Telegram*. Appetizers include "No Bull" fried mushrooms and breaded Cowboy shrimp. Center-cut pork chops and grilled shrimp dinner are two among the Brau corral specials. The costliest steak is the 24-ounce sirloin, followed by 16-ounce Texas T-bone, eight-ounce bacon-wrapped tenderloin filet, 12-ounce ribeye,

12-ounce Lone Star strip, and ten-ounce sirloin. You can enjoy "The Good, The Bad, and The Ugly" 8-, 12-, and 16-ounce prime ribs after 5 pm. There are at least half a dozen chicken dishes on the menu, as well as burgers and sandwiches.

In addition to Hoffbrau and Owens, there are several other restaurants in the shopping center; Courtyard by Marriott is also nearby (see individual listings).

Riscky's Steak House, 120 East Exchange Ave. at North Main St.; (817) 624-4800. M. Open Mon-Fri 4-10 pm, Sat 11 am-11 pm, Sun noon-10 pm. Located in the historic Stockyards district, about two miles north of downtown, diagonally from the Stockyards Hotel and a few doors from the White Elephant Saloon (see individual entries).

"Mountain oysters are just one of the delicacies served at this barbecue legend's Northside offshoot," says *FW Weekly* about the restaurant, which in the early 1920s opened here under the name of The Saddle and Sirloin Inn. Beyond the soups and salads, you will find appetizers, such as grilled shrimp, Riscky's pork ribs, escargot, stuffed jalapenos, and calf fries. Texas T-bone is the most expensive steak on the menu, followed by New York strip steak, and ribeye. Tenderloin fillet and peppered strip steak, catfish filet, and chicken-fried steak are also on the menu. Grilled pork chops and cowboy chicken breast round out the menu.

Rodeo Steakhouse, 1309 Calhoun at East 12th St.; (817) 332-1288. M. Open Tue-Thu 5-10 pm, Fri-Sat 5-11 pm, bar open Mon-Sat 4-10 pm. Surf the Internet free. Located a block from the Water Gardens downtown and as close to Ramada Plaza Hotel (see individual entries).

"Popular not just with locals but conventioneers, as it's right next to the Fort Worth Convention Center," says *Fort Worth Star-Telegram.*

Appetizers include Wild West escargot-stuffed mushrooms and stampede cheese nachos. Rodeo specials, such as lobster and king crab dinners, are the costliest, followed by grilled shrimp and chicken. If you love steaks, you can dive into a prime rib, sirloin marinated in soy sauce, teriyaki sirloin, and filet. There are also prime rib and barbecue ribs, as well as baked red snapper and yellow fin tuna.

PERFORMING ARTS

Perhaps the best known Cowtown cultural sight outside the Metroplex is the Kimbell Art Museum. There is the symphony, now located in the Bass Performance Hall, a handsome new downtown structure that also serves a ballet company the city shares with Dallas, and the quadrennial Van Cliburn International Piano Competition for those who like to speculate on who the next Horowitz might be. There are some ten theaters and the summer Shakespeare in the Park festival, which is more than twenty years old.

Your best bet to find out which events take place where and when is the tabloid-sized "Star Time," a pullout section in the Friday's *Fort Worth Star-Telegram*, the *Dallas Morning News*' "Friday's Guide," or the complimentary *FW Weekly*. The monthly *D Magazine* and *Texas Monthly* also carry some Fort Worth events.

DANCE

Dance is perhaps the Metroplex's weakest cultural link, although as early as February 7, 1911, Dallas welcomed the famed ballerina Anna Pavlovna with the Imperial Russian Ballet. Since the Dallas Ballet was dissolved in 1988 and Ballet Dallas went out of business early in 1996, only these ensembles might be worth mentioning:

Bruce Wood Dance Company, 2260 College Ave.; (817) 926-9151. Performs at the Fort Worth Convention Center and William Edrington Scott Theatre—a four-and-a-half-level theater with main auditorium seating nearly 500—at Will Rogers Memorial Center, as well as Bass Performance Hall (see individual entries).

Founded in Austin in 1996, the company moved to Fort Worth the following year and has a budget of about $500,000 a year. It consists of nine dancers, including three from Fort Worth Dallas Ballet (see below) and focuses mostly on the works by its founder. It presents three productions in Fort Worth, with additional performances in Dallas. "It

114

took the company about 15 minutes to leave all rivals in the dust," says the *Dallas Morning News.* "Mr. Wood has money and taste, evident in spare but striking stage designs and enormously assured choreography."

Its founder, Bruce Wood, the son of a Haltom City school athletic coach, went to high school in Fort Worth, began dancing at fifteen and has performed with Les Ballet Jazz de Montreal, New York City Ballet, San Francisco Ballet, and Twyla Tharp Dance Company.

Contemporary Dance/Fort Worth, Post Office Box 11652, Fort Worth; (817) 922-0944, Internet www.cdfw.org. *NCH.* It usually performs at the 385-seat Orchestra Hall in south Fort Worth or the 1,200-seat Ed Landreth Auditorium on the Texas Christian University campus (see entry).

Founded in 1990 by alumni of the Texas Christian University, both of whom had studied modern dance at TCU and the University of Illinois at Champaign-Urbana. It has a budget of about $200,000 a year, consists of nine to 15 dancers, and presents five productions each season.

"It's not the ballet. We fall down . . . on purpose. We dance barefoot," informs the company's Internet page. "New music. No Swans. No limits."

Fort Worth Dallas Ballet, 6845 Green Oaks Rd., Fort Worth; (817) 763-0207, Internet www.fwdballet.com. Located in Fort Worth, but claiming the Metroplex as its home.

The Fort Worth Dallas Ballet was founded in 1961 as a civic troupe and reorganized as a professional ballet organization in 1985. Since then, the company has performed throughout Texas, as well as in Chicago, New York, Washington, D.C., Japan, and Taiwan. Dallas performances are usually given at Music Hall in Fair Park. In 1999, the company had a budget of over $4 million and 31 dancers.

Since the demise of Ballet Dallas in 1996, both Dallas and Fort Worth claim the company as their own. Sometimes, like in the case of *Cinderella,* the 32 dancers have to perform 52 roles, not counting the scores of children's parts. Otherwise the troupe performs to the music from Albinoni to Stravinsky.

Its long-time artistic director, the Peruvian-born Paul Mejia, had danced with George Balanchine's New York City Ballet from 1964 to 1969, when he married Balanchine's favorite ballerina, Suzanne Farrell, which led to his break with the master. Mejia and Farrell joined Maurice Bejart Ballet in Belgium. "In a city that boasts the largest honky-tonk in the world but could never muster up a following for ballet, Mejia looked like the Ballet's last best chance," says *D Magazine.* In 1987, he became the artistic director of the Fort Worth Dallas Ballet and held the job until 1998, when he abruptly resigned at age 50. Later that year, Mejia joined Ballet Arlington (see entry in ARLINGTON chapter).

He was replaced by Benjamin Houk, 38 years old in 2000, a former dancer who had been artistic director of the Nashville Ballet for two seasons.

JAADE Dance Theatre, 506 Main St.; (800) 535-4715, Internet www.jaade.org, E-mail jaadedance@aol.com.

An African-American modern-dance company—originally named Jubilee African American Dance Ensemble—JAADE began performing in 1992. The five-member professional group moved in 1997 to Lancaster Avenue, where it holds dance and tap classes. The company's budget is $35,000 a year, two-thirds of which comes from an Art Council of Fort Worth and Tarrant County grant. The company's repertoire consists of works depicting African-American culture.

Keisha Breaker-Haliburton, 28 years old in 2000, is its dancer, teacher, choreographer, artistic director, and business manager. A native of Washington, D.C., she grew up in Houston. She was hired to lead JAADE fresh out of Texas Women's University in 1993 and organized dance classes in a storefront across the street from Texas Wesleyan University in Fort Worth the following year.

MUSIC

The first known symphony concert in Fort Worth was given by the Boston Orchestral Club in 1890, when the city had a population of 23,000. The first home orchestra had a 14-concert season in 1913-14 under the direction of conductor Carl Venth.

Since then, the Metroplex has become a regular stop for many of the world's finest classical musicians, singers, and chamber groups. While the Fort Worth Symphony Orchestra does not command the respect of a first- or second-tier American orchestra, you will find its concerts an enjoyable experience and its program varied enough to satisfy your thirst for the classics.

Fort Worth Symphony Orchestra, Commerce and East Fourth streets; (817) 921-2676, Fax 921-9795, Tickets 926-8831, Internet www.fwsymphony.org. Located downtown in Sundance Square at the new Bass Performance Hall. Barnes & Noble Booksellers and Angeluna restaurant (see individual entries) are across the street.

The Fort Worth Symphony Orchestra grew from a community effort behind the dream of conductor and violinist Brooks Morris, the orchestra's founder and first conductor. The orchestra debuted in 1925 before an audience of 4,000. Morris served as conductor until 1943. The orchestra—one of only four full-time professional ones in Texas—has an annual budget of about $8 million, in range with Buffalo, New York, Columbus, Ohio, and Salt Lake City, Utah, orchestras.

In 1976, the **Fort Worth Chamber Orchestra** was created and has since then toured the People's Republic of China, Mexico, and Spain. When performing in Carnegie Hall in 1976, the *New York Times* noted, "It was what one might expect to hear from a good, provincial German orchestra—lyrical, relaxed, idiomatic, expressive."

The chamber orchestra employs 36 full-time professional musicians and the symphony orchestra another 39, both under the artistic leadership of music director John Giordano. The symphony is the principal orchestra for the Fort Worth Opera and Ballet. The symphony orchestra presents masterpiece concert performances annually. The chamber orchestra gives a virtuoso series and a casual series at Texas Christian University's Landreth Hall. Both have recorded for several labels.

The symphony also serves as the host orchestra for the Van Cliburn International Piano Competition (see entry below). In 1994 the Symphony hosted the first preliminary round of the Tokyo International Conducting Competition ever to be held in the U.S. The orchestra has performed with pianist Van Cliburn and in 1992 with operatic tenor Luciano Pavarotti for 14,000 at the convention center arena.

John Giordano, 62 years old in 2000, was appointed the music director of the symphony orchestra in 1972. He is credited with founding the chamber orchestra in 1976. A graduate of Haltom High School and Texas Christian University, the New York-born maestro also studied as a Fulbright scholar at the Royal Conservatory in Brussels, where he earned the Prix and the Diplome Superieur. He appeared as a guest conductor with the national symphonies of Argentina, Belgium, Brazil, and Portugal, as well as the Amsterdam, Hong Kong, and London philharmonics. He has conducted concerts with the Symphony Orchestra of Bilbao, Spain, for four seasons. Giordano retired at the end of the 1999-2000 season.

Miguel Harth-Bedoya, 31, succeeded Giordano in 2000. A native of Lima, Peru, he holds conducting degrees from the Curtis Institute of Music and the Julliard School. At the time of his appointment, Harth-Bedoya was associate conductor of the Los Angeles Philharmonic, and music director of the Eugene, Oregon, Symphony Orchestra and the Auckland Philharmonia in New Zealand. He is making Fort Worth his primary residence. His guest-conducting credits include the New York Philharmonic, the Philadelphia Orchestra, and Chicago, Baltimore, and Seattle symphony orchestras.

The associate conductor of the symphony and chamber orchestras is Ron Spigelman, who was born in Sydney, Australia, and served as assistant to the chief conductor of the Adelaide Symphony Orchestra, also in Australia.

Van Cliburn International Piano Competition, 2525 Ridgmar Blvd.; (817) 738-6536, E.mail cliburn@startext.net, Internet www.cliburn.com.

The Tenth Cliburn Competition—which is held every four years—took place May 23-June 8, 1997, at Texas Christian University's 1,200-seat Ed Landreth Auditorium, which the *Dallas Morning News* singled out for "its formality, its claustrophobic lobby, its flat acoustics."

Although of English, Scottish, and Irish ancestry, Van Cliburn—an only child—was born in Shreveport, Louisiana, and "from the age of three, he studied piano with his mother. When he was twelve, he made his orchestral debut with the Houston Symphony," according to his Internet biographical sketch. He was a young pianist from Kilgore, Texas, where his father worked for the Magnolia Petroleum Company, until he won the G. B. Dealey Award in 1952 and appeared with the Dallas symphony orchestra. His debut with the New York Philharmonic took place two years later. In 1958, at age 23, he won against all odds the first International Tchaikovsky Piano Competition in Moscow, although Nikita Khrushchev himself—in office only 17 days—had to approve the award going to the young capitalist.

"Why are you so tall?" asked Khrushchev, who invited him to play several concerts in the Soviet Union. "Because I'm from Texas," answered Van Cliburn, who was six feet and four inches tall.

Van Cliburn won the hearts of the Russian people when he won the piano competition. According to Hugh Best in *Debrett's Texas Peerage:* "Tickets to Cliburn auditions were in such demand that people queued up for three or four days in advance." Best continues: "the Russians showered him with so many gifts, he left Moscow with 17 pieces of luggage to carry them all home."

Van Cliburn was the first classical musician to be honored with a ticker-tape parade and received the keys to New York City. President Eisenhower invited him and his parents to visit the White House. Reviewing his first concert in New York after winning the medal in Moscow, the *New York Times* noted that Van Cliburn "had lived up to expectations, something that hardly seemed possible after so great a buildup."

When the young pianist returned to the Soviet Union that same summer, as part of the U.S. Department of State cultural exchange program, his final performance in Moscow's Sports Palace was heard by 20,000, even as thousands of others had to be turned away for lack of space.

The Van Cliburn competition in Fort Worth, started in 1962 to honor the pianist for his Moscow success, was not initiated by Cliburn, although he has lent it his attention and stardom. The pianist, born in 1935, dropped out of the performing circuit in 1978 and surfaced again in 1987 at the White House, where he played at a state dinner for the Soviet premier Mikhail Gorbachev.

The competition is produced by the Van Cliburn Foundation on a budget of more than $4 million and 650 volunteers. Chopin is usually the most represented among the composers.

Of the 146 pianists from 18 countries heard in the preliminary 1997 Van Cliburn auditions, 35—aged 19 to 30 years—were accepted to take part in the contests, 15 were from Russia or one of the former states of the Soviet Union. The U.S. had four entrants.

The 35 competed for the first prize, valued at more than $250,000, including $20,000 in cash, as well as two seasons of tours and a record-ing. Silver and bronze medalists also received cash awards, tours, and recordings. The participants benefited by free round-trip air fares and have been required to reside in the homes of Tarrant County residents since the competition began. Steinway and Yamaha pianos are often installed by the piano makers in the homes of their hosts.

During the first round, all 35 performed 50-minute recitals of their own selections. Twelve progressed to round two, when they performed 75-minute recitals, which included a commissioned work. In the third round, six finalists played two concertos, each with the Fort Worth Chamber and Symphony orchestras. More than 50,000 attended the concerts.

Jon Nakamatsu, a 28-year-old high school teacher of German ances-try, became in 1997 the first American in 16 years to win the gold medal and the third in the competition's history. Russian Yakov Kasman—at 30 the oldest finalist—"given to grand gestures, both phys-ical and musical," took the silver medal, and Israeli Aviram Reichert the bronze.

The eleventh Van Cliburn competition will be held May 25-June 10, 2001 in the new Bass Performance Hall downtown. Check the Internet site, starting in the year 2000, for details. In a change from pre-vious competitions, the judges may from now on award more than one gold medal to dispense with "the artificiality of ranking musicians."

OPERA

The first opera house in Fort Worth, named Evans Hall, was opened shortly after the coming of the railroad in 1876 and it presented most-ly traveling shows and revues. "But grand opera arrived two years later with the Adah Richmond English Opera Troupe," says historian Leonard Sanders, "consisting of 40 singers, an orchestra and chorus. The company presented *Les Cloches de Corneville* for its first night per-formance and *La Perichole* on the second night." The Fort Worth Opera House emerged in 1883 and was later renamed Greenwall Opera House. In 1908, the Northside Coliseum (now known as Cowtown

Coliseum), housing the world's first indoor rodeo, opened; it was here that the legendary Italian tenor Enrico Caruso performed in 1920, the year before his death.

Fort Worth Opera, 3505 West Lancaster Ave.; (817) 731-0200. Located in the Fort Worth's cultural district, about one and a half miles west of downtown, but performs mostly in the new Bass Performance Hall (see entry).

Fort Worth Opera was introduced as a professional opera company in the fall of 1946 under the direction of Walter Herbert, followed by the Berlin-born Rudolph Kruger, who guided the company for twenty-eight years until his retirement in 1983. One might consider his tenure as "opera's golden years here," observes *FW Weekly*. Kruger signed Luciano Pavarotti for his American debut, but he made that debut at the Met in New York. The Fort Worth Opera is not only the oldest continuously-operating opera company in Texas, but also one of only fourteen opera houses in the nation to have achieved this distinction.

Fort Worth Opera claims to have launched the careers of many talented opera singers, among them John Alexander, Luigi Alva, Enrico di Guiseppe, Placido Domingo (who sang here at age 21 in 1962), Beverly Sills, Diana Soviero, Norman Treigle, and William Walker, its current general director, who was a guest on Johnny Carson's *Tonight Show* more than sixty times.

Walker, a former member of the Metropolitan Opera, returned home in 1991 to take over the nearly bankrupt company, which in 1998 had an annual budget of $2.5 million and an endowment of about one million dollars. The general director, who was 68 years old in 2000, announced that he would retire at the end of the 2001-2002 season.

Born in Waco, south of the Metroplex, Walker grew up in Fort Worth and studied voice at Texas Christian University (see entry) before moving to New York to pursue a career as an opera singer. In 1961, he was accepted in the Metropolitan's training program and a year later earned a contract with the opera company by winning its national auditions. Only three singers have supposedly ever gone from winning the auditions to getting principal roles at the Met and he was one of them. Walker, who sang at the Met for the last time in 1980, developed hearing problems and his last public performance was in 1982 with the Fort Worth Symphony.

Fort Worth Opera employs 500 performers and production people. About 50,000 Metroplex residents attend its programs annually. The company produces three main-stage operas each season, which is not nearly enough for the classical music critic of the *Fort Worth Star-Telegram*, who notes: "No city that produces only three full-scale operatic productions annually has any claim to being anything but a

backwater of the operatic world." Much of the answer is money, he continues. While in Tarrant County the opera is budgeted at $2.10 per per-
son, Dallas County residents allocate $5.30 per person. "Though it
pains me to say it, our neighbors to the east in Dallas, as well as our
cousins on the coast in Houston, are way ahead of us, both in quantity
and quality, when it comes to opera."

Among the company's recent productions have been Gounod's
Faust, Donizetti's *The Elixir of Love*, Verdi's *Rigoletto* and *Il Trovatore*,
Rossini's *Barber of Seville*, and Bizet's *Carmen*.

THEATER

The first dramatic performances in the Metroplex go back to the
Civil War, when shows that traveled by wagon provided a somewhat
questionable entertainment. During the late 1800s theaters, to the dismay of the city fathers, often featured crude burlesque shows and several of them were alleged to harbor "the most depraved characters in
the country." The first vaudeville theater of note was the Adelphi,
which opened at Third and Main streets downtown in 1876. Although
providing some serious entertainment, the theater's owners skipped
town after a few performances, unable to cover their debts. Within a
few weeks, the facilities were taken over by the Theater Comique,
which entertained patrons with crude acts. It was replaced by My
Theater, which stood where Riscky's Bar-B-Q stands today (see restaurant entry in DINING chapter).

A somewhat more respectable theater, Evans Hall was opened in
1876 by merchant B. C. Evans on the second floor of his store at First
Street, between Main and Houston streets. Although *Romeo and Juliet*
was initially performed here, sales dropped until Evans brought from
Paris Madame Rentz's can-can dancers, who scandalized Fort Worth
with the new dance. "A former employee shot Evans to death in 1889,"
writes city historian Bill Fairley. "His partner in Evans-Brown Dry
Goods took over the business and closed the theater."

In 1881, a three-story Fort Worth Opera House was built at Third
Street and Commerce, which was then known as Rusk Street. Italian
opera tenor Enrico Caruso, actor Edwin Booth, and Polish pianist
Ignace Paderewski all performed in this handsome building, which
burned down in 1890. A year later, Henry Greenwall and his brothers
Mitchell and Phillip opened Greenwall Opera House at East Seventh
and what is now Commerce Street, on the spot where the Continental
Plaza/Union Pacific Plaza (see entry) stands today. The building was
condemned and razed in 1908 and a new opera house built for

Greenwall. By the early 1930s, Greenwall's became the Palace, a fine cinema, which was torn down in 1976.

Two other theaters opened in Fort Worth at the turn of the century, both in 1903. One was the Standard Theater, which stood at 1301-3 Commerce Street, the other Crown Theater, at 1213 Calhoun Street; they featured vaudeville acts.

Casa Manana Theatre, 3101 West Lancaster Ave. and University Dr. Tickets (817) 332-2272, Fax 332-5711, Internet http://www.iminet.com/casamanana. Located 1.5 miles west of downtown Fort Worth, east of Will Rogers Memorial Center (see entry), and across the street from the 1939 Farrington Field stadium.

Casa Manana (which translates as the House of Tomorrow) is an 1,800-seat playhouse-in-the-round. It was designed by engineer, inventor, and architect Buckminster Fuller (1895-1983) and built by the city in 1958, east of the old 1939 Casa Manana revolving stage that figured prominently in the 1936 Fort Worth Frontier Centennial Exhibition. This venue for popular Broadway musicals, touring companies, special performances, and children's theater is covered by one of the nation's first geodesic domes, a Fuller invention, that Dallas's alternative weekly *The Met* described as ugly and noted that "if the wind blows from the west during the [Southwestern Exposition and Live] Stock Show, every production smells like *Oklahoma!*" But "despite such architectural and locational hazards, it was one of the first theaters anywhere to present musicals 'in the round' (a seating arrangement that places the audience on three sides of the stage rather than just the front) successfully."

Casa's annual budged is about $11 million, although the theater "has piled up more than $1 million in debt," according to the *Dallas Morning News*. More than 300,000 attend its year-round live comedy, drama, and musicals. In 1999, Casa underwent a $5 million reconstruction—the first in 40 years—which reduced the number of seats to 1,500.

The site was originally home of the Casa Manana Revue, then the world's largest production staged by New York showman Billy Rose. Fort Worth publisher and civic booster Amon Carter (1879-1955) hired Rose in 1936 for a hundred days at $100,000 to lure the visitors from the competing Texas Centennial Exposition celebrations in Dallas's Fair Park to Fort Worth. The theater seated 4,500 people; the floor level provided dinner seating for at least 1,000, surrounded by tiers and balconies for those who came just for the show. The circular stage was surrounded by a 600,000-gallon moat, where gondolas with singers floated until showtime. The Casa Manana shows played to full houses for five months.

While the Texas Centennial Exposition took place in Dallas, the Fort Worth Frontier Exposition ran in Cowtown to show "those dudes over there," in Dallas, what Fort Worth could do. The Dallas Centennial counted 6.3 million paid admissions in all, while the "dudes" in Fort Worth coughed up only 986,000. Carter lured the Dallas visitors with advertising slogan, "for education go to Dallas, for entertainment come to Fort Worth."

President Roosevelt opened the first Casa open-air night show by remote control from a fishing boat off the coast of Maine. The renowned band leader Paul Whiteman and his orchestra inaugurated the revue, attended by 4,800, with *Rhapsody in Blue*, and were followed by two hundred dancers and principals on the revolving stage three times larger than that of Radio City Music Hall in New York City. Of all the major Frontier Centennial attractions, only Casa Manana proved profitable. It ran for two more years after the centennial celebrations, but was torn down because it was too expensive to produce the large-scale shows required by the big stage.

Casa Manana now stages musicals, such as *Oklahoma!*, *Mame*, *The Sound of Music*, and *The Phantom of the Opera*.

Casa on the Square, a 128-seat downtown theater on Sundance Square, next to 8.0 restaurant, opened in 1991 and closed eight years later.

Circle Theatre, 230 West Fourth at Throckmorton St.; (817) 877-3040. Located in the basement of the Sanger Brothers Building, now Sanger Loft Apartments, downtown, roughly between The Modern Museum at Sundance Square Annex and the Convention and Visitors Bureau, on Sundance Square (see individual entries).

Founded in 1981 by Rose Pearson and Bill Newberry, who married each other in 1985, Circle Theatre is a nonprofit company that presents a year-round season of comedies, dramas, and musicals. Its mission is the advocacy of contemporary plays rarely seen in the community. The founders claim that former rancher Ann L. Rhodes, a major supporter of Fort Worth theaters, "has singlehandedly been responsible for us continuing because she undertook to underwrite the risky shows, so it gave us the ability to take some chances." The benefactress, in turn, says, "They do top-quality work." The theatre derives its name from its original location on Bluebonnet Circle, at South University Drive, where it staged its first production in a converted Mexican restaurant.

In 1987, the Circle moved to Magnolia Avenue in Fort Worth's historic south side, and in 1994 to its present location downtown. The auditorium seats 125 patrons arena style around an open thrust stage. There is a large lobby displaying local art.

The theatre produces works by Texas playwrights, such as Robert Schenken, Larry L. King, Oliver Hailey, Del Shores, and Horton Foote. Recently it staged A. R. Gurney's canine comedy *Sylvia*, whose title character is a stray dog adopted by a New Yorker mired in a mid-life crisis. *Sordid Lives,* a bittersweet homosexual comedy filled with sordid language by Del Shores, was also shown.

Fort Worth Theatre, At Orchestra Hall, 4401 Trail Lake at Grandbury Rd.; (817) 921-5300. Located east of Hulen Mall (see entry) and north of Interstate 20.

Founded in 1955, this community playhouse is Tarrant County's oldest live theater. It has been at its current address since 1996. In recent years, the company staged Tennessee Williams' *Cat on a Hot Tin Roof* and *Love! Valour! Compassion!* by Terrance McNally, winner of the 1995 Tony award for best play.

Hip Pocket Theatre, 1620 Las Vegas Trail North at 820 North; (817) 237-5977. A theater company located at the outdoor 175-seat Oak Acres Amphitheatre, northwest of downtown and near Lake Worth, on five acres of privately-owned land. Oak Acres barbecue restaurant is nearby.

Established in 1977, the theater's primary thrust is to showcase original theatrical works by regional playwrights. It is a nonprofit company. Performing from June through October, Hip Pocket presents an eclectic mix of musical theater, comedy, and drama on its outdoor stage. More than 125 productions have been mounted by this company and some 80 of the plays have been penned by its artistic director and playwright-in-residence, Johnny Simons. *FW Weekly* readers named it the "best theater troupe," although the weekly's staff picked the Jubilee Theatre (see listing).

Like Pegasus Theatre in Dallas, Fort Worth's Hip Pocket specializes in humorous plays and frequently presents world premieres. In 1983, Hip Pocket performed at a theater festival in Edinburgh, Scotland. It was also the first American company to perform in London's Queen Elizabeth Hall.

Among its recent productions was *Eggheads,* a comedy that takes place on a transcontinental train trip and calls for seventy characters played by a dozen actors.

Jubilee Theatre, 506 Main, between East Fourth and Fifth streets; (817) 338-4411. Located downtown between the Historic Burke Burnett and Sinclair Buildings in the heart of Sundance Square (see individual entries). The theater is situated in the Jarvis Building, constructed in 1884 and one of the oldest commercial buildings still standing downtown. It is named for J. J. Jarvis, a member of one of Fort Worth's founding families.

Founded in Fort Worth in 1981, Jubilee Theatre is the home of African-American musical theater; it is the only African-American community theater in Texas and producing seven shows and 170 performances each season. Its mission is to produce theatrical works that reflect the African-American culture. In 1993, the company moved into the current 100-seat theater downtown.

In its struggle for audiences black and white, perhaps the only time Jubilee plays to a full house is when presenting a gospel show, like *God's Trombones* in 1988 or *The Book of Job*, which ran for twelve weeks in 1996.

Recently, the Jubilee performed *Back on the Corner*, a 1992 musical about downtown life among the poor, and *Dirty Laundry*, a comedy set in Harlem during the Jazz Age, by Charles C. Cole, adapted from Richard Brinsley Sheridan's *The School for Scandal*.

Main Street Theatre, 107 North Main St., Mansfield; (817) 473-6060. Located in the historic Farr movie theater building in downtown Mansfield, a town of 25,000 in Tarrant County.

Established in 1988, the Main Street Theatre presents six shows each season in the 124-seat theater. It also has managed the Backstage Cafe next door since 1996.

Sage & Silo Theatre, Victory Arts Center, 801 West Shaw at Hemphill St.; (817) 924-6243. Located in south Fort Worth in a historic 90-year-old building that formerly was Our Lady of Victory Convent.

"When we first started, the place was a wreck," cofounder Jeff Sprague told the *Fort Worth Star-Telegram*. There was no stage platform, no seating, and the middle of the floor contained just a huge pile of plaster. John Templin, his partner, was a theater major and "convinced I was going to be the world's greatest actor. . . . But when you find yourself lying in bed hoping that a meteor hits your house so you don't have to go to work the next day, you know that it's the time to do the things that are really important to you." This theater was his dream.

It did well in its opening season in 1998. Among its performances have been an "exceptionally well done production" of *Driving Miss Daisy*, and Tennessee Williams' play *Small Craft Warnings*.

Shakespeare in the Park, 3113 South University Dr. #310; (817) 923-6698, Internet www.shakespeare.vt1.com. Summer performances are held every Tuesday through Sunday at the Trinity Park Playhouse on Seventh Street, seven blocks east of University Drive, and attract up to 15,000 people each summer.

Shakespeare in the Park (SITP) was founded in 1977 as a pilot project for Casa Manana (see entry). SITP's original philosophy was to present the classics in a unique atmosphere while keeping Casa Manana children's theatre actors employed during the summer. The plays are performed in front of the 1936 Work Projects Administration (WPA) picnic shelter, which resembles an Elizabethan manor house, on the north end of Trinity Park, near downtown.

In 1999, Shakespeare and Stage West combined their administrative functions and merged into Allied Theatre Group. The names of the individual troupes have not changed.

Stage West Theatre, 3053-55 South University Dr. and Berry St.; (817) STG-WEST, Tickets 924-9454. Located in southwest Fort Worth, near Texas Christian University (see entry).

Established in 1979, Stage West is a nonprofit theatre company "committed to challenging artists and audiences with plays that explore the diversity of human condition." Among its benefactors was F. Howard Welsh, a most generous Fort Worth millionaire oilman who died at age 85 in 1998. The company stages eight to ten productions every year. Each season its patrons can see a classic by playwright such as Shakespeare, Bernard Shaw, or Molière. Contemporary offerings might include plays by Arthur Miller, Edward Albee, Sam Shepard, Neil Simon, or August Wilson.

Stage West secured its current 10,000-square-foot home in 1993, when it purchased and five years later renovated the first theater built in Fort Worth after World War II. The theater seats 192.

Stage West's recent productions include *Ion*, an ancient Greek play about a mother yearning for her abandoned son, by Euripides, whose *Medea* was performed in 1999. Also staged was *Simpatico*, by Sam Shepard, a tale of revenge in the world of horse racing.

In 1996, the *Dallas Morning News* named *Travels With My Aunt*—a Graham Greene comedy adaptation at which the show's 16 male and nine female characters, without makeup or accessories, are played by four male actors—as the top production in the Metroplex. It was also a hit in London and New York. The *Fort Worth Star-Telegram* named Stage West productions as "the top rated theatrical production in Tarrant County."

Texas Christian University Theater, University Drive at Cantey St.; (817) 921-7626. In addition to its regular undergraduate productions, the TCU's theater arts department has a partnership with the State Theater Koleso based in Togliatti, Russia, says the *Fort Worth Star-Telegram*. Every other year, professional actors from the Russian troupe present Russian-language plays on the campus and sometimes appear with student actors in bilingual productions. On the off years, TCU actors travel to Russia.

NIGHTLIFE

See also the DINING chapter, which features a few like establishments, including a couple of brewpubs.

Aardvark, 2905 West Berry St.; (817) 926-7814. Open Tue-Sun 5 pm-2 am, closed Monday. Live music Thu-Sun. Cover charge.

"This landmark hole in the wall has had more owners than a '79 Monte Carlo," says the *Fort Worth Star-Telegram*, "but the songs remain the same: pop, rock, folk, hard stuff, light stuff, mostly locals but sometimes not. A little cramped, a little seedy—just the way we've always liked it." Readers of the *Star-Telegram* voted it the "best" for a couple of years. Popular with the Texas Christian University (see entry) crowd. Menu includes burgers and chicken. Also a swing club, with free swing lessons Wednesday nights.

Billy Bob's Texas, 2520 Rodeo Pl. and North Main St.; (817) 624-7117 or 589-1711, Internet www.billybobstexas.com. CH and parking fee. Open Mon-Sat 11 am-2 am, Sun noon-2 am. Free Family Line Dance lessons Thursdays at 7 pm.

Located in the northern part of the historic Stockyards district, about two miles north of downtown, north of Cowtown Coliseum (see individual entries). Arcadia discotheque is across the street and Luskey's Ryon Western gear store is on the other side of North Main.

While country & Western dance bands perform every night, starting at 8 pm, Friday and Saturday shows with big-name entertainers start at 10:30 pm. Real bulls and real cowboys perform Fridays and Saturdays at 9 and 10 pm and compete for prize money.

Having a capacity to accommodate 6,000, Billy Bob's advertises itself as "the world's largest honky-tonk," a word that Webster's dictionary defines as "tawdry nightclub or dance hall." Hopefully it is not tawdry to many, but measuring 127,000 square feet (almost three acres) it is the largest indeed. There is plenty of food, from barbecue to fajitas, and plenty to drink, from draft beer to Stolichnaya vodka. It has a showroom for 1,800, a dance floor for 10,000, 31 bar stations, and the bull-riding arena, which was once an auction ring. More than 700,000 visitors drop in every year.

Billy Bob's Texas, advertising itself as "the world's largest honky-tonk," is located on the northern edge of the Stockyards. Measuring almost three acres, it can accommodate 6,000 patrons, has dance floors for 10,000, 31 bar stations, and a bull-riding arena that features cowboys on Friday and Saturday nights. (Photo by Yves Gerem)

Also on the premises are slot machines and casino arcade, where players are rewarded with noncash merchandise or redeemable coupons, a restaurant, and its own dry goods store, where you can buy embroidered denim shirts, jackets, caps, and T-shirts. But if you can't make it to Texas, you can order the merchandise by calling (800) 940-1865. There are even free country-Western dance lessons Thursday evenings; you pay $3 on Saturday and Sunday.

Billy Bob's was built as a cattle barn in the early 1900s and had a tower added in 1936. The slope of the club was built for easy cleaning and runoff of the cattle pens. In the 1950s it became a department store so vast that the stock boys wore roller skates to get around. It was reopened in 1981 by a Fort Worth entrepreneur. The biggest names in country music—Garth Brooks being just one—play here, along with entertainers such as the Beatles' Ringo Star and Bob Hope. Among all, Hank Williams, Jr., still holds the record for selling 16,000 bottles of beer during his show. Movies filmed at Billy Bob's have starred Willie Nelson, Sylvester Stallone, and George Strait. The club figured prominently on the TV soap opera *Dallas*.

Other country & Western music venues include:

Big Balls of Cowtown, 302 West Exchange Ave.; (817) 624-2800. Live music Fri-Sun.

The Branding Iron, 2700 N.E. 28th St.; (817) 838-8173. No cover charge.

Circle M Saloon, 2929 Alta Mere Dr.; (817) 763-8686. No cover charge.

Country Connection, 3137-C Alta Mere Dr.; (817) 763-5799. Live music. No cover charge.

Ernest Tubb Record Shop No. 6, 140 East Exchange Ave.; (817) 624-8449. No cover.

Mike & Mo's Toucan Too, 3408 Indale Rd. at Camp Bowie Blvd.; (817) 377-1233. No cover.

The New West Club, I-30 at Linkcrest; (817) 560-4043. No cover charge.

Red's Lounge, 3700 Hemphill Rd.; (817) 927-9243. Live music. No cover charge.

The Rig Steakhouse, 6308 South Freeway; (817) 293-7027. Live music. No cover charge.

Billy Miner's Saloon, 150 West Third at Houston St.; (817) 877-3301. M. Open Sun-Thu 11 am-10 pm, Fri-Sat 11 am-11 pm, bar until midnight. Located in a four-story building downtown on the Sundance Square, across the street from the Caravan of Dreams club (see individual entries). This former City National Bank Building, designed by Haggard and Sanguinet, was built in 1884 and is one of the city's oldest commercial facades still intact; its interior was rebuilt in 1981 as part of the Sundance Square development.

Billy Miner's is "rowdy," large and friendly, just the spot to drop by to study local characters after a day of sightseeing. There is a bar, with several television sets tuned to ballgames, as you enter and a patio in the back. Serves juice-dripping burgers and sandwiches that you can customize to your taste at a condiment bar.

The Black Dog Tavern, 903 Throckmorton at West Eighth St.; (817) 332-8190. Open Mon-Fri 2 pm-2 am, Sat-Sun 6 pm-2 am. No cover charge. Bands start playing at 9 pm. Located downtown, a block from the Fort Worth Convention Center and Flatiron Building, next to Bryce Building (see individual entries).

A jazz club named after a dog that the co-owner rescued from the Lancaster Street pound. Located where Blarney Stone Pub (see entry) was once situated. "We're proudly an American neighborhood bar," says one of the owners. In a city that seems to have ceased exporting jazz legends, such as the city's native son, Ornette Coleman, "the Black Dog has become the only outlet in Fort Worth hosting the kind of jazz that is imperfect and improvisational," says *FW Weekly*.

The Blarney Stone Pub, 904 Houston at West Eighth St.; (817) 332-474. Open Mon-Fri 2 pm-2 am, Sat-Sun 6 pm-2 am. Located downtown, a block from the Fort Worth Convention Center, across the street from Randall's Cafe & Wine Bar, which boasts 60 flavors of cheesecake, Peters Bros. Hats, and next door to Terry's Grill, which claims to be the oldest downtown restaurant (see individual entries).

When Matt McEntire (who still owns a pub in Ireland) decided to open The Blarney Stone on Throckmorton Street downtown, the walkdown space it occupied was hardly anything more than a cellar. According to the *Fort Worth Star-Telegram:* "There was no plumbing, no electricity, and the floor was simple Texas clay. McEntire, a former construction worker from Ireland who came to the U.S. in 1990, created the place virtually from scratch, modeling it after the pubs he had known in his homeland."

In addition to Bass, Fosters, Harp, and Guinness on tap, it also stocks 80 bottled beers from Belgium, Germany, and Scotland and 100 liquors. Has two pool tables.

Caravan of Dreams, 312 Houston at West Third St.; (817) 877-3000. Club hours 7 pm-2 am, showtimes Wed-Sun 8 pm and 10:30 pm. Located diagonally across the street from the 1907 building, which displays Richard Hass's 1986 *Chisholm Trail* (see entry) storefront mural, and next to the AMC Sundance 11 cinema.

Inaugurated in 1983 on the design by architect Margret Augistine and opened by the Fort Worth billionaire Edward Perry Bass. Caravan of Dreams is a multilevel entertainment complex, including a concert

Open-air rooftop Grotto Bar atop Caravan of Dreams entertainment complex downtown is a local hangout. The geodesic dome cactus garden atop the building (not seen here) served as a research prototype for the Biosphere II, a self-contained environmental indoor habitat near Tucson, Arizona, where eight persons lived for two years. (Photo by Yves Gerem)

venue, auditorium, dance facility, and the Rooftop Grotto Bar, which the readers of *FW Weekly* named the "best place to take a blind date." The club is a new building behind the original facades of two 1880s structures. In 1999, rumors were rife that Caravan may change its format and name.

The Caravan, once said to showcase cutting edge performing arts—emphasizing hard jazz and experimental theater—is sometimes accused of hosting mostly mainstream touring acts that appeal to masses. "The dark, cozy, 500-seat room is an essential stop for contemporary jazz, R & B and rock road acts, yet small enough that there isn't a bad seat," claims *D Magazine*. The renowned jazz musician and Fort Worth native Ornette Coleman recorded his inaugural performances at the club, which launched its Caravan of Dreams Records label with those recordings and stayed in business for five years.

Coleman (b. 1930) originally appeared at the Five Spot club in New York in 1959 with Oklahoman Don Cherry "in the quartet that helped alter the face of jazz." But afficionados were hard to come by for the revolutionary modernist, for even the legendary bassist Charles Mingus had his doubts about "Coleman's credibility. Just pushing the melody out of line here and there," commented Mingus. "Trouble is, he can't play it straight." Coleman received a Guggenheim Fellowship for composition in 1967 and 1974.

Above the concert venue on the second level is the lobby, which opens into a 212-seat auditorium-style theater and adjoining dance studio. The open-air rooftop grotto bar is a local hangout and particularly popular at night. The geodesic dome cactus garden atop the building served as a research prototype for Ed Bass's Biosphere II. A self-contained environmental indoor habitat near Tuscon, Arizona, it was a $100-million ecosystem where eight persons lived for two years.

Next door is the **Marble Slab Creamery,** a "superpremium" ice-cream shop franchise, where a dozen flavors go for $2.50 a scoop; it tastes rich and delicious, but not quite like the flavors you will find at The Back Porch restaurant, across Camp Bowie Boulevard from the Kimbell Art Museum (see individual entries).

DanceMakers of Texas Ballroom, 8674 Hwy. 80 West at Las Vegas Trail (Spur 580); (817) 244-8500, Internet www.dancemakers.com. Ballroom dancing every Saturday 8:30 pm-midnight with Joey Vaughn and His Big Band. Swing dancing every Thursday 9 pm-midnight with DJ Alan. Country and Western/Swing dancing every Friday 8:30 pm-midnight.

A similar Fort Worth venue is **Stardust Ballroom,** 3316 Roberts Cut-Off Rd.; (817) 624-1361. Open Fridays 9 pm-midnight. Women must wear dresses, men jackets and ties.

Horny's Cowtown Blues Cafe, 2731 White Settlement Rd. at Foch St.; (817) 336-HORN. Open Tue-Sat 2 pm-2 am, closed Sun-Mon. Live music most nights, cover charge. Located northwest of downtown and east of University Drive.

"Low-key and friendly, outdoor patio, good jukebox, crowded dance floors and a solid mix of local and regional blues acts," describes the *Fort Worth Star-Telegram*.

Hyena's Comedy Night Club, 604 Main at West Fifth St.; (817) 877-LAFF. Shows Thu 8:30 pm, Fri 8 and 10 pm, Sat 7 and 9 pm, Sun 8 pm. *CH.* Located downtown across Main Street from Courtyard by Marriott, formerly the Blackstone Hotel, and across West Fifth St. from the Sinclair Building (see individual entries). This Art Deco structure, designed by New Yorker Edward F. Sibbert and built in 1936, is known as the Kress Building, which once housed one of the Kress stores.

It features national comedy acts and variety entertainment. Thursday is amateur talent night. While being entertained, you can put away a chicken basket and have a drink. Readers of the *Fort Worth Star-Telegram* picked it as the most popular live comedy club.

Fridays and Saturdays "Swank is what happens to Hyena after the last comedian leaves the stage; staffers swoop in, remove the tables and chairs, and let in the youngsters waiting outside," says the *Fort Worth Star-Telegram*.

J & J Blues Bar, 937 Woodward Ave.; (817) 870-BEER, Internet www.jjbluesbar.com. Open Wed-Sat noon-2 am, Sun 6 pm-2 am, closed Mon-Tue. Located northwest of the Tarrant County Courthouse, between Heritage Park and Henderson Street. Live music most evenings, jam nights are Wednesdays and Sundays.

"For more than a decade, the top blues club in the city," notes the *Fort Worth Star-Telegram*. "This durable Fort Worth joint comes close to creating an authentic Texas roadhouse atmosphere," says *D Magazine*, adding that "foil-wrapped barbecue is usually available." *FW Weekly* readers and staff named it the "best blues venue."

Keys Lounge, 5677 Westcreek Dr. and Walton Ave.; (817) 292-8627. Open daily 11 am-2 am. Live entertainment Thu-Sun, jam nights Thursday and Sunday. No cover charge. Located in south Fort Worth, west of Interstate 35 West, between McCart Avenue and Woodway Drive. Hulen Mall (see entry) is northwest of here.

"A neighborhood bar that doubles as a blues venue, the Keys is a small room where local and regional acts burn up the frets," says the *Fort Worth Star-Telegram*.

Pig and Whistle, 210 East Eighth at Calhoun St.; (817) 882-9966. Open Mon-Sat 4 pm-2 am. Located downtown diagonally across from

Radisson Plaza Hotel (see entry) and next to the bus depot. Live pop and rock bands play every night, but Saturdays are particularly crowded.

This pub moved downtown in 1997 after 13 years off Camp Bowie Boulevard. Jo Meredith, the owner, calls her place "Texopolitan. My background is Commonwealth. You can say British, too." She has lived in Beirut, Singapore, South Africa, South America, and the Philippines. Pig and Whistle stocks extensive selection of bottled beers. "Guinness and Harp are always available," says *FW Weekly*, "and the bartender will pour you a black and tan the proper way, using a spoon to keep the brews separate in the glass." The ladies' room is marked "Sows."

Red Star Lounge, 700 Carroll at Sixth St.; (817) 870-2525. Open Mon-Fri 3 pm-2 am, Sat-Sun 7 pm-2 am. No food. Located in west Fort Worth about a mile and a half from downtown, across from Montgomery Ward's on Seventh St. A full-service bar with television and pool.

Formerly a Southwestern and Mediterranean cuisine restaurant that became a music venue after the mealtime was over. Owned by a transplanted New Yorker who also manages the Wreck Room club (see entry) and The Screaming Peanut Sports Bar nearby.

Springbok Pub, 600 Houston at West Fifth St.; (817) 878-4284. Open Mon-Sat 4 pm-2 am. Located downtown on the second floor of Houston Street Mall, behind the elevator, on the southern edge of Sundance Square (see entry). Big Apple Bagels, next door, also caters to Springbok patrons.

Owned by a South African and claims to be one of only two South African pubs in the U.S., with the other being in Washington, D.C. Has a somewhat limited selection of bottled and on-tap beers. Not the best location for a pub. "We have an excellent clientele here," says the pub's manager, "older, more mature, established, even the Texas Christian University people who come in are very well behaved."

Tatoo Bar, 6463 East Lancaster Ave.; (817) 429-3341. Open Wed-Sun 7 pm-2 am. Closed Mon-Tue. No cover charge Wed, Thu, or Sun. Located east of East Loop 820 and north of Lake Arlington.

Loud regional rock groups will be heard here, although the *Fort Worth Star-Telegram* claims, "This is a really cool and usually safe haven for lovers of insanely noisy hard-rock stuff."

Next door to it is **Randy Adams Tattoo Studio,** which the staff and readers of the *Star-Telegram* voted as the best tattoo parlor in the county.

A few blocks from here, at 5309 East Lancaster, stands **John Carter Place,** (817) 446-3045, which the staff of the *Star-Telegram* named as the best in Tarrant County for home cooking as well as for its "soul food."

We Can Do It Club, 711 Barden St. off Camp Bowie Blvd.; (817) 335-4999. Open Thu-Sun 4 pm-2 am. Located in west Fort Worth.

Originally located downtown on Main Street, across the street from Sid Richardson Collection of Western Art, the White Elephant Saloon now stands on East Exchange Avenue in the Stockyards. The famed Jim Courtright-Luke Short Annual Shootout is reenacted in front of the saloon every February 8. (Photo by Yves Gerem)

Readers of the *Fort Worth Star-Telegram* voted it the "best" live Tejano club in Tarrant County.

White Elephant Saloon, 106 East Exchange Ave. at North Main St.; (817) 624-1887/8273. Open every day at noon, Sun-Thu until midnight, Fri-Sat until 2 am. Outdoor beer garden open Apr-Oct. Live country and Western music seven nights a week.

Originally located downtown in the Morris & Conn Building, at 308 Main Street, directly across from Sid Richardson Collection of Western Art (see individual entries). Fort Worth civic booster and publisher Amon Carter drank and played poker here.

It has been situated in the Stockyards (see entry) in this building, which was erected in 1931 by architect L. B. Weinman, since 1974. There has been a saloon here since 1906. *Esquire* magazine voted White Elephant one of the "100 Best Bars in America." Has long wooden, stand-up bar with brass footrail and dance floor. The saloon is known as CD's Bar & Grill in the television series *Walker, Texas Ranger,* which stars Chuck Norris. The Stockyards Hotel (see entry) is situated across the street.

See also Jim Courtright-Luke Short Annual Shootout—which is re-enacted here every February 8—in the SIGHTS chapter.

Wreck Room, 3208 West Seventh St. near Camp Bowie Blvd.; (817) 870-4900. Open daily 6 pm-2 am. Bar open every night, live music now and then. Cover charge. Located just north of the cultural district, next to a Seven-Eleven convenience store and a block from Seventh Street Theatre.

"I said 'let's call it the Wreck Room because it's a dump dive,'" says the owner, a transplanted New Yorker whose family has been in the bar business for fifty years. "We have a hard-core group of 100 people who hang out there, and everybody knows each other."

"Casual, everyone-knows-your-name-and-they'll-probably-buy-you-a-beer type of hangout," says the *Fort Worth Star-Telegram,* whose staff selected as the "best" in Tarrant County. Now and then you will hear a local alternative rocker here. Also a swing club with free swing lessons Thursday nights. *FW Weekly* readers voted it the "best rock venue" in the city with the "best jukebox."

The owner's mother runs The Screaming Peanut Sports Bar, at 2736 West Sixth St., northeast of the cultural district. They also manage the Red Star Lounge, at 700 Carroll, nearby (see entry).

SIGHTS

Nearly seven million visitors come to Fort Worth every year and spend about $800 million on lodging, dining, shopping, and entertainment. About one-fifth come to Cowtown on business, the rest are leisure travelers. They collectively spend about $225 million on food, $200 million on entertainment, $195 million on shopping, and $150 million on lodging. By comparison, the number of visitors to Dallas is double the Fort Worth figure.

Fewer than 2 percent of the visitors to Fort Worth come from outside the U.S., even though many—particularly European travelers—have up to six weeks of vacation and often spend twice as much per day as domestic tourists. Their favorite pastimes are shopping, dining, and visiting historic places.

Mexican, Canadian, British, German, Japanese, and French visitors are the most common. While in Texas, the French spend an average of $146, Japanese $131, Mexicans $113, British $105, Germans $94, and Canadians $64 a day per person, compare that to Americans, who spend $78 daily on average.

More than half of those visitors to Cowtown who were surveyed to obtain the above figures say there is almost nothing they dislike about Cowtown, although about 15 percent say that traffic congestion is the city's biggest problem.

There is plenty to see and enjoy in Fort Worth, as long as you keep in mind that 50 years, not 500 like in Europe, means history in Cowtown. Please note that Six Flags Over Texas and Hurricane Harbor theme parks are listed in the ARLINGTON chapter. Here are some of the better known sights, listed in alphabetical order.

The *CH* abbreviation indicates there is a charge, *NCH* that there is none.

400 Block of Main and Third Streets ——
Richard Haas's *Chisholm Trail* mural and the site of the El Paso, Pickwick, Delaware, and Westbrook hotels.

Three sides of the 1907 commercial building—until recently housing the Fort Worth-based Pangburn's Chocolates storefront—have trompe-l'oeil paintings by Richard Haas. *The Chisholm Trail* mural is on the south side of the building. Fort Worth was a rest stop on the Eastern Cattle Trail that connected with the Chisholm Trail. This building was a terminal and business office for the Interurban rail line between Fort Worth-Dallas and Fort Worth-Cleburne from 1902 to 1934; it was discontinued when commuters began relying on their private automobiles. (The 33-mile Trinity Railway Express, a $324-million version of a new Interurban, is slated for completion in the fall of 2000.)

The **El Paso Hotel,** the first Fort Worth lodging equipped with gas lights, opened at this site in 1877 to satisfy the hordes of newcomers arriving on the newly opened railroad line the year before. It was the first three-story building in the city. That year, the longest mail and passenger stagecoach line in the country departed every morning from the El Paso and headed 1,560 miles west to Yuma, Arizona Territory, which it reached 17 days later—provided it could escape frequent robberies.

The El Paso became the **Pickwick Hotel** in 1885. Quanah Parker (1845-1911), the legendary Comanche Indian chief—whose white mother, Cynthia Ann Parker, was eleven years old when taken captive by Comanches—had often visited Cowtown. He and his friend Yellow Bear stayed at the Pickwick. Unfamiliar with gas lights, Yellow Bear turned off the light when retiring for the night, apparently not closing the valve completely, and died of gas inhalation. Quanah was unconscious for three days but survived. Electric lights began replacing the gas jets that same year.

The Pickwick became the **Delaware Hotel** in 1891. In 1910, the building was razed and the **Westbrook Hotel** built on the very block where Maj. K. M. van Zandt bought his first house and placed his pigpen and cow lot in 1866. It was so crowded with oil traders that "the management was forced to clear the furniture from the lobby." The hotel was torn down in 1978. The Golden Goddess statue, which once stood in the Westbrook hotel lobby as a source of good luck, can now be seen in the Old Spaghetti Warehouse restaurant in the historic Stockyards (see entries).

The 900 Block of Houston Street ————

This block of Houston Street has one of Fort Worth's highest concentration of turn-of-the-century buildings.

Terry's Grill, built in 1909, at 902 Houston St. Originally a meat market. The building has housed restaurants since 1936, the year when the temperature rose to 120 degrees in the northwest-based town of Seymour, a Texas state record.

Houston Place, built in 1907, is a building designed by Sanguinet and Staats for William Harrison Eddleman to house his Western National Bank. Eddleman came to Fort Worth from Weatherford to establish this bank, which failed in 1914.

Between 1904 and 1978, his family occupied the **Eddleman-McFarland mansion** that you can see on the bluff overlooking the Trinity River, at 1110 Penn Street, roughly between the cultural district and downtown Fort Worth. The house was originally built in 1899 for a wealthy Galveston widow for $36,000. McFarland's daughter Carrie (who lead a life of luxury and wore pink at every party) lived in the house for 75 years and died at the age of 100 in 1978, when the house was purchased by the Junior League of Fort Worth for $270,000 and restored. The house, which author Laura Trim calls "the finest in Fort Worth" is usually open for tours Tue-Fri. CH. For group tours, call (817) 332-5875.

Shelton Building, constructed in 1910, at 901 Houston St., was a general merchandise store leased by S. H. Kress Company until 1936, when it was remodeled, then used by McCrory's Variety Store for the next three decades.

Peters Brothers Hats Building, (817) 335-1715, Internet petersbros.com, across the street from the **Flatiron Building** and next door to **Randall's Cafe** (see individual entries), was built in 1911 at 909 Houston St. It is home of the oldest continuous hat-making business in Texas, also begun in 1911, and its shabby interior will attest to it.

The company made hats for every American president from Warren G. Harding through Richard Nixon. It originated the extraordinary Stetson's Amon Carter Shady Oak Western hat, which the civic booster Amon Carter gave to all visiting celebrities, several thousand in all, at a cost of at least $35 each. The hat was named after Carter's Shady Oak Farm, set along the shores of Lake Worth, where a reconstructed log cabin in which Cynthia Ann Parker, Chief Quanah Parker's mother, once lived. "Harry Truman, whom Amon did not like because of Truman's anti-Texas position on offshore oil, was given only the standard Shady Oak hat, as were Presidents Coolidge and Hoover, who, being Republicans, weren't considered very important," notes Carter's biographer Jerry Flemmons.

Peters Brothers was started by Jim and Tom, Greek immigrants who began their business shining shoes in nearby Waco during the Cotton Palace Celebration. After saving $600, the brothers moved to Fort Worth and purchased a 17-by-10-foot wood building at Ninth and Houston streets. They renovated the building and hired four men.

By World War I, the business was so robust that the store employed 36 men shining shoes in two shifts. On the side, the Peters brothers operated a hat renovation department. In 1921, Tom went to work for

the master hatter John B. Stetson in Philadelphia and on his return
started making hats. The shoeshine business was discontinued in 1973.
Jim Peters died in 1933, his brother Tom in 1991.

If you are looking for a hat, a fifth-generation Peters will make one
for you on the premises for up to $800 or will sell you a ready-made one
from the rack for $25.

Barber's Books, at 215 West Eighth and Throckmorton streets,
started out as the Adams Hotel in 1908. The building was modernized
in 1935 and occupied by Barber's, perhaps the most beloved bookstore
in Cowtown until 1998. It was one of the oldest bookshops in Texas.
Even comedian Red Skelton stopped by, "just to relax out of the public eye for a while." The *Fort Worth Star-Telegram* called it and its owners "eclectic" and "quirky." Opened in 1925 by Bert and Alice Barber
and owned since 1960 by Brian Perkins, the cramped store held thousands of used books, many of which were not likely to be found anywhere
else in Tarrant County. In 1998, the entire inventory of more than
70,000 volumes was bought by Larry McMurtry (b. 1936), the 1986
Texas Pulitzer Prize-winning author of *Lonesome Dove*. McMurtry's
antiquarian bookstores, bulging with 300,000 volumes, are scattered in
four buildings about downtown Archer City (pop. 1,918), northwest
of Fort Worth, where Dairy Queen is the town's social hub and there's
"a sky so vast and blue it makes your heart ache," according to
Newsweek magazine.

Around the corner, at West Eighth Street, between Barber's and former Thompson Book Store, you will notice the **Atelier Building,** a
brick structure with two chimneys that was constructed in 1905 and in
1936 served as a temporary Carnegie Library.

American Airlines C. R. Smith Museum, 4601 Texas State Hwy.
360 at FAA Rd.; (817) 967-1560. Open Tue-Sat 10 am-6 pm, Sun noon-
5 pm. NCH. Located about four miles south of the Dallas-Fort Worth
International Airport, immediately south of the intersection of State
Highways 183 and 360. American Airlines Training & Conference
Center is located within walking distance (see individual entries).

The museum is named after the "paternalistic, very tough and no-
nonsense" founder, who served as chief executive of American Airlines
for 35 years and was commerce secretary under Pres. Lyndon B.
Johnson. He died in 1990. It is funded mostly by American Airlines, so
it should come as no surprise that it chronicles the history of the company, as well as America's love affair with flying. Almost 100,000 visit
it every year.

Having touch-screen video monitors, motion sensors, and other
exhibits, this is one of the technologically more advanced museums in
the Metroplex. It also features the Flightlab, with simulated cockpits
and hands-on demonstrations of aerodynamics, airplane design, and

flight principles. The *Dream of Flight* film short is shown every half-hour in the theater. A gift shop is on the premises.

Outside the museum stands a fully restored DC-3 airliner, named *Flagship Knoxville*, one of the few remaining pre-World War II DC-3s that were delivered to American Airlines in 1940. *Knoxville* served as a mosquito sprayer in South Carolina and was saved for posterity in 1991. Two modern jet engines, a Rolls-Royce RR-211, and an Allison D-501 were acquired in 1997. A wing addition is planned for to enclose the *Flagship Knoxville*.

The museum is staffed mainly by volunteers, most of whom are retired American Airlines employees. The company's roots go back to the 1920s, when it was called Texas Air Transport and located in the Aviation Building downtown, where Continental Plaza/Union Pacific Plaza (see entry) stands today. Among the interesting tidbits in this museum you will learn that until World War II all stewardesses were required to be registered nurses.

Bank One Tower, 500 Throckmorton, between East Fourth and Fifth streets. Borders on Sundance Square, diagonally across from the Sanger Brothers Building (see individual entries).

The 454-foot-tall, 37-story building, designed by John Portman of Atlanta, was constructed in 1974 and formerly housed Fort Worth National Bank. It has 620,000 leasable square feet of space, which makes it one of the ten largest office buildings in the city. Author Laura Trim calls it the "one modern building in Fort Worth that never fails to intrigue us. From the exterior, it looks like a glass pyramid that straightened up, but inside the geometry of that form provides all sorts of fascinating nooks." Portman was the designer of the original Hyatt Regency hotels.

In May 1995, softball-sized hail knocked out 15 large sloping panels on the ground of this building, but because the original manufacturer went out of business, the owners had to replace all the panels to preserve the uniformity of the glass.

Reata restaurant, located on the 35th floor of this tower, serves Southwestern cuisine and is described in the DINING chapter.

Note: Please see page 216 for details on the March 2000 tornadoes.

Bass Performance Hall, Commerce St., between East Fourth and Fifth streets; Box Office (817) 212-4280, Internet www.basshall.com. Wheelchair-accessible from the east and west entrances, and elevators on each side of the hall. Located on Sundance Square downtown, across the street from Barnes & Noble Booksellers and Angeluna restaurant (see individual entries).

The ten-story **Nancy Lee and Perry R. Bass Performance Hall,** largely spearheaded by the billionaire Bass family, which is known for its success in oil and other investments, was dedicated in 1998, five blocks from the Tarrant County Convention Center (see entry). It is

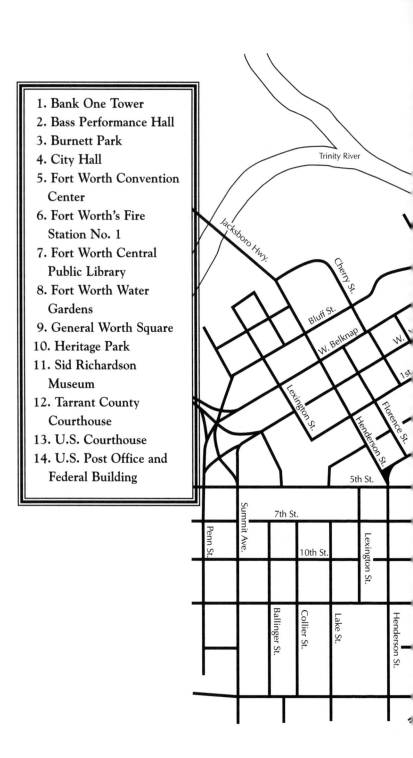

1. Bank One Tower
2. Bass Performance Hall
3. Burnett Park
4. City Hall
5. Fort Worth Convention
   Center
6. Fort Worth's Fire
   Station No. 1
7. Fort Worth Central
   Public Library
8. Fort Worth Water
   Gardens
9. General Worth Square
10. Heritage Park
11. Sid Richardson
    Museum
12. Tarrant County
    Courthouse
13. U.S. Courthouse
14. U.S. Post Office and
    Federal Building

Trinity River

Jacksboro Hwy.

Cherry St.

Bluff St.

W. Belknap

W.

Lexington St.

Florence St.

Henderson St.

1st

5th St.

Summit Ave.

7th St.

Penn St.

10th St.

Lexington St.

Ballinger St.

Collier St.

Lake St.

Henderson St.

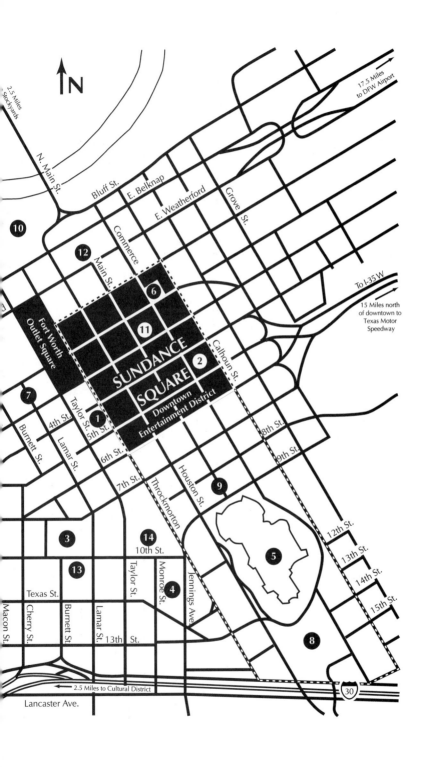

N

2.5 Miles Stockyards

17.5 Miles to DFW Airport

N. Main St.

Bluff St.

E. Belknap

E. Weatherford

Grove St.

Commerce

To I-35 W

15 Miles north of downtown to Texas Motor Speedway

Main St.

Fort Worth Outlet Square

SUNDANCE SQUARE
Downtown Entertainment District

Calhoun St.

4th St.

Taylor St.

5th St.

Lamar St.

Burnett St.

6th St.

7th St.

Throckmorton

Houston St.

8th St.

9th St.

12th St.

13th St.

14th St.

15th St.

10th St.

Taylor St.

Monroe St.

Jennings Ave.

Texas St.

Cherry St.

Burnett St.

Lamar St.

Macon St.

13th St.

2.5 Miles to Cultural District

Lancaster Ave.

30

10

12

6

11

2

7

7

3

14

13

4

9

5

8

named after the parents of the four Bass brothers, who are all active in Fort Worth's affairs and have invested hundreds of millions of dollars in downtown real estate.

About $18 million of the $65 million it cost to build the privately-funded hall came from the Sid W. Richardson Foundation, named after the Bass brothers' great-uncle, who, at his death in 1959, left the four brothers—Lee Marshall, Robert Muse, Edward Perry, and Sid Richardson—$2.8 million each. Their father Perry pooled the sons' $11.2 million inheritance into Bass Brothers Enterprises and increased it many times over. *Forbes* magazine estimated in 1998 that every one of the Bass brothers was worth anywhere from $1.1 to $3.3 billion. Even Sid Richardson Bass's wife Anne Hendricks, whom he divorced in 1989, had no less than $560 million to her name. The patriarch Perry Richardson Bass, 85 years old in 2000, himself had a net worth exceeding $1.3 billion.

Inspired by the Theatre des Champ-Elysees in Paris, the hall was built on the one-acre block in a Beaux-Arts revival architectural style with two copper domes, a slate roof, and a limestone-and-stucco facade. The 2,054-seat six-level hall is home to the Fort Worth Symphony, the Opera, the Fort Worth Ballet, Van Cliburn International Piano Competition, and select Casa Manana (see entry) shows. A 425-ton acoustical ceiling made of nine-and-a-half-inch thick concrete is suspended from the massive roof trusses. The ceiling mural was created by Fort Worth artists, twins Scott and Stuart Gentling. The seven-foot-tall gilded-bronze statue of Diana that you see in the lobby, sculpted by Augustus Saint-Gaudens (1848-1907), is on a long-term loan from the Amon Carter Museum (see entry).

According to the *Fort Worth Star-Telegram*, "Assuming you don't mind the climb, you'll get the best sound and the most spectacular view from up in the gallery. But there don't appear to be any bad seats." The music critic noted that it would appear that the less you pay for your ticket, the better your seat.

Two 48-foot-tall trumpet-blowing overscaled angels, chiseled by the Hungarian-born Marton Varo alone in Texas limestone and weighing 148 tons, grace its facade. Varo spent a year and a half working 12-hour days to carve the angels that *FW Weekly* labels "tacky," adding, "If the exterior of the hall seems out of tune with itself and the site, the inside elements work in perfect harmony."

"The compact, vaultlike structure with a native limestone facade would have fit right in, in turn-of-the-century Stuttgart or Paris," according to *Texas Monthly*. Fueling the state's most antagonistic urban competition, the magazine went on to point out that the Bass Performance Hall seems to be everything the Morton H. Meyerson Symphony Center in Dallas not, even quoting one of the Basses as saying that the Bass will

The $65-million Bass Performance Hall downtown was largely underwritten by the billionaire Bass family of Fort Worth and inaugurated in 1998. The 2,054-seat, six-level hall, home to the local symphony, opera, and ballet company, as well as the prestigious Van Cliburn International Piano Competition, occupies an entire block in Sundance Square. (Photo by Yves Gerem)

serve many functions, while the "Meyerson is strictly a concert hall." The *Wall Street Journal* adds that "unlike the Meyerson, whose vast lobbies can intimidate and chill, the Bass Hall is all gemutlich and comfy, as well as civilized and dignified." The hall's boxes sold for up to $2 million each, with many going to companies, such as the *Fort Worth Star-Telegram*.

Pianist Van Cliburn collapsed on stage during the first full orchestra concert at the hall in May 1998. The 63-year-old adopted son of Fort Worth was just a few minutes into the third movement of Rachmaninoff's *Piano Concerto No. 2*, when he suddenly hit the keyboard with both hands. "As the long dissonant tone resounded through the packed concert hall, Cliburn slumped to his left and fell off the bench to the floor," reported the *Star-Telegram*, adding that several doctors leaped onto the stage. "Conductor John Giordano turned to reassure the frightened audience, which was sitting in dazed silence." He was taken to a hospital and recovered in a few hours.

The Bass most involved in the development of Sundance Square, where the hall stands, was Edward Perry (b. 1945), a Yale-educated "Texas-bred cross between Prince Charles and Lorenzo de Medici." The "lanky, soft-spoken, courtly man" was "raised in a privileged family on the city's west side." After dropping out of Yale, he opened a hotel in Katmandu, Nepal, invested in a 1,042-acre rain forest in Puerto Rico, and lived on a 300,000-acre ranch in the Australian Outback. It was he who financed the Biosphere II. The Arizona-based project was a $100 million 3.15-acre glass-and-steel terrarium with a tropical rain forest to create a self-sustaining ecosystem indoors, where eight persons lived for two years. Edward Perry Bass, worth $1.1 billion, was the 157th richest American in 1998, according to *Forbes* magazine.

Blackstone Hotel/Marriott, 601 Main at East Fifth streets. Located in Sundance Square downtown, about a block southwest from the Bass Performance Hall (see individual entries).

This 22-story hostelry with 284 guest rooms and luxury suites on the 15th and 18th floors opened a couple of weeks before the stock market crash of October 1929, when singles went for $7.50 a night. It was designed by the Kansas City architectural firm of Mauran, Russell & Crowell, which also drafted the Rice Hotel in Houston, the Galvez Hotel in Galveston, and the St. Anthony Hotel in San Antonio. It was the first Art Deco high-rise in Fort Worth. Built by oilman Christopher Augustus O'Keefe as Fort Worth's "Hotel of Distinction," this was the only building in the city constructed in the true Art Deco, ziggurat style.

In its heyday, the Blackstone welcomed such luminaries as Presidents Herber Hoover, Lyndon Johnson, and Richard Nixon; musicians Benny Goodman, Lawrence Welk, and Elvis Presley; actors Clark Gable, Bob Hope, and John Wayne. Bob Wills recorded the hit song

"San Antonio Rose" in the WBAP radio studios on the 22nd floor of the hotel.

From 1952 to 1962, The Hilton Hotel Corp. leased the Blackstone and renamed it the Hilton. Afterwards, the building was sold at foreclosure auctions twice and has had several owners since. The small size of its concrete-clad rooms did not lend itself to remodeling and the Blackstone closed permanently in 1982.

Sixteen years later, it was gutted to make space for a 203-room Courtyard by Marriott hotel, while the 1950s-era annex was turned into a parking garage. See the LODGING chapter for more details.

Bryce Building, 909 Throckmorton at West Ninth streets. Located across from the Public Safety & Courts Building (former City Hall) and across from the postage-stamp-sized Hyde Park (see individual entries).

Until 1939, this small building, constructed in 1910 by the mayor of Fort Worth—from 1927 to 1933—shared a lawn with the Carnegie Library and later the Fort Worth Public Library until 1990. Its owner, William J. Bryce (1861-1944), purchased the oddly-shaped lot in 1909, after part of it had been deeded to the city for right-of-way. The structure is located across the street from the building that served as Fort Worth's city hall during Bryce's contracting business. A native of Scotland, he moved to Winnipeg, Canada, when nineteen years old and learned bricklaying. He arrived in the U.S. in 1881 and Fort Worth two years later. He owned a brick company in nearby Denton, but sold out to Acme Brick in 1912. Bryce paved Camp Bowie Boulevard in west Fort Worth. After his death, the 2,900-square-foot building was bought by a business associate and housed a variety of tenants until it caught a fire in 1982, when it served as a German Hamburg House restaurant. In 1990, when the Public Library was demolished, the building, which was hidden from view, became much more visible. It now houses law offices.

The parking lot in front of the Bryce Building is being considered as the site of a new downtown public square.

The **Fairview/Bryce House,** built in 1893, can be seen in Arlington Heights neighborhood, at 4900 Bryce Avenue. It was designed by Messer, Sanguinet, and Messer, architects who designed nearly all houses in the area in the early 1890s. Marshall R. Sanguinet, whose own house is located at 4729 Collinwood Avenue, became one of Texas' best-known architects and practiced in the city until his retirement in 1926.

Burger's Lake Water Park, 1200 Meandering Rd. in River Oaks, just off Roberts Cut-Off Rd. and River Oaks Blvd. Open daily 9 am-8 pm, spring through Labor Day. CH for children over 5 years; 50-visit punch card is $200. Located east of the NAS Joint Reserve Air Base (formerly Carswell Air Force Base) in west Fort Worth, near West Fork Trinity River.

A 27-acre park was once a goldfish hatchery and has two shoreline beaches. Century-old pecan, oak, and birch trees surround the one-acre sandy bottom pool with diving boards, a 20-foot slide, and a trapeze. In the pool's center is a dock for lounging. The water is usually a bit cooler than at other pools because the lake is spring-fed. Going to this swimming hole "is like stepping back in time," says the *Dallas Morning News*. "The wood-framed buildings look like summer camp quarters."

Burk Burnett Building, 500 Main at West Fourth streets. Located on Sundance Square downtown, facing the *Chisholm Trail* mural by Richard Haas, painted on what is today the Pangburn Chocolates storefront. Jubilee Theatre is next door and the handsomely reconstructed Sinclair Building farther up the block (see individual entries).

This attractive 12-story Neoclassical structure was erected as the home for the State National Bank in 1914 and bought by cattle baron Samuel Burk Burnett (1849-1922) the following year. It was designed by the prolific Fort Worth architectural firm Sanguinet and Staats and stands midway in age and size between Sanguinet's two other high-rises, the 1909 Flatiron Building and the W.T. Waggoner Building of 1920 (see individual entries). The base of the building is white terra-cotta with granite columns on the Main Street facade.

Burnett—who was born in Missouri in the year that Fort Worth was founded and came to Texas in 1857—is said to have paid cash for the building, which was advertised as the tallest in Fort Worth. Because of its steel frame construction, it was believed "absolutely fireproof." It had its own artesian well, elevators that ran at a speed of 600 feet a minute, and an observation deck on the roof. Owned by Burnett and his heirs for almost 70 years, the building was purchased by Bass Brothers Enterprises in 1974 and renovated six years later. It has been listed in the National Register of Historic Places since 1980.

Burnett Park. Located downtown between West Seventh and Tenth, Cherry and Lamar streets. The U.S. Courthouse and St. Andrew's Episcopal Church (see individual entries) are situated across the street.

For details about Henri Matisse's female *Backs* on display in the reflecting pool here, please see the section Art in Public Places in the VISUAL ARTS chapter.

Rancher and oilman Samuel Burk Burnett (1849-1922) donated the land for this three-acre park to the city in 1919 in honor of his children and specified that the land was never to be used for any other purpose. On the corner of Ninth and Lamar streets, about where the park is located, Burnett had built his luxurious home. Burnett Street nearby was named after the first Republic of Texas president, David G. Burnet, but when new signs were erected someone mistakenly added another *t* to the name.

"At age 15, Samuel Burk Burnett was one of the first cowboys to herd Longhorns north to Kansas, and the following year, he was boss of a cattle drive up the Chisholm Trail for his rancher-father," according to a Stockyards Visitors Center brochure. In 1881, he established 6666 Ranch, near Wichita Falls, one of Texas' largest, winning some of the land by holding four sixes in a poker game. "Oil discovered on the ranch increased his wealth, as did banking and milling interests. Today, the ranch contains over 200,000 acres and is known for having pioneered importation and breeding of Herefords and champion race and show horses," notes one observer. The property is now owned and operated by Burnett's great-granddaughter, Anne Windfohr Marion, in 1998 one the nation's richest persons, according to *Forbes* magazine.

"He was daring and courageous, never afraid to try new and challenging enterprises, managing to rise and conquer every obstacle which commonly confronted young pioneers in the untamed west of the 1800's," writes the Fort Worth historian Bill Fairley, adding that the rancher had many gun confrontations. Burnett married the daughter of a leading Cowtown banker in 1870, but the marriage lasted for a year only and he remarried in 1892. For a quite different glimpse of a married Burnett, see a note about Mary Couts Burnett Library at Texas Christian University in the NEW RESIDENTS chapter.

In 1881, Burnett confronted the notorious rustler Jack King, who supposedly stole several of his steers whose brand was covered with another. King rode to Burnett's ranch house, demanded the return of the animals and when Burnett refused, pulled his gun. Burnett beat him to the draw. Twelve years later, a desperado named Farley Sears "was only the second man to attempt to rustle cattle from Burk Burnett. He was apprehended and tried for cattle thievery, but in a change of venue, was acquitted in Benjamin, Texas," continues Fairley. The two men finally met in a hotel washroom in Paducah, Texas. When confronted, Burnett drew his gun first and killed Sears, while his companions fled the scene. Burnett was acquitted on the grounds of self-defense.

Burnett was on friendly terms with the legendary Comanche Chief Quanah Parker (1845-1911), a rarity in those days, when Native Americans seldom trusted a white man. After he was exiled to Kiowa-Comanche reservation in southwestern Oklahoma, the chief signed lucrative agreements with the ranchers allowing them to lease reservation land for cattle grazing. Quanah adopted many of the white man's customs, assembled a fortune in cattle and land, and hunted with Pres. Theodore Roosevelt.

Across Seventh Street, you can see Isamu Noguchi's three-piece *Texas Sculpture* in front of the NationsBank Texas Building, which was constructed in 1962 for the First National bank of Fort Worth, at 500 West Seventh, and is now part of the Bank of America. There is a restaurant located inside the bank building.

Burnett Plaza, 801 Cherry St. at West Seventh; (817) 828-7000. Located downtown, across the street from the U.S. Courthouse and overlooking Burnett Park (see individual entries).

With 1.08 million leasable square feet of space, this 558-foot-tall, 40-story tower is the single largest office tower in Fort Worth. Designed by Sikes, Jennings, and Kelly, the building was originally constructed in 1983 as headquarters for InterFirst Bank, or what was until 1998 known as NationsBank and then absorbed into the Bank of America. There are Binyar Hunt's sculptures on display in the lobby. One notable tenant at Burnett Plaza is the U.S. Securities and Exchange Commission.

Samuel Burk Burnett (1849-1922), a trail driver at age 15, was one of the founders of the Texas and Southwestern Cattle Raisers Association, and the first president of the Southwestern Exposition and Livestock Show (see listing). "At the outbreak of World War I, Burnett's wealth was estimated at $7.5 million—at a time when there was no income tax," notes Fort Worth historian Bill Fairley. He later became the largest stockholder in the First National Bank of Fort Worth, now also part of the Bank of America.

Burnett died at age 73. His great-granddaughter still lives in Fort Worth, overseeing the philanthropic activities of the Burnett Foundation.

The Chisholm Trail Roundup, Stockyards National Historic District; (817) 625-7005, Internet www.chisholmtrail.org. Held one weekend in mid-June. Admission for those over age of 12.

This trail roundup once led along what is now U.S. Highway 81, from Brownsville, through Lockhart and Waco to Fort Worth, with cowboys who drove more than six million longhorns up the trail into Kansas.

A trail drive usually numbered from two to three thousand head of cattle driven by at least a dozen cowhands, often not yet 20 years old. They brought along many horses for the dangerous journey that took as long as three months to complete. Most earned about $30 a month and all the beans they could eat. The cook, incidentally, was an important man on the trail drive because good food went a long way to keep the cowboys satisfied.

The demand for red meat in the victorious north after the Civil War provided ready market for Texas ranchers. "Christopher Columbus Slaughter, who in the 1880's had been declared the state's largest single taxpayer, owned three West Texas ranches containing approximately a million acres," writes Dallas historian Darwin Payne in his book *Big D*. He continues, "Along with his father, a friend of Sam Houston's, he had been one of the first Texans to drive herds of cattle north to Kansas along the Chisholm Trail."

Although most drives originated in south Texas, they split into the Western and Eastern cattle trails even before reaching San Antonio. The Eastern divided into Chisholm and Shawnee trails. However, after settlers encroached on the path used by the cattlemen, the Western trail shifted to the west, either as the Potter-Bacon trail, or Goodnight-Loving, which led to New Mexico, Colorado, and Wyoming.

This trail gets its name after Jesse Chisholm (1805-1868), a half-Scottish, half-Cherokee trader born in Tennessee, who married a Creek woman. From 1832 until his death, he operated trading posts in the Indian Nations, driving his wagon and goods from Oklahoma to Kansas. Chisholm, who died from cholera, also was employed as a guide.

The cattle drovers, who later extended the route to the Mexican border, followed his wagon. The drives took place as early as 1846, but particularly between 1865 and 1876, when the first railroad reached Fort Worth and soon began moving millions of head of cattle. An animal worth $5 in Texas could fetch $50 in Chicago. Gambling halls, saloons, and houses of ill repute that popped up all over the newly-founded Cowtown eased the drovers' hard life a bit. "Fort Worth," says historian Leonard Sanders in *How Fort Worth Became the Texasmost City*, "was the last chance for drovers to buy flour, bacon, beans, dried fruit, coffee, and other necessities for the long drive across the Nations." It was an outpost of civilization before the drovers entered the dangerous Indian Territory of Oklahoma. In Cowtown, cowhands had some fun before it was time to push on.

Sanders says that more than 150,000 cattle passed through Fort Worth in 1880. "By the end of the 1884 season, the Chisholm Trail was virtually closed." Ranchers began turning to rail shipments.

In this Fort Worth's roundup reenactment, which started in 1977, the trail riders usually start out at YMCA Camp Carter, near Lake Worth, and continue on to the Stockyards (see entry), at about 1 pm. Afterwards, they follow the Trinity River horse trails, crossing bridges and water, and conclude their journey in the Stockyards. Rest and water stops are scheduled every couple of hours. By 6 pm, a barbecue dinner is served on the veranda of the Livestock Exchange Building (see entry).

In the reenactment, more than 1,000 modern cowboys in wagons or on horses make their way to the Stockyards to celebrate the Chisholm Trail spirit. To relieve their boredom, they participate in three days of events, which include live gunfights and a Quanah Parker Comanche Indian Pow-Wow and Honor Dance—named after the fierce Comanche chief whose mother was a kidnapped daughter of a white Texas settler. There are also Cowtown Chili and Trailblazer Barbecue Cook-Offs, live armadillo and pig races, a street fair, carnival rides, a parade, and a fiddler's contest, all held at the Stockyards.

The Churches of
Downtown Fort Worth

These are among the most notable of the Fort Worth churches. Most may be seen inside, but make arrangements before you go, (800) 433-5747 or (817) 336-8791.

Allen Chapel African Methodist Episcopal Church, 116 Elm St. at East First St.; (817) 332-5071. Located six blocks from the Tarrant County Courthouse (see entry) on the northeastern edge of the central business district. This buff-yellow brick Gothic Revival structure, which contains a number of fine stained-glass windows, houses one of Fort Worth's oldest African-American congregations. The church was founded in 1870 and the building, the church's fifth one, was constructed in 1912-14. Architect William Sidney Pittman (1875-1958), the son-in-law of Booker T. Washington, who also drafted the Twelfth Street YMCA in Washington, D.C., designed it. The interior includes a well-preserved Estey pipe organ and pressed metal ceilings.

First Christian Church, 612 Throckmorton and West Sixth streets; (817) 336-7185. Located in the central business district. Founded in 1855, two years after the U.S. Army abandoned Fort Worth, this is believed to be the oldest congregation in Cowtown. The current building was designed by E. W. Van Slyke and Clyde Woodruff and erected in 1914-15 in the Renaissance Revival style with a Greek cross plan, a tower, and copper-clad dome. Among the church members who provided financial support were cattleman Samuel Burk Burnett and banker, Maj. K. M. van Zandt. Two pedimented porticos, each with six Corinthian columns, are located on the front and south side of the building. Burnett also donated the organ. The Tarrant County Gen. R. M. Gano, rancher, physician, minister, and noted Confederate soldier, who was the great-grandfather of billionaire Howard Hughes—the recluse who died in 1976—preached regularly here. His great-grandfather, Rev. John Gano, established the first Baptist church in New York City.

First United Methodist Church, 800 West Fifth St., between Henderson and Macon; (817) 336-7277. Located on the western edge of Fort Worth's central business district, this is the city's largest church, with more than 10,000 members. Designed by local architect, Wiley G. Clarkson, in the Gothic Revival style, the ground for this church was broken in 1929 and it was completed two years later, when the congregation symbolically closed the doors of the old church at Seventh and Taylor streets and walked to the new structure. With its twin Gothic towers, the building seems to draw its inspiration from Notre Dame in Paris. In 1965, a Reuter organ with 6,610 pipes was installed in the main sanctuary. Guided tours are available the first Sunday of the month. Clarkson also designed the nearby Cook Children's Hospital.

First United Methodist Church, located at 800 West Fifth Street, on the western edge of downtown, was completed in 1931. Designed by local architect Wiley Clarkson in the Gothic Revival style, the twin-tower structure perhaps drew its inspiration from Notre Dame in Paris. (Photo by Yves Gerem)

Methodist Episcopal Church Vestry is located at East Fourth and Jones streets. The vestry portion of the Fourth Street Methodist Episcopal Church is the forerunner of today's First United Methodist Church, which was utilized from 1887 to 1908. As time passed, portions of the 1887 church were demolished, but some walls remained encased in an attached warehouse.

Missouri Avenue Methodist Church/St. Andrew's United Methodist Church, 522 Missouri Ave.; (817) 336-2117. The Missouri Avenue Methodist, founded about 1889, was originally located on the southeast corner of Missouri and Annie Street. In 1904, Dallas architect James Flanders designed the current building. The yellow-brick church has a sandstone base and a steeply pitched roof. In 1950, the congregation sold the church to St. Andrew's Methodist Church, an African-American congregation. St. Andrew's remodeled the building and held the first services the following year.

Mount Gilead Baptist Church, 600 Grove and Fifth streets; (817) 336-2695. Located on the east side of the central business district in an African-American neighborhood. The church was founded in 1875 and is Fort Worth's oldest African-American congregation. Designed by architects Sanguinet and Staats of Fort Worth and Dallas—or possibly the African-American architect Wallace Rayfield of Alabama—it was constructed in 1912-13 in the Neoclassical temple-form style with Tuscan columns. When it opened, the church had a daycare nursery, swimming pool, gymnasium, library, and roof garden. During its early years, it also ran a business school and operated a hospital nearby.

St. Andrew's Episcopal Church, 901 Lamar and West Tenth streets; (817) 332-3191. Located across the street from the U.S. Court House (see entry). Like Mount Gilead Baptist, above, it was designed by Sanguinet and Staats in the Gothic Revival style and erected in 1909-12 for the congregation that traces its beginnings to 1873. Built of gray dolomite, a hard limestone from Carthage, Missouri, this church is reminiscent of an English medieval parish church. The modified cruciform plan structure has a nave with single-side aisles and a single transept crossing. The rose window over the altar was crafted in England; other stained-glass windows were made in St. Louis. The pulpit is from the 1877 wooden church building that stood on the corner of East Fifth and Commerce (formerly Rusk) streets.

St. Demetrios Greek Orthodox Church, 2022 Ross Ave, is located far north of downtown, actually rather close to the Stockyards (see entry). It is believed to have represented the first Greek Orthodox parish in Texas. There were some 2,000 Greeks living in Fort Worth by 1916, predominantly immigrants. Many were Armour and Swift packing house workers living mostly in north Fort Worth, an area now known as the North Side. In 1910 a group of them met to organize this church, which was designed by local architect Ludwig B. Weinman.

St. Mary of the Assumption Catholic Church, 509 West Magnolia Ave.; (817) 923-1911. Established in 1909 as the city's fourth Catholic parish, St. Mary's was first housed in a wooden building that was destroyed in 1922. Two years later, architects Sanguinet, Staats, and Hedrick designed this Romanesque Revival red-brick building that could accommodate 500 worshipers. The bells, which were originally intended for a church in Muenster, Texas, were installed in 1956. The stained-glass windows are from a Bavarian craftsman. St. Mary serves mostly Hispanic worshipers today. It was listed in the National Register of Historic Places in 1984.

St. Patrick Cathedral, 1206 Throckmorton and West Eleventh streets; (817) 332-4915. Located across Jennings Avenue from the Fort Worth City Hall and a block from the Fort Worth Convention Center (see individual entries).

Designed by local architect James J. Kane (1822-1901), this Gothic Revival structure was erected in 1888-92. The oldest continuously used church building in Fort Worth, it replaced the wood-frame St. Stanislaus Catholic Church nearby. Kane had also designed Fort Worth's City Hall, which has since been demolished. The cathedral has a gabled nave flanked by buttressed aisles. The original hand-painted stained-glass windows came from Munich in 1892. A bell cast in Troy, New York, has been used since 1889. Twin towers, designed as a base for spires, were never completed, although in 1997 plans were to construct 105-foot-high spires on top of the current structure. St. Patrick became the cathedral of the Fort Worth diocese in 1969. It has been listed in the National Register of Historic Places since 1908.

Chase Texas Tower/City Center I, 201 Main and Second streets; (817) 390-8700. Located downtown between Fire Station No. 1 and the Renaissance Worthington Hotel (see individual entries), where once stood the high-end Stripling's department store.

Designed by architect Paul Rudolph of New York City and built by Bass Brothers Enterprises in 1982, this 33-story 720,000-square-foot tower, formerly known as City Center I and later Texas Commerce Tower, houses several of the Basses' offices. It has a three-story granite lobby.

"The huge gray towers near the courthouse, One City Center, have strange bulges at the tops that have been described as 'turrets' but which my companion said looked more like 'warts,'" wrote author Laura Trim.

City Center II Tower, 301 Commerce at Third St.; (817) 390-8700. Located downtown across East Third Street from Barnes & Noble

Booksellers and 8.0 restaurant and diagonally from City Center I, now known as Chase Texas Tower (see individual entries).

Like Chase Texas Tower, above, designed by architect Paul Rudolph, the 38-story office building has 820,000 square feet of office space. Owned, like so much of the city real estate, by the billionaire Bass clan, the Medicis of Fort Worth, it opened in 1984. Sid Richardson Bass (b. 1942), the oldest of the four Bass brothers, was the man most instrumental in opening City Center I and II after his father installed him as leader of Bass Brothers Enterprises. In 1998, Sid Bass had a net worth of $2.9 billion, according to *Forbes* magazine, this even after divorcing his wife of 23 years, Anne Hendricks Bass, in 1989. The "Indianapolis-born socialite now poster dame for First Wives Club," says *Forbes* "got 1.38 million Disney shares, real estate, art" worth more than $500 million. "The Vassar graduate divides time between boards of 12 ballet troupes, libraries, art museums because 'sharing beauty is a responsibility.'"

City Club, (817) 878-4000, Internet www.cityclub-ftw.com, "one of Fort Worth's most elegant membership clubs," is located here and includes a fitness center with sauna, steam room, and Jacuzzi. Racquetball courts are also on the premises.

Continental Plaza/Union Pacific Plaza, 777 Main at East Seventh St.; (817) 870-6501. Located downtown one block north of Radisson Plaza Hotel and another block from the Fort Worth Convention Center (see individual entries).

Having 955,000 leasable square feet of space, this 40-story tower is the third largest office tower in Fort Worth. It was designed by Jarvis, Putty, Jarvis, a Dallas architectural firm; the Jarvis Brothers were from a prominent early Fort Worth family. The 40-story, 525-foot-tall glass and steel structure is connected by skywalks to the Radisson Plaza Hotel (see entry). The Fort Worth **Petroleum Club,** (817) 335-7571, is also housed in the tower.

Continental Plaza—now also known as Union Pacific Plaza, after the oil and gas exploration and production company that occupies its top twenty floors—was built in 1981. On this site formerly stood the 1930 Art Deco Aviation Building, which was the original headquarters of American Airlines' predecessor company. Palace Theater also had to go to make space for this building.

Cook Children's/HealthSouth Rehabilitation Hospital, 1212 West Lancaster Ave.; (817) 870-2336. Located just west of downtown.

W. I. Cook was a cattle rancher near Albany in Shackeldorf County, west of Fort Worth. When oil was discovered on the ranch three years after her husband's death, Mrs. Cook honored him and their daughter, who had died in childbirth, by erecting a hospital for children and working women and named it W. I. Cook Memorial Hospital. The private 30-bed hospital was designed by Wiley G. Clarkson and stood on her land and was paid for by her oil royalties. The three-story Renaissance Revival-styled facility constructed of Indiana limestone opened in 1929.

In 1952, the general hospital was converted into a children's hospital and was renamed W. I. Cook Children's Hospital. It was expanded in 1958 by a two-story addition on top of the front wing and increased its capacity to 100 beds. In 1985, it merged with Fort Worth Children's Medical Center in the hospital district. Cook sold this building to HealthSouth Rehabilitation Corp. in 1989.

Cow Bell Indoor Rodeo, 1263 North Main St., Mansfield; (817) 477-3092. CH, free parking, no credit cards. Open year-round. Rodeo held Sat-Sun, starting at 8 pm. Bull riding takes place year-round every Monday and Friday at 8 pm.

Mansfield, a town of about 22,000, is located midway between Dallas and Fort Worth, south of Arlington and Interstate 20. From either direction take the Mansfield exit, 157, and continue for eight miles. This authentic (some would say broken down) arena has been home to rodeo for 42 years, and it shows its age for all to see. Up to 50 bull riders could be seen on an average night.

The Filling Station Barbecue, for a real Texas meal, is just across the street.

In 1998, plans were afoot for the Fort Worth's Trinity Valley Railroad Club to transfer its railroad museum to Mansfield permanently. The club holds hundreds of artifacts, ranging from lanterns to a 1912 steam locomotive and full-size freight cars, and wants to display them next to an active railroad. When realized, it would be the second largest such museum in Texas, surpassed only by the railroad collection in Galveston. Until 1984, some of the club's artifacts were displayed in a small museum in Weatherford, Texas, and have since then been held in storage.

Cowtown Coliseum, 121 East Exchange Ave. at Rodeo Pl.; (888) COW-TOWN or (817) 625-1025. Rodeo Fri-Sat at 8 pm. Located in the historic Stockyards, next to the Livestock Exchange Building (see individual entries) and across the street from the Visitors Information Center.

The mission-style, 2,447-seat Coliseum was constructed in 88 working days in 1908 at a cost of $250,000. Hailed as the largest show arena at the time, it was home of the world's first indoor rodeo in 1918, and hosted shows as varied as Enrico Caruso performing for 8,000 in 1920 and Elvis Presley who played with his band in 1956 for a mere $500. Pres. Theodore Roosevelt addressed 5,000 here in 1911, Sergey Diaghilev's Ballet Russe performed in 1916.

The city purchased the 12,000-seat brick arena, which was designed by Chicago architect Berkley Brandt, in 1936. The Coliseum hosted the Southwestern Exposition and Livestock Show until 1942, when it was moved to Will Rogers Memorial Center (see individual entries). In 1986, the arena underwent a $3-million restoration. There are professional rodeo events, such bull riding, steer wrestling, calf roping, and barrel racing. Pawnee Bill's Wild West Shows of the early 1900s—including trick roping, bull whip acts, trick shooting, and cowboy music—are recreated on some weekends. While here, cross East Exchange Avenue and have a look at **Saunders Park** and **Marine Creek** behind the avenue, two of the lesser known sights in the Stockyards.

Thomas Bailey Saunders (1816-1902) migrated to Texas in 1850. He started a cattle ranch near Gonzales and had 12 children. The park is named after his family. Marine Creek, so named because marine fossils were found here, was the site of a bloody battle between early settlers and Comanche Indians in the summer of 1871.

Cullen Davis Mansion, 4200 Stonegate Blvd. at South Hulen St. Located in southwest Fort Worth, southwest from the cultural district, south of Interstate 30 West (also known as West Freeway), and west from Texas Christian University (see entry), just behind Calloway's Nursery.

Kenneth Davis (1895-1968) was an oilman who operated several oil-drilling, manufacturing, and supply businesses under the umbrella of Kendavis Industries International. Davis Sr. provided funds for the Noble Planetarium at today's Fort Worth Museum of Science & History (see entry). T. Cullen Davis is one of his three sons.

This gaudy, desolate-looking, sprawling white former $6.6-million, 19,000-square-foot, 20-room mansion, sitting on three acres of land, was once home of the one-time Fort Worth multimillionaire Cullen Davis and his wife Priscilla. It remained vacant and was vandalized before a Fort Worth businessman reopened it as the Stonegate Mansion in 1996.

After one unprofitable year, it became the Stonegate Steakhouse, but its owner told the *Fort Worth Star-Telegram*, "I have never lost as much money in my life in any other restaurant venture." The following two years, until the fall of 1998, it served steaks, along with such Tex-Mex fare as beef fajitas, under the name of Mercado Juarez, a restaurant chain that still has several other Metroplex locations.

Some blamed the closures on a curse, but when the *Dallas Morning News* reviewer sampled its wares, he noted that the food and service didn't fit in with the atmosphere. "The seafood was rubbery and the cocktail overloaded with peppers. A 14-ounce ribeye was tough and overly fatty."

"Cullen and Priscilla Davis had been locked in a nasty divorce battle," reported the *Fort Worth Star-Telegram*. "A judge had awarded Priscilla temporary ownership of the mansion and granted a restraining order barring Cullen from the property." The mansion became the scene of a much-talked-about crime on August 2, 1976, the day that the judge approved Priscilla's request for a postponement in the divorce trial. That evening, when Priscilla and her live-in lover returned to the mansion, they were met by a "man in black" wearing a woman's wig and carrying a revolver. He wounded Davis's estranged wife, and killed her lover and a 12-year-old daughter from a previous marriage. Survivors identified Davis, then one of the richest men in America, as the gunman, but he was acquitted twice in high profile trials. The police investigator assigned to the case, now an assistant district attorney in Tarrant County, told the *Fort Worth Star-Telegram* in 1999: "There is absolutely no doubt in my mind that Cullen Davis is responsible for those murders."

By 1987, Davis's "company owed $500 million, and he personally owed $300 million to banks," according to *Fort Worth, Texas*, magazine. He is now a distributor of a skin cream product, working out of his home in the wealthy town of Colleyville. "Cullen Davis now lives quietly with his wife, Karen, surrounded by a close circle of friends and neighbors who almost never talk with them about the past, and who consider the couple exemplary Christians and model citizens," notes the magazine.

Believe it or not, Davis was the restaurant's regular customer, along with his third wife. The glass hilltop residence with a large indoor swimming pool was refurbished at a cost of $2.2 million and opened as a restaurant 20 years after the crime. The cellar where Priscilla's daughter was murdered was used as a dining room for private parties. The restaurant seated 300 and afforded a view of downtown Fort Worth.

The **Electric Building,** 410 West Seventh at Taylor streets. Located next to the Fort Worth Star-Telegram building and across Seventh from the Neil P. Anderson Building (see individual entries).

Designed by Wyatt C. Hedrick, this was one of several buildings erected for financier Jesse Jones, Franklin Delano Roosevelt's Secretary of Agriculture. The building was constructed in 1930 as headquarters for the Fort Worth Light & Power Co. The structure housed the Hollywood Three, one of the three downtown first-run cinemas. The Worth and Palace, both on Seventh Street, have been torn down, but the Hollywood remains largely intact if hidden behind a 1979 first-floor office renovation.

In 1984, the building was purchased by Robert Muse Bass (b. 1948), the third of the four Bass billionaire brothers, and ten years later converted it into 106 apartments. For more, see Apartments in the LODGING chapter. The Stanford-educated Robert Bass—having a net worth of $2.5 billion in 1998—and his wife led the fight against expansion of Interstate 30 overhead downtown.

FAIR PARK, 3809 Grand Ave., in Dallas. Bounded by Parry Ave., Robert B. Cullum Blvd., South Fitzhugh Ave., and Union Pacific railroad tracks, Fair Park is a 277-acre cultural and entertainment complex owned by the city of Dallas in a mostly black neighborhood two miles east of downtown.

Some 150 events take place in the park annually, but the biggest is the State Fair of Texas (see below), now the largest state fair in the U.S. More than 3.5 million attend it annually.

The complex includes the African-American Museum of Life & Culture, Age of Steam Railroad Museum, Dallas Aquarium, Dallas Horticulture Center, Dallas Museum of Natural History, Dallas Music Hall, The Science Place, Texas Hall of State, Women's Museum, and Texas Vietnam Veterans Memorial. Some charge admission, others do not. For more details, please see *A Marmac Guide to Dallas*.

The Dallas Opera and the city-owned 24-hour all-classical radio station WRR-FM, on 101.1 FM band, are also headquartered here. The Coca-Cola Starplex Amphitheater is an outdoor performing arts theater with celebrity entertainment and the capacity to hold 20,100.

The Cotton Bowl stadium is the 28,000-square-foot arena with Coliseum, where rodeos take place. Built in 1930, the Cotton Bowl is Dallas's largest outdoor stadium with a capacity for 100,000 spectators. Until 1971, when Texas Stadium opened in the suburb of Irving, Dallas Cowboys played their home games here.

Fair Park's 1936 Centennial Exposition—In 1936, when Dallas's population was 265,000, Fair Park was the sight of a lavish event that's never been repeated. The 185-acre grounds were transformed into a $25-million World's Fair that was visited by 6.3 million. Dallas, Houston, San Antonio, and Fort Worth all wanted to host the exposition, but only Dallas's leaders agreed to host it without any state or federal aid.

The chief architect of the fair complex, Harvard-educated George Dahl was hired at $1,500 a month; this was at a time when a good secretary earned $125. By May 1936, ten thousand men in three shifts completed the impossible task of opening the exposition by the next month. Seventy-seven buildings were completely remodeled or constructed just for the fair.

After ten months of breakneck construction and $5.5 million in local funding, the gates opened on June 6. The first day 117,600 visitors passed through. Ginger Rogers and Lucille Ball, Clark Gable and Robert Taylor were just some of the Hollywood personalities who came. Fairgoers were entertained by Duke Ellington's, Cab Calloway's, and Tommy Dorsey's orchestras.

Meanwhile, Fort Worth's civic booster Amon Carter felt that Cowtown must not be outdone and convinced his colleagues that an

unofficial **Fort Worth Frontier Centennial Exposition,** also to cele-
brate the state's freedom from Mexico, was just what Texas needed.
This, after all, was Amon, who "learned to yell 'Yippee' and
'Whooppee' without a shred of shame," says journalist Jerry Flemmons.
"He could bellow ridiculously, 'Hoooooo-e-e-e! Round 'em up! Head
off that lit'l dogie yonder!"

Carter hired New York showman Billy Rose, at $100,000 for one hun-
dred days, to put on the greatest extravaganza Fort Worth has ever seen
"and teach those dudes over there [in Dallas] where the West really
begins."

Rose engaged Sally Rand, a Quaker farm girl from Missouri and a
nude dancer, who stirred a predictable local response, just the controversy he hoped would sell lots of tickets. It focused around the newly-
built Casa Manana (see entry), the world's largest open-air theater that
could seat more than 3,800.

In mid-April, while "two thousand men toiled at the centennial site,
rushing to meet an impossible June opening date," Rose kept inspect-
ing acts as varied as a promoter with a frog circus and a snake with two
heads, each of which could be fed separately.

During that summer and autumn, at least four thousand people
packed Casa Manana each night. "The crowd often was mixed with
tuxedos and overalls, ball gowns and print dresses, but nobody cared,"
writes author Jerry Flemmons. "They came, ate the $1.75 dinner, and
sighed as Everett Marshall sang, 'The Night Is Young and You're So
Beautiful.'" But nothing compared with the finale, when the stage—
136 feet in diameter and three times the size of that at Radio City
Music Hall in New York City—rolled back, and the entire cast assembled, while 85 fountains exploded with colored water.

November 6 was designated as Sally Rand Day, and Fort Worth publicly thanked her for bringing "culture and progress to Tarrant County"
with her Nude Ranch, where replicas of bare-breasted classic statues
were on exhibit out front at 25 cents per person. Inside, eight girls
lounged on swings and beach chairs, some played with a beach ball,
others shot bows and arrows. For another two bits an educational view
of a young woman bathing in milk could be had 25 times daily. To really irritate those dudes over in Dallas, a green and red 130-foot-long and
60-foot-high neon sign was erected opposite the main entrance of
Dallas's exposition proclaiming: Forty-Five Minutes West to Whoopee.

The FBI's J. Edgar Hoover and Ernest Hemingway were among the
celebrities visiting. But trying what they might, the Fort Worth
Frontier Fair was a financial flop and only 986,000 showed up, even
though "illegal liquor openly was poured everywhere." The two-headed
snake died from the heat.

State Fair of Texas, General Information (214) 565-9931, Internet www.texfair.com. Held annually September 27-October 20. CH, but some museums are free. Fair grounds are open daily 10 am-10 pm. Paid parking for 8,000 vehicles.

Fair Park has been the site of the state fair since 1886. By 1905, when the famed French actress Sarah Bernhardt performed here in a tent for 4,000 spectators, 300,000 fair visitors passed through the gates. In 1956, Elvis Presley gave a concert here.

To enjoy the fair at its merriest, bring your children. The fair is rides or trying your luck at a game of skill. It is parades and contests. It is shows of every kind or walking around and indulging yourself in many varieties of foods. It is the place to watch, listen, shop, browse, eat, and relax—and spend money.

In a long Texas tradition, thousands of steers, cows, horses, hogs, sheep, goats, rabbits, even broiler hens, are judged in the livestock arenas during the fair for first-place prizes as high as $65,000.

The Old Mill Inn, near Big Tex, serves lunch and dinner during the fair. Big who? Big Tex. Texas' contribution to American folklore is a cowboy larger than life and this fair is the place where you will find Big Tex, the gigantic monument to the Western way of life. Fifty-two feet tall, he booms out, "Howdy, folks, this is Big Tex."

While at the fair, also try the *tornado taters* (long ribbons of entire potatoes deep-fat fried), *Fletcher's corny dog* (stick-mounted wiener hand-dipped in cornmeal batter and deep-fried), *turkey legs* (pre-smoked and baked while you wait), spicy *sausages on sticks*, and *funnel cakes* (sweet pancake batter with cinnamon and nutmeg, fried and sprinkled with powdered sugar).

For more details about the fair, please see *A Marmac Guide to Dallas*.

Flatiron Building, 1000 Houston St. Located on a triangle-shaped lot at the intersection with Ninth St. and Jennings Ave. downtown, a block from Radisson Plaza Hotel and across the street from the Fort Worth Convention Center (see individual entries).

This is believed to be the earliest high-rise still remaining in Fort Worth and the only true flatiron building in Texas. Built as a seven-story steel-framed structure in 1907 to emulate similar flatiron buildings in Chicago and New York, it was then said to be the tallest in the southwest. Only the Tarrant County Courthouse and Thistle Hill mansion (see entries) are said to be equally recognizable historic buildings in Fort Worth.

Its owner, Fort Worth surgeon Dr. Bacon Saunders (1855-1925), also dean of the Fort Worth Medical College, decided on the triangular shape of the building after seeing the 1902 Flatiron Building in New York. The local architectural firm of Sanguinet and Staats originally designed a ten-story structure, but it was scaled down for economic reasons. Dr. Saunders' offices and laboratory were on the top, while other physicians occupied the lower floors. A band around the building, above the second floor, displays carved heads of lions or panthers.

"Before the railroad arrived in 1876," writes historian Carol Roark, "a Dallas newspaper charged that Fort Worth was such a sleepy little town that a panther could sleep undisturbed in its streets. Local residents saw the reference to the panther as a compliment—perhaps because they liked the cat's spirit and temperament—and Fort Worth adopted the nickname of 'Panther City.'"

Fort Worth Botanic Garden, 3220 Botanic Garden Blvd. and University Dr.; (817) 871-7689, Tours 871-7682, Internet http://fort-worth.org/local/botanic.htm. CH for the Conservatory and Japanese Garden. Open daily 8 am-11 pm. Wheelchair accessibility is limited. Located in Trinity Park, just southeast of the cultural district and north of the Fort Worth Zoo (see entry), north of Interstate 30, also known as West Freeway.

In 1907 the city hired noted city planner George Kessler to develop the site of the current Botanic Garden, which was purchased in 1912. That year, Rock Springs Park was established on a 37-acre tract just west of the Trinity River. It is believed that the area served as a camp site for Indians before the first military fort was established. Fort Worth banker and civic leader K. M. van Zandt operated a mill here in 1868, three years after his family settled in the city. In 1925 voters approved a bond issue to improve public parks and develop Rock Springs as a municipal rose garden, but very little came of it because of the approaching Great Depression.

Finally, in 1933, the Garden became the first federal relief project in Tarrant County. More than 750 out-of-work stonemasons were hired at $2 a day and completed it in 15 months. The cactus garden was laid out in 1935. With the construction of the freeway just to the south of the garden during the 1950s, the natural springs dried up and water for the park is now pumped from the Trinity River, "a dowdy, vermicular stream that either flooded or puddled and that, until 1913, served as a convenient garbage and sewage dump."

What is today a 114-acre garden is the oldest such institution in Texas. Fulfilling the dream of an "outdoor library of plants," it contains more than 2,500 native and exotic species of plants and 150 varieties of trees. More than 600,000 visit its 21 specialty gardens annually.

The 10,000-square-foot botanical **Conservatory** within it brims with plants, birds, and trees from around the world. The rose gardens are of European design and will delight you with more than 3,400 roses reaching their peak of bloom in late April and October.

The 7.5-acre **Japanese Garden,** constructed in 1970, complete with a pagoda, teahouse extending over the pool filled with koi (or imperial carp) that annually eat 5,000 pounds of Purina catfish chow, waterfalls,

Entrance to the Fort Worth Botanic Garden, which is located southeast of the cultural district. The 114-acre garden, the first federal relief project in Tarrant County in 1933, is the oldest such institution in Texas. It contains more than 2,500 native and exotic species of plants and 150 varieties of trees. (Photo by Yves Gerem)

and a meditation garden styled after one in the city of Kyoto. The Japanese Garden, whose three gates are symbolic of heaven, man, and earth, was originally the site of an old gravel pit.

The Japanese Garden, (817) 871-7685, is open daily 9 am-7 pm from April through October, and the Conservatory daily from dawn to dusk. Both have an abbreviated schedule November through March and charge an admission fee to those over the age of four.

The Gardens restaurant is open Mon-Fri 10 am-3 pm, and Sat-Sun noon-4 pm. The gift shop, which recalls the waterside structures characteristic of medieval Japan, is open daily 10 am-4 pm.

Fort Worth City Hall, 1000 Throckmorton at Tenth St.; (817) 871-8900. Located across Jennings St. from the St. Patrick Cathedral and John Peter Smith Monument (see individual entries).

It was built in 1971 on the design by Edward Durrell Stone, "a master of simple, elegant designs" who had also drafted the American Building at the World's Fair in Brussels in 1958 and the American Embassy in New Delhi, India. The three-story municipal building was constructed to house the expanded operations of the city government, which had been located across the street from this building since 1893.

The **Old City Hall & Public Safety and Courts Building** was designed by Wyatt Hedrick and constructed with the help of a 45-percent share of the $500 thousand construction cost from the Public Works Administration grant. The four-story polished Minnesota black-granite-faced structure built of reinforced concrete served as city hall from 1938 to 1970. Jail operations were located in the basement until 1985, when a new city and county jail was built near the Tarrant County Courthouse (see entry). The building lies on the site of the 1893 Victorian city hall and the old Main Street fire station.

City Store, on the ground floor at the south end of the City Hall, sells everything from T-shirts to fire hydrants. It is open Mon-Fri 9:30 am-5:30 pm.

Fort Worth Club Building, 306 West Seventh and Throckmorton streets. Located across the street from the First Christian Church, "the spiritual home of the Texas Christian University," and near the Texas Building, a 30-story office tower that by the year 2000 is to sport 159 luxury apartments with swimming pool and tennis court.

Designed by Sanguinet, Staats & Hedrick and constructed in the Spanish Renaissance style in 1925, this 13-story building has played a large role in the history of Fort Worth as the gathering place of the business community. Still today, you will find the movers and shakers enjoying its benefits. The Club was organized in 1885 as the Commercial Club and was renamed as the Fort Worth Club in 1906. It has served as the city's social and political base since its inception.

Amon Carter, the ego of Cowtown, practically lived at the club, "where, amid the sodality of men, he drank and played poker, often forty-eight hours without a pause," writes Carter's biographer Jerry Flemmons. And so did many of his chums, such as the wildcatter Sid Richardson. Carter's pal, Will Rogers, also stayed in the publisher's suite when in town; the two "would sit all night in Suite 10G, Amon drinking his scotch." After the club was remodeled, Suite 10G "was designed away," says Flemmons.

Fort Worth Convention Center, 1111 Houston St.; (817) 884-2222, Fax 884-2323. Encompassing what was once a 14-city-block area—eight under one roof—the Convention Center is located inside Houston and Commerce, Ninth and Thirteenth streets, in the southwestern part of downtown. Fort Worth Water Gardens, St. Patrick Cathedral, Flatiron Building and General Worth Square are across the street (see individual entries).

The largest meeting facility in Tarrant County is located on the site of Hell's Half Acre, a large concentration of bars, dance halls, and bawdy houses that flourished from the trail-driving era and into the first decade of the twentieth century. Many of the old buildings here were similar in style to those in Sundance Square. The train and stagecoach robber Sam Bass used it as a refuge from the law, as did the Hole in the Wall Gang of Butch Cassidy and the Sundance Kid in the late 1890s. They often stayed at Fannie Porter's bawdy house, which also stood here and where Sundance became infatuated with Etta Place, his girlfriend.

After 1911, these were also the stomping grounds for a fiery Baptist preacher, J. Frank Norris, the son of an alcoholic who campaigned tirelessly to close down some 80 bordellos in the red-light district, as well as stop alcohol and drug use. He read the names of the bordello landlords from his pulpit at the First Baptist Church and endured dozens of threats to his life. In 1912, the preacher, his wife, and their three children escaped from their burning home by leaping from a second-floor window, nothing new for the man who was shot at by horse thieves at age 15. By then his congregations were so huge, Norris had to buy an old circus tent that had once been used by the French actress Sarah Bernhardt (1844-1923) and erected it on Tenth Street, between Throckmorton and Houston streets.

In the mid-1920s, the minister accused the Fort Worth mayor Henry C. Meacham of being a man of low moral character. A mayor's close friend entered Norris's church to complain and was shot four times and killed. A trial was held in Austin and the preacher was found innocent. He was befriended by Pres. Franklin Roosevelt and met Winston Churchill more than once. It is said that during an audience, Pope Pius XII blessed Norris, "after which the Baptist blessed the pope." Born in

Alabama, he arrived in Fort Worth in 1909 and died of a heart attack in Florida in 1952 at the age of 74.

The 200,281-square-foot Convention Center opened in 1968 and was bought by the city in 1997. It consists of a 14,000-seat arena, a 3,054-seat theater, 25 meeting rooms, and banquet space for 10,000. State, regional, and national meetings and trade shows are held here, as well as Democratic and Republican conventions, car, truck, and boat shows, circuses, even the Miss Texas Pageant. The *Fort Worth Star-Telegram* in 1998 quoted professionals as labeling the "doddering" 30-year-old center "tired, worn-out, undersized," an "albatross" and a "clunker." A major renovation was planned for the aged facility starting with the demolition of the JFK theatre in 2000 and completion the following year. More than 200,000 square feet of exhibit space will be added at a cost of $60 million.

Where the convention center is located now there also stood until 1959 the Metropolitan Hotel, one of the finest lodgings in Fort Worth. Built in 1898 and renovated in 1905, the three-story, red-brick Metropolitan ruled proudly on the corner of Main and Ninth streets. Owned for a while by the millionaire cattleman Winfield Scott, the hotel also had one of the best restaurants in the city and it was located just a few blocks from the train depot.

The Metropolitan gained nationwide notoriety for two gruesome killings that both occurred in its lobby. Beautiful women were the cause of both. In the first, in 1913, the wealthy 70-year-old cattle rancher Capt. A. G. Boyce was shot point blank over his son's entanglement in a romance with another man's wife. Almost twenty years later a 46-year-old drilling contractor, E. L. Churchill, dallied with someone else's girlfriend and was also knocked off at the Metropolitan.

Also on the convention center property, then at 1101 Commerce Street, once stood the elegant Majestic theater, whose marble lobby displayed red velvet drapes. Built in 1910, it seated more than 1,500 patrons. When talking pictures began replacing operatic concerts and stage plays, a motion picture screen was installed; the movie *The Westerner*, with Gary Cooper, held its world premiere here, at which the actor appeared on stage after its screening.

A station is under construction nearby for the Trinity Railway Express, a commuter-rail project that will link up with downtown Dallas in 2001. A 55-minute ride from Fort Worth to Dallas will cost about $3 each way. Amtrak Rail Station and the bus depot are also nearby.

Fort Worth's Fire Station No. 1, Commerce and East Second streets; (817) 732-1631. NCH. Open daily 9 am-7 pm. Located downtown at the northeastern edge of the Sundance Square, conjoined with the City Center Tower II, and across from City Center Tower I, which is now known as the Chase Texas Tower (see individual entries).

Fire Station No. 1 was the site of Fort Worth's original city hall, with the mayor's office located on the second floor. The volunteer fire fighters with their hook and ladder wagon occupied the ground floor of the building, which served as a fire station for more than a century. The idea of a volunteer fire department was first proposed by B. B. Paddock, a former mayor, in 1873. Fort Worth's first mayor, Dr. W. P. Burts, donated the land. The present structure, designed by Sanguinet and Staats, replaced the original building in 1907.

The first central fire station, on Main Street, between Eleventh and Twelfth streets, opened in 1883; a 3,000-pound bell was placed in its tower.

Through a permanent exhibit, on display since 1984, you can trace Fort Worth's development from its beginnings as a frontier outpost, through its rowdy youth as a cattle town, and to its maturity today. It is a satellite exhibit of the Fort Worth Museum of Science & History (see entry).

B. B. Paddock (1844-1922) arrived in Fort Worth in 1872. He was instrumental in bringing the railroad to Fort Worth and served as both the city's mayor and state legislator. He is honored by having Paddock Park (see entry) near the Courthouse Square named after him. In 1981, a statue of the business and civic leader Charles David Tandy was placed nearby.

The Fort Worth Trail Herd

Receipts from hotel-bed taxes are financing 20 longhorns that have been driven from the historic Stockyards (see entry) district along the Trinity River to downtown since 1999, when Fort Worth celebrated its 150th anniversary.

In warmer months, typically March through October, cowhands drive part of the herd from the Purebred Barn, north of the Livestock Exchange Building, across Exchange Avenue each day and south along the Trinity River's West Fork toward downtown. Drives are coordinated with the Tarantula Train (see entry) arrivals and departures to maximize tourists' exposure to the herd. Some longhorns remain in the Stockyards at all times for display. In winter, the herd is driven downtown if the weather permits, otherwise it is presented inside the Cowtown Coliseum (see entry). "I don't care what people say, we're still a cow town, and we should have cattle that people can come and see," says a city councilman. "This wouldn't work in Dallas or San Antonio, but it works in Cowtown, Texas, because it's real here."

Although cattle raisers donated the longhorns, the city is paying the salaries and equipment for an "ethnically diverse group of cowboys" to manage the herd, whose annual operating costs are about $350,000.

Hundreds wanted the jobs, even though salaries range from $10,000 a year for a part-time wrangler to $33,000 for the trail boss overseeing the program. The trail boss is a 6-foot-2 horseman and bull rider from Alvorado, Texas, who has competed at Cow Bell Indoor Rodeo (see entry) in Mansfield and was nearly killed by a bull named Bad Hombre in Minnesota. The cowboys wear period costumes from the late 1880s, when the Stockyards were an important hub for the cattle business on the Chisholm Trail (see entry).

Before the Civil War there were more than ten million Texas long-horns in the U.S., notes the *Fort Worth Star-Telegram*, but by 1927 the number had dwindled to fewer than 30. When the Texas Longhorn Breeders Association was formed in 1964, there were only 1,400 head left in the world, according to its president, who says that today there are 250,000 registered longhorns. Within the Texas longhorn breed there are only seven different blood lines, with each having a distinc-tive horn pattern ranging from straight to curved or upright. The length of the horns ranges from two to eight feet.

"The longhorn created the cowboy, created the need for such a crea-ture, and once present, he became the essence of legends and myths," says Texas author Jerry Flemmons.

The original cowboy was West Texan, but the profession actually began with the Mexican vaquero. Although historically the cowboy is thought of as white Anglo-Saxon, he was actually brown or black and usually had a European accent. "But whatever else he may have been, he was Texan and his life was far less romantic and adventurous than John Wayne led us to believe," says Flemmons.

Fort Worth Log Cabin Village, 2100 Log Cabin Village Ln. at South University Dr.; (817) 926-5881. CH. Open Tue-Fri 9 am-4:30 pm, Sat 11 am-4:30 pm, Sun 1-5 pm, closed Mondays. Located on 2.5 acres in Forest Park, about one-half mile west of the Fort Worth Zoo (see entry) and near Colonial Parkway.

Pioneers from Arkansas, Missouri, and Tennessee began moving to north-central Texas in the 1840s. Here they found cedar and oak trees to build log cabins for their families. The Log Cabin Village, which opened to the public in 1964, has seven restored log cabins from the 1850s that will give you a good idea what life was like on the Texas frontier.

Shaw Grist Mill was built on a 160-acre tract located on what is now Shaw Creek, on the extreme frontier; only five miles away, Tonkawa Indians were camped along the Brazos River. Thomas Shaw was born in 1819 in Tennessee, married in 1845, and settled in what is now Parker County, Texas, in 1854. The Shaws had 14 children, four of whom died in infancy. This cabin was moved to the Village and restored in the 1950s. **Tompkins Cabin** belonged to John Tompkins, a breeder of fine horses, who was born in Virginia in 1820. He married in 1844 and moved to Missouri where his four children were born. The family settled in Parker County in 1857 and bought a farm with this one-room cabin, where five more children were born.

The two-story, nine-room **Foster Cabin** was built in the 1850s from oaks and cedars that grew in the Brazos River bottoms. Harry Foster was born in 1814 in Tennessee and moved to Mississippi, where he married and had six children. In 1852, the family made the long wagon trip to Port Sullivan, Texas. In 1969, a Foster great-grandson donated the log home to the Village.

Pickard Cabin belonged to William Pickard, who was born in 1834 in Tennessee, married in 1856, and moved to Texas; in 1863, he purchased this 1850s cabin and 90 acres on a tributary of Spring Creek, near Mount Nebo, in Parker County. The Pickards bred horses and raised eight children.

Seela Cabin belonged to Isaac Seela, who married in 1827 and had 13 children. In 1854, the Seelas sold their farm in Missouri and moved in their wagons to Texas, where they homesteaded 160 acres on Spring Creek, about 12 miles south of Weatherford, Texas, also in Parker County. Their original cabin was lost in the flood of 1860 and another one was built above the flood plain; a Seela grandson donated it to the Village.

The double log cabin with a dogtrot (breezeway), now known as **Parker Cabin,** was the Birdville, Texas, home of Isaac Parker, for whom Parker County was named. Parker was born in 1793 in Georgia, married in Tennessee, and had five of his eight children in Illinois. The family migrated to Elkhart, Texas, in 1833 and ten years later to Birdville, where Parker purchased this home that was built in 1848.

Hartsford Howard was born in 1819 in Georgia, married in 1845, and had eight children. It is doubtful that he built what is now known as **Howard Pioneer School.** Howard's son Billy once drove off an Indian attack by firing from the upstairs windows of this cabin until help arrived. The cabin was remodeled in 1995 to depict a typical one-room school, with living quarters for the teacher on the second floor.

The reproduction **Blacksmith Shop** was added to the village in the 1980s.

Demonstrations held in the Log Cabin Village include spinning yarn and weaving, candle-making, and corn-grinding.

A somewhat similar experience could be had at the **Old City Park** on the edge of downtown Dallas (see A Marmac Guide to Dallas for details).

Fort Worth Museum of Science & History, 1501 Montgomery St.; (817) 732-1631. CH. Open Mon 9 am-5 pm, Tue-Thu 9 am-8 pm, Fri-Sat 9 am-9 pm, Sun noon-8 pm. Located in Fort Worth's cultural

district, about 1.5 miles west of downtown, near the Modern, Amon
Carter, and Kimbell art museums (see individual entries).

The more than 100,000 artifacts and specimens displayed here
trace man's history on earth and illustrate the wonders of the uni-
verse. Exhibits encompass centuries-old relics, turn-of-the-century
Texas dioramas, the mystery of extinct dinosaurs, computer technology, and wonders of the human body. Among the fossil exhibits is a
mold of *Tenontosaurus dossi*, a one-ton dinosaur unearthed in nearby
Weatherford, in Parker County, in 1988, that is big even by the often
exaggerated Texas standards. *Tenontosaurus dossi*, named after the family on whose farm it was unearthed, was officially classified as a new
species in 1997. These creatures are said to have lived in the area 115
million years ago.

Dino Dig is an outdoor discovery area where the younger visitors
can become amateur paleontologists and dig for dinosaur bones.

The museum also is home to the 80-seat **Noble Planetarium,** where
30-minute astronomy and laser light shows are presented daily every
half-hour between 11 am and 4:30 pm. CH. For those interested, there
is also the **University of North Texas Planetarium,** (940) 565-4561,
on the corner of Hickory Street and Avenue C in Denton, a city of
75,000 north of the Metroplex.

The newest museum attraction is the 385-seat **Omni Theater,** one
of the largest theaters in the world that surrounds viewers with sight
and sound using 70mm film format. You can see films, such as the scal-
ing of the 29,028-foot Mount Everest, while the winds howl at 80 mph.
The theater's projector, weighing one ton, projects onto a domed
screen 80 feet in diameter, tilted at a 30-degree angle to the horizon.
There are 72 giant speakers around the theater driven by 19,000 watts
of power. Admission is charged.

Fort Worth Nature Center & Refuge, 9601 Fossil Ridge Rd.; (817)
237-1111. NCH, except for guided hikes. Open daily 9 am-5 pm. Visitor
Center is open Tue-Sat 9 am-4:30 pm, Sun noon-4:30 pm, closed
Mondays. This 3,500-acre sanctuary is located ten miles northwest from
downtown Fort Worth, also two miles past Lake Worth Bridge on State
Highway 199, which is also known as Jacksboro Highway. The entrance
is off Highway 199, four miles west of Loop 820.

This is the largest city-owned park in Texas and in the nation. Set
aside in 1964, the refuge also protects wildlife habitat—1,700 acres of
post-oak savannah, 1,000 acres of wetlands, and 800 acres of prairie.
Forests, marshes, and the Trinity River remain here much as they were
150 years ago, when the first white settlers arrived. A 25-mile trail provides opportunities to see native wildlife and plants, including a small
bison herd cohabitating with a prairie dog colony, white-tailed deer, and
Texas wildflowers. The park is home to 213 migratory birds, including

black vultures. Post-oaks that are up to 400 years old will be found on the Wild Plum Trail. Some 150,000 visit the park annually.

All plants, animals, and natural objects inside the sanctuary are protected. You may not pick plants or feed animals. No vehicles, bicycles, or horses are allowed on trails. Fishing is not permitted and you can picnic in designated areas only. There is no camping and dogs must be on a leash.

Nature programs, maps, and exhibits are available at Hardwicke Interpretive Center, which is wheelchair-accessible.

The 3,560-acre Lake Worth—a reservoir on the West Fork of the Trinity, to protect the city's water supply—is located nearby and is best known as a recreational boating lake. Most of the lakeside is private property so access is not the easiest. The lake has four public boat ramps and picnic areas. Fishing is poor.

Fort Worth Central Public Library, 300 Taylor at West Third St.; Information, (817) 871-7701; Business & Technology, 871-7727; Children's Services, 871-7745; Internet http://198.215.16.7:443/fort-worth/fwpl. Open Mon-Thu 9 am-9 pm, Fri-Sat 10 am-6 pm, Sun noon-6 pm. Wheelchair-accessible. Located downtown on the edge of Sundance Square, borders on Tandy Center, a block from the Fort Worth Outlet Square shopping mall (see individual entries). The library and the Outlet Square are connected underground.

It was originally designed in 1978 as an underground library, most of which still is below the street level. The library was redesigned in 1993 by having a facade and a roof over the old library added to solve the problem with roof leaks. It incorporated a Neoclassical facade design by architect David M. Schwarz that *Texas Monthly* labeled "the Supreme Court Jr. facade," judging it "underwhelming at best, ugly at worst." Covering two city blocks and labeled a "world-class library that we can be very, very proud of," by a mayor pro tempore, it is connected to the Tandy Center. A 20,000-square-foot street-level youth library with a media center and 6,000-square-foot art gallery was built in 1999, along with a new entrance from Third Street. Schwartz also designed the Bass Performance Hall nearby (see individual entries).

With a Fort Worth Public Library card you can borrow materials from Fort Worth, Haltom City, and Keller public libraries. Cards are available free of charge to Fort Worth residents, although proof of residency or property ownership is required. Fees for non-residents are based on the per capita rate paid by Fort Worth residents. Most materials may be checked out for three weeks and returned to any Fort Worth public library.

Most collections are located on the lower level. Materials in Spanish, Vietnamese, Chinese, French, German, Russian, and Greek are also available. Internet is accessible in all city libraries. Up to 40,000 visitors use the library every month.

In addition to the downtown location, there are 12 other library branches throughout the city. Arlington's four library branches, in addition to the main library at 101 East Abram St., can be accessed by calling (817) 459-6900 or on the Internet at www.ci.arlington.tx.us.

Fort Worth Star-Telegram Building, 400 West Seventh at Taylor St.; (817) 390-7400. Located downtown next to the Electric Building and across the street from the Neil P. Anderson Building (see individual entries).

After he arrived in Fort Worth in 1905, the notorious Amon G. Carter (1879-1955) discussed with two reporters "the possibility of creating a new daily afternoon newspaper to contend with the Fort Worth Telegram. Colonel Paul Waples rounded up a few friends and they laid out $50,000" to finance a new daily, the *Star.* Carter had no money to invest, but received a $35-a-week job as advertising manager. By 1908, the investment was gone and so were the two original reporters.

Instead of going bankrupt, Carter used his four diamond rings as collateral for a $2,500 down payment to acquire the competing daily. He wound up with a 10-percent ownership of the combined *Star-Telegram* "and did not stop until he owned it all." As early as 1918, the newspaper publisher William Randolph Hearst (1863-1951) wanted to hire Carter by trying to buy the *Star-Telegram,* but Carter refused. In a moment of pique, Hearst bought the *Star-Telegram's* competitor, the *Fort Worth Record,* but his purchase did not pan out and by 1924 the frustrated Hearst sold the competing morning daily to the Cowtown publisher.

The original four-story building was designed by Sanguinet and Staats and constructed in 1921 at the height of a Fort Worth building boom as headquarters of what is today the second largest daily in the Metroplex. Carter, a shameless promoter of Fort Worth, well known for his antipathy of anything connected with Dallas (see Fair Park's 1936 Centennial Exhibition entry in this chapter) became *Star-Telegram's* president and publisher in 1923. By then the daily had built the highest circulation in Texas and held it until the 1950s. Carter's Western art collection formed the base for the Amon Carter Museum (see entry).

In 1922, Amon Carter established radio station WBAP—still operational today—which was one of the first in the nation. In 1948, his WBAP television station was also one of the first to broadcast in the southwest and was later renamed KXAS-TV, Channel 5.

Fort Worth Union/Santa Fe Depot, 1501 Jones at East 14th streets. Located east of Fort Worth Gardens, a block from Ramada Plaza Hotel, and southeast of the Fort Worth Convention Center (see individual entries).

When inaugurated in March of 1900, the Fort Worth Union Depot served six railway companies: Gulf, Colorado and Santa Fe, and the

Houston and Texas Central railroads. Also operating here were the Cotton Belt, Rock Island, Southern Pacific, and the St. Louis and San Francisco Railway (also known as Frisco). Less than a year later, a 5 am fire burned the wooden framework between the station roof and the metal ceiling, but the ticket office remained.

The Beaux Arts-style terminal was renovated in 1938 and continued serving several lines until 1960, when the Santa Fe became the only railroad using it, so the facility was renamed the Santa Fe Depot. Presidents Franklin D. Roosevelt, Dwight Eisenhower, and Lyndon Johnson have all been welcomed here. Amtrak has operated passenger rail service out of the station since 1973. The depot was listed in both the National Register of Historic Places and designated as a Recorded Texas Historic Landmark in 1970. The red-brick structure is unfriendly, shabby, and deserted now, with its paint peeling and the bathrooms locked; you will probably be asked to leave unless you come about the time when the few trains pull in or out of the station.

Fort Worth Water Gardens, 1502 Commerce St.; (817) 871-5700. NCH. Open daily 8 am-11 pm, although the water fountains sometimes do not function until 10 am. Located south of the Fort Worth Convention Center, across the street from Ramada Plaza Hotel (see individual entries), north of Interstate 30, between Commerce and Houston streets.

A 4.3-acre water park with a miniature forest, pools, and waterfalls—designed by noted architects Philip Johnson (b. 1906) and John Burgee—uses water to create various effects. The gardens, which cost $7 million to construct, were paid for by the Amon G. Carter Foundation.

Completed in 1974, after eight years of construction, they feature a complex of sculptures and fountains. There is a terraced walkway that allows you to stand 38 feet below ground level and observe 19,000 gallons of water rushing from 710 feet of hidden troughs each minute. The gardens, which are illuminated at night, contain more than 500 species of plants and trees. Author Laura Trim calls it "a place contrived to blend with city streets, indeed to invite people off the streets for refreshment in its cool places. The effect is not unlike the ancient pyramids in Mexico."

Parts of the 1976 film *Logan's Run*, depicting life in the year 2274, with Michael York, Peter Ustinov, and Texas native Farrah Fawcett-Majors, were filmed here.

Water Garden Place, at 100 East 15th Street, across the street from Ramada Plaza Hotel, was built by William Monnig for his wholesale business in 1925. The building has since been renovated and now faces the gardens.

South of here, at the intersection of Main and Lancaster streets, stands the 1893 Hayne Memorial (see entry), where the Texas Spring Palace once stood.

Fort Worth Zoo, 1989 Colonial Pkwy.; (817) 871-7050, Internet www.fortworthzoo.com. Open Mon-Fri 10 am-5 pm, Sat-Sun 10 am-6 pm. CH for admission and parking, children under 2 get in free. On Wednesdays admission is half-price and parking is free. There is an ATM near the entrance. Located in the Forest Park, at University Drive and Colonial Parkway, about three miles southwest of downtown Fort Worth. To get to the zoo, take the University exit off Interstate 30 and go south for a mile to Colonial Parkway, then take a left turn.

This is the oldest continuous zoo site in Texas and was established in 1909, when three park commissioners bought a group of animals from a traveling carnival. Some 732 species and 5,000 native and exotic specimens can be seen, including a Sumatran tiger, a black rhino, and Malayan bears, in addition to longhorns, buffaloes, and other native Texas animals. More than 30 endangered species live in this 60-acre zoo, including the Mexican and red wolf, the Asian elephant, and harpy eagles. There is an aquarium and a herpetarium, as well as a diorama of Texas frontier life. *Travel America* magazine named it one of America's 14 best zoos in 1997; two years earlier, the zoo was selected as one of the "Top Five Zoos in America." It is the only American zoo to house all four species of great apes. It has an annual budget of $12 million and more than 1.2 million visitors.

Film actor James Stewart first came to Cowtown in 1948 and served on the board of directors of the zoo from the early 1950s on. At the time of his death in 1997, the Fort Worth *Star-Telegram* wrote that "for decades, Stewart and his wife, Gloria, were strong supporters of the zoo, donating time, talent and money. In 1988, they helped break ground for facilities for rhinoceroses, giraffes and apes, filmed public service announcements declaring their support and attended a $150-a-plate dinner to raise money to transport ten black rhinos to the United States." Stewart hunted with his Fort Worth friends in Africa and went on dove-hunting trips to Possum Kingdom Lake, west of Fort Worth, but "never shot anything except birds." If Stewart was the most famous supporter, Lee Marshall Bass and his wife Ramona, worth an estimated $3.3 billion, must be the wealthiest: both have espoused its value for years and "shivered" in the November 1998 chill to help raise funds for a $35-million eight-acre **Texas Wild!** interactive exhibit—to feature 75 species of Texas animals—that is scheduled to open in the year 2000. They gave the zoo $12 million in 1999 alone, according to *Texas Monthly*.

This is also the home of one of the most respected insectaria in the country: from hairy spiders to fist-sized beetles, from venomous centipedes to jumbo roaches from the rain forest where they grow to the size of a soft-drink can, but still are just a fraction of the insect world, which includes more than a million species, most of which have been around for 350 million years. Dirt-filled aquariums feature assassin bugs, baboon spiders, Madagascar hissing cockroaches, and more.

In 1997, the zoo unveiled two Philippines crocodiles, who share an indoor pool next to the Komodo dragons exhibit. Of the 23 world's crocodile species, the Philippines is considered most endangered, with only an estimated 100 remaining in the wild. There is also the Penguin Island with underwater viewing areas. Gerenuk, an antelope that acts like a giraffe, also joined the zoo that year. It has overdeveloped hind legs, a curved spine, and wedge-shaped hooves that allow it to step sideways as it stands and to graze on tree branches higher than six feet. The following year, the zoo completed the 14,000-square-floor animal clinic that accommodates some of the largest animals.

The zoo also has a gallery of sorts: it features 28 oil paintings by German wildlife artist Wilhelm Kuhnert. He was one of the first European artists to travel to Africa in the late 1800s to paint exotic animals in their natural habitat. There are food and gift shops.

Fort Worth fondly recalls its former zoo director Lawrence Curtis, who had served in this capacity for 14 years, until 1975. Clever at publicity stunts, he once made international headlines with the supposed two-week disappearance of an 18-foot python. When someone would call in with a question, according to the *Fort Worth Star-Telegram*, Curtis was in the habit of saying, "Just a minute," looked up the caller's answer, and returned to the phone saying, "I'm awfully sorry to keep you waiting. A hooded cobra escaped and I had to recapture it before it could hurt some little child. Now what was your question again?" Curtis had the answer ready, of course. Once a woman called and asked how long a rooster has to be with a hen before the egg is fertilized. The zoo director, again, said, "Just a minute" to gain time. "Oh, thank you," said the woman and hung up. In the 1980s Curtis became director of the Royal Zoo in Riyadh, Saudi Arabia, which cost $48 million to build.

In 2000, the zoo received an eleven-year-old Asian elephant, Angel, who had shared a Nevada casino stage with some of the best-known performers. She played the harmonica and keyboard. Her stage partner for ten years, another elephant, died, and since elephants are highly sociable, the Nugget Casina in Reno decided to donate Angel to Fort Worth.

General Worth Square, 900 Block of Main Street downtown. Located just north of the Fort Worth Convention Center and across Eighth Street from Radisson Plaza Hotel (see individual entries).

This square is dedicated to Gen. William Jenkins Worth (1794-1849), for whom Fort Worth was named. A native of Hudson, New

York, Worth was severely wounded during the war of 1812. Eight years later, he became instructor of infantry tactics at the U.S. military academy at West Point. In 1825, Worth was appointed the first Commandant of Cadets at West Point. When he was reassigned in 1828, Robert E. Lee was serving as cadet adjutant. Worth was involved in defense along the Canadian border in the 1830s and in 1841-42 led an expedition against the Florida Seminole Indians. During the Mexican War, he fought at the battle of Monterrey. He received a sword of honor from the U.S. Congress and a promotion to major general. While serving as commander of the Texas and New Mexico military districts, he died of cholera in San Antonio, Texas, before being informed that the fort was named after him. Buried in New York City, his grave at Broadway and Fifth Avenue is marked by a 500-foot-high monument.

Worth ordered the founding of a frontier fort, now known as the city of Fort Worth, in 1849 to protect the growing number of settlers in this area. The park was built on the former site of the Washer Brothers clothing store. Jacob and Nat Washer came to Fort Worth in 1882 from Tennessee. Their first store was located at Fourth and Main streets. They moved here in 1900. The original two-story building was expanded to four by 1927, when the store was recognized as a fashion center for women.

Grapevine Opryland Hotel & Convention Center, Ruth Wall Rd. at State Hwy. 26, Grapevine. Located north of the Dallas-Fort Worth International Airport, near Grapevine Mills (see individual entries), a $200-million shopping center, and the 197,000-square-foot Bass Pro Outdoor World hunting, fishing, and camping gear superstore (Internet www.basspro.com) across from it, which opened in 1999.

A 77-acre, $300-million Opryland hotel and convention center is being built by the owners of the Nashville, Tennessee-based Opryland on a peninsula overlooking Grapevine Lake. It will include a 1,500-room hotel, a 200,000-square-foot exhibition hall, 350,000 square feet of convention and exhibit space, a giant indoor garden atrium, a 27-hole golf course, restaurants, a supermarket-sized country-Western entertainment venue, and retail shopping space. The complex is expected to attract about four million visitors annually.

The seven-story Opryland Hotel-Texas—the third largest in the Metroplex, after Adam's Mark and Wyndham Anatole, both in Dallas—will be completed in 2003. A 120-foot glass ceiling over the hotel's atrium and shaped like a giant star will feature a four-acre indoor garden. Dozens of themed restaurants and stores are planned for. Opryland's convention center will be the largest in Tarrant County. To unwind, guests will be able to pick from a golf course or a sailboat at nearby Silver Lake marina, which will be upgraded. A 20-acre entrance along State Highway 26 will sport a new four-lane road and bridge over the southern corner of the 7,280-acre Grapevine Lake for those arriving in their own vehicles. The complex is owned by the Gaylord family, whose patriarch Edward K. Gaylord came to Oklahoma from Missouri in 1903, four years before it became a state.

Grapevine, a cantaloupe and cotton farming town of 40,000, promotes itself as the wine capital of Texas, the state with 27 wineries, although only one vineyard actually grows grapes and manufactures wine in Grapevine. The town is believed to be the oldest settlement in Tarrant County and named after the wild mustang grapes that covered the area when the first settlers arrived in 1844. A three-day **Grapefest** wine-tasting festival takes place in September.

The Nashville Opryland complex, next to the Grand Ole Opry House, is twice the size of Grapevine's, with a 2,883-room hotel, and the largest combined hotel-convention center in the world. *FW Weekly* calls it the "kitschiest tourist trap."

Hayne Memorial, Lancaster at Main and Houston streets. Located near the Fort Worth Water Gardens and the U.S. Post Office building downtown (see individual entries).

At this intersection there is the **Alfred S. Hayne Memorial** with his bronze bust, originally sculpted by local marble cutter Lloyd Brown. In 1934, the bust was cast in bronze by Fort Worth sculptor Evaline Sellors (b. 1908) and erected in 1937.

Near here stood the magnificent **Texas Spring Palace,** designed to house a trade fair promoting the Texas agricultural products. Designed by local firm of Armstrong and Messer, it was built of wood, with ornamentation using Texas agricultural products. The first exhibition was held in 1889 and attracted visitors from as far away as Boston, Chicago, and New York.

The following year, while the 225-by-375-foot building was jammed with 7,000 people attending a dress ball in the 16,000-square-foot ballroom, a fire broke out in the evening of May 30 and engulfed the structure that cost $100,000 to build. "In four minutes the building was a mass of flame, inside and out, and in eleven minutes the building fell to the ground." While rescuing "fainting women and terrified children" from the burning building, Al Hayne, a civil engineer from Scotland who had worked in Fort Worth, leaped from the window with a fainting woman whose dress was already ablaze and in the fall broke several bones. He died of burns three hours later and is buried in Oakwood Cemetery, northwest of downtown.

Heritage Park, North Main and Bluff streets. Located just northwest of the Tarrant County Courthouse (see entry). Overlooking the Trinity River, this 112-acre park has hiking and biking trails and is landscaped with gardens, ponds, walkways, and waterfalls. It was dedicated in 1980.

There is a marker in the park commemorating the first school dating from the mid-1850s, when it started with twelve students. It was established by civic leader John Peter Smith, after whom a hospital was named. A metal plate on an old oak tree indicates the site of the Fort Worth's first hotel. Capt. Ephraim M. Daggett's lodging house was located in the old cavalry stable of the Second U.S. Dragoons. In 1853, a two-story hotel was erected on the site. For more details about *Continuum,* by Texas sculptor Brad Goldberg, please see the Art in Public Places section in the VISUAL ARTS chapter.

Nearby, at Belknap and Houston streets, you will find a bronze plaque on a boulder commemorating the military fort that was established in 1849-1853 by Maj. Ripley Arnold, who had served in Indian wars in Florida and came to Texas with Zachary Taylor (1784-1850), the twelfth president of the U.S. The marker is placed on the site of the former parade grounds and was dedicated in 1921.

Hyde Park, 200 block of West Ninth and Throckmorton streets. Located downtown in the shadow of Flatiron Building and behind Park Central Hotel (see individual entries).

Inaugurated in 1873 and part of the 1836 Sarah Hyde Jennings 980-acre land grant, this is believed to be the oldest park in the city and was named in honor of Mrs. Jennings' parents. Her husband, Thomas J. Jennings, served as attorney general of Texas. This handkerchief-sized patch of green is so tiny you may bypass it without knowing when. Most of the city's park lands in the late 1800s and early 1900s were open lawns, called "pleasure grounds," where residents could enjoy a picnic or take a stroll or a carriage ride.

The artillery shells mounted in the park are a memorial to the city veterans serving in World War II in the U.S. Navy.

Jim Courtright-Luke Short Annual Shootout, in front of the modern-day White Elephant Saloon, 106 East Exchange Ave., near North Main St., in the Stockyards district; (817) 624-9712. Reenacted every February 8, starting at about 7 pm.

On February 8, 1887, something unexpected happened in front of Ella Blackwell's shooting gallery, on the 300 block of the east side of Main Street, between Second and Third streets, downtown.

Luke Short, who owned the gambling concession at the White Elephant Saloon and Fort Worth Marshal Timothy Isaiah "Long Hair Jim" Courtright settled their differences with guns, something that was not uncommon at that time.

Courtright, who had years earlier performed in Wild West shows and killed several outlaws, was a two-time Fort Worth marshal. After his first election, he and his wife, Sarah Elizabeth Weeks, herself a crack shot, moved to downtown Fort Worth and settled in a house on Calhoun Street, just a block from the Tarrant County Courthouse (see entry). A six-foot-tall man who loved to gamble, he had his own ideas of how to clean up the prostitution-filled Hell's Half Acre area, where the Fort Worth Convention Center (see entry) stands today. The merchants felt that he exceeded his authority and drove away the paying customers. Courtright quit in disgust and left for the New Mexico Territory, where he worked first as a marshal, then as a guard for a silver mining company. After killing several men there, he was indicted for murder and fled back to Fort Worth.

Courtright was always a flamboyant figure followed by a colorful reputation. In 1884, he was pursued by the Albuquerque chief of police and two Texas Rangers and tricked into another man's hotel room, where he was arrested and thrown in jail. The Fort Worth populace was so taken in by Courtright they threatened to storm the jail and release him. The prisoner was taken to the county jail and the Merchants Restaurant, near Houston and Second streets, for his meals. He received word he would be assisted in his escape. After finishing his supper, Courtright dropped his napkin and asked the sheriff to pick it up for him.

"Pick it up yourself," snapped back the sheriff. Courtright reached for the guns that had been hung by hooks under the table. Following some tense moments, he escaped on a horse that his friends had left waiting for him outside. After almost two years as a fugitive in New York, Toronto, and Washington Territory, Courtright grew tired of hiding and turned himself in in New Mexico and was acquitted on all charges. He returned to Fort Worth.

Courtright learned that his acquaintance, Luke Short, was cheating as a gambler. Short, a former cattle drover who also had a reputation as a gunfighter, owned the gambling concession at the White Elephant Saloon (see entry), then at 308-310 Main Street, and was supposedly fleecing his customers at the keno tables, a game similar to bingo.

When the two met in front of Ella Blackwell's shooting gallery nearby, no one expected such a violent confrontation. There was a brief conversation, perhaps about Short cheating his customers. Luke stood facing Courtright, his thumbs in the arm holes of his vest. When he lowered his hands, Courtright warned him not to reach for his gun. "I have no gun there," Short said as he lifted his vest to show that he did not have one. Perhaps misinterpreting the gesture, Courtright now reached for his pistol, but Short drew a Colt .45 revolver from his hip and fired. He shot Courtright in his right hand. Before the marshal could shift his gun to his other hand, Short fired three more times and killed him.

Luke Short became the first man ever to outdraw Marshal Courtright. Legend has it that while lying in the dust, Courtright yelled, "Shoot, Luke, or give up your gun," and in reply Short shot him again, saying, "Goodbye, Jim."

Courtright's wife Betty later claimed that her husband was killed because Luke Short was in love with her. After the shooting, she said, Short came to her and said he wanted to marry her. Betty ran him off with a shotgun.

Courtright's funeral was the largest ever held in Cowtown up to that time, stretching for more than six blocks. Luke Short spent some time in jail and was then quietly let go. He went to Kansas and is said to have died there in 1891 at the age of 39. Others claim that both men are buried in Oakwood Cemetery, which opened halfway between Sundance Square and the Stockyards in 1879.

Come to the Stockyards any February 8 and see the reenactment of that shootout in front of the modern-day White Elephant Saloon on East Exchange Avenue that opened in 1976.

The only lawman who came even close to Courtright was the 6-foot-4, 225-pound "lummox" of a Tarrant County sheriff, James Ralph "Sully" Montgomery (1901-1970). After three years in professional football, he entered a boxing career and was rated as the nation's No. 7 contender until he lost by a decision to Jack Dempsey. "In 1942, he was elected Constable of Precinct 1, where he served two terms before being elected sheriff," writes historian Bill Fairley. "In 1952, the Internal Revenue Service went after the sheriff for taxes owed from 1948-50." He was sentenced to seven years in prison, but the second jury acquitted him.

John Peter Smith Memorial, 1100 Jennings at Throckmorton streets. Located across Jennings from City Hall and St. Patrick Cathedral, and a block west of the Fort Worth Convention Center (see individual entries).

John Peter Smith (1831-1901), born in Owen County, Kentucky, was one of the earliest residents of Fort Worth. Losing both of his parents at age 12, he lived with a cousin, attended Franklin College in Indiana, and graduated from Bethany College, now located in West Virginia. Smith arrived in Dallas in 1853, but was disappointed with the "muddy village that had grown up to be a trading post." He walked most of the way to Fort Worth. There, he opened a school with 12 students in the old Dragoon's Army hospital, near today's Tarrant County Courthouse square, and worked there as a teacher. Later he became a clerk and surveyor, for a short time even a Texas Ranger. Smith studied law and was admitted to the bar.

The marker at this location notes that he was opposed to the secession of Texas from the Union, but nevertheless raised a company of 120

Tarrant County volunteers for the Confederacy in 1861. While in the war, he served in the unsuccessful invasion of New Mexico, the recapture of Galveston from Union forces in 1863, and was severely wounded at Donaldsville, Louisiana, later that year.

After the war, in 1867, he married a young widow with whom he had four children. He helped organize a bank, a gas light company, and a street railway. He contributed more than $7,000 toward bringing the railroad to Cowtown. Smith served as the mayor of Fort Worth from 1882 to 1885, overseeing the development of a municipal water supply, a modernized fire department, the first streets being paved, and the construction of the city's first sanitation sewers.

In 1901, aged 70, Smith went to see a friend off at the railway station in St. Louis and was beaten and robbed while returning to his hotel. He died six days later. He donated land for parks, cemeteries, and a hospital that was named JPS Hospital (see entry). Smith is buried in Oakwood Cemetery—between Henderson and North Main streets—a site he donated to the city (see entry). This marble bust on a pedestal was made from his death mask.

Knights of Pythias Castle Hall, 313 Main at East Third streets. Located in Sundance Square downtown, next door to Sid Richardson Collection of Western Art, and three blocks south of the Tarrant County Courthouse (see individual entries).

The first Knights of Pythias Castle Hall in the world was built here in 1881, nine years after this charitable, benevolent, and fraternal order was established in Houston. After the original structure burned down, the present building, which was designed by Marshall R. Sanguinet, was constructed in 1901 by brick mason and former Cowtown mayor William Bryce (1861-1944) (see Bryce Building listing in this chapter). The original seven-foot-high knight was made in New York in 1882 to stand guard in a high niche on the front of the building; a replica of the knight was installed during the 1982 renovation after the original was damaged.

The Knights sold the building in 1975. Bass Brothers Enterprises acquired it in 1978 and renovated it four years later as part of the Sundance Square project. The interior, which has been adapted, now houses Haltom's Jewelers, whose two-and-a-half-ton cast-iron clock in front of it dates from 1914.

Landreth-Davis House, 900 Rivercrest Rd. Located on a three-and-a-half-acre site near River Crest Country Club, west of the cultural district.

Edward A. Landreth (1881-1962) made his fortune in west Texas oil fields in the 1920s. He moved to Fort Worth shortly before he sold several million barrels of oil he had in storage to Texaco for an astounding $6.5 million in 1928. He lost a small fortune in the stock market crash of 1929, but made up the difference in other business dealings.

Landreth retired in 1941 and devoted himself to civic projects. The Ed Landreth Fine Arts Building at Texas Christian University (see entry) is named after him.

The well-known Dallas architects Marion Fooshee and James Cheek—who had also designed the Highland Park Shopping Village in Dallas—drew plans for this two-and-a-half story Tudor Revival mansion overlooking the bend in Rivercrest Road. It was built in 1928.

In 1943, Landreth and his wife sold the mansion to Kenneth Davis (1895-1968), an oilman who was associated with the Mid-Continent Supply Co., an oil-field equipment firm. Over the years, he also operated several other drilling, manufacturing, and supply businesses. One of his sons, T. Cullen Davis, became infamous for two unresolved murders that cling to his former residence, Cullen Davis Mansion, first a steakhouse, then a Tex-Mex restaurant. Kenneth Davis financed the Noble Planetarium at the Fort Worth Museum of Science & History (see individual entries).

Land Title Building, 111 East Fourth at Commerce streets. Located downtown, on the edge of Sundance Square, across Main Street from Haas's *Chisholm Trail* Mural. Today, the old bank lobby houses The Flying Saucer Beer Emporium (see individual entries).

"Sitting alone on a square city block, the Land Title Block is Fort Worth's best surviving 19th century commercial building," says historian Carol Roark. "The small Victorian Romanesque structure showcases a rich variety of materials including pressed red brick, red sandstone, multi-colored glazed brick, cast iron, and stained glass."

The two-story building was designed by Haggart and Sanguinet—the predecessor of the local architectural firm of Sanguinet and Staats—and constructed in 1889 by the Land Mortgage Bank of Texas, whose offices were on the first floor. The interior was frequently altered to accommodate tenants, such as banks, and real estate and title companies.

Leonard Brothers Department Store Marker, 100 Houston at West Belknap streets. Located across the street from the Tarrant County Courthouse (see entry) downtown.

John Marvin Leonard (1895-1970), better known as "Mr. Marvin," opened a 25-by-60-foot storefront in the morning shadow of the courthouse with $600 in 1918. He was later joined by his brother Obadiah Paul (1898-1987), nicknamed "Obie." They built it into a department store with 185 departments and 2,500 employees that stretched over an area larger than a city block by the time the Depression struck and to a behemoth sprawling over six and a half blocks of downtown by the early 1960s. The store sales topped a million dollars by 1928. It sold everything from pastries to high fashions, from canned tuna to tractors. "Low prices were the foundation of Leonards' appeal," write Victoria and Walter Buenger in *Texas Merchant,* a 1998 history of the store. "Profit came from high volume, not high markups." The brothers issued Leonard scrip in 1933, when checks were difficult to cash, and cashed more of them "than any downtown bank." Until Obie bought out Marvin in 1967 for more than $10 million, Leonards was "the epicenter of the city." Less than three years later, the store was sold to Charles Tandy for $8.5 million and became part of the Tandy Corporation. In 1974 Dillard's bought it for $5 million, but closed it for lack of profitability.

To alleviate the parking congestion downtown, Obie Leonard constructed in 1963 a $500,000 privately-owned M & O Subway, utilizing "the old Washington, D.C. street cars that Obie had found and refurbished." It connected the store with an off-site parking lot a mile north, providing free transportation for 12,000 shoppers and downtown workers each day. It "postponed the decay of downtown," according to the authors. "When the store was sold to the Tandy Corporation on October 30, 1967, the complex covered six blocks, offered over 500,000 square feet of merchandise, and employed 1,800 people," notes the marker. Tandy built its Tandy Center on the site and preserved the subway that you can still ride to and from the Fort Worth Outlet Square (see individual entries).

On the $1,500-an-acre property near today's Ridgmar Mall (see entry), which was once owned by Amon Carter, the blasphemous ayatollah of Fort Worth, Marvin Leonard also built in 1958 the $3.5 million Shady Oaks County Club, where the initial membership fee was $6,500. In 1935, he established the 140-acre Colonial Country Club, where the annual MasterCard Colonial (see entry) golf tournament has been held since 1946. In 1935, Leonard built an orange-brick Tudor Revival residence at 600 Alta Drive, overlooking the River Crest Country Club golf course.

Livestock Exchange Building, 131 East Exchange Ave. Located in the historic Stockyards district, next to the Cowtown Coliseum, and across the street from the Tarantula Train Depot (see individual entries). Stockyards Hotel and White Elephant Saloon are also nearby.

The two-story brick adobe-style Livestock Exchange faces the Visitors Information Center. Built in 1902-1903—at the same time as the Armour and Swift meat-packing plants nearby, which sustained the area economically—it was for many years the site of animal auctions. By 1915, several additions were made to the building. Amazingly, the name of its architect is not known. All cattle, hogs, sheep, mules, and horses sold in the stockyards were processed or cleared through this exchange at one time. When it opened, livestock pens stretched for acres around the building.

During the 1950s and 1960s, the building deteriorated severely, although the auction barn was added in 1960. It was only in the mid-1970s, with both the Armour and Swift plants closed, that plans were born to resurrect it as a monument to the cattle industry's legacy. The building was renovated in the late 1970s and in 1994 purchased by entrepreneur Holt Hickman, who has redeveloped the stockyards as an entertainment district. The building also houses the Stockyards Museum (see entry).

Mesquite Championship Rodeo, 1818 Rodeo Dr., Mesquite; (800) 833-9339, (972) 222-BULL or 285-8777. CH and parking fee. Open April 4 through October 4, Fri-Sat 8-10 pm. Located at LBJ Freeway and Military Parkway, behind the Trail Dust Steak House.

You can recapture the flavor of the West at the 5,300-seat covered Mesquite Arena, where some of the most daring cowboys show off their stuff with often uncooperative and potentially deadly livestock. Mesquite rodeo, established in 1957, is to the Metroplex what going to the Bolshoy Theater is to Moscow. You will see saddle and bareback riders, calf ropers, steer wrestlers, and bronc and bull riders perform with courage and skill that you have seen before only on screen. While sitting in the stands, you can munch on cotton candy. The carnival atmosphere is enhanced by barrel racers, clowns, and country music. There are so many first-timers at the Mesquite rodeo that organizers regularly explain each event's rules and scoring procedures.

The $10-million arena, which opened in 1986, features luxury boxes, modeled after the suites at Texas Stadium, home of the Dallas Cowboys, in Irving. More than a quarter-million spectators come every year. Texas has more professional rodeos than any other state, 110 a year, compared with about 62 in the second-ranked California.

Bull riders score points for style and skill, not just for staying atop the fierce animal for at least eight seconds. If you want to know how the real cowboys of yesteryear handled their daily chores, watch for steer wrestling, where the cowboy ropes a 600-pound animal and wrestles it to the ground in about four seconds using leverage and strength. In calf roping—whose roots date to the Old West when a calf might be injured and had to be immobilized quickly for treatment—the contestant ropes a calf, gets off his horse, and ties the calf's any three legs together using a pigging string he carries in his teeth.

For children there are also a petting zoo, pony rides, and a calf-catching contest.

Come early enough and you can sit down to a real hickory-smoked barbecue, barbecued brisket of beef, or sliced smoked sausage before the show starts; then you can work off the calories by visiting the gift shop nearby.

The Miller Marketplace & Brew Kettle Museum, 7001 South Fwy. at the Sycamore School Road exit; (817) 568-BEER. NCH. Open Wed-Sat 11 am-5 pm. Located next to the Miller Brewing Co. plant in far south Fort Worth, on Interstate 35 West (also known as South Freeway), south of Altamesa Boulevard East.

The 9,000-square-foot center chronicles Miller Brewing Company's years in Fort Worth and traces 5,000 years of brewing history. The museum features a brew-kettle dome that measures 22 feet in diameter and weighs two tons, as well as other machinery, bottles, beer glasses, bottle openers, signs, and postcards. It is said to be the only museum of its kind in the Southwest. While you cannot watch the actual brewing, because the brewery is not designed to handle tours, the process is depicted through illustrations and narratives. If age 21 or older, you may taste a free seven-ounce sample of the Miller beers on tap.

The museum traces the roots of beer back to 3000 B.C., when a recipe was inscribed on an Egyptian clay tablet. The Pilgrims opted to stop at Plymouth Rock when supplies—including their beer—ran low. "We could not now take time for further search or consideration, our victuals being much spent, especially our beere," reads a shipboard Pilgrim diary passage re-created on the museum's time line. George Washington and Thomas Jefferson had brew houses on their estates. At the turn of the century, there were 1,500 breweries in the U.S., but the Prohibition cut that number in half. Frederick Miller III founded the Miller Brewing Company in 1855 and the company opened its Fort Worth brewery in 1969.

Morris & Conn Building, 308 West Main, between Second and Third streets. Located directly across the street from Sid Richardson Collection of Western Art and from the former Savoy and Plaza Hotels, now La Madeleine French Bakery & Cafe (see individual entries).

The building was the original site of the legendary White Elephant Saloon (see entry), where gambler Luke Short outdrew and shot Fort Worth Marshal Timothy Isaiah "Long Hair Jim" Courtright on February 8, 1887. The saloon has moved to the Stockyards (see entry), but the legend is perpetuated by the yearly reenactment of the gunfight in front of the new White Elephant Saloon in the yards. For more details about that, please see entry on the Jim Courtright-Luke Short Annual Shootout in this chapter.

National Archives & Records Administration, 501 West Felix St.; (817) 334-5515; Genealogy, 334-5525. Located in south Fort Worth, west of Interstate 35 West and north of Southwest Loop 820.

This musty World War II ensemble has been home to federal archives of Texas, Arkansas, Louisiana, New Mexico, and Oklahoma for more than 30 years. With about 67,000 cubic feet of records from 90 federal agencies, the Fort Worth center is one of the 13 largest such regional archives. Original records are kept in acid-free folders and boxes, and some documents and photos are kept in polyester film sleeves for additional protection.

Most among the 1,600 visitors each month are genealogists research-ing their own or someone else's family's history. Among the most inac-cessible items is the disassembled Parkland Memorial Hospital emergency room, where President Kennedy died on November 22, 1963. Floor and ceiling tiles, cabinet, gurney, and various medical instruments from the Dallas hospital are boxed-up here. The Kennedy Library refused the materials and the Sixth Floor Kennedy Museum (see entry) in Dallas cannot have them because it is not federally owned.

Among the records found here is a document from 1934, indicting Bonnie Parker and Clyde Barrow in the theft of rifles and pistols from the Texas National Guard Armory in Ranger. Also in storage is an offi-cial refusal by Pres. James Monroe to pardon 15 pirates sentenced to death in the case of the *U.S. vs. John Defargues*. Several presidential pardons are stored a few aisles from the *Apollo 11* flight plan. The old-est records date back to 1806.

The former 150-acre Army Quartermaster Depot here was turned into a prisoners-of-war compound after World War II. "In May 1945, the same month that Germany capitulated to the Allies, 250 German prisoners of war arrived in Fort Worth," writes Fort Worth historian Bill Fairley. When the POW's left the area in the fall of 1946, their number had doubled. They were enclosed behind two high, mile-long barbed-wire fences that were guarded 24 hours a day by military police in sev-eral tall watch towers. Each tower, equipped with powerful searchlights, also held loaded machine guns that were ready to be fired at any time. "The captives worked eight-hour, six-day weeks with Sundays off." The prisoners, some of whom worked for civilian enterprises in the area, only received 80 cents a day.

Neil P. Anderson Building, 411 West Seventh at Lamar streets. Located across the street from The Electric Building and the Fort Worth Star-Telegram editorial offices, overlooking the nearby Burnett Park (see individual entries).

Neil P. Anderson (1847-1912) established a cotton brokerage firm soon after his arrival in Fort Worth in 1882. After Anderson's death, the business was continued by his son and son-in-law. In 1919, the two purchased a homestead on the corner of West Seventh and Lamar streets, a gateway to the central business district. Architects from Sanguinet and Staats drew plans for the building that housed the Fort Worth Cotton and Grain Exchange, U.S. Department of Agriculture, Anderson & Company, and several other cotton and grain merchants. This informal cotton exchange had seven skylights over the top floor showrooms.

The 11-story brick building has a curved facade with terra-cotta ornamentation. Although Anderson & Company closed for business in 1939, the building ownership stayed in the family and the structure was renovated in 1959. Four years later the building was sold and had several owners until 1977, when it was purchased to prevent demolition. The following year it was designated as a Texas Historic Landmark.

NRH₂O Family Water Park, 9001 Grapevine Hwy., North Richland Hills; (817) 656-6500, Internet www.nrh2o.com. Open from mid-May to mid-September, hours vary by time of year. Admission depends on height. Season passes are available. Free parking. Located in northeast Tarrant County.

A 15-acre $7.8-million city-owned water park that opened in 1995 with a 16,000-square-foot wave pool, water slides, a two-person tube slide, a water playground, and other attractions visited by more than 200,000 every year. A good choice for families with smaller children. The Green Extreme, a 65-foot-tall and 1,161-foot-long water "coaster" with lots of twists and turns, is the most popular distraction. For a fast drop, try also Black Falls slide. Master Blaster, a $2-million roller coaster-type water ride, opened in 1998. Picnics are allowed.

Next door to the water park is **Mountasia Family Fun Center,** 8851 Grapevine Hwy.; (817) 788-0990. It has a 36-hole miniature golf course, can-am racers, batting cages, and a 6,000-square-foot game room. Mountasia in Arlington is located at 111 Wet & Wild Way; (817) 460-3600.

Also in this entertainment district are the **Mid-Cities Combat Zone Paintball, Southwest Golf** driving range, and **Northeast Tarrant County Inline Hockey Center** that hosts inline hockey tournaments and public skating.

Down the road, at **Indoor Grand Prix,** (817) 335-3646, you can speed in race cars, at $5 for five minutes, or enjoy the 21st-century combination of tag and hide & seek at the 8,000-square-foot multilevel **Laser Quest,** 7601 Grapevine Hwy.; (817) 281-0360.

Oakwood Cemetery, located at 701 Grand Ave., between North Main and Henderson streets, northwest of downtown and south of the Stockyards district (see entry).

In 1879, **John Peter Smith,** one of Fort Worth's earliest settlers, gave 20 acres to the city for this cemetery, which was later enlarged to 100 acres. It actually consists of Oakwood, Cavalry, and Trinity cemeteries. Some call it "Westmister Abbey of Fort Worth."

Smith is just one notable Fort Worthian whose remains are located here. Others include **Belle Burchill,** the postmistress, appointed in 1881, who started home delivery in Cowtown. Also buried here is **Winfield Scott,** a rancher and oilman who came to Tarrant County in 1868 and built the Plaza Hotel downtown, where La Madeleine French Bakery & Cafe is located today. Then there is **W. T. Waggoner,** another cattleman and oilman and one of the richest Texans of his time.

Another one is **Charles A. Culberson,** who served as governor of Texas from 1895 until 1899 and later also served four terms in the U.S. Senate. Rancher and oilman **Samuel Burk Burnett** was buried here in 1922. Former mayor of Fort Worth and brick mason, **William Bryce,** also rests here. City Marshal **"Longhair" Jim Courtright** and gambler **Luke Short,** who fought it out on a downtown sidewalk on February 8, 1887, supposedly both rest here, according to some (see Jim Courtright-Luke Short Annual Shootout entry in this chapter). **Al Hayne,** a civil engineer from Scotland, who rescued "fainting women and terrified children" from the burning Texas Spring Palace, which in 1890 was jammed with 7,000 people, is also buried here. The remains of World War II hero **Horace Carswell,** after whom a local Air Force Base was named for many years, are also interred at Oakwood.

Among those buried in **Greenwood Cemetery,** located northwest of downtown and southwest of Oakwood Cemetery, across from North Henderson Street, are the publisher and self-proclaimed Fort Worth cowboy, **Amon Carter,** along with his longtime adversary and former Cowtown mayor, **Henry Clay Meacham,** even though Carter later married his second daughter Minnie Meacham Smith. **Marvin Leonard,** the founder of Leonard Brothers Department Store, rests in the family mausoleum here.

The Oil Information Library, basement of Mallick Tower, 1401 West Fifth St. at Summit Ave.; (817) 332-4977. The charge is $50 for one-day visit by nonmember. Membership fee is $110 a year. Located on the northern end of Summit Avenue on the western edge of downtown.

The nonprofit and tax-exempt 2,900-square-foot library contains more than 2.5 million completion cards going back to the 1930s, each card representing one oil well. It also has drilling logs on more than 100,000 projects dating back to 1916. Production and county maps are also available.

The library's main purpose is for small independent producers with limited resources to get information about wells, although the Texas Railroad Commission in Austin also maintains much of this data.

The library is in the process of computerizing its card system, a legacy of Fort Worth oilman Clayton Valder, who died in 1991. The information library began in 1985 with more than 100 members.

Paddock Park & Viaduct, North Main and Bluff streets. Located north of Tarrant County Courthouse (see entry).

This park is named after the Cleveland-born Buckley Boardman Paddock (1844-1922), a newspaperman, civic leader, four-term Fort Worth mayor, and member of the Texas legislature from 1912 to 1913. Paddock joined a Confederate cavalry, married a southern woman after the war, and settled in Mississippi. He came to Cowtown on horseback in 1872 after meeting former Texas governor J. W. Throckmorton, "who suggested Fort Worth as a town of promise," and became editor of the *Fort Worth Democrat*. Although Paddock gave up running the newspaper around 1884, he was a civic booster of Cowtown for almost 40 years, perhaps surpassed in his zeal only by the publisher Amon Carter. It was B. B. Paddock who envisioned a network of rail lines centered in Fort Worth that looked like a tarantula spider. (See Tarantula Train in the Stockyards entry in this chapter.)

Paddock Viaduct nearby, which connects downtown with the North Side, was the first reinforced concrete arch bridge in the nation in which self-supporting steel was used. Engineered in 1914 by Brenneke & Fay of St. Louis and built at a cost of $400,000, the 1,172-foot-long bridge has been designated a Texas Historic Civil Engineering Landmark by the American Society of Civil Engineers. Originally a two-lane wire suspension bridge, it was built here for $10,250 in 1889 and later replaced by an iron bridge. Before that, ferries provided the only regular access across the Trinity River at this point.

In this area, the Eastern Cattle Trail/Chisholm Trail longhorns were driven north of Rusk Street (now Commerce) through downtown Fort Worth "into the bluff and then across the Trinity River to the broad valley below, where they rested before continuing their long drive north," according to a marker near the viaduct. On the viaduct's other side, another marker in Heritage Park identifies the site of Fort Worth's first school established in 1853 by former mayor John Peter Smith, who came from Kentucky.

Pioneer Days, Stockyards Historic District; (817) 625-9839 or 626-7921. Fri-Sun around the Labor Day weekend. Admission CH, children under 12 free. Takes place along Exchange Avenue.

This is just one event celebrating the city's cultural heritage, in addition to a dance festival, parade, rodeo, live country music, and street performers. Attendance reaches up to 200,000. Gunfighting competitions are held Sat noon-3 pm and Sun 1-3 pm. Other events start at 6 pm Friday and conclude at 6 pm on the following Monday.

The West was booming during the decade of the 1880s, America was still young, and the times were rough. Known as the decade of the gunfighters, it was also the time when the Colt .45 cartridge revolver was popular in the taming of Texas. Like the Texans said, "God made some men big and some men small, but Sam Colt [its New Jersey inventor] made them all equal."

Several gunfighting teams, with more than 100 desperadoes in authentic costumes, have kept memories of the times alive for 40 years in Cowtown's Stockyards district, where many a gunfighter passed through in those days. There is also recreation of a Western village with a pioneer camp, barbecue cook-off, and old-fashioned games for children. If you do not have a chance to participate in the Chisholm Trail Roundup (see entry in this chapter), this would be a good choice to acquaint yourself with the life in the West gone-by.

The gunfighters at Pioneer Days, who compete for cash prizes, are judged on originality, plot, dialogue, character portrayal, and overall impression, not who draws the fastest or kills the most bad guys. The costumes, too, are important, for a cowboy of the 1880s did not wear Levi's jeans and pointy-toe cowboy boots, but canvas or wool pants held up by suspenders, and rounded or square-toe boots.

Pioneer's Rest Cemetery, 626 Samuels Ave., one mile northeast of downtown, between Arnold and Heritage Parks, west of Interstate 35 West.

Samuels is one of the oldest Fort Worth streets on which the first civilian trader near the original fort set his establishment. Military regulations forced him to remain some distance from the fort. The cemetery was laid out near a tavern and a crossing point of the Trinity River used by drovers moving herds to the stockyards. During the 1890s, Samuels Avenue was a popular residential street.

The earliest known graves in Fort Worth will be found at this six-acre cemetery, which has more than 1,000 plots. This is the largest burial site of Confederate soldiers in Fort Worth, some 75 in all. At the rear of the cemetery, where a rough granite boulder bears the inscription, is the grave of **Maj. Ripley Arnold,** the founder of the original fort, and two of his children. Also buried here is **Susan Brown,** granddaughter of statesman Daniel Webster, who died in 1864 at the age of 52. **Capt. Ephraim M. Daggett,** sometimes called the Father of Fort Worth, his brother, and his mother are all buried here. You will also find here the grave of **Gen. Edward H. Tarrant,** who was born in South Carolina, came to Texas in 1835, and became a brigadier general in the Texas Militia. He died in Fort Belknap. Tarrant County is named in his honor.

Other lesser notables interred here include among others Sam Houston's friend, Fort Worth merchant and Texas Ranger **Charles Turner,** who fought in the Mexican War. Turner had 150 slaves working his 640-acre farm, which was located where Greenwood Cemetery now stands. **William Thomas Gray,** who operated a water supply company in Fort Worth and had fought with the Confederate general Robert E. Lee, is also buried here, as is **Dr. Carroll Peak,** one of Fort Worth's first physicians. Twenty prostitutes killed in an Indian raid are buried along one wall without a marker.

In 1998, the cemetery was severely damaged by vandals.

Ripley's Believe It or Not/The Palace of Wax, 601 East Safari Pkwy., Grand Prairie; (972) 263-2391. Open daily 10 am-9 pm. CH. Located at Interstate 30 and Belt Line Rd., a ten-minute drive east of Six Flags Over Texas (see entry).

Ripley's, named after the American literary critic and socialist, Robert Ripley (1802-1880), features his collection of oddities from 198 countries that he visited. You can experience an earthquake and find yourself on the ocean floor, you can step into a real Texas twister and see what a 200-mph tornado can do, and you can walk over a bed of fiery coals, if you dare, although the place is air-conditioned.

A new exhibit since 1997 is the Lost Ship Marlborough, the ship that sailed from New Zealand in 1890 and 23 years later was sighted off Cape Horn. When boarded, the entire crew found on board had turned to skeletons. You will see the leaning Tower of Pisa made of matchsticks. Check out the real shrunken human skull. See how African women from Tchad look, after they had their lips pierced in their youth and wooden plates inserted to make them unattractive to raiders from other tribes.

The Palace of Wax displays life-like figures of Jesus Christ, Mother Theresa, former South African president Nelson Mandela, and well-known film actors from Hollywood and even Sleeping Beauty and her Prince.

Sanger Brothers Building, West Fourth, between Houston and Throckmorton streets. Located diagonally across from Bank One Tower and next to the Modern at Sundance Square Annex. The Circle Theatre and Milan Gallery (see individual entries) are also located in this building downtown.

The Fort Worth Convention and Visitors Bureau has its offices on the western side of the building, at 415 Throckmorton St.

The Dallas-based Sanger Brothers department store inaugurated its Fort Worth store in 1918. Alex and Philip Sanger were among the most innovative merchants of the day. In 1925, they erected a new store at 515 Houston Street, not far from the future site of this five-story building, which was founded in mid-1929. The stock market collapse was just a few months away and the Great Depression on the horizon. The architect of this building was Fort Worth designer Wyatt C. Hedrick. Its builders boasted that the lighting was powerful enough to "illuminate the entire town of Weatherford, Texas." Also widely publicized was the store's "manufactured weather," which included not only heating but also being the first air-conditioned building in the city.

The store closed less than a year after opening and the building stood vacant until 1943, when it was rebuilt as the largest United Service Organization (USO) in the country. Three years later, J.C. Penney purchased the structure and moved into it from the store next door, staying here until 1981. Sanger's, later absorbed by Foley's, did not return to Fort Worth until 1977, when it opened a store at Hulen Mall (see entry).

In 1993, the Sanger building became part of the Sundance Square (see entry) development and its upper floors were converted into loft-style apartments.

Sanguinet House, 4729 Collinwood Ave. in Arlington Heights neighborhood. Located east of the cultural district and north of West Freeway, also known as Interstate 30.

Marshall R. Sanguinet (1859-1936) was perhaps the most prolific Fort Worth architect and is particularly well known for his partnership with architect Carl Staats.

Sanguinet built this house for his family around 1894 "from the ruins of his earlier home of the same design, constructed in 1890 but damaged by fire," says historian Carol Roark. This was the first house in the Arlington Heights development, an exclusive Fort Worth suburb that featured its own Lake Como, Ye Arlington Inn, and an electric streetcar line running to downtown. Sanguinet and his original English-born partners, Arthur and Howard Messer, designed most of the twenty homes constructed in this area between 1890 and the financial panic of 1893.

Sanguinet enlarged the house in 1906, when he added a wood-paneled dining room and enlarged the front porch; it initially stood on a lot that covered a full city block. The architect lived here with his wife until his death. She remained in the house until 1948, then moved to Dallas, where she died two years later. The Sanguinet House was listed in the National Register of Historic Places in 1983.

Sinclair Building, 512 Main at West Fifth streets. Located on the edge of Sundance Square and next to Jubilee Theatre. The former Blackstone Hotel, now Courtyard by Marriott is diagonally across the street (see individual entries).

This was one of the last high-rises built in Fort Worth before the onset of the Great Depression. On this site since 1903 stood the Van Zandt Building, which housed his Fort Worth National Bank and was named after the Confederate veteran from east Texas, Maj. Khleber Miller van Zandt (1836-1930), whose family settled in Fort Worth after the Civil War. Oilman Richard Otto Dulaney and his architect Wiley Clarkson scoured many new buildings in major cities in the north before Dulaney decided to build "the most perfect" structure in the Southwest.

Originally named the Dulaney Building, the structure was named after Sinclair Oil Company when the firm leased seven of its 16 floors and moved in in 1932. Completed in 1930, the tower was built of Texas limestone and Minnesota granite. It has lobby entrances on Main and West Fifth streets. The lobby features dark green marble walls and richly ornamented surfaces that were restored in 1990 by architect Ward Bogard. You will not fail to notice the zig-zag motif, Mayan accents, and terra-cotta detailing. The Italian-cuisine Picchi-Pacchi restaurant is located on the ground floor.

For a peek at Dulaney House, an elaborate Mediterranean Revival-style private residence, stop at 1001 Elizabeth Boulevard, in this historic residential district. The oilman made his initial fortune in real estate in Oklahoma, then founded an oil and gas company in 1916. He moved with his wife to Fort Worth three years later and built this opulent residence in 1923. By the time of his death in 1966, the area lost some of its prestige, but the two-story residence was still most impressive. In 1979, the boulevard was listed in the National Register of Historic Places as the city's first residential historic district.

In 1927, Dulaney constructed the Petroleum Building, also known as Rattikin Title Building, at 611 Throckmorton Street, where Gulf Oil Company was a major tenant for more than 20 years. After World War II, Dulaney invested in a Colorado uranium mine speculating that atomic energy might become a major source of power.

Southfork Ranch, 3700 Hogge Rd., Parker; (800) 989-7800 or (972) 442-7800, Internet www.foreverresorts.com. *CH.* Open daily 9 am-4:30 pm. Located northeast of Dallas and bordering on Plano. Go north on North Central Expressway (or U.S. Highway 75) to Exit 30, at Parker Road, then continue east for about 6.5 miles and turn right on FM 2551, Hogge Road.

Depicting an improbable lifestyle, at least for most Dallasites, the television show *Dallas* implied to viewers in 96 countries that the television soap opera *Dallas* was real Dallas. It was not, but it was fun pretending, even if much of the actual filming of the show was done in Hollywood.

The trial run started in 1978 and dealt with two generations of the fictional Ewing family, whose fortunes had been made in the oil business; all of them supposedly lived at this ranch in the fictional Braddock County. By the 1989-90 season, the 13th, no exteriors were filmed in Dallas and the series finished in 43rd place. Actor and Fort Worth native Larry Hagman, portraying J.R., was one of only two continuously serving members left from the original cast.

Once a working ranch, the 41-acre Southfork was built in 1970 by a Dallasite J.R. (no kidding) Duncan. In 1992, it was bought at auction by an Arizona businessman for $2.6 million and extensively renovated to include conference rooms, rodeo arena, Oil Baron's Ballroom, and Miss Ellie's Delicatessen shop. More than 100,000 tourists a year still visit the Ewing family home, supposedly the second-most visited Metroplex sight after the Sixth Floor Museum in Dallas (see entry). Your best bet is to visit the fantasy ranch with a tour operator.

Southwestern Exposition & Livestock Show, Will Rogers Memorial Center, One Amon Carter Square; (817) 877-2400, Tickets 877-2420, Internet www.fwstockshowrodeo.com. *CH.* Grounds are open daily 7 am-midnight for about 17 days from the second half of January through the first week of February. Rodeo is held nightly at 8 pm and some afternoons at 2 pm. Shuttle runs every 20 minutes, from noon to midnight, from the parking lot at Billy Bob's Texas in the

Stockyards (see individual entries) to the Will Rogers Center. Located near the brick-paved Camp Bowie Boulevard, Montgomery Street, University Drive, and West Lancaster Avenue. Amon Carter, the Kimbell, and Modern art museums are all nearby, as is the Fort Worth Museum of Science & History (see individual entries).

If you want to understand the old-fashioned Texas living and enjoy Western-style family entertainment, see the stock show, which has been around for more than a hundred years. Its original intent was to offer a central meeting place where animals could be judged for quality and stockmen could compare breeding practices. Everyone involved agreed on a date in early March of 1896. According to J'Nell Pate in her *North of the River* history of the Stockyards, "Excitement prevailed the day before the show as railroad cars of cattle arrived to be unloaded and cowboys herded others from surrounding pastures into the yard." But as can be expected in Texas during the early spring, a sleet and snowstorm hit the area overnight. "When they [the organizers] got to the stockyards, they found the animals huddled under the trees, their backs covered with icy whiteness." But by later in the morning, the sun shone brightly and the snow and sleet began to melt. Rodeo was added in 1918 and in 1933 was broadcast live on the radio.

Today, nearly every farm animal—from Hereford cows to llamas, from donkeys to pigeons—is displayed, bought, and sold on the 100-acre site that has more than 39 acres under its roof. More than $1 million in premiums and prize money is awarded every year. Well over 21,900 animals were entered in the stock show competition in 2000. During the reign of Amon Carter (1879-1955), the civic booster "purchased the stock show grand champion steer each year, paying up to $6,000 for the prized animal." In 2000, Del Frisco's Double Eagle Steakhouse of Fort Worth (see entry) bought the grand champion steer for a record $104,000, or about $125 a pound of its edible parts. Average stock show attendance is estimated at almost 800,000 annually and, despite the addition of several buildings, the space to exhibit animals is still in short supply. Since 1918 it includes an indoor rodeo show at which hundreds of cowboys and cowgirls compete for $400,000 in rodeo prizes. A 21-year-old college student won the calf-roping championship in 2000 and took home $15,858. There is a two-mile parade through downtown, the midway with 45 rides, a Cowboy Poetry Gathering, and stock show exhibits.

There are 162 boxes in the Coliseum for those privileged to have one at the rodeo and the demand for them is so great that some hopefuls have remained on a waiting list for 25 years. Many of the boxes are still reserved for the same old-guard ranch families that supported the stock show in its early years and were rewarded with box seats when the rodeo was added in 1918. When the show moved from the North Side

Coliseum in the Stockyards to the Will Rogers in 1944—when it was called Southwestern Exposition and Fat Stock Show—the same families were assigned the new boxes, which now cost upward of $1,250 a year.

During the Exposition and Livestock Show, the entire Will Rogers Memorial Center—which in 1917 was part of Camp Bowie military training center—is utilized. It was named after Amon Carter's close friend and the humorist who had perished in an airplane crash over Alaska in August 1935.

But all is not peaches at the show, according to *FW Weekly*, particularly when it comes to rodeo. "Hamstrung by its long-in-the-tooth managers and their old-fashioned ideas and unwillingness to court the big-name sponsors and TV revenues, the Fort Worth Rodeo has become a nice little regional rodeo that's slowly going nowhere." Some cowboys complain that a third generation of general managers, all from the Watts family, "is too much. Of course, they don't want to lose their 50-year-long gravy train, but it's time for them to go." The catering contractor, the rodeo manager, and the midway operator have all been exclusive providers for at least 20 years. That, say detractors, is why the Fort Worth rodeo is ranked eighth nationwide in a city that calls itself Cowtown.

Stockyards Historic District, a 258-acre area around Exchange Ave. and North Main St.; (817) 624-4741. Located two miles north of downtown Fort Worth. There is a regular bus service from Throckmorton St. downtown and back. For events, see the *Stockyard Gazette* or its Internet site www.fwsg.com.

The Stockyards is home to weekly rodeos, Stockyards Museum, Western nightlife, horseback riding, Stockyard Station, and the Livestock Exchange Building (see individual entries in this chapter).

The Stockyards grew as a satellite of the old Fort Worth. In the fall of 1865, Capt. Ephraim M. Daggett drove a herd of cattle to Shreveport, Louisiana, but the longhorns brought only six dollars a head above expenses. The following year, more than 200,000 longhorns were driven northward and the Texas cowboys sold their cattle at a better profit in Abilene, Kansas. Afterwards, the Stockyards became a stop for cowboys driving cattle from south Texas to Kansas along the Eastern Cattle Trail, one of the routes that fed Jesse Chisholm's trail to Abilene, Kansas. Between 1866 and 1890, more than four million head of cattle were driven through Fort Worth.

In 1873 Fort Worth was incorporated as a city and devastated by a financial panic that greatly affected the cattle drives for lack of markets. Three years later, rail lines extended from Fort Worth and included the Fort Worth Stockyards Belt Railway, which moved livestock from the Stockyards area to the Kansas packing plants. Cattle drives

A typical view on Exchange Avenue at North Main Street in the Stockyards historic district. Located two miles north of downtown Fort Worth, the 125-acre yards are home to weekly rodeos and other western-inspired entertainment. Cattle pens once extended for nearly a mile and the area was called the "richest little city in the U.S." (Photo by Yves Gerem)

became a thing of the past. The stockyards were opened for business in the summer of 1889, about the same time that Fort Worth businessmen built a ten-mile electric railway from downtown to the stockyards at the cost of $60,000, the first such street railway in the Southwest. In 1902, Swift & Company and Armour & Company, the country's largest meat packers, built slaughter houses and packing plants in the Stockyards. North Main Street gained in prestige by becoming the only road north of downtown that was paved.

By the end of that same year, the city of North Fort Worth officially became a separate entity and by the following spring grew so rapidly that "the city council had adopted a resolution prohibiting the hitching of horses on Main Street for longer than thirty minutes." It remained an independent municipality for seven years only, although Fort Worth purposely did not annex the industrial area of the stockyards and packing plants outside the city limits, which later became Niles City.

"By 1909, the two companies [Armour and Swift] were processing 1.2 million cattle and 870,000 hogs each year," says Caleb Pirtle in his history of Fort Worth. "And the town's population had jumped from 26,688 to 73,312." Fort Worth ranked as the nation's third largest livestock market, after Chicago and Kansas City.

Cattle pens extended for nearly a mile and property values were so high in the area, which was incorporated in 1911 as Niles City, that it became known as the "richest little city in the U.S.," until annexed by Fort Worth for tax reasons in 1923. Niles City, which originally extended for half a mile around the stockyards, was named for Louville Veranus Niles (1839-1928), a Boston businessman who first visited Fort Worth in 1893. His reorganization of the Fort Worth Packing Company in 1899 led the firms of Swift and Armour to locate here in 1902. The economic impact of these plants was immense and it was just a question of time before Fort Worth found a way to annex the community, which had a taxable property value of $30 million and its own police and fire department, five schools, and three grocery stores.

During World War I, Cowtown's yards became headquarters to the largest horse and mule market in the world, serving foreign governments who bought millions of dollars' worth of cavalry animals here. It was reported in 1999 that a horse museum was planned for in these barns to showcase America's major horse breeds. By World War II, it ranked as the largest sheep market in the world. The livestock industry was the largest single employer in the city until the end of the 1940s, when aircraft manufacturers overtook them.

In the years that followed, other railroads came to Fort Worth, making the cattle drives superfluous; the cattle industry slowed to a crawl and the area deteriorated. Armour closed in 1962, Swift, relying on immigrants getting the minimum wage, lingered on until 1971. The market held its last auction in 1992. Today, the Western atmosphere and architecture have been preserved. About one-eighth of the original stockyards are being restored, just enough for the area to maintain its Western flavor.

In the shops that line brick-paved Exchange Avenue, craftsmen use time-worn tools to hand-craft saddles, chaps, and boots. There are many Western-wear shops here, as are a number of restaurants and saloons, including the legendary White Elephant Saloon (see entry).

The old hog and sheep pens have been restored and now house the 125,000-square-foot **Stockyard Station,** (817) 625-9715, a 125,000-square-foot marketplace and the depot for the **Tarantula Train,** (800) 952-5717 or (817) 625-RAIL, Internet www.tarantulatrain.com. Trains run daily year-round, except Thanksgiving and Christmas, leaving Stockyards Mon-Sat at noon, and Sundays at 3 pm. *CH*.

Named after the myriad rail lines envisioned by the Cowtown publisher and mayor B. B. Paddock, the *Tarantula* makes the daily one-hour or so ten-mile cross-city excursion from Stockyards, at 140 East Exchange Avenue, via the Eighth Avenue train yard. It is pulled by an authentic 1896 Steam Locomotive No. 2248 built by Cooke Locomotive Works of Paterson, New Jersey, and purchased by Tarantula in 1990. When retired from regular service in 1959, it was bought by a private collector, Charles T. Brown. He and Walt Disney planned to build a full-size steam railroad around Griffith Park in Los Angeles. Instead Disney opened Disneyland. In 1974, 2248 was purchased by the Texas State Railroad, but became obsolete after five years and was stored in Rusk, Texas. "Puffy" is the only before-the-turn-of-the-century operational steam engine remaining in Texas. *Tarantula's* four 1925 Victorian coaches, which seat 72 passengers, were purchased from the Strasburg Railroad in Pennsylvania and the windowless touring coaches were built in 1927.

The name Tarantula has nothing to do with spiders; it derives from a railroad map dreamed up by Captain Paddock in 1873 and showing the city as a future railroad hub with tracks radiating out in many directions.

The train runs from the Cotton Belt Depot, at 707 South Main Street in the town of Grapevine, which is located roughly between the Dallas-Fort Worth International Airport (see entry) and the 7,280-acre Grapevine Lake. It goes to the Stockyards station on East Exchange Avenue, Wednesday through Friday, starting at 10 am, Saturdays at 8:30 am, and Sundays at 1 pm. The trains run for 21 miles through Haltom City (once known as Birdville), North Richland Hills (previously called Smithfield), Colleyville, and Southlake, but do not stop until arriving at Grapevine, a town named after the area's mouth-puckering wild grapes. There the engine is turned on a 180-ton 1927 Santa

Fe Railroad turntable, which was originally installed in Brownwood, Texas. If in the mood for shopping, consider taking a shuttle from the Cotton Belt Depot to the Grapevine Mills mega shopping mall (see entry in the SHOPPING chapter).

The **Texas Star Clipper dinner trains** began operating on the Tarantula track early in 2000. They leave the Stockyards station at 7 pm every Tuesday, Wednesday, Thursday, and Saturday, but at 7:30 pm on Fridays, and at 5 pm on Sundays. It takes three hours to make the round trip, long enough for you to have a leisurely meal, a drink or two, and enjoy some entertainment.

The dinner trains run six nights a week, while a five-course meal is being served along with the show. On some nights, you can participate in a "comedy murder mystery," instead of light musical entertainment. When making reservations, you can choose a prime rib, fish, or chicken meal prepared fresh on board. Two waiters, a bartender, and a cocktail waiter are stationed in each dining car. The cost is about $75 per person. A dress code requires "jackets for gentlemen and appropriate attire for ladies."

The dining cars were built in the 1950s, the kitchen car dates back to 1920, and both are pulled by a mid-1950s diesel locomotive. They were all meticulously restored and are operated by Michigan-based Coe Rail, Inc., the company that also runs the *Tarantula*. The cars seat 60-plus passengers, each at tables of four.

The 52-room Stockyards Hotel (see entry), at East Exchange and North Main streets, where infamous bank robbers Bonnie and Clyde once stayed, has been restored to its original 1907 state, its lobby decorated in "Cattle Baron Baroque." Adjoining the hotel are Hunter Brothers' H3 Ranch steakhouse and Booger Red's Saloon, where patrons sit on saddles.

The White Elephant Saloon, where the gun duel between the City Marshal Jim Courtright and Luke Short took place downtown (see Jim Courtright-Luke Short Annual Shootout entry in this chapter) and is still re-enacted here each February 8, is just across the street. The saloon is a backdrop in the *Walker, Texas Ranger* television show.

Billy Bob's Texas (see entry in the NIGHTLIFE chapter), located north of Cowtown Coliseum, is advertised as the world's largest "honkytonk" and features good country-Western music entertainment.

Among restaurants located in the Stockyards, some of which are described in the DINING chapter, you will find the Cattlemen's Steak House, the renowned Joe T. Garcia's, Los Vaqueros, Riscky's Bar-B-Q, Old Spaghetti Warehouse, and Star Cafe. The Swift & Company office building, built on a hill overlooking Exchange Avenue, now houses the Old Spaghetti Warehouse (see entry), decorated with an eclectic assortment of objects.

One hundred years after being established as the stopping point along the legendary Chisholm Trail, the Stockyards is on the National Register of Historic Places.

Sundance Square, Second to Fifth between Throckmorton and Calhoun streets; (817) 390-8711, Internet www.fortworth.com/sundance. Business office at 505 Main St., 5th Floor. Free parking after 5 pm weekdays and all day on weekends and holidays is available in City Center II Tower (see entry) and parking garages on Calhoun between Third and Fourth streets.

Located about two miles south of Stockyards and 1.5 miles east of the cultural district. Convention & Visitors Bureau is at 415 Throckmorton St., (817) 336-8791, Internet www.fortworth.com, in the Sanger Brothers Building (see individual entries).

Sundance Square sits just a couple of blocks south of the bluff above the Trinity River where Fort Worth was established in 1849. Begun in 1982 with a two-block renovation of the turn-of-the-century buildings downtown, the square is now a nationally recognized model for urban revitalization. The billionaire Bass family, the Medicis of Fort Worth, which in 1998 controlled about 40 blocks downtown, has been the main force behind its development. The 14-block Sundance development features a unique architectural blend of historic buildings and modern glass skyscrapers. Its chief architect, David Schwartz of Washington, also designed The Ballpark in nearby Arlington and Bass Performance Hall (see individual entries).

The square is named after the gun-slinging Sundance Kid, a.k.a. Harry Longabaugh, the famed outlaw who once lived in these parts. In 1902, he and his girlfriend Etta Place, and Butch Cassidy (Robert Leroy Parker) left for Argentina and did not return until the Sundance Kid had to bring the ailing Etta to the U.S. to have her appendix removed in Denver. The two men returned to South America after the Sundance Kid shot a policeman in the leg. They died following a train robbery in Bolivia, when a cavalry detachment finally caught up with them. The Sundance Kid bled to death during the night. Cassidy shot himself with his last bullet at dawn.

In addition to the city police, the area is patrolled on bicycles, horseback, and skates by some 115 private security officers, headed by a former Secret Service agent, all of which makes it one of the safest places anywhere.

Sundance Square contains dozens of shops, restaurants, theaters, cinemas, galleries, and entertainment venues to suit most tastes. Among the best-known finds are these.

• **AMC Sundance 11 Theatres,** at 304 Houston St., (817) 336-4262, across the street from the Renaissance Worthington Hotel, opened in 1991 and features 11 cinemas with 1,850 seats in the heart of the Square. **AMC Palace 9 Theatres,** 220 East Third St., (817) 870-1111, around the corner from Barnes & Noble Booksellers, with its stadium-style seating, is a four-level, nine-screen, 1,940-seat cinema. *The Met* alternative weekly in 1998 rated them "clean, classy, with unique design and huge variety of films to choose from." Their sound, says *The Met*, is "sharp, crisp, and loud without being painfully so," while seats are "big, comfy."

Fort Worth has now joined Dallas, Houston, and Austin in staging a film festival. During Fort Worth's first festival, held in 1998, actress Tippi Hedren introduced Alfred Hitchcock's classic *The Birds*.

Actor Gregory Peck was the guest of honor in 1999, when several of his films were shown at these and other Sundance Square locations. The four-day event had movies ranging from low-budget independent films looking for a distributor to classics, such as *To Kill a Mockingbird*. The cofounder of the festival works in the *Star-Telegram's* obituary department. For more details on future festivals, please call (817) 237-1008, e-mail fwff@fortworthfilmfest.com, Internet www.fortworthfilmfest.com.

• **Barnes & Noble Booksellers,** (817) 332-7178, at 401 Commerce St., next to Bass Performance Hall, situated on two levels, stocking 150,000 titles, is the largest and the sole bookstore downtown. Check out the two-story replica of a 20-foot-high bucking bronco done after Frederick Remington. Has a spacious Starbucks coffee shop.

• **Caravan of Dreams,** (817) 877-3000, at 312 Houston and West Third streets, was in 1983 the first live music venue in Sundance Square. You can hear some decent jazz and blues and admire the downtown skyline from its rooftop grotto bar.

• *The Chisholm Trail,* Richard Haas's tromp-l'oeil three-story-tall mural on the southern facade of the 1902 Jett Building, is now a location of the Pangburn's chocolate store at 400 Main St. The mural commemorates a cattle drive on the Chisholm Trail between 1867 and 1875. This was once the main terminal for the Interurban rail line, then a bookstore and a series of restaurants. "Unverified reports say it was the site of a suicide in the 1940's, or perhaps a murder, or even multiple murders," notes the *Fort Worth Star-Telegram*.

• **Classic Carriages,** (817) 336-0400 or 444-1557, at 200 Main St., will take you on a moonlit Sundance tour in an antique, horse-drawn carriage after your dinner at the Renaissance Worthington's Reflections or another restaurant. Rides take place Wed-Sat evenings after 7:30 pm. The charge is $20 for four and $5 each additional person.

• **Etta's Place,** (817) 654-0267, Fax 878-2560, at 200 West Third St., next to Caravan of Dreams club, was the first downtown bed & breakfast and named after the Sundance Kid's girlfriend, whose whereabouts were unknown after she returned from Argentina in 1906, when

Caravan of Dreams entertainment complex (center), with its popular rooftop Grotto Bar, the 12-story Art Deco Sundance West luxury apartment building behind it on the left, and the Renaissance Worthington Hotel on the right, are all part of Sundance Square downtown. (Photo by Yves Gerem)

she had her appendix removed in Denver. Butch Cassidy and the Sundance Kid were killed in Bolivia after her departure.

• **The Flying Saucer Beer Emporium,** (817) 336-PINT, located in a 100-year-old two-story building—supposedly one of the first brick structures in the city—at 111 East Fourth and Commerce streets, is a brewpub boasting German-style food that will make you drink more than one of the 150 varieties of beer available. There are another 17 food and drink establishments on the square, including Angeluna.

• **Jubilee Theatre,** (817) 338-4411, at 506 Main St., whose plays and musicals were originally aimed at African-Americans, but now draw mixed crowds.

• The **Knights of Pythias Castle Hall** was built here in 1881, nine years after this fraternal order was established in Houston. The building, which was designed by Marshall R. Sanguinet, was completed in 1901. Bass Brothers Enterprises acquired it in 1978 and renovated it in 1982 as part of the Sundance Square project. The Haltom's Jewelers' two-and-a-half-ton cast-iron clock stands on the corner.

• The **Bass Performance Hall** opened in 1988, across the street from the Barnes & Noble Booksellers and Angeluna restaurant. The 2,056-seat six-level hall is home to the Fort Worth Symphony, Fort Worth Opera, Fort Worth Ballet, Van Cliburn International Piano Competition, and Casa Manana shows. Two 48-foot-tall trumpet-blowing angels chiseled by the Hungarian-born Marton Varo in Texas limestone and weighing 250,000 pounds each grace its facade.

• **Reata,** (817) 336-1009, located on the 35th floor of Bank One Tower, at 500 Throckmorton St., borders on Sundance Square and serves Southwestern cuisine, which is described in the DINING chapter, along with a spectacular 360-degree view of Cowtown. This was once Fort Worth National Bank, which was established by two Confederate veterans in 1873. It was chartered in the 1880s and is the city's oldest bank.

• **The Sid Richardson Collection of Western Art,** (817) 332-6554, at 309 Main St., displays works of Western artists Frederick Remington and Charles M. Russell. They were collected by Sid Richardson, who made his fortune in oil and was great-uncle to the Bass brothers. The museum is housed in a building that replicates the original 1885 structure.

• The 12-story Art Deco red-brick **Sundance West** building, (817) 339-7777, at 505 Main St., across the street from the Fort Worth Outlet Square, was designed by architect David Schwarz, who also drafted the Bass Performance Hall, and developed by the billionaire Bass family, a few of whose members live here. It contains 59 luxury apartments, beginning on the sixth floor, as well as retail establishments.

• **Western Union Telegraph Co. Building,** at 314-316 Main St., is a 1931 Art Deco-style building designed by James Davis, Sr., that has been converted to retail use.

• The **Renaissance Worthington Hotel,** (817) 870-1000, and its classy, but expensive restaurant Reflections, located at 200 Main and West Second streets, was constructed in 1981 and is described in the LODGING chapter.

Tandy Center, 100 Throckmorton St. Located downtown between West Weatherford and Third streets, on the edge of the rejuvenated Sundance Square. The Center was built on the site of the Leonard Brothers Department Store (see individual entries).

Designed by M. Growald & Associates, the center consists of two 19- and 20-story office towers, constructed in 1976 and 1978, with a mid-section housing an ice rink and the Fort Worth Outlet Square (see entry). The center is the fourth largest office complex in the city. It is the headquarters of Tandy Corporation, a consumer electronics retailer and one of the largest Metroplex companies, with revenues of more than $7 billion and 6,000 local employees. Tandy's Radio Shack, which it acquired in 1963, opened its first store in downtown Boston in 1921. It introduced the first mass-marketed personal computer in 1977.

Adjacent to it is the 270,000-square-foot **Tandy Technology Center,** built in 1990 and home of the company's research and development activities. An amphitheater, with seating for 400, is part of a one-acre park at the Center.

The former Leonard Brothers M & O Subway, now the Tandy Subway, remains a privately-owned mass transit system. It arrives and departs from the lower level, still providing free transportation between the business district and the river-front free parking area.

Tandy Center is named after civic and business leader Charles David Tandy (1918-1978), who with his father started out in the leather business until, in 1963, he went to Boston and purchased a small chain of nine stores called Radio Shack. Fifteen years later the company passed $1 billion in sales and Tandy was earning $800,000 a year. He died of a heart attack when Radio Shack had 7,353 stores; the number has since declined to 6,900. Tandy was once the leader in calculators, personal computers, and cordless and cellular telephones, but lost its lead in all of these fields and is back to square one again, retailing knick-knacks. For more, see Tandy's Internet site www.tandy.com.

Tarrant County Courthouse, 100 East Weatherford and Main streets. Open to the public Mon-Fri 8 am-4:40 pm; for a free tour call (817) 334-1116. Located a block north of the Renaissance Worthington Hotel (see entry), at the head of the nine-block-long Main Street, where the parade grounds of the original fort stood, overlooking the Trinity River Valley.

"When Major Ripley Arnold's scouting party first searched for a military post site 'near the confluence of the Clear and West forks of the Trinity River,' they chose a place on a bend in the river below the

The Tarrant County Courthouse downtown stands near where the original fort was laid out in 1849. Its construction was delayed by the Civil War, then destroyed by fire in 1876. Seventeen years later, a new courthouse was built for $500,000, an expense that so infuriated the voters they threw out every single county commissioner in the next election. (Photo by Yves Gerem)

bluff," says historian Carol Roark. About a month later, they came back
and established the fort on June 6, 1849. But following a late July flood,
they moved it "to the top of the bluff overlooking the Trinity River."

The fort was laid out just northwest of the present courthouse site.
Tarrant County, named after the state legislator, Gen. Edward Tarrant,
was established on December 20, 1849. After the army left the fort in
1853, nearby settlers moved into the army's abandoned buildings. It
can be said that Fort Worth began on the bluffs and the county government has been headquartered there for more than 135 years, according to Roark in her 1995 *Fort Worth's Legendary Landmarks*.

When Fort Worth became the county seat in 1860, construction of
the permanent courthouse began. The two-story stone building was
completed after the Civil War and served until it was destroyed by fire
on March 29, 1876. The stones from the burned courthouse were used
in construction of a new building, which was again overcrowded by the
early 1890s.

In 1893, the county commissioners funded a new courthouse, which
was constructed below the $500,000 allocation. But, according to his-
torian Roark, the Tarrant County citizens were shocked by the building's cost and were themselves struggling to overcome the current
economic depression. At the next election they firmly voiced their dis-
approval by replacing all of the county commissioners.

Designed by the Kansas City firm of Gunn and Curtis, the red-gran-
ite courthouse is patterned after the Texas State Capitol in Austin. Its
tower includes a 103-year-old Seth Thomas clock, which until 1944
was driven by a weight and pendulum. About that time other major
changes took place inside and out; elevators, steam heating, and air
conditioning were added. During the 1950s, a 1,250-pound electrified
metal American flag was placed atop the dome.

In 1958, the Tarrant County Civil Courts Building was constructed
on the west side of the courthouse as drafted by the Fort Worth designer Wyatt Hedrick. It was not originally designed to be part of the
Courthouse complex. "This building owes its current appearance to a
1988 project to create a trompe-l'oeil facade to match the 1893-1895
courthouse," says Roark. "Muralist Richard Haas designed the illusion-
istic facade" in 1988.

Although it was occasionally singled out for demolition, the courthouse instead underwent a $3-million restoration in 1983 by architect
Ward Bogard. Authors of the official visitor's guide to Fort Worth call
it, with a straight face, "one of the most magnificent county buildings
in America."

Texas & Pacific Terminal/Renaissance Plaza, 1600 Throckmorton
St., at West Lancaster Ave. and Main St. Located on the southern edge
of the central business district, south of Interstate 30 and the Fort

Worth Water Gardens, between the U.S. Post Office and Alfred Hayne Memorial (see individual entries).

Texas & Pacific railroad was extended to Fort Worth in 1876. In 1929, John L. Lancaster (for whom Lancaster Avenue is named), president of the Texas & Pacific Railway, and Fort Worth mayor William Bryce (see Bryce Building in this chapter) announced a huge project to build a passenger terminal and a freight warehouse. The Texas & Pacific committed $13 million and the city $3 million.

Designed by Wyatt C. Hedrick (1888-1964) in the Art Deco style, the 13-story brick office building and passenger station were built of granite. The passenger terminal opened in 1931, was largely finished by 1933, although the construction nearby continued until 1937. The terminal served four railroad lines: Texas & Pacific, Fort Worth & Denver City, International-Great Northern, and the Missouri-Kansas-Texas. The warehouse, also dating from 1931, is an eight-story building, located one block west of the terminal.

The terminal operated until March 22, 1967, when the last train, the Texas & Pacific Eagle, pulled into the station from El Paso. Ten years later, both the terminal and warehouse building were sold and stood vacant for twelve years. The passenger terminal was resurrected as an office building in 1978 and served as the regional office for the Housing and Urban Development agency until 1999, when it moved to the 40-story Burnett Plaza (see entry) downtown.

That year, a $1.4-million facelift took place in the 60-by-90-foot lobby. "This is the Sistine Chapel ceiling of Fort Worth," said the chief restoration architect.

The building is being considered for retail and residential development after Interstate 30 is reconfigured and moved farther south. The commuter rail service from Dallas will reach Cowtown on the Trinity Railway Express in 2001. The terminal will then be the westernmost stop in Fort Worth. A transit center is under construction at Ninth and Jones streets.

Thistle Hill Mansion/Wharton-Scott House, 1509 Pennsylvania Ave. at Eighth Ave.; (817) 336-1212, Open Mon-Fri 11 am-2 pm, Sun 1-3 pm. Weekday group tours can be booked at 10 am and 2 pm. CH. Located in the hospital district of southwest Fort Worth, across Interstate 30 (also known as West Freeway) from the cultural district, northwest of here.

"No home in Fort Worth evokes the city's 'Cowtown' heritage as does Thistle Hill," writes historian Carol Roark in her book *Fort Worth's Legendary Landmarks*. "Although the house was constructed in 1903, just after the Armour and Swift meat-packing plants opened, its legacy is rooted in the cattle drives that followed the Civil War and in the subsequent establishment of the state's large cattle ranches."

Thistle Hill Mansion in the hospital district of southwest Fort Worth was constructed in 1903 by the wealthy cattleman W. T. Waggoner as a honeymoon cottage for his only daughter Electra when she married a Philadelphia socialite. Electra was the first customer at Neiman Marcus to spend $20,000 in a single day.
(Photo by Yves Gerem)

Legend has it that the wealthy cattleman William Thomas Waggoner (1852-1934), "Pappy" to his friends, had this mansion built as a "honeymoon cottage" for his only daughter Electra Waggoner Wharton (1882-1924) when she married a Philadelphia socialite, Albert Buckman Wharton, who had captured her heart in the mountains of Nepal, in 1903. A. B. Wharton owned Fort Worth's first car dealership.

Electra's clothes were ordered from Paris; she was believed never to have worn the same dress twice. "She owned hundreds of pairs of shoes, and she was the first customer at Neiman Marcus to spend more than $20,000 in one day," says author Laura Trim. She came back the following day and spent another $20,000, for a total of close to $200,000 in today's dollars. As an example of excesses, see the inkstand in the parlor with Electra's bridal portrait; the Venetian lace veil that she wore cost $1,000 at a time when a good man's suit could be had for $25 and an average Texas schoolteacher's salary was $320 a year.

The prolific Fort Worth architectural firm Sanguinet and Staats designed the 18-room, 11,000-square-foot, three-story red-brick Colonial Revival-style house, which stands southwest of downtown.

The Whartons lived here from 1904 to 1910, when Waggoner gave his daughter large parcels of land, cattle, and horses. After "the Princess of the Panhandle" and her husband moved to their new ranch near Vernon, Texas, Thistle Hill was purchased, in 1911, by cattleman and hotel builder Winfield Scott for $90,000. The Whartons divorced in 1921 and Electra died four years later from cirrhosis of the liver. Scott owned Fort Worth real estate and made money in ranching. He once owned the White Elephant Saloon, later transplanted to the Stockyards (see individual entries). Thistle Hill underwent substantial remodeling, coordinated by the original architects, and acquired more of a Georgian Revival style. The wooden columns at the entrance were replaced by massive limestone columns and the balustrade gave way to a balcony above it. "You'll marvel at the rich, highly polished oak flooring and walls," promises *Texas Highways* magazine. Although Scott died before the house was completed, his wife and her son lived here until 1938. The son squandered most of the family fortune and by 1940 sold the house to the Girls Service League, an organization that provided housing for young women working in bomber factories during World War II. It served neglected teens in the fifties and delinquent teenagers in the sixties. By 1968, the mansion had fallen into disrepair, but was saved by preservation efforts. It was listed in the National Register of Historic Places two years later.

While here, check out also the Mitchell-Schooner Home designed by the same architectural firm for jeweler Mitchell and built in 1907.

U.S. Courthouse, 501 West Tenth at Lamar streets. Located across the street from St. Andrew's Episcopal Church and facing the Burnett

Park (see individual entries) with the four Matisse's reliefs, titled *Backs*.

The U.S. Courthouse and the U.S. Post Office (see below) are two large federal projects from the early 1930s that benefited Fort Worth. The combined post office and courthouse dated from 1892-1896 was overcrowded and led to badly needed Depression-era federal jobs. The reputable Philadelphian Paul Philippe Cret, who had also created a master plan for the University of Texas in 1930, was the courthouse architect, along with the local draftsman Wiley G. Clarkson. The $1.2-million, five-story building was constructed in 1933. It is a "sophisticated Classical Moderne building which combines elements of the classical Beaux Arts and Moderne form with elaborate details drawn from Classical, Native American, and Moderne sources," says historian Carol Roark. A reconstruction took place in 1992-1993, when suspended ceiling panels were removed in the lobby and corridor of the first floor.

The fourth-floor court of appeals courtroom features two murals painted by Frank Mechau and are the sole examples of Depression-era public art in the city.

U.S. Post Office, 251 West Lancaster Ave. at Jennings St. Located next to Texas & Pacific Terminal and southwest from the Fort Worth Water Gardens (see individual entries). Still functioning as a post office and open the regular business hours.

Postal service was established in Fort Worth in 1856, when settler Julian Feild was named the first postmaster. Service was not always regular, however, and frequently it was necessary to send a rider to Dallas to pick up the mail. In 1896, a federal building and post office was constructed on Jennings Avenue at Eleventh Street, but was overwhelmed by a growing demand for a larger postal facility. The central offices, designed by Wyatt C. Hedrick, opened here in 1933 and were located near the Texas & Pacific Terminal because most incoming and outgoing mail was handled by railroads that used the station.

Constructed of Cordova limestone quarried near Austin, it draws inspiration from Beaux Arts design and occupies a full city block. The front facade features a colonnade of 16 classical columns with capitals featuring Texas longhorns and Herefords. The marble-lined lobby, which stretches the length of the building and features recessed ceiling panels, is perhaps the most arresting interior. The facility served as the main processing center until 1986. The building was listed in the National Register of Historic Places in 1985.

Van Zandt Cottage, 2900 Crestline Rd. Located on the north side of what was called the Old Weatherford Road, which served as a cattle trail and stage road, the cottage stands on the western edge of Trinity Park. This was an early home of the van Zandts before they built their mansion overlooking the Trinity River on Penn Street, surely the most impressive residential street of the old.

This is believed to be the only cabin still standing on its original site. The cabin's construction date is not known and early ownership of the property unclear because the Tarrant County Courthouse (see entry) burned in 1876 and deed records were destroyed.

Maj. Khleber Miller van Zandt (1836-1930) bought the property around 1871, about six years after his family settled in Fort Worth. He was the son of Isaac van Zandt (1813-1847), a minister from the Republic of Texas who negotiated the annexation of Texas by the Union and died of yellow fever while campaigning for governor. Although a lawyer by training, the younger van Zandt preferred banking, merchandising, and the cattle business. He was a founder of the Fort Worth National Bank and its president for 46 years. No one seems to know whether the major ever lived in the cabin, although speculation has it he did between 1871 and 1878. By the 1880s, the van Zandts were living at the corner of Penn and Seventh streets, roughly between today's central business and cultural districts.

The van Zandt Land Cattle Company still owned the site in the early 1930s. When plans for the celebration of the 1936 Texas Centennial Fair were made, the organizers of the Fort Worth Frontier Centennial allocated $2,000 for the restoration of the cottage, so that it could be opened to the public in conjunction with the Centennial celebration, says historian Carol Roark. What was before 1936 a deteriorated two-room, dogtrot cabin with an open, roofed passageway between the rooms was renovated under the direction of architect Joseph R. Pelich. Windows were replaced by larger ones, shutters were added, and a large porch on the north side of the house was enclosed to form a small room, a dining room, and a kitchen. Although the cottage does not look as it did during the nineteenth century, says Roark, Pelich's alterations are significant as an early attempt to preserve Fort Worth's frontier heritage.

The drag stone in the yard of the log house was dug from the courthouse bluff by a German who arrived in the U.S. in time to fight in the Mexican War, from 1846 to 1848, with Maj. Ripley Arnold. He was with Major Arnold when Fort Worth was founded, but was killed in the Civil War. He pulled the stone by oxen to smooth rutted roads and knock down high grass so surveyors could mark boundaries.

A few blocks away, at 4926 Crestline Road, you can see the King-McFadden-Dupree House, a mansion built on a bluff overlooking the West Fork of the Trinity River that was owned by candy manufacturer John P. King (1861-1946). His Candy Store and Tearoom, located during the 1920s on Houston Street downtown, was popular with shoppers.

Veterans Memorial Park, 4100 Camp Bowie Blvd. at Crestline Rd.
Headquarters of the 36th Division, U.S. Army, from 1917 to 1919,
Camp Bowie was established to train National Guard units from Texas
and Oklahoma for service in World War I. It was named for James
Bowie (1796-1836), a colonel in Texas army killed at the Alamo and
credited with invention of the bowie knife.

"When the first units arrived at the camp, it was open prairie, still
used for grazing, and soldiers slept in knee-deep Johnson grass," writes
historian Ruby Schmidt, adding that some 25,000 men were shipped to
France from the camp in July 1918. The camp reverted to civilian use
by mid-1920.

The roadway running through the camp, now called Camp Bowie
Boulevard, was originally known as Arlington Heights Boulevard.
Camp Bowie Boulevard was paved with Thurber bricks in the late
1920s. When the city wanted to repave the road and cover the bricks
in the 1980s, the opposition was so strong the idea was abandoned.

Barvo Walker's larger than life-size 1987 bronze, titled *Duty,* is on
display here.

W.T. Waggoner Building, 810 Houston at West Eighth streets.
Located across the street from the Peters Brothers Hats (see entry under
900 block of Houston St.) and across the street from General Worth
Square (see entry).

Designed by Sanguinet and Staats, this 20-story high-rise was built
in 1920, after oil was discovered on Waggoner's DDD Ranches. The
owner of the U-shaped, steel-framed brick tower, built at a cost of $1.5
million, boasted in a promotional brochure that "no feature of the
building has been stinted" and "no money has been wasted in useless
ornamentation." For a year or so it was the tallest building in Fort
Worth. The first-floor bank lobby had marble paneling and vaulted
ceilings. Refrigerated water from its own artesian well was also available. From 1920 to 1957, the building was home of the Continental
National Bank. The Waggoner family owned the structure until 1962.
Twenty-two years later it was completely refurbished.

William Thomas "Pappy" Waggoner (1852-1934) was born on the
family stock farm in Hopkins County, Texas. His mother died a year
after his birth and the child lived with Waggoner's sister. By 1869, Tom
became his father's partner in the cattle business and the following year
the Waggoners drove a herd of cattle to Abilene, Kansas, and netted an
astounding $55,000, the foundation of the Waggoner fortune. In 1877,
Tom married Ella Halsell, a younger sister of his stepmother.

By 1900, Tom was so wealthy, he was able to give each of his children 90,000 acres of land and 10,000 head of cattle. Eleven years later,
he drilled water wells on his cattle ranch near Electra—located at U.S.
Hwy. 477, 15 miles northwest of Wichita Falls—and struck oil.

"Damn the oil, I want water. Cows can't drink this stuff," was his reported reaction, but being a shrewd businessman he did not mind amassing a fortune from it over the years in cooperation with Texaco. His descendants today continue to manage the W.T. Waggoner Estate, the largest single ranch inside one fence in Texas, where 520,000 acres of ranch, farm, and oil properties are managed out of Vernon. The property runs 30 miles east and west and 25 miles north and south. Waggoner moved to Cowtown in 1904. He played host to Teddy Roosevelt the following year and took him on a wolf hunt on his ranch in Oklahoma.

Waggoner is also known for his one-and-a-quarter-mile Arlington Downs Racetrack with 6,000-seat grandstands that he built at a cost of $3 million in 1929, when pari-mutuel betting was still illegal. It was located on 400 acres of his 3,300-acre Thoroughbred horse farm, across from today's Six Flags Over Texas (see entry) theme park. The 1933 Texas pari-mutuel racing bill passed the legislature largely through his efforts. During its first year, the profits averaged $113,000 a day. He suffered a paralyzing stroke in 1933 and died the following year. The state legislature reversed itself in 1937 and repealed the pari-mutuel laws. Waggoner is buried near the grave of his longtime friend, Samuel Burk Burnett.

His favorite story takes place at the Decatur train station, where he once talked with his friends. When a salesman got off a train, he said he would pay $1 to the person carrying his suitcase to the nearby hotel. Waggoner picked up the salesman's case. As they were passing the mansion on the hill, the salesman asked who lived there. Waggoner said he did.

"How can you afford to live in a house like that?" asked the man.

"I carry my own suitcases," replied Waggoner.

To many in Fort Worth, Waggoner is also known as the builder of the 11,000-square-foot mansion Thistle Hill (see entry) for his daughter. His granddaughter, Electra Waggoner Biggs (b. 1914) still lives on the ranch in Vernon. She sculpted the Will Rogers' statue at Will Rogers Memorial Coliseum (see Art in Public Places in the VISUAL ARTS chapter). In 1959, Buick Motors named the Electra luxury model after her.

Tom's father, Daniel (1828-1903), was born in Lincoln County, Tennessee, and moved to Texas about 1848. In 1859, the 31-year-old Daniel married the 16-year-old Sicily Ann Halsell and in 1883 built a $50,000 Victorian mansion on a rocky hill overlooking Decatur.

Will Rogers Memorial Center, 3300 West Lancaster Ave.; (817) 871-8150, Internet www.fortworth.com/willrog.htm. Located at Camp Bowie Blvd., Montgomery St., University Dr., and West Lancaster Ave. Amon Carter Museum and Kimbell Art Museum are north of here, Fort Worth Museum of Science & History and Modern Art Museum (see individual entries) west of the complex. A $2.2 million Visitors Center and ticket office opened at the north entrance of the complex, near West Lancaster, in 1998.

The memorial center has 134,000 square feet of space and is the second largest meeting facility in Tarrant County, after the Fort Worth Convention Center (see entry).

The coliseum, designed by engineer Herbert M. Hinckley, was supposedly the world's first domed structure with a steel-framed roof that allowed for unobstructed views because it had no visible supports. It seats 5,900 and is home of the Southwestern Exposition and Livestock Show (see entry) rodeos.

Initially, the assistance requested from the federal government toward its construction was denied. It was authorized when Fort Worth publisher Amon Carter appealed directly to Pres. Franklin Delano Roosevelt. The center was built in 1936 as a federal Public Works Administration project and supplemented by a local bond issue and private donations.

It includes the 2,856-seat **Will Rogers Auditorium,** and the **Pioneer Tower,** a soaring brick-and-stone column with an octagonal aluminum crown. The facility was named after Amon Carter's friend Will Rogers, a cowpoke and grassroots philosopher who perished in a 1935 airplane crash. Of all Carter's celebrity friends, only Will Rogers had his complete admiration and love, says Carter's biographer Jerry Flemmons.

William Penn Adair Rogers was born on a ranch near Claremore, Oklahoma, in 1879. He ran away from home at an early age and worked as a ranch hand in the Texas Panhandle. Once he accompanied a shipload of cattle to Argentina, worked on a freighter going to South Africa, then joined a circus where he performed rope tricks. He went on to star in the Ziegfield Follies, then movies, and wrote several books. Rogers first came to Cowtown in 1913, but met Carter in 1922. By the time of his death, Rogers was an American institution. "The death of Will Rogers was a national tragedy," notes Flemmons. "All America mourned, and afterwards there was a clamor for suitable memorials to America's most beloved man." The center was named after him and Rogers' bust sits on a pedestal in the Pioneer Tower's rotunda.

Wyatt C. Hedrick was the center's chief architect and it cost almost $1 million. The *Fort Worth Star-Telegram* publisher petitioned Roosevelt after it became obvious that Dallas—not Houston or San Antonio, which had historic ties to the 1836 revolution—was to be the locale for the 1936 Texas Centennial Fair (see the Fair Park listing in this chapter). By the time the buildings were completed, the Centennial celebration was officially over.

In 1984, the 100,000-square-foot **Amon G. Carter Exhibits Hall** opened in the 85-acre memorial center to host consumer shows and conventions. Three years later, the $16-million, 215,000-square-foot **Will Rogers Equestrian Center** opened. The $11-million **Moncrief Building,** which includes a 1,000-seat arena and meeting rooms, opened in 1996; the 170,000-square-foot structure includes a 1,000-seat arena and space for 260 horses.

Also part of the memorial center are the 197,000-square-foot **Burnett Building,** the 215,000-square-foot **Richardson-Bass Building,** and livestock barns covering twenty acres in nine connected buildings that were constructed between 1935 and 1955.

Five people died—two were blown from their cars into the nearby Trinity River—and more than 100 were injured when separate tornadoes struck downtown Fort Worth and Arlington at 6:15 on the evening of March 28, 2000, just days before this guide went to print. Fort Worth's streets were littered with broken glass, debris, damaged cars, and downed trees when the twisters cut through the Cowtown with winds of up to 157 miles per hour. At least 100 homes were destroyed and more than 200 severely damaged in Fort Worth, and about half as many were destroyed and damaged in Arlington. Scores were left homeless and 30,000 remained without power. Within hours, more than 2,100 calls were made to 911 emergency lines. Damage was estimated at up to $500 million. Several large downtown skyrises, such as the Bank One Building (see entry), had thousands of large-pane windows blown out—at least half of the 5,200 14-foot-tall by 5-foot-wide glass panes on the Bank One Building alone—and it was estimated that it would take up to six months to replace them all. Reata restaurant (see entry), atop the 35-story Bank One tower, sustained $300,000 in damage and had furniture blown to the streets below. Fort Worth's museum district was barely touched. All affected businesses, particularly in Sundance Square, planned to reopen within weeks, or earlier. Gov. George W. Bush declared the affected Tarrant County a disaster area.

VISUAL ARTS

According to the *Forbes* list of the 400 wealthiest Americans, there are seven Dallas families or individuals worth at least $475 million each, which is the magazine's cutoff for tracking such riches. New York City has 38 and Fort Worth nine. Probably only the Internal Revenue Service keeps score on the countless other multimillionaires in Fort Worth. Excluding a handful, such as the Kimbells and the Basses, there are not many that have made a major contribution to the Fort Worth cultural pool. One cannot help but speculate on the riches of Fort Worth if they contributed according to their ability.

"Fort Worth has the museums but not the galleries; it has the artist support (in spirit, anyway) but few showcases for those artists," noted the *Dallas Observer* in 1998. "Dallas has the galleries but not the museums, and little incentive for artists to stick around."

But for its size there is still plenty to see in Cowtown, even if the galleries sometimes exhibit cheesy art that would not have a chance elsewhere.

MAJOR FORT WORTH MUSEUMS

The history of art in Fort Worth is not dissimilar from that of many other southwestern American cities. Fort Worth residents were often preoccupied with more immediate concerns about their survival than having time to worry about artistic inclinations of the few among them. Artistic expression was usually limited to portraits of the well-to-do who could pay for them. Texas' struggle for independence was another favorite subject.

Please note that practically all museums are closed on holidays, such as the Fourth of July, Thanksgiving, Christmas, and New Year's.

Amon Carter Museum, 3501 Camp Bowie Blvd.; (817) 738-1933. *NCH.* Open Tue-Sat 10 am-5 pm, Sun noon-5 pm, closed Mondays and holidays. Tours of the collection are given at 2 pm daily. Wheelchair-accessible from Lancaster Avenue. Located about 1.5 miles west of downtown in the city's cultural district.

The Amon Carter Museum opened in 1961 to house the collection of 200 paintings by Frederic Remington and Charles M. Russell, 60 of Russell's and 14 of Remington's bronzes—admired by Fort Worth publisher Amon Carter (1879-1955), who was introduced to Russell by his friend Will Rogers, born in the same year.

"The cowboy began assembling his artwork before Amon could afford such effete foolishness," writes Carter's biographer Jerry Flemmons. "In 1928, New York art dealer Bertram Newhouse showed the publisher six watercolors and an oil by Russell." These paintings reminded Carter of the West as he'd always imagined it; he immediately "signed a $7,500 note" and paid for "his new treasures in two yearly installments." After that he continued to obtain Russell's work, and paid $5,000 for his first Remington oil in 1935. In 1952, Carter purchased the entire Russell collection housed in the Old Mint Saloon of Great Falls, Montana, according to *Time* magazine.

You will not find Remington's or Russell's name in Janson's 850-page *History of Art,* but the artists have a huge following in the southwest. Remington (1861-1909) was a painter and sculptor of the American West, but born in Catskills, New York, the son of a cavalry colonel and Civil War commander. His artistic career lasted less than twenty years. He traveled widely in the western U.S., while working as a cowboy, and in 1898 was a correspondent in Cuba during the Spanish-American war. A docent at the Amon Carter museum called Remington "a male chauvinist and a racist" in an interview in the *Fort Worth Star-Telegram.* He went on to say that Remington didn't portray the Indian very well in his paintings and didn't seem to know the West as well as Russell did—but he did think that Remington's bronzes are wonderful.

Russell (1865-1926) was a painter of Western scenes of cowboy and Indian life, who was born in St. Louis, Missouri. "Unlike Remington, who I don't think ever did a painting of a woman, Russell painted a lot of scenes with women, and in a kind way," noted the same docent, adding about *The Swimming Hole,* an 1885 oil of a group of nude boys, by Thomas Eakins, on display at the Carter, "I'm so impressed that the women of the Fort Worth Art Association, back in the '20's had the audacity to acquire such a painting." The Eakins was bought from the Modern Art Museum of Fort Worth (see entry).

Since its founding, the Carter has broadened the scope of the original collection with works of 19th- and early 20th-century American art and artists like William Merritt Chase, Stuart Davis, Charles Demuth, Winslow Homer, Thomas Hovenden, and Georgia O'Keeffe. It now "houses more than 358,000 objects—including paintings, drawings, watercolors, prints, sculptures, and photographs" and welcomes 100,000 visitors a year. Carter stipulated in his will that no admission ever be charged to the museum.

Amon Carter, later known "as the most devoted, determined and downright fanatical promoter Fort Worth could have," was born in a log cabin in Wise County in 1879, a failed blacksmith's son. His mother—who had lived at La Reunion, an experimental French commune near Dallas—died when he was 13 years old. Carter left his home at the age of eleven to live with an aunt and worked at a variety of odd jobs before moving to Cowtown. His first job was as a "handyman, chambermaid, and janitor" in a boarding house in Bowie for $1.50 a week. "He sold chicken sandwiches to passengers traveling on the Fort Worth & Denver City Railroad, which had no dining car," says historian Leonard Sanders. He sold peaches, assisted a doctor, and resold empty whiskey bottles. Still later, he worked as a salesman for a portrait firm; the portraits were given free, but "the price of the frame more than offset the cost of the free portrait."

He came to Fort Worth in 1905 from San Francisco and became advertising manager of the *Fort Worth Star*. The *Star* published its first issue on February 1, 1906, when Fort Worth numbered about 40,000 and there were "more outdoor privies than indoor bathrooms." Carter and his partners subsequently bought the paper and merged it with the *Fort Worth Telegram* two years later. By 1919, the daily had the largest circulation in Texas, a position it did not relinquish until the 1950s. He became president of the *Star-Telegram* in 1925. An unapologetic booster of Fort Worth, it is said that when Carter attended a luncheon in Dallas, he carried his own sack lunch and a thermos bottle of Fort Worth drinking water. He is also credited with coining the phrase that you can see to this day under the masthead of his former daily—"Where the West Begins." Even Pres. Franklin Roosevelt used it in his speeches.

But Carter's health began to deteriorate in the early 1950s, when he suffered a series of debilitating heart attacks, notes Fort Worth historian Bill Fairley. In June 1955, his family and his close friend Sid Richardson were summoned to his bedside to discuss his plans for the museum. "Carter lingered, in and out of consciousness, for four days after that bedside meeting and died June 23," says Fairley. Did he die with his boots on? No. Amon didn't care for boots because "they hurt his feet. He preferred the $150 slippers handcrafted for him by a New York shoemaker," writes Flemmons.

A year after his death, Carter's net worth was estimated at

$10,252,294.51. The estate's balance of $7,285,990.22 was given to the Amon Carter Foundation, which he and his wife Nenetta endowed in 1945.

His son, 2nd Lt. Amon G. Carter Jr., served in the 91st Armored Field Battalion in central Tunisia, where Allied forces were encircling Rommel in 1943. Lt. Carter and his sergeant were sent on a reconnaissance mission and, after hiking across the desert for ten days, hiding in caves and ravines, until February 24, when they were confronted, beaten, stripped, and robbed by some 30 bedouins, spat upon by women, and sold to a passing German patrol, according to Fairley. Amon was first taken to Tunis, from there to Italy, and shipped by a cattle car to Poland. Carter was notified by the military in March that his son was presumed missing in action, then received a note from his son, almost two months later, telling him he was interned in Poland. His father Amon then wired President Roosevelt and requested of his friend that the Allies not bomb the Polish camp, according to Fairley.

In May, the publisher reached the camp near Szubin, southwest of today's Gdansk, but his son was taken by the retreating Germans to the Luckenwalde camp near Berlin, which was liberated by the Russians on April 22. Painfully thin due to near-starvation, his son had also sustained extreme frostbite on his feet from a forced march from Poland to the Luckenwalde camp. Seeing that his son was safe and going home, his father followed two weeks later.

In New York, he telephoned his secretary to tell her to send a thousand dollars to every church in Fort Worth. When she paused and asked about "the colored churches," he retorted, "They pray, don't they?" After she said she thought they did, he instructed her to go ahead and send the money.

Carter Jr. succeeded his father at the *Star-Telegram* in 1955. He revisited Szubin the following year. Upon his death from a heart attack in 1982, at age 62, while driving on a Dallas freeway, the two Polish families that assisted him in 1943 were rewarded with "substantial sums of money," according to Fairley.

In 1936, Carter Sr. was instrumental in organizing Fort Worth's Frontier Centennial Exposition (see Fair Park entry in the SIGHTS chapter), which unsuccessfully competed with the Dallas fair and in the process only deepened the mistrust between the two cities. While Dallas, Houston, and San Antonio submitted bids for their cities to host the Texas Centennial and celebrate Texas independence from Mexico, Fort Worth "quietly withdrew from the competition," but later changed its mind. "This celebration would have nothing to do with patriotism and Texas' century of progress," wrote author Kenneth Ragsdale in his 1987 history of the Centennial, continuing, "The Fort Worth business community for whom Carter spoke was creating an entertainment package for one purpose only—to switch the nation's economic spotlight to Fort Worth, and Dallas be damned." While Amon Carter may not have created the rivalry between Dallas and Fort Worth, he definitely added great fuel to the fire.

He hired the New York showman Billy Rose at an unheard of $1,000 a day for 100 days to put on an extravaganza that focused on a slogan, "For education go to Dallas, for entertainment, come to Fort Worth." More than 6.3 million paid to see the Dallas exposition, but only 986,000 to see the circus in Fort Worth. But it was a jolly good show and "Carter loved crowds like a pickpocket."

The following year, Carter struck oil and sold his holdings in the pool to Shell Oil Company for $16.5 million, until then the largest oil transaction in Texas.

Carter identified with the American West so it was only natural that he should turn to painters like Remington and Russell. "Blatantly non-intellectual, he rarely attended theater or ballet or opera and, said daughter Ruth, 'if he ever set foot in a museum, I don't know about it.' But he became Fort Worth's largest contributor to the arts merely because he thought them necessary for his town's completeness," writes journalist Jerry Flemmons. *Time* magazine noted that Carter did not read a dozen books in his lifetime. He established a foundation and left instructions in his will that a museum to house his collection be established by the foundation, leaving details to his children.

Carter, who died six years before the museum opened, only stipulated that it be located on a hill with a view of downtown Fort Worth—and a pleasing view it is. He is buried in the Greenwood Cemetery, northwest of downtown Fort Worth. Philip Johnson (b. 1906) was commissioned as its architect and since the museum's 1961 opening has had two additions, in 1964 and 1977, when it expanded by some 50,000 square feet. "It was the beginning of my classical period," the architect told the *Dallas Morning News*. "I was getting tired of Mies van der Rohe and the Bauhaus and wanted to try something different." The building is constructed of Texas shell limestone and faces a terraced plaza in which Henry Moore's (1898-1986) three-piece bronze abstraction *Upright Motives* (1955-56) has been installed.

The collection of 350 paintings includes early landscapes from the Hudson River School, luminist paintings, trompe l'oeil still lifes, and examples of early 20th-century modernism. Two galleries are devoted to the work of Remington and Russell. Complementing their paintings is a collection of more than one hundred sculptures by these two artists. Also included here is work by artists, such as Kiev-born Aleksandr Arkhipenko (1887-1964), a major sculptor and painter in the development of Cubist sculpture in Paris.

The more than 500 watercolors in the collection span American art history from early Western artists to early abstract watercolors by Georgia O'Keeffe, and drawings by Winslow Homer. The museum also has a collection of 5,000 prints, including those of Currier and Ives. Other well-known artists on display are Mary Cassatt and Edward Hopper. In 1997, the museum acquired the 1925 painting titled *White Birch*, by the modernist O'Keeffe, to bring the total of her works to a dozen. That same year, the Basses, the city's billionaire family, made possible the museum's acquisition of Stuart Davis's 1939 abstraction, *Bass Rocks No. 2*, which is valued at $2.5 million, and complements the artist's four other paintings on display. The museum also holds a collection of more than 350,000 photographs and many other pieces, most of which are rarely shown.

In 1998, Amon Carter's daughter, Ruth Carter Stevenson—variously described as "extraordinarily thoughtful," "impatient," "a very complex woman"—announced plans for most of the museum to be replaced by a three-story triangle extension. It was to be clad in brown Arabian granite. It was to triple the current exhibition space to showcase its collection of American art. Only the original 1961 memorial to Carter, with its plaza and view of downtown, is to remain and be devoted to Carter's original collection of Remingtons and Russells. The new $26-million building—about 107,000 square feet, with 27,000 square feet of gallery space—was also designed by Philip Johnson. It is to include some 5,330 square feet for special exhibitions, such as works on paper and photography. Completion is scheduled for 2003.

Carter Downtown, 500 Commerce St., (817) 738-1938. Open Tue-Wed 10:30 am-5 pm, Sun noon-5 pm.

To make up for the closure of the main museum in mid-1999, Carter Downtown opened in 1999 across the street from the Bass Performance Hall and next door to Grape Escape wine bar, located in the former Southwestern Bell retail store. Carter Downtown measures only 2,700 square feet.

While the main museum is closed, you can also surf the website www.museumshop.com and buy replicas of Amon Carter's family china, in addition to the more traditional prints and mugs.

Kimbell Art Museum, 3333 Camp Bowie Blvd. at West Lancaster Ave.; (817) 332-8451, Internet www.kimbellart.org. Open Tue-Thu & Sat 10 am-5 pm, Fri noon-8 pm, Sun noon-5 pm. Wheelchair-accessible. Exhibition tour of loan exhibits Tue-Fri & Sun at 2 pm, Introductory walks through permanent collection Sun at 3 pm. Kimbell Buffet is open Tue-Thu & Sat 11:30 am-2 pm, Fri noon-2 pm and 5:30-7:30 pm, Sun noon-2 pm. Patio smoking only.

Since its opening in 1972, the Kimbell has won acclaim for its classic modern building designed by the American architect Louis I. Kahn

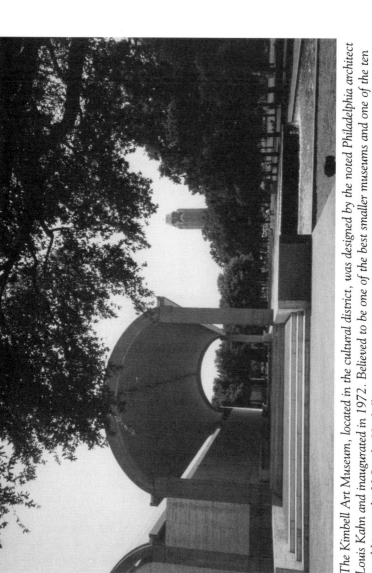

The Kimbell Art Museum, located in the cultural district, was designed by the noted Philadelphia architect Louis Kahn and inaugurated in 1972. Believed to be one of the best smaller museums and one of the ten wealthiest in the U.S., the Kimbell possesses an eclectic selection of some of the finest artworks. Shown at right is Will Rogers Tower. (Photo by Yves Gerem)

(1901-1974) from Philadelphia. As the last building completed under the architect's personal supervision, the museum is perhaps his finest creation. In the galleries, Kahn's innovative use of natural light and subtle articulation of space and materials enhance the art experience. It is regarded as an outstanding modern art gallery. Almost 600,000 visit it every year.

The Kimbell Art Foundation was established by Kay Kimbell—a successful entrepreneur in the grain business, retailing, real estate, and petroleum—and his wife Velma Fuller Kimbell in the 1930s, shortly after they purchased their first paintings.

Throughout the following decades the Kimbells continued to collect artworks and when Kimbell died in 1964, he bequeathed his art collection and entire personal fortune to the foundation to establish and maintain a public art museum in Fort Worth. He attached no conditions on the use or retention of his collection. By 1966, the foundation board of directors had appointed its first director and adopted the policy to "form collections of the highest aesthetic quality in any medium or style."

When in 1966 the museum considered acquisition of Picasso's 1911 cubist painting, *Man with a Pipe*, Mrs. Kimbell set the tone by declaring, "Mr. Kimbell wouldn't have liked it or understood it, but if you believe we should have it, then we should have it."

Its founding director, Richard Brown, paid $205,800 for Frans Hals' *Portrait of a Man*. "It did not worry Brown that the painting was first purchased by a Russian cabaret pianist at a county fair for $7. He had been prepared to spend over $400,000 if necessary to acquire the painting," writes historian Caleb Pirtle, adding the Kimbell also snatched Paul Cezanne's late 19th-century *Peasant in a Blue Smock* from one of Paris's biggest art dealers by bidding $3.9 million for the painting.

The Kimbell's holdings range in period from antiquity to the 20th-century. Here are a few examples of the museum's chronological acquisitions between 1965 and 1995:

Francisco de Goya's *Matador Pedro Romero*, painted 1795-98; Aristide Maillol's *L'Air*, 1938; Edgar Degas' *Dancer Stretching*, 1882-85; Claude Monet's *Pointe de la Heve*, 1865; Canaletto's *Venice*, 1735; Camille Pissarro's *Near Sydenham Hill*, 1871; Peter Paul Rubens' *The Duke of Buckingham*, 1625; Rembrandt's *Portrait of a Young Jew*, 1663; El Greco's *Portrait of an Ecclesiastic*, 1610-14; Edouard Manet's *Georges Clemenceau*, 1879-80; Paul Cezanne's *Maison Maria with a View of Chateau Noir*, 1895-98; Piet Mondrian's *Composition No. 7*, 1914; Nicolas Poussin's *Venus and Adonis*, 1628-29; Fernand Leger's *The Red Wheel*, 1920; Eugene Delacroix's *Selim and Zuleika*, 1857; Titian's *Madonna and Child*, 1530s; Caravaggio's *The Cardsharps*, 1594-95;

Georges Braque's *Girl with a Cross*, 1911; Henri Matisse's *L'Asie*, 1946; and Joan Miro's *Constellation*, created in 1941. The Kimbell also owns four other Picassos.

"Mind you, this isn't New York City's Frick Collection; you can't really get a sense of the continuity of artistic schools or traditions, a shortfall that makes it hard to comprehend, say, how Carvaggio's style presented a radical departure from a hundred mannerist painters of the day," noted the *Dallas Observer* in 1998, when reviewing a Renoir retrospective that was supposedly pandering to the masses and the weekly noted that the Kimbell does not even own a Renoir. "The Kimbell is a collection of masterpieces, not an encyclopedic art historical survey," writes a *Dallas Morning News* art critic.

The museum is believed to be one among the ten wealthiest in the U.S. It is the only institution in the Southwest with a substantial collection of Asian arts, and has also assembled small but select groups of Mesoamerican and African pieces, as well as Mediterranean antiquities. Going to the Kimbell's website, you will see many of these works in brilliant color and good detail; from there you can also explore museums worldwide, be it the Louvre or Moscow's Pushkin Museum.

In 1998, Edmund P. "Ted" Pillsbury, its director since 1980, stunned the art world by resigning his Kimbell post. An Italian Renaissance scholar and former curator of European art at Yale University's Art Gallery, he was perhaps the highest-paid museum director in the world, at about $450,000 a year. During his 17-year tenure in Fort Worth and having millions to spend, Pillsbury acquired for the Kimbell masterpieces by Caravaggio, Cezanne, Gaugin, La Tour, Manet, Matisse, Miro, Mondrian, Picasso, Titian, and Velazquez.

Before the year-end, the Kimbell appointed Sydney native, Dr. Timothy F. Potts, as his successor. Dr. Potts, 42 years old in 2000, had been since 1995, director of the state-owned 140-year-old National Gallery of Victoria in Melbourne—with 70,000 objects Australia's largest public art collection. He taught ancient art at Oxford University in London, did research for the British Academy and the Louvre in Paris, and led archeological excavations in Greece, Jordan, and Iraq. Reflecting on his life in Fort Worth, he told the *Fort Worth Star-Telegram:* "The hardest thing about coming here has been getting a strong cup of coffee that isn't a gallon."

On the grounds surrounding the Kimbell, you will find these sculptures:

• ***Running Flower*** (*La Fleur Qui Marche*), created in 1952 by the French painter Fernand Leger (1887-1975), who was influenced by Cezanne and industrial technology, and who also executed murals for the U.N. building the same year as this ceramic sculpture.

• *Figure in a Shelter,* a 1983 large bronze by the British sculptor Henry Moore (1898-1986), who also has his work on exhibit at Amon Carter Museum (see entry) nearby, as well as at the Southern Methodist University in University Park and in front of the Dallas City Hall downtown.

• *Constellation (for Louis Kahn),* consisting of four carved stones realized by Isamu Noguchi (1904-1989) in 1980. The sculptor created set designs for dancer Martha Graham for decades. Noguchi's three-piece granite ensemble could also be seen in front of the NationsBank, now Bank of America, at 500 West Seventh Street and Lamar downtown, as well as in the Meadows Sculpture Garden at the Southern Methodist University in Dallas.

• *Woman Addressing the Public,* a large bronze by Spaniard Joan Miro (1893-1983) was installed in 1997.

In 1996, the Kimbell purchased a rare Nigerian terra-cotta sculpture of a male figure (195 B.C. to A.D. 200) from the Nok culture that is a thousand years older than any of its other African objects and valued at more than $125,000. The following year, the museum acquired A *Franciscan Friar,* a rare painting created in the early 1540s by the Venetian Renaissance master Jacopo Basano, valued at more than $2 million.

In 1999, the Kimball offered a British earl $24 million for Botticelli's *Virgin Adoring the Christ Child,* one of the great images of the Renaissance artist, which was subject to strict British export laws. Much to the Kimball's disappointment, the National Gallery of Scotland pre-empted the Fort Worth museum bid and Botticelli went to Edinburgh instead.

"We were impressed with the individual quiche, the chicken quesadillas, and especially a magnificent wedge of vegetable torta, with layers of poblanos, squash, eggplant and cheese topped with blue-cheese sauce," noted the *Texas Monthly* restaurant reviewer about the Kimbell Buffet.

Modern Art Museum of Fort Worth, 1309 Montgomery St. at Camp Bowie Blvd.; (817) 738-9215, Internet www.mamfw.org. *NCH.* Open Tue-Fri 10 am-5 pm, Sat 11 am-5 pm, Sun noon-5 pm. Closed Mondays and holidays. Wheelchair-accessible. Located north of Interstate 30 and west of University Drive, in the cultural district, less than two miles west of downtown. Kimbell Art Museum is northeast of here, the Fort Worth Museum of Science & History (see individual listings) south.

The Modern at Sundance Square Annex, 410 Houston St.; (817) 335-9215. *NCH.* Open Mon-Wed 11 am-6 pm, Thu-Sat 11 am-8 pm, Sun 1-5 pm. Wheelchair-accessible. It has a gift shop almost as large as the gallery, selling pottery, jewelry, clocks, glassware, books, T-shirts, and toys. Located in the Sanger Building in Sundance Square (see individual entries) downtown in a building constructed in 1929 that once housed the first department store to be air-conditioned west of the Mississippi.

The Modern is believed to be the oldest art museum in Texas, although it adopted its present name in 1987. It was chartered in 1892, when Texas was only 42 years old and electricity had only been available in Cowtown for seven years. It is the achievement of twenty dedicated women, who were determined to bring learning and culture to what was then a rough and tumble town. It focuses on modern and contemporary American and European art, including paintings, sculpture, and works on paper.

With a $50,000 donation from the philanthropist Andrew Carnegie and $150,000 in other donations, a new library building with a gallery opened at Ninth and Throckmorton streets downtown in 1901, when the city had grown to 26,000 inhabitants. Three years later the museum acquired George Inness's *Approaching Storm* as the first artwork for its permanent collection. It took until 1940 before the first full-time employee was hired.

Six years later the citizens of Fort Worth approved a $500,000 bond issue for the construction of the city's first building exclusively for the museum at its current site.

During the 1960s, the permanent collection of the museum added Vassily Kandinsky's *Above and Left* and Picasso's *Reclining Woman Reading, Suite Vollard,* and *Head of a Woman.* Since then the Modern has also acquired 21 works by Jackson Pollock and 13 by Milton Avery, as well as those by Mark Rothko, Robert Rauschenberg, Claes Oldenburg, Roy Lichtenstein, and Andy Warhol. In 1998, it added to its permanent collection the work of Dennis Blagg, Anselm Kiefer, Tatsuo Miyajima, and Warhol.

The Modern's director E. A. Carmean was asked to resign in early 1991 because he "plunged the museum into scandal when he engineered the sale of its most revered painting, *The Swimming Hole* by Thomas Eakins, which eventually was purchased by the Amon Carter Museum," says the *Fort Worth Star-Telegram.*

In 1995, the museum opened its annex in Sundance Square downtown.

On view on the grounds outside the museum are these sculptures:

• **Hina,** a life-size bronze abstraction of a horse by Deborah Butterfield (b. 1949).

• **Ball Contact,** a 1990 steel abstraction by Tony Cragg (b. 1949).

• The 1987 **Sculpture for Derry Walls** by the British artist Anthony Gormley (b. 1950), who came to Fort Worth to supervise its installation.

• **Texas Shield,** a 1986 work by Rockport, Texas, native Jesus Bautista Moroles (b. 1950), "who has his granite monoliths in collections in Italy and Japan and just about everywhere in the United States," according to the *Fort Worth Star-Telegram*. The daily in 1998 labeled Moroles one of the "top five overhyped artists" in Texas. Declaring that his works have "become the Holiday Inns of stone sculpture," the daily opines that "this innovative sculptor has been on autopilot for way too long."

• **Chance Meeting,** a life-size bronze group by American George Segal (b. 1924).

In 1997, the Modern invited six well-known architects to submit proposals for a new $50-million building for the museum, which is to occupy an 11-acre site adjacent to the Kimbell Art Museum and made possible by a grant from the Burnett Foundation. It is bounded by the brick-paved Camp Bowie Boulevard, as well as University Drive and Darnell and Arch Adams streets.

The design of the Osaka-based Japanese modernist architect Tadao Ando was selected after six months of frenetic activity, although his design was refined to withstand extremes of Texas weather. "Its serene yet audacious poetry captivated members of the Modern's building committee," says the *Fort Worth Star-Telegram*. A former Pritzker-award winner, Ando donated the $100,000 award to victims of the 1995 earthquake that struck Kobe, Japan, where the self-taught architect designed 35 buildings.

The new Modern is to consist of five concrete-and-glass pavilions containing galleries, offices, and public spaces, and will be surrounded by a shallow reflecting pool and trees. The pavilions are to contain 150,000 square feet of space, about 50,000 of it for the galleries, as opposed to the current 15,000 square feet. The ground level will contain an auditorium and a cafe, the second floor will be devoted to the permanent collection. The northeast corner of the site is to be screened out by trees. The new Modern is expected to open in the year 2002.

The 55-year-old Ando—who refers to himself as a builder rather than an architect—has no formal architectural training and has learned his craft from the carpenters in his native Osaka. He said he never apprenticed to another architect because every time he tried he was fired for his stubbornness.

OTHER MUSEUMS

The Cattleman's Museum, 1301 West Seventh St.; (817) 332-7064. Open Mon-Fri 8:30 am-4:30 pm. *NCH*. Located north of Lancaster Ave., between Summit Ave. and Henderson St.

You will relive the time of cattle drives, of longhorns and cowboys in this museum maintained by the nonprofit Texas and Southwestern Cattle Raisers Association, which is also headquartered here. TSCRA was formed in 1877 in Graham, Texas, to "bring to justice cattle rustlers who were taking advantage of the wide open range." The story of the cattle and ranching industry is told through life-size cattle, films, artifacts, and interactive exhibits. Youngsters will enjoy the "talking longhorn" in the entrance of the museum's diorama.

In the **Branding Iron Room,** you will see the branding irons of Stephen F. Austin (1793-1836), a colonizer and secretary of state of the Republic of Texas, of Pres. Lyndon B. Johnson, of film star John Wayne, and of baseball player Nolan Ryan. In the **Brand Inspectors Hall,** you will learn how these lawmen fought against cattle thieves for more than 100 years. The **Memorial Hall** honors cattlemen and women who were responsible for the development of the cattle industry, Samuel Burk Burnett, Charles Goodnight, and Cornelia Adair being just three among them.

For details about Jim Reno's *Brand Inspector,* located in front of the building, please see the Art in Public Places section.

Leonards Museum, Fort Worth Outlet Square Mall, Tandy Center, Third and Throckmorton streets; Open Mon-Fri 10 am-noon and 1-5 pm. *NCH.* Located in Sundance Square downtown, on the lower level of the mall, near the ice rink, and across the street from the Renaissance Worthington Hotel (see individual entries).

Leonard Brothers Department Store (see entry) was a downtown institution for nearly fifty years in the area where the museum now stands until it was closed in 1967. The museum is a labor of love by the daughter of Marvin Leonard, who with his brother Obadiah founded a giant department store that at one time encompassed six and a half city blocks. Leonards was for many years Fort Worth's largest store, occupying more than half a million square feet and catering to people who came from hundreds of miles away. It had a grocery, bakery, creamery, clothing and appliance shops, and automobile service.

The store presented each newcomer to Fort Worth with a Welcome Box that included a pound of coffee, a loaf of bread, an egg separator, and a map of the city. The Newborn Welcome Box included a rattle and other baby necessities.

Among its many items, the museum displays a Leonards bicycle, a Leonards refrigerator, its Velvet Cut Lawn mover, a Leonards sewing machine, and a 1936 model Leonards All-Steel Speeder, a child's wagon that sold for $2.29. Also on display are photos, posters, billboards, and magazine and newspaper clippings. Leonards spent more than a million dollars on newspaper advertising in 1957 alone.

In the 1930s, according to the founder's daughter, the Leonards even printed their own money. The store cashed checks when the banks could not and checkholders were given cash and Leonards' money.

Obie Leonard, like his brother a native of Linden, northeast Texas, also built the nation's first private subway, which still serves the Tandy Center (see entry).

National Western Heritage Center, Crestline Rd. and Gendy St. To be located in the cultural district, about 1.5 miles west of downtown, across from the Fort Worth Museum of Science & History, also near the Kimbell, Modern, and Amon Carter Museums (see individual entries).

The National Western Heritage Center is planned for on publicly-owned land in the cultural district in the year 2000. The $30-million center, to be located on the 1.5 acres of land, has been drafted by the noted architect David Schwartz who has also designed the Texas Rangers Ballpark in Arlington and Bass Performance Hall on Sundance Square (see individual entries).

Two among its tenants will be the Texas and Southwestern Cattle Raisers Foundation, (817) 332-7064, now located at 1301 West Seventh Street, and the National Cowgirl Museum and Hall of Fame, (817) 336-4475, whose temporary headquarters in 1999 were located at 111 West Fourth and Houston streets, next to Burk Burnett Building (see entry) downtown. Cowgirl Museum's hours are Mon-Sat 10 am-6 pm, Sun noon-5 pm. It includes cowgirl-inspired gifts, such as T-shirts, books, and the like.

One 20,000-square-foot building will house the cattle raisers foundation and the Cattleman's Museum (see above).

The second building, which will measure about 28,000 square feet, will house the National Cowgirl Museum and Hall of Fame and its collection of show saddles, Western wear, scrapbooks, and rare photographs. This is the only museum in the world dedicated to honoring the women of the American West.

The cowgirl museum, which was founded in 1975, moved from Hereford, Texas, to Fort Worth in 1993 because of its increasing popularity. But until exhibit space is finished in the year 2000, displays of the group's Western collection are limited to trade shows, rodeos, and its headquarters. Much of the group's collection is in storage at the Milan Gallery on Houston Street until the opening of the Heritage Center. The cowgirl museum will have five permanent galleries that will highlight ranchers, trailblazers, writers and artists, entertainers, and rodeo champions.

Sid Richardson Collection of Western Art, 309 Main at East Third St.; (817) 332-6554, Internet www.txcc.net/~sidr. *NCH.* Open Tue-Wed 10 am-5 pm, Thu-Fri 10 am-8 pm, Sat 11 am-8 pm, Sun 1-5 pm, closed Mondays and major holidays. Located near the 1901 Knights of

Pythias Castle Hall in the historic Sundance Square (see individual entries), an area of restored turn-of-the-century buildings downtown.

Sid Williams Richardson (1891-1959), great-uncle to the Fort Worth billionaire Bass brothers, made his fortune in oil and was an avid collector of Western art. While playing poker in Wichita Falls in 1919, Richardson was told by his boyhood friend Clint Murchison about a secret well that was to be tested that night. The two men raced to the site and arrived at the well by 3 am. The drilling crew believed they were owners and they all brought the well in. Richardson—"a natural trader with nerves of a riverboat gambler"—and his friend raced back and by nine o'clock the next morning bought up $75,000 worth of acreage surrounding the well, then sold off five percent of it for $200,000. Within a couple of years, the two men had earned $2 million each. Richardson, a "taciturn and unassuming" man, went broke as fast as he got rich. When the price of oil dropped to a dollar a barrel, he was wiped out. Eight years later, he hit a producing well in the vast Keystone oilfield in west Texas and rolled in money all over again. He is said to have drilled 385 wells, only 17 of which came up dry. Richardson was on a first-name basis with Franklin Roosevelt and Dwight Eisenhower and, together with Amon Carter "was pressuring Dwight Eisenhower to run for president."

In 1935, Richardson made Perry Bass, who was at the time a sophomore at Yale, his business partner in his oil enterprise, according to the *Fort Worth Star-Telegram*. "It was payback for a $40 loan from Perry Bass' mother after Richardson went broke at the start of the Depression." In 1956, Richardson gave Perry Bass the company. Richardson died in 1959 and "left an estimated $2.8 million to each of Perry Bass' four sons—Lee Marshall, Robert Muse, Edward Perry and Sid Richardson, then ages 3 to 17." Richardson's remaining wealth went into the Sid Richardson Foundation, which funds education, health, human services, and the artistic endeavors in Texas. *Fortune* magazine called him the wealthiest man in America the year before his death.

On display here is a permanent collection of 55 paintings of Western art by Frederick Remington and Charles M. Russell, which were acquired by Richardson from 1942 until his death in 1959. The museum, which replicates the original 1885 structure, was opened in 1982 by the Bass family.

Between the Sid Richardson Collection and Knights of Pythias Castle Hall stands, at 311 East Main, the two-story Domino Building, which was built in 1885 and reconstructed in 1981. It was originally known as Buck's Domino Parlor gambling house, which had the reputation as the Casino of the Wild West, where fortunes were won and lost. Butch Cassidy, the Sundance Kid, and gambler Luke Short frequented this area in the late 1880s.

Stockyards Museum, 131 East Exchange Avenue; (817) 625-5087. *NCH*. Open Mon-Sat 10 am-5 pm. Located in the Livestock Exchange Building in the Stockyards district, two miles north of downtown.

The Livestock Exchange Building, which was erected at the same time as the Armour and Swift packing plants that brought prosperity to northern Fort Worth, was for many years the center of stockyards business operations. All animals sold in the yards were processed through this exchange. Livestock pens stretched for acres around the Mission Revival-style building, when it opened in 1903. By the mid-1970s, both packing plants were closed, but the building was to be renovated. In 1994, it was purchased by an entrepreneur as part of his plan to redevelop the Stockyards as an entertainment district.

More than 100,000 visit it each year. The museum gives visitors a peek into an era "when man's word was his bond and a handshake was his contract." It displays photographs, documents, and artifacts from the 1920s and 1930s.

FORT WORTH ART GALLERIES

Fort Worth is not London, Paris, or Vienna when it comes to art galleries. You do not come here to admire Picassos, although you will find several, and Henry Moores are scattered all over the Metroplex. But you will always bump into some good regional art, particularly depictions of the West.

You will get a good overview of what the Fort Worth galleries offer during the **Gallery Night,** held annually in mid-September, when more that two dozen houses display a variety of art for sale in a relaxed atmosphere and available well into the night. "One night each year the seemingly subterranean art world surfaces to reveal its growing population to local citizens, some of whom wouldn't know an artist if they struck one with their car," says *FW Weekly*. "For a town deeply committed to bovine traditions, Gallery Night is a slice of SoHo."

Edith Baker, owner of the respected **Edith Baker Gallery** in Dallas, was quoted in a local weekly saying that "Texas has more artists per capita than any other state, yet they must leave the state to make a name for themselves." Adds the *Fort Worth Star-Telegram*: "More artists live in Texas than in any state except New York and California."

Be aware that a surprisingly large number of Fort Worth establishments that call themselves galleries are in reality antique, home furnishings, or gift shops.

Janis Bryant Art Centre, 4319-A Camp Bowie Blvd. at Ashland Ave.; (817) 737-6368. Open Mon-Sat 11 am-4 pm. Located in southwest Fort Worth, a block from Isabella's Italian Bistro (see entry).

Oil and watercolor paintings from emerging Metroplex and Texas artists are available and priced $250-$900.

The Contemporary Art Center, Gainsco Bldg., 500 Commerce and West Fourth streets; (817) 877-5550. Open Wed-Thu 11 am-6 pm, Fri-Sat 11 am-8 pm, Sun noon-5 pm.

Until 1920, when destroyed by fire, this was the site of the Mansion Hotel and in 1924 the original three-story concrete garage that served the nearby Blackstone Hotel (see entry). In 1990 the building was reconstructed to become the headquarters of Gainsco Insurance Company. The art center, designed by architect Norman Ward, is located on the ground floor.

CAC, a gallery and museum, was started by 65 local artists, each of whom contributed $100 in seed money, while "Fort Worth's museum directors and other arts community leaders were named to the advisory board. Since its auspicious opening in 1996, the Center has become known more for in-fighting, quarrelsome egos, and a serious lack of leadership than for nurturing local talent," says *The Met*, a Dallas weekly. The center sells a variety of products, from beaded jewelry to glass and ceramic wares.

William Campbell Contemporary Art Gallery, 4935 Byers Ave.; (817) 737-9566, Fax 737-9571. Open Tue-Fri 10 am-5 pm, Sat 10 am-4 pm. Located in west Fort Worth, one block west of Camp Bowie Blvd.

"The classiest sometimes-close-to-the-cutting-edge gallery," according to one *Fort Worth Star-Telegram* critic. Open in 1974 under another name, this is Fort Worth's oldest continuously operated art gallery, now located in a converted duplex. It is run by Campbell, who has a fine arts degree in sculpture, "a Bubba in Geoffrey Beene suits," in the *Star-Telegram's* words, and his wife Pam, a former Neiman Marcus fashion merchandiser, both "consummate professionals." The daily's art critic writes that "Among Fort Worth dealers, their gallery is more contemporary than Evelyn Siegel Gallery, rarely as aggressive as Gallery 414, not quite as adventuresome as Handley-Hicks Gallery and not as commercial as Milan Gallery." It focuses on paintings, sculpture, graphics, and ceramics by contemporary artists; "most of what we show is made in Texas."

Artists: Fort Worthian Anitra Blayton, Christopher Brown, Stephen Daly, Billy Hassell, Fort Worthian Val Hunnicut, Jun Kaneko, Texan Patrick Kelly, Julie Larazus, Jesus Bautista Moroles, Scottie Parsons, Richard Thompson, Cecil Touchon, Karl Umlauf, and Bob Wade.

The Edmund Craig Gallery, 3550-C Seventh at Montgomery St.; (817) 732-6663. Open Tue-Fri 10 am-5 pm, Sat 11 am-3 pm. Located west of downtown, a couple of blocks north of the Amon Carter Museum; Michael's contemporary ranch-cuisine restaurant is two blocks east of here (see individual entries).

Presents a diverse selection of Texas artists, offering oil paintings, acrylic, pastel, and watercolor works, also bronze sculptures. Prices range $300-$10,000.

There are several other galleries in the vicinity, including Carol Henderson/Artenergies, at 3409 West Seventh, and Strings, next to it, which is primarily a home furnishings store.

Dow Art Galleries, 3330 Camp Bowie Blvd. at Arch Adams; (817) 332-3437. Open Mon-Fri 9 am-5 pm, Sat 9 am-noon. Located across the street from the Kimbell Art Museum (see entry).

Specializes in art and frame restoration, as well as appraisals. Sells primarily traditional art, mostly oil paintings, priced from $200 "to several thousand dollars." Percy Dow moved to Fort Worth in 1918 after a drought made cattle ranching impossible and took over a frame shop in 1935, when the store was netting about $15 a week. Publisher Amon Carter, whose museum is nearby, was a major client.

Dutch Phillips & Co., 4125 Modlin Ave. at Washington Terrace; (817) 732-3067. Open by appointment only. The owner of this gallery and its former Dallas location, established in 1976, now conducts business from his home, not far from the cultural district.

Aside from some pre-Colombian and African art, American paintings and sculpture since 1940 are also available. **Artists:** David Barbero, James Blake, Bill Bomar, Veronica Helfensteller, Sharon Kopriva, Gene Owens, Dickson Reeder, Juergen Strunck, Bror Utter, Byrd Williams, Charlie Williams.

The Edge of Glass, 4911 Camp Bowie Blvd. at Penticost St.; (817) 731-8388. Open Mon-Fri 10 am-6 pm, Sat. 11 am-5 pm. Located southwest of the cultural district and downtown, a couple of blocks south of William Campbell Contemporary Art Gallery (see listing). Marty's Gallery, mostly a frame shop, is a block away; it usually displays a couple of local artists whose works sell for up to $1,000.

Hand-blown cold-glass artworks—including vases, beads, and lamps—by north Texas artists.

Fort Worth International Center, 711 Houston at West Seventh St.; (817) 212-2666. Open Mon-Fri 8:30-5 pm. Located downtown, roughly between Sundance Square and Fort Worth Convention Center (see individual entries).

The center facilitates contact between Fort Worth and international companies and organizations. There is a domestic or international artist on exhibit here for a couple of months at a time and most of the works are usually for sale.

Gallery 414, 414 Templeton Dr.; (817) 336-6595 or 926-4111. Open Sat-Sun noon-5 pm and by appointment; closed part of summer. Located in west Fort Worth, a block east of University Drive and northeast of the cultural district.

"Consistently showing work of high quality by emerging local artists, Gallery 414 is the only gallery of its type in the city and one space that is truly local-artist friendly," says *FW Weekly*, adding that the gallery has no operating budget. Artists exhibiting here are responsible for creating and mailing their own invitations. Established in 1995, the gallery takes no commission on works sold; the exhibiting artists make all sales. "Cool gallery where you can actually afford the art," says the *Fort Worth Star-Telegram*. A Dallas alternative weekly calls it "Fort Worth's hippest, noncommercial gallery." In 1998, the gallery exhibited 12 works entitled *Muffler Man*, collected from local muffler shops.

Galerie Kornye West, 4000 Camp Bowie Blvd. at Clover Ln.; (817) 763-5227. Open Mon-Sat 10 am-5 pm. Located three blocks from the Kimbell and Amon Carter museums (see individual entries).

Features mostly American traditional art—oil on canvas and oil on wood panel from national and Texas artists whose work is priced at $225-$25,000. Also has access to antiques from its Dallas location.

On the next block, at 3923 Camp Bowie, is located Pease-Cobb Gallery, (817) 763-5108. Three blocks in the opposite direction and on the other side of Clover Ln., at 4319-A Camp Bowie, is Janis Bryan Art Centre (see listing).

Handley-Hicks Gallery, 6515 East Lancaster Ave. at East Loop 820; (817) 446-5004. Open Tue-Sat 10 am-4 pm. A 700-square-foot gallery located in the historic Handley section of southeast Fort Worth.

Established in 1993, Handley-Hicks showcases several contemporary Metroplex and Texas artists working in various media, including oil, acrylic, ceramics, and photography. Prices range $200-$7,000.

Carol Henderson Gallery/Artenergies, 3409 West Seventh and Montgomery streets; (817) 737-9910. Open Mon-Sat 10 am-5:30 pm. Located in the cultural district one block from the Kimbell Art Museum (see entry).

Established in 1989, Carol Henderson moved "into new digs on artsy Seventh Street" in 1998. Focuses on emerging Fort Worth artists and sells everything from oils to watercolors to acrylic. Representational to abstract painting in oil, watercolors and acrylic, as well as sculpture, glass, and pottery are featured. Prices range from $30 prints to $5,600 oils on canvas. **Artists:** Alvis Ballew, Michael Bane, Ann Ekstrom, Teri Goldstein, Cindi Holt, Sue Kemp, Wayne McKinzie, Doris Miller, and Hungarian-born Marton Varo, who created the Bass Performance Hall angels (see entry).

There are several other galleries in the vicinity, including Henson-McAlister, in the next block, which is a picture-framing business, but also exhibits a couple of artists at a time.

Kabin Fever, 3408 Camp Bowie Blvd.; (817) 338-1912. Open Tue-Sat 9:30 am-6 pm. Located west of downtown and across the street from the Kimbell Art Museum (see entry). There are several other galleries in the vicinity.

Oils, pastels, watercolors of wildlife, outdoor scenes, and big game are priced $200-$5,500, sculptures $200-$300.

Thomas Kinkade Gallery, 302 Main St. on Sundance Square downtown; (817) 335-2060, Internet www.kinkadeart.com. Open Tue-Thu 11 am-6 pm, Fri-Sat 11 am-9 pm, Sun 1-5 pm. It is located in the Weber Building, which was constructed in 1885, remodeled in 1915, and restored in 1981, was among the first structures rehabilitated in the Sundance Square development.

Syrupy art for the masses and, according to a visitor's guide, "Features the works of Thomas Kinkade, the most published artist in the U.S. and the living master of Luminism, a studio technique that causes a completed painting to literally glow from within."

This is one of 248 Kinkade galleries in malls and tourists spots nationwide, where mass-produced paintings by his assistants sell for $500 to $5,000, while the "semi-originals highlighted by Kinkade himself cost up to $35,000—while the 15th-century woodcuts by the great German Renaissance artist Albrecht Durer, for example, sit unsold at $5,000 each. A Gugenheim Museum curator was quoted by the *New York Times* as saying that Kinkade's work "strikes him as vapid and repetitive," while the *San Francisco Chronicle* art critic "found much of the imagery 'clumsy' and 'cheesy.'"

The Kinkade Gallery in Fort Worth is run by his brother, Patrick, a sociology professor.

Rebecca Low Sculptural Metal Gallery & Studio, 7608 Hwy. 80 West (also known here as Weatherford Hwy.), between Regan and Bonnie Dr.; (817) 244-1151. Open Wed-Fri 10 am-5 pm, Sat 11 am-4 pm. Located in southwest Fort Worth, four blocks west of Alta Mere Drive (also known as State Highway 183) and south of Interstate 30, also known here as West Freeway.

Rebecca Low opened this 1,500-square-foot gallery and 3,000-square-foot sculptural garden in 1998 after realizing that most galleries cannot accommodate her 6- to 7-foot-high contemporary sculptures. A former interior designer, who appears to enjoys herself, she has been sculpting her unusual pieces and furniture since 1992 and seems to defy conventional wisdom. Most of her work sells for $1,000-$4,000. Some 20 pieces are on display at all times.

McAnthony's Multicultural Gallery, 3270 Canberra Court at East Berry St.; (817) 536-5750. Located in southeast Fort Worth, east of Interstate 35 West and south of Interstate 30 that leads to Dallas. Open by appointment.

"For 20 years, this gallery has operated as an act of love on the part of artist and teacher Eddie McAnthony," says the *Fort Worth Star-*

Telegram. He founded the gallery and has maintained it with the help of longtime friend and co-artist Anita Knox. Among other artists, they have also cultivated the talents of Dan Williams, "whose vivid drawings tell stories old and new from African-American life."

Milan Gallery, 408 Houston St.; (817) 338-4278. Open Mon-Thu 11 am-6 pm, Fri-Sat noon-9 pm, Sun 1-5 pm. Located in the Sanger Brothers Building in Sundance Square downtown (see individual entries). Readers of the *Fort Worth Star-Telegram* picked it as the most popular gallery in Tarrant County. Modern at Sundance (see entry) is next door.

Features representational to expressionistic paintings, sculpture, and graphics. **Artists:** keyboard compositionist Gregory Arth, Seppo Aarnds, Cynthia Bryant, George Hamilton, Edna Hibel, Siri Hollander, Covelle Jones, Charles Middlekauff, international artists and local residents Henrietta Milan and Rome Milan, and modernist Terri Thornton, who is a curator of the Modern Art Museum of Fort Worth.

Evelyn Siegel Gallery, 3700 West Seventh St.; (817) 731-6412, Fax 731-6413. Open Mon-Fri 11 am-5 pm, Sat 11 am-4 pm; Est. 1982. Located west of downtown, on the northwestern edge of the cultural district.

"The icon of the Seventh Street art scene" according to the *Dallas Morning News*. Displays 20th-century paintings, sculpture, drawings, graphics, ceramics, and Native American art. **Fort Worth artists:** painter Betty Alcorn, acrylic artist Margo Bartel, folk artist Jim Clark, ceramicist Jane Cranz, photographer Mary Anne Fittipaldi, painter Shirley Kellerman, wood artist Raymond Luther, watercolorist Jane Molpus, sculptor Michael Pavlovsky, pastelist Judy Pelt, photographer Michelle Perlmutter, sculptor Deran Wright, and painter Eloise Wright. The gallery also represents the Romanian-born Alexandra Nechita, a teenager who bears the burden of being labeled the "Petite Picasso." In addition to museums—from Alexander Brest Museum in Jacksonville, Florida, to the Vatican Collection in Rome—actress Catherine Deneuve, designer Calvin Klein, and television hostess Oprah Winfrey also own the works of this "pure prodigy."

Uncommon Angles Gallery, University Park Village, 1616 South University Dr., Suite 303; (817) 335-9933. Open Mon-Thu 10 am-8 pm, Fri-Sat 10 am-9 pm, Sun noon-5 pm. Located in southwest Fort Worth and south of Interstate 30, which leads to Dallas.

Functional and sculptural ceramics, glass, wood, jewelry, and wall art from some two hundred American artists is for sale in a 2,000-square-foot store.

Yellow House Gallery, 1112 Norwood St.; (817) 332-2885. Open Mon-Fri and first Saturday of the month 11 am-4 pm. Located in the cultural district, about two blocks east of Kimbell Art Museum (see entry).

Named after Vincent van Gogh's French Riviera house. Exhibits original contemporary paintings, photographs, and ceramics; holds art classes. "Art galleries don't have to be snobbish and exclusive, they can be warm and fuzzy," owner Michaele Ann Harper is quoted as saying.

ART IN PUBLIC PLACES

There are fewer than two dozen public art works on display in down-town Fort Worth and they are mostly funded by private donations and corporations. Loveland, Colorado, with a population of 40,000, in contrast, boasts more than 160. Seattle, with a population not much larger than Cowtown, has 250.

Dallas, where ordinance requires 0.5 to 0.75 percent of the budget to go to arts, has about 160 public art works. The suburb of Euless has dedicated two percent of its half-cent sales tax to art since 1997. "Although Fort Worth boasts some impressive public art—such as Calder's The Eagle, an orange stabile downtown, and Backs by Henri Matisse—it does not have a program that earmarks funding for the arts, according to city officials," reported the Fort Worth Star-Telegram in late 1997, before the Calder was taken to Philadelphia. "Most of what is on city streets has arrived through donations by individuals or private business."

These are some of the better-known examples of public art in Fort Worth.

Downtown

The Eagle, a "stabile" type of non-moving sculpture, by Alexander Calder (1898-1976) was on display on the plaza in front of the Bank One Tower (see entry), at Fifth and Throckmorton streets. The 40-foot-high, 16-ton painted-steel abstraction dates from 1974, when it was valued at $144,000. Today it could sell for $2 million. Bank One in 1994 had considered selling the orange abstract sculpture, says the Fort Worth Star-Telegram, but decided not to after news of the potential sale created a public outcry.

On Sunday, April 11, 1999, workers hurriedly dismantled the sculpture, loaded it onto two flatbed trucks, and drove off, supposedly to have it restored. The Dallas company that bought the sculpture along with the Bank One Tower the year before refused to tell where the Calder went. The Fort Worth art community was in disbelief. "It's a desecration of Fort Worth," said Ted Pillsbury, former director of the Kimbell Art Museum.

Three months later, rumors swept Cowtown that *The Eagle* landed in New York City. On August 3, nearly four months after its removal, the *Star-Telegram* told its readers in a front-page story that the sculpture was on display on the terrace of the Museum of Art in downtown Philadelphia.

Inside the Bank One Tower are featured the works by Texas artists Richard Davis, David Demins, Gene Owens, Mac Whitney, and Charles Truett Williams.

John F. Kennedy Memorial. Plans were underway in 2000 for an eight-foot bronze statue of Pres. John F. Kennedy that would stand in General Worth Square downtown, across from the entrance of the Radisson Plaza, the former Texas Hotel, where the slain president spent his last night.

Houston sculptor Lawrence M. "Larry" Ludtke (b. 1929), a fellow of the National Sculpture Society and member of the Royal Academy of British Sculptors, has been commissioned to create a figure depicting an active president. Ludtke has already sculpted bronzes of Abraham Lincoln, Lyndon Johnson, and Ronald Reagan, and his work can be seen all over Texas, including at College Station, Houston, San Angelo, and San Antonio.

The Dallas-based Remington Hotels group, which has owned the Plaza since 1994, has committed $50,000 toward the sculpture, while the nonprofit John F. Kennedy Museum Foundation of Dallas attempted to raise twice as much.

Kennedy came to Cowtown on November 21, 1963, as part of a five-city tour of Texas and spent his last night at what is now the Radisson Plaza. He addressed the crowd about 8:45 the next morning in front of the Hotel Texas in what turned out to be his last public address. He was cut down by an assassin's bullet about three hours later, allegedly by the 24-year-old New Orleans native who had attended Ridglea West Elementary and Arlington Heights High School, both in Fort Worth, and who is buried in east Fort Worth.

The handsome three-acre Burnett Park (see entry) downtown, between West Seventh and Tenth, Cherry and Lamar streets, contains a series of four life-size bronze studies of a female back immersed in a reflecting pool. Progressively more abstract and titled **Backs,** they were created by the noted French artist Henri Matisse (1869-1954) between 1909 and 1930, a time before he traveled in Europe and the United States. The Tandy Foundation of Fort Worth purchased *Backs* in 1982 as part of a $5-million renovation of Burnett Park.

The Texas Sculpture, an abstract three-piece work carved of Japanese granite, created by Isamu Noguchi (1904-1989), stands on the NationsBank plaza, at 500 West Seventh and Lamar streets downtown.

It was commissioned by the First National Bank of Fort Worth, the predecessor of NationsBank. In 1998, NationsBank merged into Bank of America, the nation's largest and first coast-to-coast bank. Noguchi also designed the plaza, which originally included 15 Japanese stones and landscaping. Twelve were removed when the plaza was paved. The building was designed by Skidmore, Owings, and Merrill and built in 1960.

For details about the **Hayne Memorial,** Lancaster at Main and Houston streets downtown, please see the entry in the SIGHTS chapter.

Adjacent to the Tarrant County Courthouse and Heritage Park (see individual entries), at North Main and Bluff streets, is the Tarrant County Plaza, which overlooks the Trinity River and was built in 1992. A five-element red Marble Falls granite sculpture there, titled **Continuum,** is the work of Dallas sculptor Brad Goldberg (b. 1954). It was funded by a descendant of John Peter Smith, who had founded Fort Worth's first school nearby. Goldberg also created nine granite boulders in the Pegasus Plaza in downtown Dallas, across from the Adolphus Hotel.

Also on display nearby is Chris Powell's **Along the River** (1994), an eight-piece Texas granite abstraction. Powell's three-piece limestone sculpture **To Stand** will be found at Broadway Baptist Church, south of downtown, at 305 West Broadway Street.

For details about the **John Peter Smith Memorial,** 1100 Jennings Avenue at Throckmorton Street, please see the entry in the SIGHTS chapter.

The life-size bronze in front of the Cattleman's Museum building west of downtown, at 1301 West Seventh Street, titled **The Brand Inspector,** was created in 1983 by Jim Reno (b. 1929) of Kerrville, Texas. It depicts a brand inspector of the 1880s, who, on horseback, is looking through his brand book for the brand of the longhorn steer in front of him. "Through his cunning and courage, along with his book of registered markings, the brand inspector was a powerful and essential figure in the establishment of the Texas cattle industry," says Carol Morris Little in her guide *Outdoor Sculpture in Texas.*

In 1981, a larger-than-life statue of civic and business leader Charles David Tandy (1918-1978), also created by Reno, was placed downtown, behind the Tarrant County Courthouse (see entry).

For description of Philip Johnson's **Fort Worth Water Gardens,** a 4.3-acre environmental stone and water creation at Interstate 30 and Main Street, please see the SIGHTS chapter.

The life-size longhorn topiary sculpture installed in Sundance Square in 1998 fell prey to an early-morning surgical squad on the orders of Fort Worth developers. A few days after the $4,000 jasmine-covered steel skeleton appeared at Fourth and Main streets, the manager for the

Square ordered that its anatomical appendage be removed with a hacksaw and the bull made a cow. The proud longhorn was allegedly too well endowed to avoid controversy.

Richland Hills sculptor Deran Wright was to create in 2000 a larger-than-life bronze of an 8-foot-long, 4-foot-wide, and 3-foot-high sleeping panther, for many years a symbol of Cowtown, for Sundance Square. It was born in the 1870s when a Dallas reporter disdainfully wrote that "things are so dull in Fort Worth that a panther was found asleep on Main Street."

Deran Wright was selected by the family of 19th-century sculptor Pierre Auguste Renoir to reconstruct his garden sculpture *Venus Victorious* with Renoir's grandson Paul. The Renoir family had deliberately broken the original statue to keep it from being stolen by Nazis when Germany invaded France.

Cultural District

At Will Rogers Memorial Center (see entry), on West Lancaster Avenue, you will find a ten-foot-high 3,000-pound equestrian bronze of humorist Rogers (1879-1935) astride his horse Soapsuds, titled **Riding into the Sunset.** It was created through ten years of dissatisfaction with her work by Electra Waggoner Biggs (b. 1912), who had received the $20,000 commission from Cowtown publisher Amon G. Carter in 1937. It was not unveiled until 1947, in part because Carter supposedly waited for a "correct dignitary" to unveil it. Dwight D. Eisenhower, who six years later became the 34th president of the U.S., and Pres. Harry Truman's daughter Margaret finally dedicated it. Carter turned a Republican in 1952 to support Ike for president. Other castings of the statue will be found in Dallas, Lubbock, and Claremore, Oklahoma, near where Rogers was born.

Biggs was a granddaughter of cattleman W. T. Waggoner (1852-1934), who built the mansion Thistle Hill (see entry) for his daughter. Although she was born on her father's land in northwest Texas, she spent most of her youth and married life in New York. Because she loathed math, she turned to sculpting to get out of taking a business class at Columbia, according to Hugh Best in *Debrett's Texas Peerage*. "Electra first established her studio in a building near the mayor of New York's Gracie Mansion." This happened to be extremely convenient for her when she needed to go next door to borrow something from her illustrious neighbor. She needed to borrow "not a cup of sugar, but a police horse . . . to pose for her life-size Will Rogers statue." She had never actually met Rogers.

At the Amon G. Carter Exhibits Hall, which is part of the Will Rogers Memorial Center, 3401 West Lancaster, there is a life-size

The ten-foot-high bronze of humorist Will Rogers (1879-1935) is on display at the Will Rogers Memorial Center. It was created by Electra Waggoner Biggs and dedicated in 1947 by Dwight D. Eisenhower and Harry Truman's daughter. An Oklahoma native, Rogers worked as a ranch hand in Texas, joined a circus, starred in movies, and wrote books. Dying in an airplane crash over Alaska, he was perhaps the most admired person in Cowtown. (Photo by Yves Gerem)

equestrian bronze of **Midnight,** the bucking horse that worked on the rodeo circuit from 1923 to 1933, a period during which only nine cowboys managed to stay in his saddle. It was sculpted in 1984 by Texan Jack Bryant (b. 1929), whose **Horse Thief** is on display nearby. Midnight (1910-1936) was believed to be the "world's greatest bucking horse."

Horse Thief, a privately owned life-size equestrian bronze of a horse rider, created by Texan Jack Bryant in 1989, can be seen at 3340 Camp Bowie Boulevard, across the street from the Kimbell Art Museum and across from The Back Porch restaurant (see individual entries).

On the south side of the Fort Worth Museum of Science & History (see entry), you will find the steel **Galapagos Tortoise,** by Jon G. Bedford, with its shell made of car bumpers. Two life-sized steel and cement sculptures of North Texas dinosaurs, **Acrocanthosaurus** and **Tenontosaurus,** also greet the museum visitors.

In the Fort Worth Botanic Garden, south of the cultural district, 3220 Botanic Garden Boulevard at University Drive, you can find these sculptures:

• **Spirit Woman,** a life-size bronze created by Texan Jack Bryant, depicts a pioneer woman calling her family in the fields, and is located on the north vista of the garden.

• The three **Naiads** consist of female figures, which are on display on your right as you enter the garden. They were created by Texas sculptor Glenna Goodacre and acquired through Alterman and Morris Gallery in uptown Dallas, where several more can usually be seen. Goodacre sculpted the Vietnam Women's Memorial in Washington, D.C. Her bronze of Ronald Reagan is on display in Oklahoma City.

• **Along Beside Me** consists of four glazed stone abstract sculptures, created by the Fort Worth artist Chris Powell and is placed in the enclosed garden adjacent to the Leonhardt Lecture Hall. His abstraction **Along the River** is located north of the Tarrant County Courthouse (see entry) downtown.

• **St. Francis of Assisi,** a bronze by Frances Rich, is located near the Botanic Garden Center and Conservatory.

• **Frog** is a larger-than-life amphibian sitting on a bronze lily pad in the Fragrance Garden Pool. It was created by Fort Worth sculptor Evaline Sellors (b. 1908).

• **Spring Ballet,** a pair of dancing bronze frogs, were installed on the pond at the entrance in 1998.

Stockyards

On the lawn in front of the Cowtown Coliseum, on the corner of Rodeo Plaza and East Exchange Avenue, you will see the ten-foot-high

1,400-pound statue, titled **Bill Pickett, Bulldogger,** created by the Montana native Lisa Perry (b. 1950), now living in Texas. It was unveiled in 1987. Cowboy Bill Pickett (1870-1932) invented bulldogging (or steer wrestling) as a rodeo event at which he bit the steer and wrestled the animal in pain to the ground. Pickett is the only African-American named to the Cowboy Hall of Fame. He died from a kick to his head by a wild horse.

In the coliseum's front lobby is a bronze statue of the Comanche chief **Quanah Parker** (1845-1911), who was on friendly terms with ranchers, like Samuel Burk Burnett, to whom he leased Indian reservation land for cattle grazing. Although exiled to the Kiowa-Comanche reservation in southwestern Oklahoma, he regularly visited Fort Worth. The son of Cynthia Ann Parker—she was taken captive by Comanches when eleven years old—the chief amassed a fortune in cattle and land, and adopted white man's customs, but kept seven wives. "Under Quanah's leadership," says Fort Worth historian Jerry Flemmons, "the Comanches became ranchers, they went to school and farmed."

Across from Billy Bob's honky-tonk nightclub, at the northeast corner of Stockyards Boulevard and North Main Street, is a massive bronze ensemble cast in 900 sections and showing a cowboy heading up the trail with seven longhorn steers, titled **Texas Gold,** by artist and rancher T. D. Kelsey. In 1984, when unveiled by Kelsey and his wife, it was believed to be one of the largest cast bronzes in the nation.

Two years after the idea was conceived, the **Fort Worth Sculpture Symposium** was held at the Botanic Garden, starting on July 1, 1999. Three sculptors from Cowtown and one Dallas sculptor worked for eight weeks, six days a week, on abstract sculpture in the broiling Texas sun, while the public watched.

The first two works, Dallas's Sandi Stein's (b. 1946) **Solar Stone: Garden of the Gods**—with a base featuring fish, frog, lizard, and cat designs—was installed next to the Garden's Dorothea Leonhardt Hall, and her **A Celestial Jazz** in the Garden's north woods in the fall. Stein's work can also be seen in Dallas and San Antonio.

They were followed by Chris Powell's three-piece **To Be With Me** in the tiny Capps Park on Fort Worth's south side, a few blocks east of the South Freeway. Powell (b. 1957) already had his work on display at the Botanic Garden and in Fort Worth's Heritage Park.

Alice Bateman's (b. 1944) **Natura**—twice the size of the sculptress and cut from 14 tons of limestone, the largest at the symposium—was installed at southwest Fort Worth's Titus Paulsel Park, north of Martin Luther King, Jr., Freeway. If you happen to in downtown Dallas, you can see her work at Harwood and San Jacinto streets.

Cameron Schoepp's **Hats**—like others' work chiseled from stone quarried near Big Spring—was installed six months later in General Worth Square, near the Radisson Hotel downtown. It consists of five aligned pieces, each with a flat, circular surface facing west.

"The symposium not only brought new artworks to a city sorely lacking in public art but also involved the public in the artistic process," observed an editorial in the *Fort Worth Star-Telegram*. The second symposium was set for the summer of 2000.

SHOPPING

When the Houston & Texas Central Railroad began service to Dallas in 1872, a group of merchants also came along selling their wares. Among them were the five Sanger brothers, who had emigrated from German Bavaria to avoid the Prussian military service and made retailing here an art. Upon opening their first store in downtown Dallas, the Sangers were the first in Texas with a buyer in New York and boasted 21 departments by 1880. Sanger Bros. was also the first to introduce monthly retail charge accounts and employee fringe benefits. "One such benefit was a delivery wagon to take unmarried female employees home after work, with Alex Sanger, one of the brothers, as guardian," notes one historian. By the mid-1890s, they were doing $3 million worth of business annually. They inaugurated their first Fort Worth store in 1918, seven years before the last of the brothers died in Dallas.

The legendary Herbert Marcus (1878-1950), founder of another celebrated emporium, trained at Sanger's and left because, when asking for a pay raise, received only two dollars more a month. Neiman Marcus is still the most prestigious store in the Metroplex. Officially, you have not been to Texas until you shop at the downtown Dallas Neiman Marcus. As far as many Dallasites are concerned, this is the one and only store in the world, even if you only buy a trinket with the store's name on it. After you have bought your obligatory $20 coffee mug at Neiman's, you can proceed to the shopping centers.

Neiman Marcus Department Store, 1618 Main and Ervay streets; (214) 741-6911, Internet www.neimanmarcus.com. Open Mon-Sat 10 am-5:30 pm, closed Sundays and major holidays. The only Neiman's in Tarrant County is located at Ridgmar Mall (see entry) and also open Sundays noon-6 pm. That store's travel service can be reached at (817) 738-3581.

According to the official legend, "in 1907, Herbert Marcus, Sr., his sister Carrie Marcus Neiman (1883-1953), and her husband A. L. Neiman founded Neiman Marcus with the concept of offering the finest, most carefully selected merchandise in the world. It was said that

246

one would have to visit 40 stores in New York to find the variety of designer names represented under one roof at Neiman's."

Fort Worth wags not long ago joked that the company initials stand for Needless Markups. "Neiman's had many customers among Fort Worth's society crowd but the Star-Telegram would accept no advertising from the elegant specialty store," writes Jerry Flemmons, who had spent 33 years with the daily. Publisher "Amon [Carter] bragged that he bought everything he needed in Fort Worth and others should, too." His wife Nenetta "kept a Neiman's charge account secret from Amon and even he sent an occasional envoy to buy special gifts not found anywhere else." Carter animosity rose from Neiman Marcus's refusal to open a Fort Worth location. Only in 1963, eight years after Carter's death, did Neiman's open its first store at Camp Bowie Boulevard and Alta Mere Drive, which relocated to the newly opened Ridgmar Mall in 1977.

Neiman Marcus is now part of Carter-Hawley-Hale Corporation. Today, the store at times appears to be just another corporation pushing the most expensive and sometimes nonsensical objects, like His and Hers Camels, or His and Hers Mummy Cases, through Neiman's catalogue, that only an idiosyncratic Metroplex billionaire would buy.

FORT WORTH
SHOPPING CENTERS

The first Dallas store was opened in 1842 by John Beeman, one of the earliest settlers whose daughter Margaret married Dallas founder, John Neely Bryan, the following year. He stocked it with tobacco, gunpowder, and whiskey. In 1845, a post was established in Dallas's Oak Lawn neighborhood, where buffalo hides were traded for gunpowder and food.

The initial trading post in Fort Worth sprouted well before the soldiers abandoned the fort in 1853 and moved to Fort Belknap. Competing merchants followed upon the departure of the military.

Fort Worth Outlet Square, Third and Throckmorton streets; (817) 415-3720; Events Hotline, (800) 414-2817; Internet www.fwoutletsquare.com. Open Mon-Thu 10 am-7 pm, Fri-Sat 10 am-9 pm, Sun noon-6 pm. Free validated parking at Taylor and Second streets. Wheelchair-accessible rest rooms are available. The Outlet Square and the central library are connected underground. Located downtown in Sundance Square, across the street from the Renaissance Worthington Hotel. The Fort Worth Public Library (see individual entries) is across Taylor Street from the outlet.

Originally designed as a regular shopping mall. When not successful it was remodeled into a discount center. The Outlet Square—until 1996 known as Tandy Center—consists of about eight women's apparel, seven men's apparel, and six children's apparel stores, in addition to shoes and luggage shops scattered over the two levels. They include **London Fog, Spiegel, Haggar Clothing Co., Carter's for Kids, Nine West,** and **Samsonite.** There are several accessories, cards, gifts, and flower stores. **Publishers Warehouse** and the 500-store **Dress Barn** have shops here. There is an ATM, a bank, and a post office. Burgers, pizza, sandwiches, and **Sonny Bryan's** barbecue are also sold at the Outlet.

There is a 56-by-128-foot **skating rink,** for which you can make reservations by calling (817) 878-4800. CH. Open Mon-Fri 11 am-5:30 pm and 7:30-10 pm, Sat-Sun 1-6 pm and 7:30-10 pm. Skate rentals are available.

You can park at the Outlet Square garage next door, or at the Bluff and Cherry Street 14-acre parking lot, a few blocks northwest of the mall, then take the nation's first private subway, which opened in 1963. "The tunnel, reaching a depth of 42 feet, had to be blasted through solid rock," says historian Ruby Schmidt. During the days of the Leonard Brothers Department Store (see entry) this was known as M & O Express. The trains arrive and depart from the lower level, providing free transportation between the business district and the riverfront free parking area.

The sunken amphitheater, with seating for 400, is part of a one-acre park located on the lower level of the Tandy Technology Center west of here.

Fort Worth Town Center Mall, 4200 South Fwy.; (817) 972-8459. Located in south Fort Worth, west of Interstate 35 West (also known as South Freeway) and north of Southwest Loop 820, or Interstate 20. A Days Inn motel is located nearby at 4213 South Freeway.

A one-million-square-foot mall, but does not measure up to Dallas shopping centers. When opened in 1962 as Seminary South Shopping Center, an open-air mall that was later covered, this was Tarrant County's first shopping mall.

It has **Dillard's** and **Sears** anchor department stores and the usual shops one would expect to find in an average mall. Town Center is "courting the minority community, bringing in retailers such as FiestaMart grocery store that specializes in ethnic foods," says the Fort Worth Star-Telegram. It also has eight low-priced cinemas and an amusement park for children. In 1997, the Star-Telegram noted that "Town Center's fortunes have been sagging for years. The mall has fallen victim to shifting demographics, stiff competition, and customer perceptions that the surrounding area is unsafe."

Hulen Mall, 4800 South Hulen St.; (817) 294-1200. Open Mon-Sat 10 am-9 pm, Sun noon-6 pm. Located in southwest Fort Worth, at

Interstate 20, Southwest Blvd. (also known as State Highway 183), and South Hulen St. (From downtown, take Interstate 30 West, about four miles to Hulen Street exit, then go south on Hulen for another four miles.)

Claiming some 360,000 shoppers a month, Hulen is Fort Worth's largest and unquestionably the most elegant shopping center. Almost one-third of all Tarrant County shoppers visit it every month. It claims more than one million square feet of leasable space and boasts such anchors as the **Dillard's** 230,000-square-foot store that opened in 1994, **Foley's** and **Montgomery Ward's,** as well as another 130 shops.

Among the women's apparel stores, you will find **Abercrombie & Fitch, Ann Taylor, Banana Republic, Express, Gap, Guess, Lane Bryant, Lerner New York,** and **The Limited.** Men's apparel is sold by **Britches, Eddie Bauer,** and **Structure.**

Other stores include **B. Dalton Bookseller, The Disney Store, Corrigan's, Gordon's,** and **Zales Jewelers, Foot Locker, Ritz Camera, EyeMasters** and **LensCrafters,** and **Coach** leather shop. **Luby's Cafeteria** and **Godiva Chocolatier** are also on the premises.

Across Hulen Street from the mall, you will find the sole Fort Worth location of **Borders Books,** and **Bookstop; Half Price Books** is a block south from here.

Nordstrom fashion retailer planned to add a 144,000-square-foot two-level anchor store in 2001.

Ridgmar Mall, 2060 Green Oaks Rd.; (817) 731-0856. Open daily 10 am-9 pm, Sundays noon-6 pm. Located west of downtown, at Alta Mere Drive (also known as State Highway 183) and Interstate 30 (known as West Freeway) and State Highway 183.

One block north of here is **American Express Travel Agency,** which exchanges foreign currencies and issues airline tickets and traveler's checks. The 284-room Green Oaks Park Hotel is also nearby at 6901 West Fry. Hulen Mall (see entry) is five miles away. Parking is scarce.

Inaugurated in 1976 and measuring 1.3 million square feet, this was Fort Worth's first fully enclosed, climate-controlled mall, and is still one of the better and larger Fort Worth shopping centers. It started taking shape in 1969, when J.C. Penney purchased 118.9 acres of land here and developed the mall. A two-year $70-million renovation of the mall was begun in 1999.

In addition to **J.C. Penney,** its anchor department stores include the sole **Neiman Marcus** in Tarrant County, **Dillard's, Sears,** and a two-level **Foley's,** which opened its 180,000-square-foot department store in 1998. Courts near entrances to Dillard's and Neiman Marcus have large skylights, ceiling cloud murals, fountains, and stone walkways. Among the specialty stores, you will find apparel stores, such as **Eddie Bauer, Old Navy,** the **Gap** and **Gap Kids.** There is also **Foot Locker,**

Ritz Camera photographic equipment, **Sam Goody** music, **Victoria's Secret** lingerie, and **Zales Jewelers.**

Among about 100 stores and food operators, you will also find **Lerner's, Lane Bryant,** and **The Limited** for women's clothes, **Waldenbooks** and **B. Dalton** bookstores, as well as **El Fenix** Mexican restaurant and **Dick Clark's American Bandstand Grill.** "Once the county's premier mall, Ridgmar is regrouping after being rocked this decade by job cutbacks at nearby General Dynamics, now owned by Lockheed Martin, and at Carswell Air Force Base, now a joint reserve base," said the *Fort Worth Star-Telegram* in 1998. It has been divided into districts: arts and fashion, kids, and sports. The fashion end, near Neiman Marcus, has Fort Worth's largest **Banana Republic** store. The children's district offers a play area.

An 18-screen AMC movie theater is planned for on the mall rooftop in the year 2000.

Stockyards Station, 140 East Exchange Ave.; (817) 625-9715. Located in the Stockyards historic district, where Tarantula Train makes a regular stop. There are more than three dozen shops and restaurants surrounding the station and many more within the walking distance, all catering primarily to tourists.

Among the restaurants reviewed in the DINING chapter are **Cattlemen's Steak House** and **Hunter Brothers' H3 Ranch Steakhouse, Old Spaghetti Warehouse, Riscky Rita, Tommy's Hamburgers,** and the renowned **Joe T. Garcia's,** which is probably beyond casual walkers. Hotel Texas and Stockyards Hotel (see individual entries) are also nearby. Billy Bob's Texas (see entry), the world's largest honky-tonk, is a couple of blocks north of here.

University Park Village, 1612 South University Dr.; (817) 654-0521. Located at South University, two blocks south of Interstate 30 (also known as West Freeway) and almost within walking distance of the Fort Worth Botanic Garden (see entry), which is located north of here. Texas Christian University (see entry) is nearby.

A handsome small shopping center that opened in 1995 and is surrounded by restaurants, hotels, and specialty stores. Among the restaurants, you will find **Blue Mesa,** with its distinct Southwestern motif, **Denny's, Good Eats,** the Italian-cuisine **La Piazza, Ninfa's,** and **Owens.**

A **Barnes & Noble Booksellers** and **Voyagers** travel bookstore are also in the mall, as are such well-known tenants as **Ann Taylor, Express, Gap, Harold's, The Limited Too, Nine West, Structure,** and **Victoria's Secret.**

The hotels within walking distance include Courtyard by Marriott, Fairfield Inn, and Residence Inn.

SHOPPING CENTERS OUTSIDE FORT WORTH

Grapevine Mills, Intersection of State Hwy. 121 and Farm Rd. 2499; (888) 645-5748 or (972) 724-4900, Internet www.grapevine-mills.com. Open Mon-Sat 10 am-9:30 pm, Sun 11 am-8 pm. Located in northeast Grapevine, a five-minute, two-mile drive north of the Dallas-Fort Worth International Airport (see entry).

The largest shopping center in Tarrant County. An 1.8-million-square-foot, $200-million project encompassing 175 acres, with 200 specialty and outlet stores, restaurants, and a 30-screen AMC cinema, which seats 5,700. It opened in 1997. Inside, rows of tenants are grouped in neighborhoods, such as Parade/State Fair, Flowers/Agriculture, Fashion Neighborhood, Sports, Vineyard Courtyard, Entertainment Zone, and Food Court.

Among the retailers you will find **Bed, Bath & Beyond, Brooks Brothers Factory Store, Dress Barn, Gap Outlet, Guess? Factory Store, J.C. Penney Outlet Store, Just for Feet, Kay Bee Toys, Levi's Outlet, Liz Claiborne Shoes, Mikasa Factory Store, Nine West Outlet, Old Navy, Oshkosh B'gosh, The Sports Authority, Virgin Megastore, Warner Bros. Studio Store,** and **Western Warehouse.** Saks has an outlet store here, **Saks Off Fifth.** There is parking for 8,500 cars at this racetrack-shaped mall. More than ten million shop here annually, 10 percent from outside Texas and international visitors.

"So adults could be kids," there is Steven Spielberg's **Sega GameWorks,** a 32,000-square-foot mall entertainment complex that houses "almost any computer game you could want to play." There is no cover charge, but game cards cost $5, $10, and $20. For those wishing to see a film, there is **Grapevine Mills 30,** one of the largest movie megaplexes in the U.S., just 200 shy of the capacity of the New York's Radio City Music Hall.

The food court can seat 1,000. The mall's 375-seat **Rainforest Cafe** rests amid a fake plastic setting designed to suggest a rain forest. "Their shrewd attempts to siphon dollars from your wallet is evident in the laborious rituals they thrust upon you before you can even get a seat in the place to buy food," says the *Dallas Observer*. A family of four can spend $100 without much effort. A better choice would be **Dick Clark's American Bandstand Grill,** owned by "America's oldest living teen-ager" and serving "good food," along with reruns of early Bandstand shows, so bring the kids. **Corner Bakery,** serving pasta, sandwiches, pizza, and baked goods, and **Chili's Too** are also in the mall.

Late in 1999, an ice rink opened at the mall, where ice skates of all sizes can be rented.

Nearby is the 197,000-square-foot **Bass Pro Shops Outdoor World** (Internet www.basspro.com), and a 330-room Embassy Suites hotel, which opened in 1999 across from the mall at Texas 121 and Farm Road 2499. Bass Pro includes a 20,000-square-foot microbrewery and restaurant, a boat and recreational vehicle service center, a 30,000-gallon aquarium, a trout pool, and a casting tank for demonstrations, as well as live archery and firing ranges, and indoor putting and driving ranges for golfers. Also scheduled for completion in 2003 is Grapevine Opryland Hotel & Convention Center (see entry), at Ruth Wall Rd. and State Hwy. 26. The 77-acre, $300-million Opryland center is being built by the owners of Nashville, Tennessee-based Opryland on a peninsula overlooking Grapevine Lake.

North East Mall, Southwest corner of Melbourne Dr. and Bedford-Euless Rd.; (972) 589-9603/1826. Located at the intersection of State Highway 183 and Northeast Loop 820 in Hurst, northeast of Fort Worth.

Established in 1971, the 1.7-million-square-foot shopping center has about 110 shops. In 1999, this was the third largest mall in Tarrant County, surpassed only by Grapevine Mills and The Parks at Arlington Mall (see individual entries). It averages almost ten million shoppers yearly. Among its anchors, you will find **Dillard's, J.C. Penney, Montgomery Ward,** and **Sears.** A **United Artists** cinema complex is also in the mall. There is parking for 5,380 vehicles.

Other stores include **Corrigan's Jewelers, The Disney Store, Express, EyeMasters, Frederick's of Hollywood, Gordon's Jewelers, Lady Foot Locker, Lane Bryant, LensCrafters, Lerner New York, The Limited, Ritz Camera, Sam Goody, Stride Rite, Waldenbooks,** and **Zales Jewelers.** The mall opened a new south wing with stores such as **Victoria's Secret, The Gap,** and **Aveda,** a high-end personal care store, in 2000.

Saks Fifth Avenue is to open here a 100,000-square-foot store on two levels, and **Nordstrom** a store measuring 200,000 square feet, both also in the year 2000. As part of its expansion, the mall is adding a second level of 185,000 square feet of shops, which would make it the largest mall in Tarrant County.

In addition, a 390,000-square-foot "power center," named **The Shops at North East Mall,** is being built between the existing North East Mall and Pipeline Road. When completed in late 2000, the combined facility will be the state's second-largest traditional mall. The $41-million addition will include such retailers as **Bed, Bath & Beyond, Just for Feet,** Irving-based **Michael's, Office Max, PetsMart,** and **T.J. Maxx.**

An ailing **North Hills Mall,** whose new owner called it "sick" before he paid $8 million to renovate it, starting in 2000, is located less than a mile away, in North Richland Hills. The 600,000-square-foot North Hills, situated on the northeast corner of Northeast Loop 820 and Texas 26/Grapevine Highway, was slated to double its size in two years and add a three-acre lake with a 200-foot laser-lighted fountain and an amphitheater for entertainment events. A creek between the mall and North Hills Hospital would become a riverwalk. Anchor stores include **Foley's, Mervyns,** and **Stripling & Cox.**

DISCOUNT DEPARTMENT STORES

If you want rock-bottom prices, forget beautiful displays and designer-clad sales personnel. These stores sell at rock-bottom prices. The service is minimal, but you do get a bag for your purchases.

Burlington Coat Factory, Euless Town Center, Hwy. 157, west of Dallas-Fort Worth International Airport (see entry), in Euless, (817) 571-2666. Open Mon-Sat 10 am-9:30 pm, Sun 11 am-6 pm. This company started out as a coat factory, but now sells practically every kind of clothing a woman may desire, but at large savings. Check telephone directory for other locations around the Metroplex.

Stein Mart, 6385 Camp Bowie Blvd.; (817) 735-4533. Open Mon-Sat 10 am-9 pm, Sun noon-5:30 pm. An apparel store for the entire family. Also has discount stores in Hurst, Arlington, and Dallas.

Syms, 844 Airport Fwy. at Precinct Line Rd., Hurst; (817) 428-5499. Located about a mile northeast of the North East Mall (see entry). Regular and designer clothing and shoes for men and women, intimate wear, casual clothes for adults and children, luggage, and more are sold at deep discount.

ANTIQUES

When collecting Texas antiques, look for good construction. Pegged, rather than glued, joints, and square, not round, nails are signs of very old pieces, says *Southern Living* magazine. Many early Texas pieces were built of longleaf pine, cypress, or a combination of the two. Ask about the history of a piece. A reputable dealer should be able to give you background information. Among the antique stores in Cowtown, you will find:

The Antique Colony, 7200 Camp Bowie Blvd.; (817) 731-7252. A consignment outlet with 120 dealers.

The Antique Connection, 7429 East Lancaster Ave.; (817) 429-0922. Some 45 dealers sell antiques and collectibles from the U.S. and Europe.

Circa fine arts and antiques gallery, at 1634 Park Place, (817) 924-4822, and **Schmedel & Reznikoff** wood furniture gallery, next door; (817) 923-5900.

Cowtown Antiques, 2400 North Main St.; (817) 626-4565. Sells Western memorabilia and antiques.

Drew's Antiques, 7113 East Lancaster Ave.; (817) 451-8822. Contains 3,000 square feet of antiques and primitive objects.

Harris Antiques, 7600 Scott St.; (817) 246-8400. This 80,000-square-foot store sells American and European antiques.

Jewelers on the Boulevard, 3911 Camp Bowie Blvd.; (817) 763-0441. Sells clocks, jewelry, gifts, and antiques. Has a gemologist on the premises.

Leigh-Boyd Gallery, 4632 Camp Bowie Blvd. at Hulen St.; (817) 738-3705. Sells antique home furnishings, also occasional art prints and oil paintings.

The Market, 3433 West Seventh St.; (817) 334-0330. Sells European antiques, china, and accessories.

Main Street Antiques, 1332 North Main St.; (817) 624-2311. Has 125 booths in an 1890s hotel. Tearoom is open daily.

Montgomery Street Antique Mall, 2601 Montgomery St.; (817) 735-9685. One of the largest antique malls in the city, with more than 200 booths. Has a tearoom.

Diane Rose Gallery, 5108 Camp Bowie Blvd. at Merrick; (817) 732-9666. Mostly antiques, but also a few oil paintings of landscapes.

BOOKS AND MUSIC

The best selection at full-price bookstores will be found at **Borders, Barnes & Noble Booksellers,** and **Bookstop,** where a membership card will save you 20 percent on every book purchase. There are 40 locations of **Blockbuster Video,** the overpriced "monster of recorded media," according to *D Magazine*. However, if you have the time, want to save money, and do not mind getting your hands dirty a bit, there are also several used and discount book and music stores.

Barnes & Noble Booksellers, 401 Commerce, between Third and Fourth streets; (817) 332-7178. Open Mon-Sat 9 am-11 pm, Sun 10 am-9 pm. Located downtown on Sundance Square, facing The Flying

Saucer pub, next to Angeluna restaurant, and across the street from the Bass Performance Hall (see individual entries).

This is Fort Worth's largest bookstore, stocking up to 180,000 book titles on two levels. That replica of a 20-foot-high bucking bronco, rearing all the way to the second floor, was done after Frederick Remington. Also part of the store is a 3,000-square-foot **Starbucks** cafe that accommodates 90 patrons.

Other Barnes & Noble Tarrant County locations are:
- 1620 South University Dr. at University Park Village mall; (817) 335-2791.
- 934 East Copeland Rd. at Collins St. in north Arlington; (817) 277-5184.
- 3909 South Cooper St. at I-20 in south Arlington; (817) 557-1171.
- 8525 Airport Fwy. at Bedford-Euless Rd. in North Richland Hills; (817) 281-7042.

B. Dalton Bookseller, has stores at Hulen, (817) 292-5388, and Ridgmar Malls, (817) 735-1977, in Fort Worth. Also at Six Flags Mall, (817) 640-9989, and The Parks at Arlington Mall, (817) 784-1188. The North Richland Hills store is at North Hills Mall, (817) 284-8113. Open Mon-Sat 10 am-9 pm, Sun noon-6 pm. B. Dalton, which is owned by Barnes & Noble, has restricted itself to mall locations. It has a fair selection of domestic travel guides, but is rather limited on foreign destinations.

Blockbuster Music, 6393 Camp Bowie Blvd.; (817) 737-8831, or 5417 South Hulen St.; (817) 346-7676. Open Sun-Thu 10 am-10 pm, Fri-Sat 10 am-11 pm. Located in southwest Fort Worth, near Ridglea Avenue. Tom Thumb Supermarket and Black-Eyed Pea Restaurant are nearby. Readers of the *Fort Worth Star-Telegram* voted this and other Blockbuster locations as the best new-records stores in Tarrant County.

The Book Shoppe, 1822 West Berry St., between Cleburne Rd. and Eighth Ave.; (817) 926-8208; Internet www.thebookshoppe.com; E-mail bookshop@thebookshoppe.com. Located in southwest Fort Worth, west of Interstate 35 and east of Texas Christian University.

A "delightful" used hardcover and paperback bookstore, according to the *Fort Worth Star-Telegram*. It measures 4,000 square feet, stocks some 100,000 titles, and keeps two cats—Simon and Schuster—on the premises, to the delight of children. Kids who buy ten books get the eleventh free. It also accepts Internet orders.

The Book Shoppe is run by two women, Kelly Chandler—who has a degree in modern and Romance languages, and who sang in the El Paso opera chorus—and Elaine Taylor, who has degrees in art, music, and theater, has worked for the Fort Worth Opera, and built harpsichords.

Bookstop, 4801 South Hulen St.; (817) 346-9055. A large Bookstop store located on the edge of Hulen Mall (see entry). Open

Mon-Sun 9 am-11 pm. This is the only Metroplex book chain where you can buy a membership card and get a 20 percent discount on books and 10 percent on magazines. There are three other Bookstop locations in Dallas, one in Plano.

Borders Books & Music, 4613 South Hulen St.; (817) 370-9473. Located across the street from Hulen Mall (see entry), at Interstate 20 (also known as Southwest Loop 820), this is the only Borders bookstore in Fort Worth. Open Mon-Sat 9 am-11 pm, Sun 9 am-9 pm. Eclectic, comfortable, and cozy, Borders locations are all inviting and have a large selection of travel guides.

Dino's Collectibles & CD's, 2800 West Berry St.; (817) 921-1441. Open Mon-Sat 10 am-9 pm, Sun noon-6 pm. Located in the Texas Christian University (see entry) vicinity, four blocks east of South University Drive in southwest Fort Worth.

Sells predominantly pop and rock, has some collectible records. Readers of the *Fort Worth Star-Telegram* voted it the best used-records store in Tarrant County.

Forever Young, 2955 South Texas 360 at Mayfield Road, Arlington; (972) 206-2727. Open Mon-Thu 10 am-9 pm, Fri-Sat 10 am-10 pm, Sun noon-6 pm. Located in a shopping center on the edge of Grand Prairie, about five miles south of Six Flags Over Texas theme park (see entry).

A 13,000-square-foot store "that's about as big as a supermarket," in the words of one employee. Staff of the *Fort Worth Star-Telegram* named it the best used-records store in Tarrant County, adding that it has "a healthy selection of new and used CD's and vinyl. Staff is made up of true music fans, not 'Can I help you even though I probably can't' robots."

Half-Price Books, 6912 Ridgmar Meadow Rd. at 183 North, or Alta Mere Dr.; (817) 732-4111. Open daily 9 am-10 pm, Sun 11 am-8 pm.

Established in 1972, the chain has 60 stores nationwide and about a dozen in the Metroplex. All stores carry used and new books, records, tapes, and CD's. Price is one-half of the original price or less.

Other Half Price locations in Fort Worth and Arlington include:

• 5264 South Hulen and South St., a block south of Hulen Mall; (817) 294-1166. The staff of the *Fort Worth Star-Telegram* named this the best used-books store in Tarrant County.

• 770 Road to Six Flags at Collins St. in north Arlington; (817) 274-5251.

• 2211 South Cooper St. at Pioneer Parkway in central Arlington; (817) 860-5247.

Thompson's Book Store, the last privately owned bookstore in a 1904 building downtown, at 900 Houston, closed in the fall of 1998.

Were it not for the Barnes & Noble superstore, Fort Worth would have joined Dallas, a city of more than a million, without a decent bookstore downtown.

The building was erected by a steamboat captain who settled in Fort Worth in 1879 and has previously housed a dentist, watchmaker, pharmacy, and a bank. It became home to a restaurant and bar in 2000.

Voyagers, The Travel Store, 1600 South University Dr.; (800) 638-9873 or (817) 335-3100, in the University Park Village shopping center. Open Mon-Sat 10 am-9 pm, Sun 11 am-6 pm.

The only Fort Worth bookstore that specializes in travel books and accessories. Has a spectacular selection of travel titles, maps, and videos, and a travel agency on the premises. Whether you go to Timbuktu or Tahiti, this is the place to stop at beforehand. The other Voyagers stores are located in Dallas.

Waldenbooks, like B. Dalton, has limited itself to shopping centers in the Metroplex. Among the Fort Worth and Arlington locations are those at Ridgmar Mall, (817) 731-2911; Parks at Arlington, (817) 784-0124; Six Flags Mall, (817) 640-3142. Another Tarrant County location is at North Hills Mall, (817) 284-1504; Open Mon-Sat 10 am-9 pm, Sun noon-6 pm. Travel titles, domestic or international, are in limited supply.

CLOTHING

Shopping centers in Fort Worth, such as Hulen Mall, Ridgmar Mall, Fort Worth Town Center, University Park Village, or Fort Worth Outlet Square, or The Parks at Arlington Mall and Six Flags Mall, probably have most of what you need in the way of regular work and casual clothes or formal wear.

There will, of course, always be specialized apparel stores, where women can sink hundreds, or even thousands, of dollars for that little black dress or some such.

An Italian couture store like that in Fort Worth, where the rich can indulge their idiosyncracies, is the 15-year-old **Maribianca Moda Italiana,** a chic west Fort Worth emporium at 3412 Westridge Ave., off Camp Bowie Blvd, and across from Frost Bank; (817) 731-9571. It is open Mon-Fri 9 am-5 pm, Sat 9 am-2 pm.

Maribianca's dresses start at $750 and some outfits cost $3,000 and more. Sweaters go for $400-$700. No shoes, handbags, or casual clothes are sold. "Absolutely not," snapped in reply the proprietress when asked whether she sells jeans. When contacted the first week in December, she claimed that most of her holiday shipment was sold out.

The boutique figured prominently during the 1998 trial of a woman accused by the Fort Worth millionaire oilman W. A. "Tex" Moncrief Jr., of stealing $400,000. She claimed the 78-year-old geezer was her lover for 16 years and authorized her to spend up to $25,000 a month, some of which ended at Maribianca. The jury found the defendant not guilty.

The Western Wear

So you want to be a cowboy, eh? All right, cover that belly and get your money ready and we will see what we can do for you. First the hat. If you plan to be a cowboy, it should be your fly swatter and a horse-whip. And in Texas you almost never take it off. John Stetson of Philadelphia introduced what is today the classic design in the 1850s with a hat made of felt. It had a wide brim to protect the eyes from the sun and a high crown to keep the top of your head cool. Cowboys also used it as a drinking vessel, to carry water to their horses, even to fan a fire. There's the Dude Stetson, Rodeo Stetson, and Joe Bob Stetson, Cowboy or Panama Straw, Oilman's Special, the Cattleman, and Baroness for his daughter.

You can't be a cowboy without the bandanna, always of bright red cotton to wipe your sweat after you have initiated a conversation with a cute blonde Texas lass or, if you are a woman, a handsome fella. You can wear it as a hatband or use it as a napkin, a handkerchief, or a dog collar.

Now the Western shirt. Until the first livestock shows and rodeos in Fort Worth, the cowboy's shirt was just that. Afterwards it became a high-fashion item with pearl snap closings, instead of buttons. Now, check out the shirt design and see what you want: Bull Rider, Honky-Tonker, Cowpoke, Rodeo Plaid, or City Slicker to wear under a suit to your Chicago office. And for you, ladies, Calico Cowgirl print in red.

Then there are the jeans. You'll never be anything beyond a circus clown without jeans. Not just anything from Guess will do. There are only three brands in which to show your stuff: Levi's, Lee, or Wrangler, the real Americana. What do those fashion-conscious Italians know about jeans! The back hem should just cover your heels and straight leg is the only authentic cut.

The boots. You may have but three strands of hair left on your head and you can be a cowboy. Wear anything but real boots and you'll look like a Covent Garden ballerina. Try Studio boot if you have cinematic aspirations or the Muleskinner if you want to be taken seriously. And you, ladies, can try the Urban Cowboy boot that gained prominence after the film with actor John Travolta.

Hold your horse, cowboy, you ain't done yet. You need a replica of the Texas state seal buckle on a cowhide belt, a bolo tie, and if you *really* want to look the part, silver spurs.

And where can you find all this? Try one of these stores:

Boot Town, 2901 Alta Mere Dr. at Calmont Ave.; (817) 654-2668. Open Mon-Sat 9 am-9 pm, Sun noon-6 pm. Located south of Ridgmar Mall (see entry), across Interstate 30, also known as West Freeway. Sells boots, sizes 4-15, such as Acme, Justin, Laredo, Lucchese, Nocona, or Tony Lama. Also Western clothing, including Wrangler and Levi's jeans, men's and women's shirts, hats, belts, some children's apparel.

Boot Town's Arlington store is located at 4115 South Cooper at Interstate 20, (817) 784-8082, near the Parks Mall at Arlington (see entry).

Cavender's Boot City, 5248 South Hulen St. near South Dr.; (817) 294-4400. Open Mon-Sat 9 am-9 pm, Sun 11 am-6 pm. Located in Hulen Fashion Center, a few blocks south of Hulen Mall (see entry).

Another Cavender's is at 2515 Centennial Dr. at Texas Highway 360, Arlington; (800) 228-2898 or (817) 640-8899. Open same hours. Located next to Sheplers Western wear super store (see entry). Second Arlington location is at 3308 East Pioneer Pwy., next to Sam's.

With eight stores throughout the Metroplex, Cavender's claims modestly to "sell more boots than anyone in the world." Most well-known brands are available, including Wrangler jeans, Tony Lama boots, some jewelry. The readers of *FW Weekly* named it the "best place to cowboy up."

Engler's Western Wear, 117 Houston and West First streets; (817) 336-7374. Open Mon-Sat noon-5 pm. Located downtown, a block from the Tarrant County Courthouse and next door to the Renaissance Worthington Hotel (see individual entries).

A family business established in 1911, this store prides itself on "fine handshaped Western hats," mostly Resistol and Stetson. Price of a hat that you can be proud of ranges around $100-$200. Also sells Western shirts and belts.

Fincher's, 115 East Exchange Ave.; (817) 624-7302. Open Mon-Sat 9 am-6 pm, Sun 1-5 pm. Located in Stockyards (see entry) historic district, a two-mile drive from downtown.

Claiming to sell Western wear since 1902, Fincher's sells men's, women's, and children's wear, such as rodeo equipment, jeans, "hand creased" hats, belts, custom shirts, and boots, including the Justin brand.

Justin Boots Outlet Store, 717 West Vickery Blvd.; (817) 654-3103. Open Mon-Fri 9 am-8 pm, Sat 9 am-7 pm, Sat noon-6 pm. Justin company outlet, located just south of downtown. Sells only Justin boots for men, women, and children.

If driving from Fort Worth to Denton, you can also stop in the town of Justin, about 20 miles north of Fort Worth, and buy at **Justin**

Discount Boots & Cowboy Outfitters (not part of the Justin company), at 101 Hwy. 156; (800) 772-5933 or (800) 677-2668. Located about five miles from Texas Motor Speedway racetrack (see entry). Open Mon-Sat 9 am-6 pm. They sell Justin and other boot brands, as well as clothing for men, women, and children.

Leddy's M.L. Boot & Saddlery, 2455 North Main St. at Exchange Ave.; (817) 624-3149. Open Mon-Sat 10 am-6 pm. Located in the historic Stockyards (see entry).

M.L. Leddy operated a shoe store, harness, and leather shop in Brady, Texas, where he learned how to make boots and saddles. His brothers came to Fort Worth in 1941 and had a small shop on the northwest corner of Main and Exchange streets, where they turned out boots and a couple of years later saddlery. By 1946, they began selling Western wear and became the largest handmade boot sellers in Texas. The Leddy brothers sold their operation to other family members in 1968, and in 1981 a son-in-law bought out the company.

Leddy's specializes in custom handmade men's and women's boots, hats, slacks, shirts, and saddles. Does not sell jeans. Another store is located in San Angelo, Texas.

Luskey's Western Store, 101 North Houston at Weatherford St.; (817) 335-5833. Open Mon-Sat 9 am-6 pm. Located downtown across the street from the Tarrant County Courthouse (see entry). Sells men's, women's, and children's apparel, boots, jeans, hats, and belts by such manufacturers as Levi's and Wrangler. Another Luskey's is located at 2601 North Main St. in the historic Stockyards; (817) 625-2391. Open same hours. Established in 1919, this is one of the oldest businesses in Fort Worth.

Sheplers, 2500 Centennial Dr., Arlington; (817) 640-5055. Open Mon-Sat 10 am-9 pm, Sun noon-6 pm. Located in central Arlington, at Centennial and service road of Highway 360, less than one mile south of Interstate 30. Cavender's Boot City and Western Warehouse (see individual listings) are located nearby.

Like a few of its competitors, promotes itself as the "world's largest Western store." Sells men's, women's, and children's apparel, boots, hats, belts, jewelry, and gifts.

Western Warehouse, 2501 Centennial Dr. at State Highway 360, Arlington; (817) 640-2301. Open Mon-Sat 9 am-9 pm, Sun noon-6 pm. Located in east Arlington, next to Sheplers and Cavender's Boot City (see individual listings).

Sells all kinds of men's, women's, and children's Western apparel, boots, hats, and belts, claims to have thousands of pairs of boots in stock. Its Grapevine store is located at Grapevine Mills mall (see entry).

Now that you are properly outfitted, you can try some real Western living. Check out the Stockyards or Southfork Ranch, from the television series *Dallas*. And, of course, you cannot say you have been in Texas unless you go to at least one rodeo. Put on your Levi's and gallop over to Cowtown Coliseum or Mesquite Championship Rodeo (see individual entries).

FOODS

Bavarian Bakery & Cafe, 3000 Southeast Loop 820 at Wichita St.; (817) 551-1150. Bakery is open Mon-Fri 7:30 am-6 pm, Sat 7:30 am-5 pm. Located since 1980 across Interstate 20 from Tarrant County Junior College's south campus in far southeast Fort Worth, east of Interstate 35 West.

A 28-year-old, family-owned bakery with hand-painted tables and chairs that is known for more than just Black Forest cake and German breads. The *Dallas Morning News* singles out "the truly wonderful apple strudel, flaky, juicy and not too tart or sugary, and swimming in decadent vanilla sauce." It also supplies food for Lufthansa German airline.

You will find here a $20,000, 14-foot-tall cuckoo clock—perhaps the largest in the south—weighing 2,500 pounds, which the Bavarian natives brought from Germany at a cost of another $15,000.

Online Supermarkets ──────────────

You can order groceries online from these vendors, who offer Web specials and accept coupons:

Albertsons.com sells 5,500 products—nonperishable items only—packaged in sealed boxes from its Fort Worth warehouse at prices equal in their supermarkets. No special software is required and orders over $60 are delivered free of charge. Tipping is not allowed.

Peapod.com or **TomThumb.com** sells 25,000 products—including perishables and frozen foods—delivered in bags and coolers at prices the same as in their supermarkets. You need specialized software to order. Offers special features, such as nutritional label information. There is a small monthly fee and $10 per order. Orders are filled at local Tom Thumb supermarkets and reward cards are accepted. You can even buy La Madeleine French Bakery products, like at Tom Thumb stores.

Netgrocer.com sells 3,500 products—nonperishable items only—delivered in sealed boxes by FedEx at prices lower than supermarkets. No special software is required. There is a $7 fee on orders up to $100. Also sells health and beauty products, electronics, some medications.

Groceryworks.com sells standard supermarket products. The minimum order is $25; there are no fees to be paid; tipping is not allowed. Frozen items are delivered in dry ice-insulated boxes. The plastic bags holding products are thicker than those in supermarkets.

Markets

Benbrook Farmers Market, 8101 Highway 80 West, two blocks west of Cherry Ln; (817) 244-6036. Open Wed-Sun 8 am-sellout, usually by early afternoon. West Side Cafe is across the street.

Benbrook (pop. 22,000) lies on the southwestern edge of Fort Worth, south of White Settlement. This is believed to be the most popular and complete farmers' market in Tarrant County, with produce grown in counties west and north of Fort Worth. Real farmers are situated in a shed in a strip shopping-center parking lot. For best selection, go before 9:30 am, particularly on Wednesdays and Saturdays.

Fort Worth Market, 2721 Rosedale at Vaughn streets. Open Fridays & Tuesdays 8 am-sellout. Operated by North Central Texas Farmers Markets.

Fort Worth Downtown Market, 900 block of Weatherford St.; west of Henderson St. Open daily 8 am-5 pm. It is operated by private individuals.

Fort Worth Summer Public Market, Sundance Square's Chisholm Trail parking lot, Main and Fourth streets; (817) 870-1692. Open June & July, Saturdays 8 am-3 pm. Farmers and other vendors sell peaches, tomatoes, cheesecakes, bagels, and God knows what else.

Town Talk Foods, 121 North Beach at First St.; (817) 831-6136. Open Mon-Fri 9 am-6 pm, Sat 9 am-5 pm. Accepts cash or Discover credit card only.

For those fortunate enough to be close to this east Fort Worth neighborhood, south of Airport Freeway (also known as State Highway 121) and east of South Freeway (also known as Interstate 35 West), there is this 40-year-old salvage grocery store located near Gateway Park and owned by a certified registered nurse anesthetist.

Now situated in a cement-floored metal building, Town Talk is for those looking to squeeze every penny from their food bill. This includes "the restaurant owners and caterers (and I recognized you, so don't duck behind the shelves), buying groceries way under wholesale and charging customers full retail. Is America a great country or what?" asks the *Fort Worth Star-Telegram's* food editor, who then explains that those low prices are possible when an 18-wheeler ditches off I-20 or a store ends in bankruptcy in Waco and Town Talk buys out their stock.

SPAS FOR WOMEN AND MEN

For information on additional day spas in the Metroplex, call New York's Spa-Finders at (800) 255-7727 or (212) 924-6800; E-mail: spa@spafinders.com. Expect to tip 15-20 percent of the total cost.

European Skin Care Institute, 3800 Camp Bowie Blvd.; (800) SKIN-CARE or (817) 731-3511. Offers a variety of services, from facials to massages, to the latest in hair removal techniques. Also provides micro-dermabrasion, acne and scar treatments, spa and steam therapy. A sampler includes an express facial, 25-minute classic massage, and spa lunch for under $100. The Ultimate provides an anti-aging facial, anti-stress massage, spa lunch, manicure, pedicure, and scalp massage for $320. Also sells gift certificates.

The Greenhouse, Box 1144, Arlington 76006; (817) 640-4000. Located "kind of near the Ballpark in Arlington" (see entry), but will not disclose the exact location "because of a lot of high profile guests," we were told on the phone. You receive the address upon prepayment of a service. The Greenhouse is located on the border between Grand Prairie and Arlington, which divides the spa in half.

Minimum stay is one week, there is room for 36 guests only, and men are not allowed at "the world's most luxurious, comprehensive beauty and fitness retreat" catering to privileged women since 1965. "Here your bags are unpacked for you," noted *Texas Business* magazine, and "dressing for dinner is de rigueur. This is a Nancy Reagan-regal kind of place, with a healthy dose of Cindy Crawford and even a touch of tough female executive mixed in." Adds *D Magazine:* "The average guest, between 45 and 65 years of age, has the fitness level of an Elizabeth Taylor or a Nancy Reagan, both of whom have stayed at The Greenhouse."

A typical days starts at 7 am with breakfast in bed, is followed by aerobics and potassium broth break at 9:45, according to a flyer. It is on to a facial at 10 am, toning exercises at noon, and luncheon at poolside at 1 pm. Massage, hydro-tone, hair and nail treatments, and yoga take place before dinner, which is served at 7 pm. "Tuck in massage" follows a couple of hours later. Not impressed? Maybe the rates will wake you up: standard room starts at $4,718.19 for "an all-inclusive Sunday-to-Sunday retreat which begins the moment you are greeted at the airport by The Greenhouse chauffeur" and goes up to $5,565.69 for a suite for two, "per person." You are assigned a "personal maid" and feast on "meals with the freshest ingredients, using fruits and vegetables at the height of their palatibility." Still feel you might not be getting your money's worth? The Greenhouse will throw in "leotards, tights, gym shorts and a terry robe." There.

Rejuvena Skin Therapy, 6038 Camp Bowie Blvd., (817) 731-0500. Specializes in facial therapies, such as chemical exfoliation, keratolyses peel, and renewal; body therapies, which include contouring program, body glow, and serenity body polish; water therapies, such as seawater or seaweed therapy, aromatherapy, and mud bath; as well as in massages, such as rejuvena, lymph drainage, and pre-natal massage; and hand and foot therapies, including manicure and pedicure. Treatments last from 30 to 90 minutes, prices range $35-$500.

SPORTS

In 1997, Arlington bid to host the 2012 Summer Olympic Games. The following year, it passed the bid over to Dallas, which raised more than $1.5 million to attract the 2012 Games as a regional effort that is estimated to cost at least $2 billion. The U.S. Olympic Committee will announce the U.S. finalist in 2002, after the Salt Lake City Games.

SPORTS TO SEE

If you love sports, the Metroplex is a good place to visit. Its residents are sports fanatics and the area will reward you with a large selection of spectator sports activities.

Paulie Ayala, born in 1970 and raised in Fort Worth's north side, won World Boxing Assocation's Bantamweight Championship in 1999. Since turning professional in 1992, he has a record of 29-1, including 12 knockouts. Ayala has also been named fighter of the year by *The Ring* magazine. Cowtown honored him with a parade through downtown. Fort Worth has had six world champions.

Auto Racing

Texas Motor Speedway, 3601 State Hwy. 114 and FM 156, Justin, about 15 miles north of Fort Worth; (817) 215-8500; Internet www.texasmotorspeedway.com; Hotel reservations, (888) FW-SPEED. Tickets $10-$100. Open daily. Call for calendar of races. Located west of Interstate 35 West in Denton County, northwest of a 23-acre lake. From Dallas-Fort Worth International Airport (see entry) take State Highway 114 west to State Highway 170 west to Interstate 35 West north.

Come at least one hour before the races start, traffic is a mess, and it can also take hours to get out. There are 1,595 seats for the handicapped. The facility attracts 200,000 yearly and accommodates about 52,600 vehicles. Alcohol is not served at the speedway.

The Ballpark Stadium in Arlington, which seats 49,178 and was inaugurated in 1994, is the home to the Texas Rangers, the Metroplex baseball team that plays in the American League. Its three-story Legends of Game Baseball Museum is the only museum of its kind in a major-league park. (Photo by Yves Gerem)

Completed in 1997, this is the first NASCAR (National Association for Stock Car Auto Racing) facility in Texas. The 151,000-seat Speedway, which is spread over 950 acres, cost $110 million to build and is the largest spectator-sport facility in Texas and supposedly the third largest in the world, behind the Indianapolis Motor Speedway and the Maracana soccer stadium in Rio de Janeiro, Brazil. The 100-acre infield is large enough to contain 91 football fields. The Speedway is a one-and-a half-mile asphalt track that has a double-dogleg front stretch and 24-degree high-banked turns. NASCAR racers ride high on the banks to take advantage of centrifugal force, which lets them maintain top speeds as they make turns. Drivers race around the track for several hundred miles at an average speed near 200 miles per hour.

You can find rooms at several hotels, about 20 minutes south of the freeway, in the Fossil Creek area along Interstate 35 West, just north of Loop 820. They include Courtyard by Marriott, Fairfield Inn, and Residence Inn. A Hampton Inn was completed in 1998 at Interstate 35 West and Westport Parkway. Downtown Fort Worth is another 15 minutes of driving time farther south.

Baseball

The Ballpark in Arlington, 1000 Ballpark Way at Randol Mill Rd., Arlington; (817) 273-5222, Internet www.texasrangers.com. Wheelchair-accessible. For tickets, call (817) 273-5100. Tickets also available on Entertainment Ticket Machines in 60-plus Kroger supermarkets—www.kroger-texas.com. Use touch-screen and select seats by location or price with credit and debit cards. Located in Arlington, halfway between Dallas and Fort Worth, it claims almost three million visitors a year more than any other Fort Worth or Arlington tourist attraction.

The five-level Ballpark Stadium, which seats 49,166, was inaugurated in 1994 and is the home of the **Texas Rangers,** the Metroplex baseball team, in the American League. The Washington Senators became the Texas Rangers in 1972, when the Dallas Cowboys were the only big-time franchise. Former Rangers pitcher Nolan Ryan was overwhelmingly elected to the Baseball Hall of Fame in Cooperstown, New York, in 1999, the first Ranger to ever do so. His major-league, 27-year career is the longest in baseball; Ryan (b. 1947) pitched with the Rangers from 1989 to 1993. Gov. George W. Bush, a former Rangers managing partner, said that "to know the hearts and minds of Texans, you'd better know Nolan Ryan. He's as Texas as a Texan can be."

The stadium is part of a $200-million, 270-acre complex that also includes a sports hall of fame, retail shopping area, riverwalk, and a man-made 12-acre lake. The playing surface is 22 feet below street level. In 1998, a Dallas businessman who already owned the Dallas Stars hockey team purchased the Rangers and the entire complex for $250 million.

The one-hour guided tours of the Ballpark are available. Surrounding the field are two restaurants, radio facilities, shops, and offices. The four-tier **Diamond Club** restaurant, (817) 795-9006, with 500 seats and a view of the playing field, is for season ticket-holders and open for lunch Mon-Fri 11:30 am-2 pm. **Front Row** sports grill, (817) 265-5191, is open Mon-Sat 11 am-2 am, Sun 11 am-midnight.

The three-story 17,000-square-foot **Legends of the Game Baseball Museum,** (817) 273-5600, located on the Randol Mill Road side of the Ballpark, is the only museum of its kind in a major-league park. It presents a general history of baseball, as well as the story of this game in Texas, through 1,000 baseball artifacts. The guided tour information line to the museum and The Ballpark is (817) 273-5099. Museum hours are Mon-Sat 9 am-6 pm, Sun noon-4 pm.

On the first floor, the museum displays the nation's legendary players and their achievements. Worn gloves, jerseys, trophies, autographed balls, and photos are shown. On the second floor, Texas baseball is explored from the founding of the Texas League in 1888 until now. On the third floor, baseball-related games and entertainment are featured, complete with interactive computers, baseball cards, and other memorabilia. A visiting exhibit from the National Baseball Hall of Fame and Museum in Cooperstown is also featured.

The Rangers season runs April-October. You can find out about availability of tickets by calling (817) 273-5100. Smoking is prohibited in all seating sections and rest rooms.

Basketball and Hockey ————————————

Fort Worth Fire Ice Hockey Club. The Fort Worth Fire of the Central Hockey League, which had been playing since 1992, ceased operating in 1999 because it drew an average of only 2,300 fans, but needed 3,500 a game to break even. It shared the Fort Worth Convention Center and Will Rogers Memorial Coliseum with the **Fort Worth Brahmas Ice Hockey Club** of the 18-team Western Professional Hockey League, which was established in 1996. The Brahmas, originally named The Bulls, has its business office at 3004 West Lancaster Ave.; (817) 336-4423, Internet www.bullshockey.com. The team is owned by a former Dallas Stars goalie and a New York bond broker.

Dallas's basketball team is the **Dallas Mavericks,** its hockey team the **Dallas Stars,** both of which use the city-owned and managed Reunion Arena, part of the Reunion complex in downtown Dallas.

The Reunion Arena, (214) 939-2770, is located at 777 Sports St., off Interstate 35. The 85-foot-high arena, which sits on 6.2 acres of land, opened in 1980. It plays host to about 200 events yearly, from circuses to concerts, and can seat 17,000-19,500 spectators, depending on the event. There is parking for 6,400 cars. Handicapped parking is in Lot B, wheelchair seating behind sections 101, 108, 116, 122. The box office is located on the north side of the arena and is open Mon-Fri 10 am-5 pm. Box office for all events can be reached at (214) 939-2800; to hear a recording about the coming events, (214) 670-1395.

The **Mavericks,** (972) 988-0117/3865, Tickets (214) 939-2800, Internet www.mavericks.nba.com, is a National Basketball Association franchise. The basketball team was bought by Ross Perot, Jr., the son of billionaire and twice unsuccessful presidential candidate Ross Perot, in 1996. Less than four years later, Mark Cuban, the 41-year-old entrepreneur who made a billion-dollar fortune with the sale of Dallas's Broadcast.com to Yahoo, Inc., bought a majority stake in the team for $280 million, more than double the previous price. The team, which came to Dallas in 1980, plays more than 50 games each season, from October through April.

Early in 2000, the flamboyant Dennis Rodman joined a losing team—the Mavericks—for the first time in his turbulent career. The Mavericks were a franchise whose nine-season playoff drought was the longest in the National Basketball Association. Rodman, who was paid $12,195 per game, has been a member of five NBA championship teams with the Chicago Bulls (1996, 1997, 1998), and the Detroit Pistons (1989 and 1990).

Also playing at this arena is the **Stars** hockey team, (972) 868-2890, Tickets (214) 467-8277, a National Hockey League franchise whose season runs September through April. The Stars moved from Minneapolis in 1993, when Minnesotans "were nursing a powerful resentment at losing their hockey team to a lot of unappreciative barbarians in Texas," according to the *Dallas Morning News*. The daily noted early in 1999 that "the team is widely regarded as a prime bet to win hockey's holy grail, the Stanley Cup."

In 1997, after four years of talks to replace the aging Reunion Arena, the city of Dallas agreed to invest $125 million in a new $230-million downtown arena—named the American Airlines Center—for its basketball and hockey teams. The Mavericks and Stars will invest $105 million and agree to remain at this facility for 30 years. The 65-acre development is to be located east of Stemmons Freeway, just north of the West End entertainment district. It is slated to open in the fall 2001 season. The sale of the franchise is not affecting an expanse of office buildings, retail shops, residential units, and entertainment being developed by Perot Jr. and owner of the Dallas Stars.

Football

Texas Stadium, 2401 East Airport Fwy., Irving; (972) 438-7676, Internet www.theboys.com. Parking gates open three hours before kick-off, stadium gates two hours before. Open Mon-Fri 8:30 am-5:30 pm. Located northwest of downtown Dallas, between John Carpenter Freeway (also known as State Highways 114 and 183) and Walton Walker Boulevard (or Loop 12).

Texas Stadium is best known as the home of the **Dallas Cowboys** football team, the five-time Super Bowl champion of the National Football League, the first time in 1972, when they beat Miami 24-3. The team was bought in 1989 by Jerry Jones, who fired the team's long-time coach Tom Landry. In 1998, Chan Gailey became the team's fourth coach in its 40-year history. He lasted only until January 2000, when replaced by Dave Campo, who has spent his entire 11-year career with the Cowboys.

The Cowboys became members of the National Football League in 1960. The team has sold out 55 consecutive home games, counting regular season and playoffs; their last home non-sellout was December 16, 1990, against Phoenix. The stadium, which now seats 65,846 and has 296 sky boxes, along with its parking facilities, occupies 140 acres and employs more than 2,000. "Building Texas Stadium is the smartest thing Irving ever did," says local historian A. C. Greene. Built in 1971, the stadium is one of the National Football League's landmarks. It was here that the concept of luxury suites, where affluent fans can watch games while enjoying catered meals began. The team's lease expires in 2008.

"Motivated in part by Jerry Jones' desire to someday host a Super Bowl in north Texas, the Cowboys are quietly making a list of potential sites for a new stadium should Texas Stadium expansion plans fizzle," reported the *Fort Worth Star-Telegram*.

Pre-season and regular season games begin in August and end in December. The Cowboys, who are identified by their silver and blue helmets and uniforms, play their home games at this stadium. This is one of the most valuable sports franchises among the more than 100 baseball, football, basketball, and hockey teams in the U.S., valued at more than $300 million.

Also part of the Texas football craze are the now-famous **Dallas Cowboys Cheerleaders,** young, enthusiastic, and pretty women who have wiggled around since 1976, for the benefit of the television cameras and mostly male audiences. About 1,000 candidates show up at Texas Stadium every April for preliminary tryouts, but only 36 finalists are retained. They earn $15 for each game, while the ball players have multimillion-dollar contracts. A yearly photo calendar and the promotional work they do seems to have invested them with glamour that has become the envy of thousands of American girls.

Public tours of the stadium are given Mon-Fri at 10 am and 2 pm and take about one hour. On weekends they take place at 11 am, 12:30 pm, and 2 pm. *CH*.

Horse Races

Lone Star Park, 2200 North Belt Line Rd. at Interstate 30, Grand Prairie; (972) 263-RACE, Internet www.lonestarpark.com. Open daily 10:30 am-11 pm, closed Tuesdays. Admission *CH* and parking fee. Live music every Friday. Located on Belt Line Road, one-half mile north of Interstate 30 and five miles east of The Ballpark in Arlington (see entry). Dallas is a little over ten miles to the east, Fort Worth about 15 miles west from here. Grand Prairie Tourist Information Center is located at Gate One, 2170 North Belt Line Road.

The 315-acre racing facility, which opened in 1997, has a one-mile oval dirt track and the seven-eighths of a mile turf course inside it, both built at a cost of $110 million. While simulcast wagering goes on throughout the year, the Thoroughbred season lasts about 73 days. In 1998, the park's attendance reached 1.3 million, ranking it among the top five of the nation's 60 race tracks, while the tracks in Houston and San Antonio filed for bankruptcy protection. It can seat 8,000 in the grandstand and another 1,500 in the Post Time Pavilion, although the total attendance capacity is 40,000. The 315-acre park was designed by the same company as The Ballpark in Arlington. The racing season is from April through November, purses go as high as $250,000. Lone Star is the area's only legal gambling option other than the Texas Lottery. There is parking for about 5,600 vehicles. "The betting lines are short and the amenities are grand," says the *Dallas Business Journal.* "But Lone Star also set its sights on the middle-class, baby boomer, married-with-children crowd."

A seven-story, glass-enclosed, climate-controlled grandstand features penthouse suites on levels five and six, a terraced trackside dining room, box seats, and outdoor seating, measuring 280,000 square feet in all. The 283 pari-mutuel windows and 176 self-bet machines are scattered on the ground floor and other levels of the grandstand, as well as inside the Post Time Pavilion. Three restaurants, 12 concession stands, and 11 bars are located throughout the complex.

The Post Time Pavilion, located 200 feet west of the grandstand, offers wagering on live racing via simulcast from several other racecourses nationwide, even during the live meets. It features Las Vegas-style racebook, sports bar, and restaurant complete with 175 television monitors and wagering windows. The Pavilion can accommodate 1,500 patrons. Adjacent to it is a 15-acre park with playgrounds for children, picnic gazebos, petting zoo, and pony rides.

In 1929, a 400-acre horse-racing facility, named Arlington Downs, was built by oilman W.T. Waggoner (1852-1934) across from where Six Flags Over Texas (see entry) stands today. In 1933 Gov. Miriam "Ma" Ferguson legalized betting on horses and by the following year the daily betting averaged $175,000. Clark Gable, Gloria Swanson, Rita Hayworth, and others visited Arlington Downs regularly. Waggoner died 13 months after pari-mutuel betting was legalized, but in 1937 Gov. James Allread outlawed betting on horses. Ten years later, the track was dismantled and an industrial park built in its place.

Just south of Lone Star and 12 miles from Dallas, a $28-million, 6,700-seat performance hall on a 30-acre site—called Texas NextStage Theater—was scheduled for completion in the fall of 2000. Some believe this will be the largest indoor performance theater in the nation. It will accommodate everything from touring Broadway shows to rock bands.

Polo

Curragh Equestrian Center, 5595 Ben Day Murrin Rd.; (817) 443-3777, Internet www.currah.com. A full-service boarding and training facility operated under the standards of the British Horse Society. Instructions and training are available for beginners to advanced competitors.

Las Colinas Equestrian Center, 600 Royal Ln. at O'Connor Rd. in Irving; (972) 869-0600, is mostly a boarding stable for horses. The 42-acre equestrian center gives riding lessons and hosts competitions. It is open Tue-Sun 7 am-9 pm. There are two polo fields, where tournaments are held. For details about **Las Colinas Polo Club,** which holds tournaments, please call (214) 373-8855 and ask for the polo information line.

The three-day Las Colinas Classic, a hunter-jumper show, normally takes place in May. Another show is held in October.

SPORTS TO DO

Bicycling

There are more than 20 miles of paved bike trails along the Trinity River. For information about the bike trails, call (817) 871-5700.

The EDS Superdrome, 9700 Wade Blvd., Frisco; (888) 4-DROME-1, Internet www.superdrome.com. CH. Open daily for year-round events. Located on land donated by Collin County Community

College on its Preston Ridge Campus, about five miles north of the EDS headquarters in Plano.

A training site for professional, amateur, and junior track cyclists, with full public certification, rental, and training programs for all experience levels. World cycling championship was held here in 1999. When it opened in mid-1998, this was the country's newest and most expensive velodrome. The 6,000-square-foot Superdrome is 250 meters long and leans in at 44 degrees on the curves. Constructed of marine-grade plywood panels, the track seats 2,200, features the timing technology of the Dallas electronic giant that sponsored it, and was built by the same firm that constructed the velodrome for the 1996 Summer Olympics in Atlanta.

Bowling

AMF Bowling Centers, with automatic scoring, bumper bowling for kids, and arcades and lounges, will be found at these locations:

- 720 West Pipeline Rd. in Hurst; (817) 282-6754.
- 1801 East Lamar Blvd. in Arlington; (817) 276-9898.
- 3149 South Cooper St., in Arlington; (817) 465-4997.

If you like "cosmic" bowling—choreographed with black lights, laser light shows, fog machine, neon bowling balls, and music videos—which seems to appeal particularly to 18- to 24-year-olds, although families like it, too—then head for **Brunswick Watauga Lanes,** (817) 485-2695, at 7301 Rufe Snow Dr. in Watauga, a town of 22,000 between Fort Worth and North Richland Hills. Open Wed 9 pm-midnight, Fri 4-6 pm and midnight-3 am, Sat 3-6 pm and midnight-3 am. There is a cover charge "to keep out the riff-raff" and fee for individual games.

Another "cosmic" bowling center, really a clever campaign to keep bowling alleys occupied late into the night, is located at **Brunswick Varsity Bowl,** (940) 383-3515, 220 San Jacinto Blvd., in Denton, a college city of 75,000 north of the Metroplex.

Don Carter's All-Star Lanes, 6601 Oakmont Blvd. at South Hulen St.; (800) 874-2695 or (817) 346-0444. Open 9 am-1 am seven days a week. Located in southwest Fort Worth, south of Interstate 20, also known here as Southwest Loop 820.

Has 64 completely automated lanes. Fee per game starts at $3 in the evening, plus $2 for shoe rental. Has a cafe and pool tables. There is bumper bowling for children and game room with video games for older kids.

Fishing and Hunting, Hiking and Sailing

Call the **Texas Parks and Wildlife Department,** (800) 792-1112, Internet www.tpwd.state.tx.us, for details about fishing, boating, hunting, camping, and Texas state parks. Check also the state's Internet site at www.texas.gov. Another useful site is www.recreation.gov, where a half-dozen federal agencies offer a comprehensive database of 2,000 recreation sites—parks, forests, and other public resources—searchable by state and activity. For each site there is a contact number, map, weather forecast, and links to related Web pages.

License sales by phone at no additional charge are available by calling (800) TX LIC 4 U (or 800 895-4248), 24 hours a day, and can be charged on your VISA or MasterCard credit cards. These licenses can be purchased by phone for immediate use without having to wait to receive a paper document by mail.

Among the top recreational lakes in the area, listed in order of preference, are

Lake Lewisville, located north of the Metroplex, has a 23,280-acre reservoir, best known for sailing, cruising, and skiing. Has good fishing for sand bass, crappie, catfish, and largemouth. More than a score of public parks are operated at lakeside, providing camping, trailer, and picnic areas.

Lake Ray Hubbard, a 22,745-acre reservoir on the East Fork of the Trinity River. Has a national reputation among sailors, also good recreational boating in the lower end. Good fishing for white bass and hybrid stripers, particularly along the eastern shore. However, surrounded by homes and apartment complexes, this is not one of the prettiest lakes. The west shore, with good water depth and windbreak, is good for skiing. **Elgin B. Roberts Park** has picnic tables. There is a restaurant, open seven days a week.

Joe Pool Lake, a 7,470-acre lake, opened to the public in 1989 and located south of Grand Prairie. Popular camping destination for nature lovers. Good recreational lake, but only fair for fishing. It borders on the 2,000-acre Cedar Hill State Park, where most of the 1,826 wooded acres have been left in a wilderness state. There is swimming and picnicking in the park.

Cedar Hill State Park, (972) 291-3900. *CH*, free for children. Guided trail rides offered periodically for horse owners. Located west of Cedar Hill. Entry fees are charged at all access points, except Britton Park, where free launching is permitted.

The horseshoe-shaped **Lake Lavon,** measuring 21,400 acres, is a Corps of Engineers lake with good parks and camping. A favorite with boaters, it has excellent crappie and white bass fishing. The best spot for skiing and tubing is the dam area because it is sandwiched between two banks, keeping the winds off and thus the waters still.

Grapevine Lake, a scenic 7,380-acre lake with a 60-mile shoreline, popular with boaters, for sailing, skiing, and cruising. Located 27 miles northeast of downtown Fort Worth. It is home to the ski shows and competitions are held in the spring and summer. Has good largemouth bass and crappie fishing. Several parks abutting the lake have hiking and biking trails, swimming, and picnic tables.

McPherson's Slew channel, on the south side of the lake, is a good spot to anchor and swim. There is a restaurant next to Twin Coves Marina on the north side of the lake.

Benbrook Lake is a 3,770-acre Army Corps of Engineers lake in southwest Tarrant County, a few miles southwest of Fort Worth. There are no homes around this lake, only wilderness, with plenty of elm, oak, and willow trees. On the north side of the lake, the city of Benbrook (pop. 22,000) has hauled in tons of sand to create **Baha Beach,** (817) 249-0009), with a roped-off swimming area and covered picnic tables. Admission is charged.

Near the lake's dam, at the eastern edge of the Pecan Valley Golf Course (see entry), at the end of Winscott Plover Road, grows the tallest bur oak in Texas. Eighty-one feet high and 17 and a half feet in circumference, it is said to produce acorns larger than hen eggs—or is it just another figment of Texas imagination. The Memorial Oak is believed to be 400 years old. The Comanches and Kiowas considered it a holy tree and conducted ceremonies underneath it. In 1884, three notorious horse thieves who were sought by the law in five states were hanged from this tree.

Golf

The legend of Fort Worth's golf is Ben Hogan, who won three majors in 1953. Following a nearly fatal car wreck, Hogan came back to win the Masters, U.S. Open, and British Open, nearly matching Bobby Jones' singular Grand Slam. He won 160 professional tournaments in all. Another great moment in Metroplex golf were Byron Nelson's eleven consecutive victories in 1945. Only Hogan has come that close.

Three professional tournaments are held in the Metroplex every May.

Perhaps the best-known is the 30-year-old **GTE Byron Nelson Classic,** Tickets (972) 717-1200, at the Four Seasons Resort & Club in Irving. It is held one weekend in mid-May and televised. The purse in 1998 was close to $2 million, with the winner taking more than $300,000. About 30,000 are expected at the four-day event. Experts say that the best place to see the action is a hill near the 15th green at the Tournament Players Course. Texas Stadium parking lots in Irving can accommodate about 15,000 vehicles; shuttle buses run to the tournament site.

MasterCard Colonial, Tickets (817) 927-4200/4280, held in the second half of May at Colonial Country Club in Fort Worth (see

Leonard Brothers Department Store Marker entry in the SIGHTS chapter), has been held since 1946 and is also televised. Marvin Leonard operated Colonial Country Club as a private venture until 1943, when he sold it to the club's members. About 175,000 attend every year. The winner takes home more than a quarter of a million dollars, with the purse amounting to more than $1.5 million. Public parking for the Colonial is at Amon Carter football stadium at Texas Christian University campus, Will Rogers Equestrian Center, as well as at nearby Farrington Field.

JC Penney/LPGA Skins Game, (972) 394-8900, is held at Stonebriar Country Club in Frisco.

There are five municipal golf courses with 108 holes in Fort Worth having 15.9 acres of greens, 20 acres of trees, and 180 acres of fairway. For reservations call (817) 926-GOLF, and follow the prompts. For fees, car rentals, and other details, call (817) 871-5748 and check the city's Internet site http://ci.fort-worth.tx.us. You must usually reserve three days ahead and the payment is due before you start playing. To reserve a public golf course, call the individual facility below.

Grapevine Municipal Golf Course, 3800 Fairway Drive, near Grapevine Lake Dam, Grapevine; (817) 481-0421. An 18-hole course rated as one of the top 75 municipal golf courses in the U.S. Open dawn to dusk.

Hyatt Bear Creek Golf & Racquet Club, West Airfield Drive, D/FW Airport; (817) 651-6808. Two 18-hole championship courses. Rated as one of the top 50 resort courses in America. The *Dallas Morning News* rated it one of the top ten public courses. Also has nine racquetball, one volleyball, four outdoor, and three covered tennis courts. Open Mon-Thu 8 am-11 pm, Fri 8 am-9:30 pm, Sat-Sun 8 am-6:30 pm. Annual passes available.

Iron Horse Golf Club, 6200 Skylark Circle, North Richland Hills; (817) 485-6666. Rated one of the top ten public courses in Texas and the best in Tarrant County by the *Fort Worth Star-Telegram* staff, which calls it "diabolically tough and immaculately maintained. Our only beef is with the outrageous green fees, but if that's what we have to pay for a course of this quality, then we'll just grit our teeth and try to stay in the fairways." Scenic, the course traverses through a hardwood forest and over meandering creeks. Open dawn to dusk.

Lake Arlington Golf Course, 1516 West Green Oaks Blvd.; (817) 451-6101/4882. Has 18 holes, is open dawn to dusk.

Meadowbrook Golf Course, 1815 Jenson Rd.; (817) 457-4616. An 18-hole championship municipal course located on the east side of Fort Worth. Open dawn to dusk. It has a Pro Shop and snack bar.

Pecan Valley Golf Course, 6800 Lakeside Dr.; (817) 249-1845.

Located in southwest Fort Worth, this popular municipal course has 36 holes, pro shop, a snack facility, and driving range. Open 6 am-7:30 pm.

Rockwood Golf Course, 1851 Jacksboro Highway, also known as State Highway 199; (817) 624-1771. Centrally located, this 1930s-era privately managed northwest Fort Worth municipal course has 27 holes. Open dawn to dusk.

Sycamore Creek Golf Course, 501 Martin Luther King Jr. Fwy.; (817) 535-7241. A Fort Worth municipal course located in southeast Fort Worth. Renovated in 1993, it has nine holes with double tee boxes. Open dawn to dusk.

Z Boaz Golf Course, 3200 Lackland Rd.; (817) 738-6287. A privately managed 1930s-era, 18-hole, west Fort Worth municipal golf course. It has a pro shop and snack facility. Open dawn to dusk.

Health Clubs

Perhaps the most frustrating chore with the health clubs is finding out what the real cost of using their facilities is. Negotiate and compare before you agree to or sign anything.

24-Hour Fitness 2, 2100 South Cooper St. at Pioneer Parkway, Arlington; (817) 860-5600. Open continuously.

With 15,000 members, this is the largest fitness club in Arlington. Has a 5,000-square-foot aerobics facility, also bikes and stair-stepping equipment, as well as sauna. The fee is $10 a day, although other long-term rates are also available.

Bally Total Fitness, Ridgmar Mall, 6833-A Green Oaks Rd.; (817) 738-8910, Internet www.ballyfitness.com. Open Mon-Fri 6 am-10 pm, Sat-Sun 8 am-7 pm.

Has locations throughout the Metroplex, with a variety of aerobic programs, racquetball, and running tracks. The Ridgmar facility has a childcare center for members. Bally said it only had three-year memberships available at Ridgmar, adding that managers sometimes give out complimentary weekly passes for international visitors.

One Arlington location is at 2306 South Collins St.; (817) 274-7177.

Dancescape Inc., 3328 West Seventh St. at Arch Adams; (817) 338-0884. Open Mon-Fri 8 am-6 pm, Sat 9 am-1 pm, closed Sundays. Located in west Fort Worth, two blocks north of Kimbell Art Museum and across the street from Michael's, a contemporary ranch-cuisine restaurant (see individual entries).

Dancescape promotes the Pilates Method, brought to New York by German acrobat Joseph H. Pilates (d. 1967), who had worked primarily with professional dancers. Strength and flexibility training, Pilates Method "is a series of controlled stretching and strengthening exercises that focus on the body's core: the abdominal and pelvic muscles," according to the *Fort Worth Star-Telegram*. The exercises are performed on floor mats and spring-operated equipment. They require intense concentration and attention to form and might be considered a cross between yoga and strength training. A one-hour session with a private instructor costs $50-$125, unlimited number of floorwork group classes is $75 a month.

Readers of the *Star-Telegram* voted this and Arlington's The Q Sports Club the most popular exercise venues in the area.

Fit for Life, Cityview Shopping Center, 6125 Southwest Loop 820, Suite 144; (817) 292-8101. Open 24 hours, seven days a week. Located in southwest Fort Worth, at Interstate 20 and Bryant Irvin Rd., a block from Hulen Mall (see entry).

A health club with 6,200 members at two locations. Monthly fee is $39 for singles, daily visits are $10 each, or 20 visits for $100. Workouts can be custom-tailored to fit individual needs, medical history, and level of activity. Has treadmills, stair climbers, stationary cycles, and cross-trainers. Sauna, whirlpool, and massage are available. Childcare is also available.

Its Arlington location is at 6031 Interstate 20 West, Suite 256; (817) 292-8101.

Get Fit Centers, 6910 Green Oaks Blvd.; (817) 737-2276. Located behind Ridgmar Mall (see entry), at Interstate 30 and State Highway 183. Open 24 hours.

The four locations of Get Fit have a total of 30,000 members, perhaps the largest fitness and health club in Tarrant County. Annual membership fee is $275 and monthly dues of $20. The monthly fee at the Green Oaks location, which measures 14,000 square feet, is $60. Childcare is available to members.

The two locations in Arlington are at 1005 Skyline, behind Hooters restaurant, (817) 860-0424, in north Arlington; and Interstate 20 at Little Road, behind Harrigans, (817) 478-8270.

Harris Fitness Center, 1616 Hospital Parkway; (817) 267-9191. Located at Harris Methodist H.E.B. Hospital in Bedford, south of State Hwy. 183, where it merges with State Hwy. 121. Open Mon-Fri 6 am-6 pm.

With 2,800 active members, one of the largest fitness centers in the Metroplex. Has three locations. Monthly fees are $35 for singles, $55 for families. Cardiovascular, strength, and aerobics workouts are available, in addition to yoga, kickboxing, and weight management. Sauna, whirlpool, and massage are at your disposal.

Health & Fitness Connection, 6242 Hulen Bend Blvd. at Oakmont Blvd.; (817) 346-6161. Open Mon-Fri 5:30 am-10:30 pm, Sat-Sun 7 am-8 pm. Located in southwest Fort Worth, across the street from Wal-Mart.

This is an affiliate of the Osteopathic Health System of Texas. Has 4,100 members. Group exercise and water fitness classes are available. Also yoga, circuit boxing, karate, indoor track, and racquetball. There are treadmills, stair climbers, and recumbent and upright cycles. Has on-site medical director, massage, and facials. Health assessment and weight loss programs. Also has programs for elderly. Childcare is available at a charge. Daily fee is $10, monthly $60. The staff of the *Fort Worth Star-Telegram* and readers of *FW Weekly* named it one of the best health clubs.

Huguley Fitness Center, 11801 South Fwy.; (817) 568-3131. Located at Huguley Memorial Hospital (see entry). Open 24 hours Sun-Thu, Fridays until 5 pm, closed Saturdays. Located in far-south Fort Worth east of Interstate Highway 35 West (also known as West Freeway), north of Rendon-Crawley Road East and north of Fort Worth Spinks Airport (see entry).

Has 6,000 members. Membership fees range $80-$120, monthly dues are $35, weekly $15. Aerobic classes, stair climbers, treadmills, racquetball, and basketball are available. There are two indoor swimming pools. Sauna, whirlpool, and massage are also available. Provides childcare at a fee.

Larry North Total Fitness Club, Commerce at East Fifth St.; (817) 336-6784. Open 5 am-11 pm. Located on the ground floor of the 15-story Crescent Realty 1,350-space parking garage downtown next to the Bass Performance Hall (see entry).

The 12,000-square-foot "signature gym" was built in 1998 at a cost of $2 million. It has 1,500 memberships, state of the art equipment, a dozen full-time employees, and twice that many contract instructors and therapists.

North, "whose father was a compulsive gambler and thief whose influence instilled a reverse motivation in his son," according to the *Fort Worth Star-Telegram,* is a fitness icon of the Metroplex. "Fleeing from his father two decades ago, North, his brother and mother were en route from Las Vegas to Houston when their car broke down in Dallas." He has since remained in Dallas. He regularly appears on television and has written three fitness books.

The Q Sports Club, 1131 West Arbrook Blvd., Arlington; (817) 465-2600. Open Mon-Fri 5 am-11 pm, Sat-Sun 7 am-8 pm. Located in central Arlington, across the street from The Parks at Arlington Mall (see entry), between Cooper Street and Matlock Road.

A workout facility with free weights, cardiovascular machines, weight machines, circuits, and personal training. Has some 300 pieces of equipment and complimentary childcare. Monthly fee is $150. Readers of the *Fort Worth Star-Telegram* voted it and Dancescape of Fort Worth as the two most popular gyms in the area.

Another Q Sports Club is located at 2100 Plaza Parkway in Bedford; (817) 545-4900. The Ohio-based chain plans to open two clubs in Fort Worth.

YMCA of Metropolitan Fort Worth, 540 Lamar St.; (817) 335-6147 or 332-3281. Open Mon-Fri 6 am-9 pm, Sat 8 am-5 pm, closed Sundays. Located downtown between West Fourth and Fifth streets.

YMCA, with 21,000 members at 14 locations, including downtown, is one of the largest fitness clubs in Tarrant County. Downtown, it provides complete workout facilities, including small indoor and outdoor track, two swimming pools, sauna, and steam room. No childcare facilities. Membership fees run $20-$150, depending on the services you use, and monthly dues are $45.

Ice Skating

Blue Line Ice Complex, Town Center, 1 Ice House Drive, North Richland Hills; (817) 788-5400. CH. Anchors Town Center, which will be in development until the end of the decade.

It has three sheets of ice, including two NHL-sized rinks and one that meets Olympic measurements. One hockey rink is home to the Texas Tornado, a junior hockey league team. A dance floor is available, where figure skaters can choreograph their routines. The facility is held at 55 degrees, even when the outside temperature is twice that. A full-service restaurant, private party rooms, and an arcade are also on the premises.

Fort Worth Outlet Square, Third and Throckmorton streets; Events Hotline, (800) 414-2817, Internet www.fwoutletsquare.com. Open Mon-Thu 10 am-7 pm, Fri-Sat 10 am-9 pm, Sun noon-6 pm. You can make reservations for skating rink by calling (817) 878-4800.

Skatin' Texas Cowtown Ice Arena, 3600 Highway 377 South, at Weatherford Traffic Circle; (817) 560-7465. Has 17,000 square feet of ice, serves as the official training facility of the Fort Worth Brahmas ice hockey club (see entry). A public skating rink. Instructions and lessons are available. Food and daycare could be had.

Skatium of Arlington, 5515 South Cooper St., Arlington; (817) 784-6222. The "largest free-standing skating center in the country," according to the *Arlington Life* guide. A popular roller skating and in-line skating venue on the city's south side.

Tennis

There are 91 municipal tennis courts in Fort Worth. Neighborhood courts are on a first-come, first-served basis. For reservations, call the individual facility.

Bayard Friedman Tennis Center, 3609 North Bellaire Dr.; (817) 921-7960. Open Mon-Fri 9 am-9 pm, Sat-Sun 9 am-7:30 pm. Located on Texas Christian University campus (see entry). It won several awards for public tennis centers. Has 16 lighted outdoor and five air-conditioned indoor courts. Reservations accepted up to one week in advance.

This facility was dedicated in honor of former Fort Worth Mayor Bayard Friedman in 2000. Friedman, also known as Mr. Fort Worth, was an avid tennis fan. He was mayor from 1963 to 1965 and died in 1998.

Don McLeland Tennis Center, 1600 West Seminary Dr.; (817) 921-5134. Open Mon-Fri 9 am-9 pm, Sat-Sun 9 am-6 pm. This municipal tennis center offers players 14 lighted outdoor hard courts and two climate-controlled indoor courts. Reservation fee. Outdoor rates are per person, indoor rates per court. Lessons are available.

Hulen Street Baptist Church, 7100 South Hulen St.; (817) 292-9787. Open Mon-Sat 9 am-dusk, Wed until 5 pm. Closed Sundays. Fort Worth's only clay tennis courts. Has ten courts open to the public. Family memberships are available.

SPECIAL EVENTS

Please check the *Fort Worth Star-Telegram*, *FW Weekly*, *Dallas Morning News*, *D Magazine*, or *Texas Monthly* for more information about these events. Telephone numbers often change from year to year, but will also be found at the time in one of these publications. Be prepared for extreme heat with the events held during the summer.

The State of Texas Internet site, www.texas.gov, which also links with cities like Fort Worth and Arlington, has a calendar of events and highway conditions.

January

Southwestern Exposition and Lifestock Show & Rodeo (see entry), the nation's oldest livestock show, is held in the second half of this month and into February at Will Rogers Memorial Center in Fort Worth's cultural district. Almost one million visitors attend the show and 30 performances of the original indoor rodeo. Call (817) 877-2400.

If you love music, opera, or ballet, check out what's happening at the **Bass Performance Hall** (see entry) in the Sundance Square downtown, (817) 212-4300, this month and beyond.

On January 17, Martin Luther King, Jr.'s birthday, events are held all over the Metroplex, including the **Multi-Cultural Festival** in Arlington.

Join the hour-long **Nature Hikes at River Legacy Park,** (817) 860-6752, a 673-acre park in Arlington, every Friday and Saturday this month and throughout the year.

February

The **Jim Courtright-Luke Short Annual Shootout** is re-enacted every February 8 in front of the modern-day White Elephant Saloon on East Exchange Avenue in the Stockyards. See the entry in the SIGHTS chapter. Call (817) 624-9712. The original 1887 gunfight between the City Marshal Jim Courtright and gambler Luke Short took place on the 300 block of east side of Main Street, between Second and Third streets downtown, but was transferred here when the White Elephant Saloon moved in 1976.

Stockyards Championship Rodeo is held every February at Cowtown Coliseum, across the street from the Fort Worth Visitors Bureau in the Stockyards, (817) 625-1025. Bull riding, steer wrestling, calf roping, team roping, and barrel racing are some of the events you can enjoy.

Also this month, you can attend a **Dallas Mavericks,** (214) 748-1808, professional basketball, **Texas Rangers,** (817) 273-5100, professional baseball, or **Dallas Cowboys,** (972) 579-5000, professional football game.

If snakes fascinate you, go to the **Walnut Springs Rattlesnake Festival & Barbecue Cook-Off,** held the last weekend of February or the first one in March. Snake-handling demonstrations, snake hunts, starting at 9 am, and country and Western dance in the evening are held in this town, between Glen Rose and Meridian, on State Highway 114. For more information call (817) 897-2176.

March

A **St. Patrick's Day Parade** and several related events are held in the city this month. See local newspapers for details.

The **Stockyards Championship Rodeo** continues at Cowtown Coliseum. Check out what the exhibits are at the **Kimbell, Modern,** and **Amon Carter** museums. Consider also the **Fort Worth Zoo,** the oldest such continuous institution in Texas.

April

NASCAR Winston Cup Race, (817) 215-8500, at the Texas Motor Speedway (see entry), the first NASCAR racing facility in Texas, at State Hwy. 114 and FM 156, about 15 miles north of Fort Worth, comes alive starting this month.

At the Will Rogers Memorial Center in Fort Worth's cultural center, **Lone Star Ranch Rodeo, National Cutting Horse Association Super Stakes,** and **North Texas Arabian Horse Championship** are all held this month, (817) 871-8150. Meanwhile, **Pawnee Bill's Wild West Show,** (817) 625-1025, takes place in Cowtown Coliseum in the Stockyards.

The **Playwright's Festival,** (817) 738-7491, consisting of One Acts, is held by local authors at the Fort Worth Theatre in the cultural district.

In the middle of April, the **Main Street Arts Festival,** (817) 336-ARTS, a three-day extravaganza stretching the entire nine blocks of Main Street downtown is held annually for 350,000 visitors. Claiming to be the third largest event of its kind in Texas, the brick-paved Main Street becomes a marketplace of food, arts, crafts, and live entertainment.

Texas Rangers, the Metroplex professional basketball team, is exciting the crowds at the Ballpark Stadium (see entry) in Arlington through October.

At the Mesquite Arena, in the city east of Dallas, the popular annual Rodeo Parade kicks off the **Championship Rodeo,** (972) 222-BULL, season, which runs from April to September.

Prairie Dog Chili Cook-Off, (972) 647-2331, the oldest and largest such event in the Metroplex, is held at the Traders Village in Grand Prairie, with some 150 chili cooking teams, usually at the beginning of April.

In Denton, north of the Metroplex, the **Annual Denton Arts & Jazz Festival,** (940) 565-0931, is held for four days at the end of April at the Civic Center Park.

Waxahachie, a town about a 30-minute drive south of Dallas, holds **Scarborough Faire,** (972) 938-3247, an annual Renaissance festival recreating a 16th-century English village. You can watch knights in armor, marvel at the falconer and his birds of prey, or watch jugglers, sorcerers, and jesters. Hundreds of entertainers and 200 merchants are on hand weekends only, 10 am-7 pm, rain or shine, from the end of April until mid-June.

Starting at the end of April and concluding in May is **Mayfest,** (817) 332-1055, a family festival on the banks of the Trinity River at Trinity Park West in the cultural district. It features food, arts, crafts, and live performances.

May

MasterCard Colonial Golf Tournament, (817) 927-4278, features the nation's top golfers who compete in this nationally televised event at the Fort Worth's Colonial Country Club, near the Log Cabin Village and the Fort Worth Zoo, in the second half of May.

Memorial Day Calf Roping, (817) 625-1025, at the Cowtown Coliseum and **Memorial Day Street Dance** are both held in the Stockyards historic district.

In Greenville, a town of 25,000 northeast of Dallas, an **Audie Murphy Day,** (903) 455-1736, named after a genuine Texas hero, is held late in May.

In Fort Worth, the quadrennial **Van Cliburn International Piano Competition,** (817) 335-9000, one of the world's most prestigious classical music pianistic events, will take place from May into June in the year 2001. Since 1997, and every three years thereafter, **Dallas International Organ Competition** takes place and the first-prize winner appears as a soloist with the Dallas Symphony Orchestra.

In North Richland Hills, northeast of Fort Worth, **NRH₂O Family Waterpark,** (817) 581-5567, opens in the middle of this month and stays open until September.

June

Texas Scottish Festival & Highland Games, (817) 654-2293, take place the first week of June, attracting 1,000 competitors and up to 60,000 visitors, at Maverick Stadium at the University of Texas at Arlington. Besides the games and music, there are kilt-clad dancers, bagpiping and drumming contests, sheep dog demonstrations, a shortbread contest, children's games, and lectures on Celtic art.

Chisholm Trail Round-Up & Chief Quanah Parker Comanche Indian Pow-Wow, (817) 625-7005, is held in mid-June in the Stockyards to celebrate the city's Western heritage and ties to the cattle drives of old. More than 50,000 attend the three-day event.

Juneteenth (Texas Emancipation Day, June 19, 1865), when General Granger arrived at Galveston proclaiming U.S. authority over Texas at the end of the Civil War and declaring slaves free, is celebrated with a parade in downtown Fort Worth and other events. Call (817) 335-9605 or go to the Internet site www.juneteenth.com/worldwide.htm and click on Texas.

Don Edwards Cowboy Gathering & Invitational Pasture Ropin', (817) 625-1025, is held at the beginning of the month at Westfork Ranch, west of Fort Worth, and includes campfire and music by the cowboy balladeer Don Edwards.

Pawnee Bill's Wild West Show, a historical reenactment of a wild west show at the turn of the century, is held this and next month at the Cowtown Coliseum in the Stockyards and includes trick roping and shooting, buffalo, longhorn cattle, and horses. Also at the Coliseum, you can see the **High School Rodeo Finals.**

There is the **Longhorn Cattle Sale,** (817) 625-9715, and the **American Miniature Horse Show** at the beginning of this month at Will Rogers Memorial Center in the cultural district.

Indy Car Races, (817) 215-8500, take place at the Texas Motor Speedway (see entry), the country's second-largest sports facility of its kind.

Shakespeare in the Park, (817) 923-6698, performances are held from June into July under the stars at the Trinity Park Playhouse on Seventh Street, seven blocks east of University Drive. Park opens for picnickers at 6:30 pm, show begins at 8:30 pm.

At the Fort Worth Botanic Garden, open-air **Concerts in the Garden,** (817) 781-7686, with performances by the Fort Worth Symphony and guests artists, take place this and next month. Grounds open at 6:30 pm, concerts begin at 8:15 pm.

July

Fort Worth Fourth!, (817) 870-1692, concludes on the banks of the Trinity River banks with fireworks that highlight a day of sporting, musical, and family events downtown and in the Stockyards historic district. **July 4 Fireworks Extravaganza,** (817) 410-3185, explodes in Grapevine, a town of 40,000 west of D/FW Airport.

Stockyards Championship Rodeo, (817) 625-1025, continues at the Cowtown Coliseum throughout this month. **Thoroughbred Horse Racing,** (972) 263-7223, starts at Lone Star Park in Grand Prairie, a city of 115,000 between Arlington and Dallas.

At the end of July, **Fiesta Fort Worth,** (817) 738-9472, celebrates the music, food, and spirit of the Hispanic culture on Main Street downtown.

In Mesquite, east of Dallas, there is an annual **Balloon Festival,** (972) 285-0211, held in Paschall Park, off New Market Road and near the Town East shopping mall, where up to 50 hot-air balloonists from all over the U.S. participate in this three-day event. More than 100,000 spectators also attend; arts and crafts fair and amusements can be enjoyed.

August

By now, it's so hot that **Six Flags Hurricane Harbor** water park in Arlington and **NRH$_2$O Family Waterpark** in North Richland Hills may be the only sensible entertainment for some. Kids don't care how hot it is as long as you also consider Arlington's **Six Flags Over Texas** theme park.

Lewisville, a city of 70,000 northeast of D/FW Airport, holds the **Texas Open Championship Chili Cook-Off,** (972) 219-3550, at the beginning of August.

In the Stockyards, **Wild West Activities** take place every Saturday this month. And the **Stockyards Championship Rodeo** at the Cowtown Coliseum is still going strong.

At Will Rogers Memorial Center in the cultural district, the **American Quarter Horse Association World Championship,** (817) 871-8150, is held for a week in mid-month.

North Texas State Fair and Rodeo, (940) 387-2632, has been held in Denton—a city of 75,000 north of the Metroplex—for more than 70 years in the second half of August. Down-home diversions include contests and dancing, barbecue cook-offs, midway rides and games, and a petting zoo.

Ringling Brothers, Barnum & Bailey **Circus,** (817) 884-2222, comes to the Fort Worth Convention Center downtown as soon as it completes its Dallas engagement. It is followed by the **RV Show.**

In mid-August, **Yellow Rose Classic Car Show,** (817) 871-8150, attracts automobile enthusiasts for a couple of days in mid-August, followed by the **Hunter's Extravaganza,** both at Will Rogers Memorial Center in the cultural district.

Meanwhile, **Texas Rangers** baseball season continues in Arlington, as does the Rodeo in Mesquite.

September

Stockyards Championship Rodeo, (817) 625-1025, will continue to thrill you with bull riding, steer wrestling, calf roping, team roping, and barrel racing in Cowtown Coliseum in the Stockyards.

This is also the month to catch **Pawnee Bill's Wild West Show,** a historical reenactment of a Wild West show that toured the world at the turn of the century. It includes trick roping, trick shooting, buffalo, longhorn cattle, and horses and is also held at the Cowtown Coliseum.

In Grapevine, northwest of the D/FW Airport, a three-day **Grapefest** wine-tasting festival, (800) 457-6338, takes place in the middle of September. Although only one vineyard actually grows grapes and manufactures wines here, Grapevine—a cantaloupe and cotton farming town of 40,000—promotes itself as the Wine Capital of Texas, the state with 27 wineries. Some 100,000 come to what is the oldest settlement in Tarrant County and named after the wild mustang grapes that covered the area when settlers first arrived in 1844.

In the second half of this month, you could participate at **Taste of Arlington,** (817) 459-5000, where food and drink are plentiful.

Right after the mid-month, **Pioneer Days,** (817) 626-7921, is held in the Stockyards. A family celebration, it commemorates the early days of the cattle industry and the pioneers who settled on the banks of the Trinity River.

Bobby Norris Roundup, (972) 644-2076, features the top cutting horse contestants and celebrities at the Cowtown Coliseum in the

Stockyards for the benefit of the Autistic Treatment Center. It is followed by the **Pioneer Days Rodeo,** (817) 625-1025, also at the Coliseum.

There are races this month at the 151,000-seat **Texas Motor Speedway,** (817) 215-8500, which measures 950 acres, cost $110 million to build, and is the largest spectator-sport facility in Texas.

At the end of this month, you can visit the three-day **Fall Home & Garden Show,** (817) 884-2222, which takes place at the Fort Worth Convention Center downtown.

The **Texas State Fair,** (214) 565-9931, the largest in the country and one of the oldest, is held annually September 27-October 20 in Dallas's Fair Park and well worth coming from Cowtown or anywhere in the Metroplex to experience if you enjoy this sort of commotion. It includes shows, exhibitions, and contests of every description. In a long Texas tradition, thousands of steers, cows, horses, hogs, sheep, goats, rabbits, even hens, are judged in the livestock arenas for prizes as high as $65,000.

October

Oktoberfest, (817) 924-5881, a Fort Worth family tradition of German and international foods, music, and performing and visual arts, is held annually at the beginning of this month at the Fort Worth Convention Center downtown. Some 40,000 attend the three-day event, which benefits 50 nonprofit organizations.

Texas Longhorn Show & Sale and **National Peruvian Paso Horse Show,** (817) 871-8150, are held simultaneously the second week of October at Will Rogers Memorial Center in the cultural district. They are followed, at the end of the month, by the **Senior Citizens Fair** and **Appaloosa Horse Club Championship,** which stretches into November.

Also around mid-month, the Fort Worth's **International Air Show,** (817) 870-1515 or 491-1092, is held at the city's Alliance Airport, 15 miles north of downtown, where stunt flying, wing-walking, and displays of military and civilian aircraft take place to the delight of some 50,000 spectators.

The annual **Fort Worth Film Festival** takes place during the second half of this month downtown.

Red Steagall Cowboy Gathering, (817) 884-1945, takes place annually in the Stockyards. Western heritage and the cowboy way of life are celebrated to the delight of 40,000 visitors; this festival features ranch rodeo, chuck wagon cooking, and cowboy poetry. Steagall has been officially recognized by the Legislature as the state poet of Texas. At the Stockyards Coliseum the **Women's National Finals Rodeo,**

(817) 625-1025, where the country's top female rodeo professionals compete, takes place at the end of the month.

The Fort Worth **Antique Show,** (817) 884-2222, is held at the end of this month at the Convention Center downtown.

For children, there is **Boo! at the Zoo,** (817) 871-7050, a "spooktacular Halloween extravaganza," where your kids could trick or treat through the Fort Worth Zoo and enjoy live shows.

November

Time again to consider visiting the **Kimbell, Modern,** and **Amon Carter museums,** all located in the cultural district, where you could also catch a show at the **Casa Manana,** or stop at the **Fort Worth Museum of Science & History.**

Stockyards Championship Rodeo, (817) 625-1025, takes place throughout the month in the historic Cowtown Coliseum, featuring bull riding, steer wrestling, calf roping, and barrel racing. The **Western Spectacular Bull Blast Benefit** is held in the second half of the month.

Parade of Lights, (817) 870-1692, an event that signals the beginning of the Christmas season, includes a parade of horses and carriages, clowns and floats down Cowtown's Main Street. There is a large Christmas tree in General Worth Square, near the Fort Worth Convention Center. Close to 100,000 spectators line the one-mile route.

At the Will Rogers Equestrian Center in the cultural district, the **National Cutting Horse Association Futurity,** (817) 871-8150, one of three such events yearly by the National Cutting Horse Association, is held from the end of November and into December, featuring the most skilled cutting horses to "separate" cattle.

December

Roland Reid Memorial Calf Roping, (817) 625-1025, is held this month at Cowtown Coliseum in the Stockyards, in addition to the **Stockyards Championship Rodeo** and **Pawnee Bill's Wild West Show.**

Christmas in the Stockyards and **The T Tour of Lights,** (817) 626-7921, are two other annual events taking place around Christmastime, as is the annual **Parade of Lights,** which features more than 100 illuminated floats, horse-drawn carriages, and and appearance by Santa Claus. Since 1999, the Christmas tree is displayed in Sundance Square.

The 300-plus homes in the upscale Interlochen subdivision in northwest Arlington have been decorated with Christmas lights for more than 25 years. The display is open from sundown to 11 pm during the last two weeks in December. A tour takes up to one hour.

SELF-GUIDED CITY TOURS

A fairly detailed walking tour of downtown Fort Worth is sketched below. Following that, we will guide you on a driving tour that will give you an overview of downtown, the cultural district, and the Stockyards area, where you can indulge your fantasy of the West.

DOWNTOWN WALKING TOUR

This is just one of many ways to sightsee downtown. We have picked a simple route to make it possible to introduce to you a number of sights that you will find described in more detail in the SIGHTS chapter. Visitors accustomed to seeing great architectural gems on many a corner when they visit other cities, should be prepared for some less than beautiful downtown real estate here and there, interspersed with a few buildings that would be a credit to any city. Wear a comfortable pair of shoes and plenty of suntan lotion if you take this tour in the summer, when the downtown streets are as hot as a boiling cauldron.

Depending on your pace, this tour could take up to two hours. As opposed to Dallas, where downtown streets seem as dead as a nail on a weekend, Fort Worth is alive, historic, and pleasant, particularly the Sundance Square, an area between Throckmorton and Calhoun, Second and Fifth streets. Numerous restaurants are listed in case you need a refreshment or want to sit down to a full meal.

Bear in mind that Main Street divides the downtown streets into east and west sides.

Let's Begin at the Convention Center ——

What better place to begin than at the **Fort Worth Convention Center?** If you stand on the corner of Main and Eight streets, for

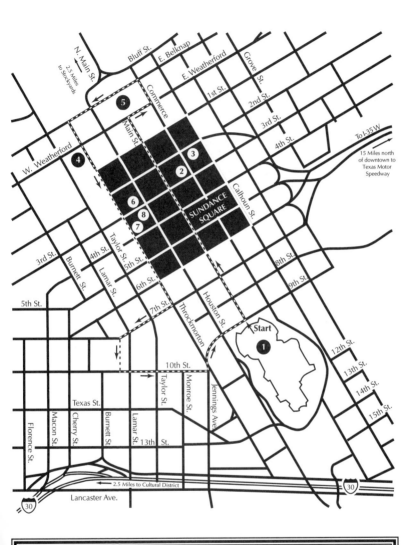

1. Fort Worth Convention
   Center
2. The Sid Richardson
   Collection of Western Art
3. Fire Station No. 1
4. Fort Worth Outlet Square

5. Tarrant County Courthouse
6. Caravan of Dreams
7. Fort Worth Convention &
   Visitors Bureau
8. Modern Art Museum

example, and face north, looking toward the **Tarrant County Courthouse,** nine blocks away, the **Radisson Plaza** hotel, where President Kennedy spent his last night before being assassinated in Dallas, is on your right. Del Frisco's Double Eagle Steak House across Main is on your left. Behind you is **General Worth Square** and another block away the Convention Center. Greyhound bus terminal is a block to your right.

Proceed in a northwesterly direction on Main Street and you will first pass on your right Radisson's Cactus Bar & Grill and across Seventh Street the **Union Pacific Plaza Building.** Across the street on the same block is Carlson Wagonlit travel agency. Cross Sixth Street and you are passing the former **Blackstone Hotel,** which opened one week before the stock market crash of 1929 and was known under several names until 1962. It closed in 1982 and was reconstructed 16 years later as a Courtyard by Marriott with 203 rooms and suites. Corner Bakery Restaurant is located in this building.

Also on Main, across from the Marriott, is the Hyena's Comedy Night Club, whose second location you will find in Arlington. As you approach Fifth Street, you will notice two blocks to your left the **Bank One Tower,** with the Southwestern-cuisine Reata restaurant and a spectacular view of the city from its 35th floor. Ahead, across Fifth Street and on your right, is a two-level Chili's Grill & Bar, and, next to it, Tex-Mex Mi Cocina.

You Are Now Entering the Sundance Square

As you cross Fifth Street—that's where **Sundance Square** begins, a 12-block retail, entertainment, and restaurant area—you will see on the west side on the corner with Main the well-known **Sinclair Building,** with Picchi-Pacchi cafe on the ground floor. Completed in 1930, it was called "the most perfect" structure in the Southwest and occupied by Sinclair Oil Company two years later. Go inside and check out the lobby.

Next door to the Sinclair building is the busy **Jubilee Theatre,** which was founded in 1981 and produces mostly works that reflect the African-American culture. On the same side and the end of that block stands the **Burk Burnett Building,** which was designed by the well-regarded architects Sanguinet and Staats and bought by the legendary cattleman Burnett in 1915. As you pause on the corner of Main and Fourth, you will see on your right ahead the huge **Chase Texas Tower,** formerly known as **City Center I,** and to the right from it **City Center II.** Flying Saucer beer emporium, with more than a 100 choices the world over, is located in that 1889 **Land Title Building** immediately to your right. The much-talked-about *Chisholm Trail* mural, painted by

Richard Hass on a 1907 three-story building, faces the Burnett Building on your left.

As you cross Fourth, you will not fail to notice on the next block on your right the most recent pride of Fort Worth, the 2,054-seat **Bass Performance Hall,** promoted here as the last major concert hall of this century. It was inaugurated in 1998 by pianist Van Cliburn and opera singer Federica von Staade. Facing it across Fourth Street is the New-American cuisine restaurant Angeluna, with cloud-painted ceilings. Keep walking and on the same block of Commerce Street, on your right, you cannot miss the gigantic Barnes & Noble Booksellers and the Surf Club USA and The Brew Co. in the basement of that building, with B & N Cafe next to it. An ATM is next door.

History, Art, and Luke Short-"Long Hair Jim" Courtright Gunfight Site ———

As you cross Third Street, there stands the 1901 **Knights of Pythias Hall,** again designed by Sanguinet and Staats, on the spot where the first Knights of Pythias Castle was erected in 1881, but burned down. Today the building houses Haltom's Jewelers, with their distinctive clock on the street corner. Farther to the right is located 8.0 restaurant, whose name stands for "eight partners, zero experience."

On the west side of Third Street stands the noisy Cajun restaurant Razzoo. Cross Main Street and you will pass on your right the **Domino Building,** where The Casino of the Wild West once stood and where the real Butch Cassidy and the Sundance Kid gambled. Next to it is the **Sid Richardson Collection of Western Art,** named after the great-uncle to the Fort Worth billionaire Bass brothers, and displaying a permanent collection of 55 paintings of Western art by Frederick Remington and Charles M. Russell. Directly across the street stands the **Morris & Conn Building,** the original location of the famed **White Elephant Saloon.** Here, the city marshal "Long Hair Jim" Courtright and gambler Luke Short squared off in a fateful encounter that left the marshal dead on the sidewalk in 1887. Want to watch the annual reenactment in front of the present Stockyard location of the White Elephant Saloon? See Jim Courtright-Luke Short Shootout in the SIGHTS chapter. Next to this sight is Thomas Kinkade Gallery, displaying the syrupy Luminist art for the masses.

More Food Choices and Famous Lodging House ———

On the southwest corner of Main and Second streets, you will find Riscky's Bar-B-Q, still another culinary venture of Mary and Joe Riscky, immigrants from Poland, who had opened the first grocery store in 1927. Once, passersby were entertained by orchestras night and day in this section of the town. On the east side of Main, there is the Ellington's Southern Table Restaurant and next to it the popular La Madeleine French Bakery & Cafe.

They both occupy the former Plaza Hotel building that originally had a saloon and "guest" rooms on the top floors where cowboys retired with their newly-met women before pushing on with their longhorns to Kansas.

Cross Second Street and there is the **Renaissance Worthington Hotel** on your left, and on your right, what is now called the **Chase Texas Tower,** but to many Worthians still known as **City Center I.** Should you decide to take the moving stairs inside, you will find that the billionaire Bass brothers have offices in this tower. A guard may remind you that copying down the names of the tenants is not allowed. A block to your right, at Second and Commerce streets, there is the **Fire Station No. 1,** the site of the city's original city hall, which features a permanent exhibit about Fort Worth, from its beginnings as a frontier outpost through its rowdy youth as a cattle town. The Renaissance Worthington—where the Van Cliburn Suite goes for $1,000 a night—boasts four stars from *Mobil Guide* and four diamonds from the American Automobile Association.

But perhaps you are not in the mood to explore the classical music pride of Fort Worth right now and want to do something more down to earth. Shopping perhaps? You are in luck because from where you stand there is the **Fort Worth Outlet Square Mall,** just two blocks to your left. But let's stop in on our way back if you don't mind. As you pass the Renaissance Worthington, you will see the China Inn restaurant behind it. Directly across Main Street, there is an ATM.

Here Comes the Tarrant County Courthouse

Long before crossing Weatherford Street, you will see from Main the **Tarrant County Courthouse,** where the parade grounds of the original fort once stood, overlooking the Trinity River Valley. In 1893, the county commissioners funded this courthouse, which was constructed below the allocated $500,000, but the "Tarrant County citizens struggling to recover from the economic depression that began in 1893 were astounded at the high cost of the building and voted all of the commissioners out of the office at the next election," says author Carol Roark. Designed by Kansas City architects, the red-granite courthouse is patterned after the Texas State Capitol in Austin. The horse fountain, to the side of it, was erected by the Women's Humane Association in 1892, and rededicated in 1999.

Turn right and walk around the Courthouse to the back, where Charles Tandy's statue stands. North Main Street starts here over the Paddock Viaduct and goes on north all the way to the historic Stockyards, which only the hardiest travelers will want to reach on foot. Before completing the rectangle around the Courthouse, consider stopping at the 112-acre **Heritage Park,** just northwest of it, although for some it may seem almost too deserted to be safe. The park lies at the confluence of the Clear Fork and West Fork of the Trinity River, where Fort Worth was first settled in 1849. Continue west on Belknap Street and pass on your left the **Tarrant County Civil Courts Building,** with Richard Haas's 1988 trompe-l'oeil facade that hid Wyatt Hedrick's uncomplimentary design. Halfway through the **Tarrant County Criminal Courts Building,** on your right, turn left on Throckmorton Street, going back south toward Sundance Square.

Near here, where 212 Taylor Street is located today, just north of West Belknap Street, the first water well was dug by French stonemason Alexandre Barbier in 1857, when Fort Worth had about 300 inhabitants. Barbier came to Texas two years earlier as part of the La Reunion communal-style colony, located west of today's downtown Dallas. Unfortunately, the treasurer ran away with the commune's assets and it went broke. The stonemason tried his luck in Fort Worth and got the commission of building the ten-foot-tall and 60-foot-deep beehive-shaped well. His house stood just 50 feet north of the well. Now the well's site is underneath the jail complex.

Shopping Anyone?

Tired, thirsty, and hungry? All right, continue south across West Weatherford Street, with the Renaissance Worthington Hotel now on your left. There, on your right, occupying an entire city block, stands the **Outlet Square Mall,** where numerous merchants will ply you with food and tempt you with merchandise priced so low you might forget your swollen joints. Join the 153,000 shoppers who throng the Outlet's two levels every month, shopping for London Fog coats, Split Rail Western Outlet denim, or Samsonite luggage. There are burgers, chicken, and sandwiches to eat, a post office, an ATM—and, thank heavens, rest rooms.

But as soon as you recharge your batteries, we must press on south. On the other side of the street, you will pass **Sundance West** apartments, where billionaire Edward Perry Bass has a "stylish two-story penthouse," then Sundance Market & Deli. **Etta's Place,** a bed & breakfast, is around that left corner on West Third Street. As a guest there you will have access to the Grotto Bar atop the **Caravan of Dreams,** which is still farther east, on West Houston Street.

As you cross West Third Street, you will pass on your left the **Fort Worth Convention & Visitors Bureau,** where a friendly receptionist will answer your questions and load you down with pamphlets, brochures, and maps. Around the corner on Fourth Street, you will find the **Circle Theatre,** entrance to Sanger Lofts in the **Sanger Brothers Building,** and on the next corner, at Houston Street, **The Modern at Sundance Square Annex,** a miniature of the Modern Art Museum of Fort Worth, the oldest such Texas museum. Diagonally across from the Visitors Bureau, at Throckmorton and West Fourth, towers the **Bank One Tower,** with Reata restaurant on its 35th floor. If you have the time, take the elevator to Reata and have a quick look at the city below you, even if you do not have time to stay for a steak.

You Are Now Leaving Sundance Square

Cross West Fifth Street farther south and there is Mikado Sushi Bar on your left, followed by The Pour House ("downtown's best sports bar") and the Fifth Street Pub downstairs with an air hockey table, all one next to the other. At the end of that block, on your right, is the **First Christian Church,** which was founded in 1855, two years after the U.S. Army abandoned Fort Worth, and is believed to be the oldest city congregation. As you cross West Sixth Street, the block-long structure on your right is the 1925 **Fort Worth Club Building,** the social and political center of Cowtown.

Turn right, or west, on West Seventh Street and as you cross Taylor Street at the end of the block, there is the **Fort Worth Star-Telegram** building on your right. Continue west until you reach **The Electric Building,** which a local billionaire Bass converted into an apartment complex. Across West Seventh from it stands **The Neil P. Anderson Building,** named for a cotton broker who had this "cotton exchange" built with seven skylights over the top-floor showrooms.

Noguchi on the Plaza, Matisse in the Park

Cross Lamar Street, in front of you, and you will find yourself on the **Bank of America Plaza,** with a three-piece Isamu Noguchi granite ensemble. Enjoy a snack or drink at the cafe on the plaza that overlooks **Burnett Park.** When ready, stroll across West Seventh Street to the park and admire the four Matisse's *Backs* in front of a tiny reflecting pool.

As you stroll across the handsome park, **Burnett Plaza,** which, among other tenants, houses the U.S. Securities & Exchange Commission, will be on your right. As you reach West Tenth Street, you will find yourself in front of the 1933 **U.S. Courthouse.** Turn left and continue to the corner with Lamar Street, where there stands **St. Andrew's Episcopal Church,** erected in 1909-12 for the congregation that traces its beginnings to 1873.

Cross Lamar, then Taylor, after which the **Federal Building** with a post office will be on your left. As soon as you pass the Federal Building, you will be approaching the intersection of Throckmorton, Ninth, and Tenth streets. The black granite-lined structure on your left is the **Old City Hall,** on your right across Tenth Street, the new **Municipal Building.** In front of you is Park Central Hotel with its grill.

That memorial on your right, across Jennings Avenue and from the new City Hall, honors the well-known Fort Worth mayor and benefactor, John Peter Smith, who was murdered while on business in St. Louis in 1901. Behind it you will see the 1892-built **St. Patrick Cathedral,** whose hand-painted stained-glass windows came from Munich and were the first in north Texas.

A Few More Historic Buildings

Cross Throckmorton at Ninth streets and continue along Park Central Hotel on your right. That tiny remnant of a brick structure ahead of you is the **Bryce Building,** named after another mayor. Farther to your left, on the corner of Throckmorton and West Eighth streets once stood the best-known downtown used bookstore, Barber's, which closed in 1998.

As you pass the Park Central Hotel, there will be on your right the tiniest **Hyde Park** and immediately following it the **Flatiron Building.** See that historical marker across the street, on your left? That's where Fort Worth's first public library was erected in 1901. Local women asked the philanthropist Andrew Carnegie to donate "the price of a good cigar" toward a new library. He gave $50,000. The old library building was razed in 1938.

The Convention Center is ahead on your right. The Peters Bros., the oldest Texas hat store is on your left, next to Randall's Cafe & Wine Bar, where "the cheesecake is to die for," according to a *Dallas Observer* review, and Branding Iron Grill. An ATM is next door. Across Houston Street from them, you will find the Human Bean Coffee House, Blarney Stone Pub, and Terry's Grill. Continue on West Ninth to Main. You are now in **General Worth Square** and Radisson Plaza is on your left. **Fort Worth Water Gardens** are on the other side of the Convention Center, across from Ramada Plaza Hotel.

1. Tarrant County Courthouse
2. White Elephant Saloon and Livestock Exchange Building
3. Stockyards Museum
4. Tarantula Steam Train
5. Stockyards Station
6. Billy Bob's Texas
7. Kimbell Art Museum
8. Amon Carter Museum
9. Modern Art Museum
10. Cowgirl Hall of Fame
11. Fort Worth Museum of Science and History
12. Will Rogers Memorial Center
13. Botanic Garden
14. Log Cabin Village
15. Fort Worth Zoo

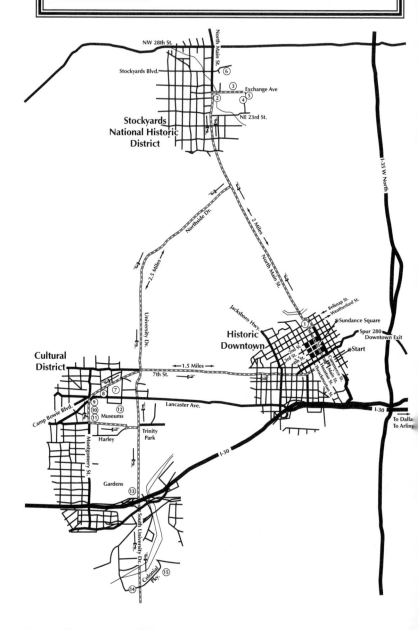

METRO DRIVING TOUR

This driving tour will take at least an hour—and more if you make detours or stop to explore other sights on the way. You will visit three parts of the city that are of greatest interest to out-of-towners: downtown, the historic Stockyards, which are located about two miles northwest of downtown, and the cultural district, about 1.5 miles west of the central business district. If you have such a luxury, ask a Fort Worth resident to do the driving for you, enabling you to concentrate on the highlights.

Details on many sights included here will be found in the SIGHTS chapter. Hotels and restaurants are usually described in their respective chapters. Main Street divides many downtown streets into east and west parts of the city.

Although Fort Worth is universally known as Cowtown, you won't find any droppings on the streets. Rather, brace yourself for some unsightly real estate between downtown and the Stockyards, as well as between downtown and the cultural district. You will drive through large stretches of the city that consist of nothing more than dilapidated buildings, one more unsightly than the next.

Begin Downtown, Near Radisson Plaza —

Like the self-guided walking tour, you can start somewhere near the **Radisson Plaza** hotel, on the brick-paved Main Street and Eighth. Fort Worth's Main Street is one of the handsomest streets in north Texas, full of little surprises, lined with pleasant eateries, not at all what you will find on its downtown Dallas namesake. However, for you to drive Fort Worth's Main Street would be to deprive yourself of a unique sight. Only nine blocks long, you would pass the length of Main and find yourself at the foot of the **Tarrant County Courthouse** before you enjoyed any of it. So, if you do drive, consider going on foot first.

But when you do drive up Main, go to Weatherford Street, turn right and drive to Commerce, then make a left turn and continue to East Bluff Street. Make a left and then right on North Main Street and drive over the **Paddock Viaduct** straight north. The building that now houses Ellis Pecan Co., at 1012 North Main, was once the Ku Klux Klan headquarters that the Klan later sold to the Leonard Brothers Department Store for a warehouse and still later became a professional boxing arena. In the early 1920s Niles City, as North Fort Worth was then called, became home to a large KKK Klavern. The Klansmen harassed not only African-Americans, but also European immigrants, many of whom worked as Swift and Armour meatpacking workers in the area. Originally, the Klan constructed a three-story brick headquarters, with

Tarrant County Courthouse photographed looking south from the Paddock Viaduct, which connects downtown with the North Side and the Stockyards. The two monstrous high-rises behind it are Chase Texas Tower/City Center I and City Center II, both made possible by Sid Richardson Bass, the oldest of the four Bass billionaire brothers. (Photo by Yves Gerem)

an auditorium to accommodate 4,000, at 1006 North Main, but the building was firebombed in 1924. On March 13 of that year, the Klan's power was still sufficient for the Fort Worth Fat Stock Show, now known as the Southwestern Exposition and Lifestock Show (see entry), to designate it as Klan Day.

Otherwise, there will be very little of interest to see on either side of North Main Street until you pass Northeast Twenty-Third Street and the Stockyards reveal themselves on your right.

As you approach the 1400 block of North Main, you will pass a block-long **Mercado de Fort Worth,** the work on which began in 1998 and is slated for completion in the year 2001. A pedestrian walkway that uses the alley to connect the buildings was constructed by the city. The municipality also acquired the historic Marine Theater and will turn it into a community performing arts center. A central plaza is being constructed to complement the theater. Mercado, which is partially funded by the U.S. Housing and Urban Development Department, will eventually include restaurants and shops and provide centralized parking.

If you are hungry and want to try some authentic Mexican cuisine, consider stopping at Joe T. Garcia's, at 2201 North Commerce at Northeast Twenty-Second streets, a block off North Main and practically on your way. It is undoubtedly the most famous Tex-Mex restaurant in Cowtown and also the largest.

You Are Now Entering the Stockyards ——

Drive up to Exchange Avenue, turn right, and you will be thick in the middle of the historic yards. Exchange Avenue is a two-way, but rather short street, so you can park at your convenience. Unless you have time to spare to crawl through the oft-encountered thick traffic and are not interested in getting out of the car, we recommend a miniature walking tour up and down Exchange Avenue so you can stop at and peek inside the **White Elephant Saloon** and **Livestock Exchange Building** and its **Stockyards Museum,** perhaps even take a ride on the **Tarantula Steam Train** from the **Stockyards Station.**

It would be a crime not stop at **Billy Bob's Texas,** or as Fort Worthians like to point out, the world's largest honky-tonk. For under $50 a night, you will have a barrel of fun and perhaps meet some interesting people.

There is a bunch of restaurants in the Stockyards, including Cattlemen's and Hunter Brothers' H3 Ranch steakhouses, Los Vaqueros and Riscky Rita Mexican eateries, Old Spaghetti Warehouse, and Tommy's Hamburgers, all of which you will find described in more detail in the DINING chapter.

For lodgings in the Stockyards, consider the Stockyards Hotel, Hotel Texas, and Miss Molly's bed and breakfast, all outlined in the LODGING chapter.

For tours of the Stockyards, go to the **Visitors Information Center,** on East Exchange Avenue and across the street from the Livestock Exchange. But beware of some tall tales from guides who would tell you, for example, that the White Elephant Saloon building was moved from downtown to its current yards location.

Ready for the Cultural District? ————

After all this Western lore, you might be thirsty for more than just a cold drink. Fort Worth boasts three museums, the **Kimbell, Modern,** and **Amon Carter,** one next to the other, that no city would be ashamed to claim. And this is how to find all three.

Return back to North Main Street and go back in the direction from where you came from. When you reach Northside Drive, turn right and go west until you get to North Henderson Street, where Northside becomes North University Drive. You will pass **Greenwood Cemetery** on your right, just before reaching White Settlement Road. When you reach West Seventh Street and Camp Bowie Boulevard, turn right and continue on Camp Bowie.

The three art museums, as well as the **Fort Worth Museum of Science & History** and **Will Rogers Memorial Center** and **Casa Manana** are all within walking distance. Please see the VISUAL ARTS chapter for the detailed description of the museums, and SIGHTS chapter for other features of the area, where in the year 2000 the **Cowgirl Museum and Hall of Fame** will be added.

A slew of restaurants is located in the area, mostly located along the brick-paved Camp Bowie Boulevard. Several are listed in the DINING chapter under the cultural district heading. The two located directly across Camp Bowie from the Kimbell are Sardine's Ristorante Italiano, which features live jazz, and The Back Porch, whose salad bar is overshadowed by the ice creams so tempting you will want to return from home just to sample them again. Oops, have we lived in Texas for too long and are given to exaggeration?

And if you want to find out what all the hoopla about Kincaid's hamburgers is, drive southwest to 4901 Camp Bowie at Eldridge Street.

Have Energy and Time for More? ————

While you are in the area, consider three more sites, the **Botanic Garden,** the **Fort Worth Zoo,** and the **Log Cabin Village** (see the SIGHTS chapter for details).

To get to the Botanic Garden, return to South University Drive and go south through Trinity Park. The Fort Worth Zoo and Log Cabin Village are on Colonial Parkway, on the opposite sides of South University, once you pass the Trinity River and reach the Forest Park. The annual Colonial Golf Tournament is held across Colonial Parkway from the Log Cabin Village.

To return to downtown Fort Worth, go back north to West Seventh Street, turn right, and you will be just 1.5 miles west of the central business district.

EXCURSIONS

There is no lack of interesting excursions for you to take out of Fort Worth in almost any direction. While some might want to consider trips to quaint Texas villages and towns, such as Granbury, most visitors staying in Cowtown seem to head sooner or later for Parker or Dallas.

In Parker, a town northeast of Dallas, you will find the **Southfork Ranch** (see entry), the make-believe abode of that lecherous celluloid intrigant, J.R., who for twelve seasons fascinated television viewers worldwide in his soap opera *Dallas*.

However, the most visited site in Dallas, more than 35 years after the unthinkable happened on Dealey Plaza, is the **Sixth Floor Museum** (see entry below). In front of it, John F. Kennedy was killed by a bullet from a Mannlicher-Carcano rifle, made in Italy in 1940, and supposedly mail-ordered by his alleged assassin Lee Harvey Oswald from a Chicago sporting goods store for $12.78.

But first things first. Since you already are in Fort Worth, let's first stop at Arlington, the entertainment center of the Metroplex, particularly for the young.

EAST TO ARLINGTON

Arlington boasts more than six million visitors a year. The average summer temperature is 95 degrees and 57 degrees in the winter. However, like anywhere in the Metroplex, it can get so hot in Arlington "it melts a monarch and makes the butter fly," as the pun goes. Public transportation is practically non-existent in Arlington, but there is a free trolley service for tourists staying at the entertainment district hotels. As a guest at a participating hotel, you can receive complimentary trolley passes. The service is available between the major hotels and the city's most popular attractions, 9:30 am-11:30 pm during Six Flags' peak season, and is scaled down at other times. Some hotels will accommodate you with complimentary transportation.

Arlington has its own **Museum of Art,** at 201 West Main St.; **Theatre Arlington,** 305 West Main St.; and **Antique Sewing Machine Museum,** 804 West Abram St. (see individual entries).

Twenty-plus-year-old live **Johnnie High's Country Musical Review** features singers, dancers, and musicians at the Arlington Music Hall, 224 North Center St. (see listing).

Other attractions include the **Air Combat School,** at 921 Six Flags Dr., (817) 640-1886, where you can strap yourself into a real jet fighter flight simulator and engage in hour-long air combat maneuvers. The 958-acre **River Legacy Park & Science Center** (see entry) is a city-run park for pre-schoolers, with trails and picnic areas. It is located one and a half miles north of Interstate 30.

Six Flags Mall, 2911 East Division St., at Division Street and State Hwy. 360, just a mile or so southeast from Six Flags, is open Mon-Sat 10 am-9 pm. **The Parks at Arlington Mall,** at the northeast corner of Interstate 20 and Cooper Street in south Arlington, is the largest city mall. (For more details, please see the ARLINGTON chapter.)

The **Arlington Convention & Visitors Bureau** is located at 1905 East Randol Mill Rd.; (800) 433-5374 or (817) 265-7721, Internet www.arlington.org. Its **Visitor Information Center** and gift shop are at the same address; (800) 342-4305 or (817) 461-3888, E-mail visitinfo@acvb.org.

The simplest way to travel to Arlington from downtown Fort Worth is by going east on Interstate 30. From south Fort Worth, you could go in the same direction on Interstate 20 until you reach Cooper or Collins streets, then turn left and continue northward.

Start with Six Flags or Hurricane Harbor

Six Flags Over Texas and **Hurricane Harbor,** which lies across Interstate 30 from it, will be particularly appreciated by families with children. If they are old enough that you can drop them off with a bundle of one- and five-dollar notes, they will probably insist on staying all day. If not, get a comfortable pair of shoes and sunscreen because you might be walking for hours in the broiling sun or standing in lines for up to one hour for the most popular rides. (For more details about these parks, please see the ARLINGTON chapter.)

The Palace of Wax/Ripley's Believe It or Not is nearby in Grand Prairie, a town of 110,000, which also boasts the Lone Star racehorse track (see individual entries).

Stop at the Ballpark

From April through October, you may want to take kids to a Texas Rangers baseball game at their Arlington home, the **Ballpark Stadium.** It is located at 1000 Ballpark Way at Randol Mill Rd.; (817) 273-5222 or 273-5100 for ticket availability. While there, see **The Legends of the Game Baseball Museum.** (For more details, please refer to the SPORTS chapter.)

If you wish to stay overnight, there are several hotels practically within walking distance of Six Flags, including AmeriSuites, Budgetel Inn, La Quinta, which is across the street from the park's entrance, and Sleep Inn. For more details about hotels and restaurants, please see the ARLINGTON chapter's lodging and dining sections.

Visit the Fielder House Museum

If this is your second day in Arlington, consider visiting the **Fielder House Museum** and **M. T. Johnson Plantation Cemetery and Historic Park,** at 1616 West Abram and Fielder streets in central Arlington. See the ARLINGTON chapter for more details.

The area was once part of large land holdings of Col. Middleton Tate Johnson (1810-1866), a former member of Texas state legislature and Texas Ranger who is buried here. Johnson founded the site for Fort Worth, gave the land for its courthouse, and is known as the father of Tarrant County, although Johnson County is named after him.

Several log structures that predate Arlington have been moved to the Johnson Plantation Cemetery and Park.

STILL FARTHER EAST TO DALLAS

From Fort Worth or Arlington, take Interstate 30 going east. As you enter downtown Dallas, take the Commerce Street exit and you will find yourself under the triple underpass with the Sixth Floor Museum (see entry below) on your left.

The lodgings and restaurants are plentiful downtown should you decide to stay overnight. Hyatt Regency, The Paramount, and Amerisuites/West End are within a few blocks of the Sixth Floor Museum and Hampton Inn is another couple blocks away. All except the Hyatt are moderately priced.

It would take you weeks to sample all the restaurants and drinking establishments in the West End, an entertainment area that borders on the Sixth Floor Museum. For details about a downtown walking tour, as well as many food establishments, please see *A Marmac Guide to Dallas*.

Many visitors first head for **The Sixth Floor Museum,** located at 411 Elm and North Houston streets; (214) 653-6659/6666. CH. Open daily 9 am-6 pm. Located in the once-warehouse district, in the former Texas School Book Depository Building. The structure was designated a national historic landmark in 1993. The entrance to the museum is on Houston Street. Only up to 300 visitors at a time are admitted so there may be a wait. No photography is allowed on the sixth floor. There is a security detector at the entrance.

On November 22, 1963, after he had spent a night at the Texas Hotel—now known as Radisson Plaza—in downtown Fort Worth, Pres. John F. Kennedy was assassinated here, an event that remains one of the most remembered and controversial in the twentieth century. Each year two million tourists flock to Dealey Plaza from around the world to try to understand how and why it happened.

The museum opened in 1989 to meet this widespread desire for information about the tragic event. The School Book Depository, then one of two textbook distribution sites for the state, was bought by Dallas County from Col. D. Harold Byrd—whose cousin was admiral and polar explorer Richard E. Byrd—for $400,000 in 1977. The museum, which is located on the floor where a sniper's nest was found after the shooting, examines the life, death, and legacy of President Kennedy.

The 9,000-square-foot museum takes visitors back to the 1960s, through the trip to Dallas, the assassination, and the quarter-century of investigations that followed. About 400 photos, interviews, artifacts, and displays, along with a 40-minute documentary—one of six—will help you to relive this tragedy. The window, from which Oswald allegedly killed Kennedy, is encased in Plexiglass in the southeast corner of the museum, only a few feet from where the crime was supposedly perpetrated. It was donated to the museum by Byrd's son in 1995. Although a caption labels it "The Original Window from the Sniper's Perch," it is widely believed this window is from another side of the building. A companion audio recording is available in English, Spanish, French, Italian, Portuguese, German, and Japanese.

You will see President Kennedy and his wife Jacqueline arrive at Love Field Airport, their ride down Main Street downtown, and the unexpected conclusion that ended in national mourning. Americans, who have seen many documentaries on this subject, will find the darkened museum more of a chapel to reflect than to see anything new. It is almost anticlimactic, except for the opportunity to look from the sixth floor down to the site where Kennedy was shot. On some days the crowds are so thick it is uncomfortable to move around the sixth floor.

On the plaza, up to half a dozen self-styled conspiracy theorists peddle their crude grainy-photo newspapers on weekends and when ticketed complain of a government cover-up to get rid of them.

No original evidence is included in the exhibits; all such documents are housed at the National Archives in Washington, D.C. There is a marker at the approximate spot where Kennedy was shot. If you look east, across Houston Street, at what is now Dallas County Criminal Court, you will see the Records Building, where Jack Ruby was jailed in Room 6M-35 after killing Lee Harvey Oswald; the bank robber Clyde Barrow was once held here on the sixth floor.

Dealey Plaza is the most visited site in the city. Many among the tourists who annually visit the plaza and the museum are foreign nationals. Oliver Stone's film *JFK* was shot here. Take the time to walk around the plaza, which was laid out in 1935-37 and still looks much as it did in 1963, except for a few additional street lamps and the trees, which are thirty-plus years older.

Traveling at a speed of about 11 miles per hour, the presidential motorcade passed down Main Street, turned onto Houston Street for one block, then turned left onto Elm. At about 12:30 pm, Central Standard Time, the presidential limousine traveled in the middle lane toward the triple underpass, which in 1935, following the westward relocation of the Trinity River, brought together Main, Commerce, and Elm streets. Suddenly shots rang out. Then-Texas governor John Connally was wounded and President Kennedy was murdered. This was the fourth presidential assassination in American history. There are fewer answers about Kennedy's death today than in 1963 and some tour guides are privately convinced the assassination was the work of the Mafia.

If you wish to take a comprehensive, 21-mile, 90-minute scheduled tour, dedicated to the JFK assassination, call **JFK, The Tour,** (214) 948-8687, which has been in business since 1994. It starts with a 20-minute walking tour of the assassination site. It then traces the entire motorcade route of the president, including Parkland Hospital, Love Field Airport, and downtown in a van with a maximum of six passengers. From there, it traces Lee Harvey Oswald's trail to his boardinghouse, police officer Tippit's murder site, Oswald's capture and arrest site, and, along the way, the site of his own eventual murder in the basement of the old city hall by Jack Ruby. The tour starts daily at 1 pm at 400 Elm St.

Kerrville Bus Co., the largest tour operator in the Metroplex, can be reached at (800) 256-4723 or (972) 263-0294. **Texas Trails Tours** also provide tours to this and other sites, (800) 785-8302 or (972) 487-9406.

THE INTERNATIONAL VISITOR

Although a noticeable portion of Fort Worthians are foreign-born and several languages are spoken in Cowtown, only a Texan might consider Fort Worth an international city. That may precisely be the reason that most Fort Worth residents will greet you warmly, no matter how far you come from. They are attentive hosts who take every opportunity to don their jeans, boots, and Stetsons and make believe they are back at the turn of the century.

Planning Your Trip

After all the Cowtown jokes, some no doubt originating in Dallas, the city will probably surprise you with its vitality, hospitality, and a few gems like the Kimbell Art Museum and the Bass Performance Hall (see

TEXAS in the U.S.A.

individual entries). If you love the Wild West lore and get to see more than the Dallas-Fort Worth International Airport, chances are you will be in heaven, even though the only shootout you will see today is a reenactment in front of the White Elephant Saloon (see entry) in the Stockyards. Whether this is your first and last visit to Cowtown, or the beginning of an exciting new destination, Fort Worth today—actually just the downtown area—is still small enough to treasure on your way home and big enough to go beyond the smell of horse manure.

Informality seems to reign in Fort Worth, whether in the Stockyards or in the cultural district. Its residents, long after the rest of the nation has gone through the exercise craze and denial of anything even resembling meat, still love to dive into a mattress-thick steak, with plenty of side dishes—or Tex-Mex fare that is available just around every corner. In Texas "women cook but men barbecue," observes one British writer. And they love anything that even remotely tastes like beer. Like their Dallas neighbors, they, too, are a bit insane about sports, be it football, baseball, or basketball, waxing on about this game and that.

Your Safety

Because gun-related injuries are the second-leading cause of death among Americans aged 10 to 24 years—no matter what anyone tells you, be careful. The police will do their best to protect you, but do not put all of your faith in them. Sometimes, the police may be unable to cope adequately with the violent crime. Only you can truly be responsible for your safety.

Crime in Texas, like nationwide, has declined to a 20-year low in 1997, taking its homicide rate to its lowest level in 31 years. Only arrests for drug possession increased.

Fort Worth saw fewer crimes in 1997 than in any other year since 1974, and violet crime declined 13 percent from 1996. Of violent crimes, only homicides rose: 74 were recorded for 1997 in Fort Worth and 12 in Arlington. In 1986, in contrast, Fort Worth had 202 homicides, an all-time record. Since then, 1998 was the first year when twice there was only one murder a month in Cowtown.

To help curb violent juvenile crime, teen curfew has been in effect in Fort Worth since 1994. During that same period, the number of juveniles arrested for murder has dropped 30 percent, while the number of youths killed has dropped 60 percent. Under the curfew, anyone under age 17 is banned from being in public and off the streets between 11 pm and 6 am Sunday through Thursday and after midnight Friday and Saturday until 6 am the next morning. Teens and their parents may be fined up to $500 a day for breaking the curfew.

Texas leads the nation in deaths related to drunken driving. The state had 1,991 alcohol-related traffic fatalities in 1996, compared with 1,606 in California.

Do not display cash, particularly since the various denominations of American currency are all of the same size and color, so a potential thief can never be sure how much cash you have on you. You would probably be wise to charge most of your purchases to an international credit card if you have one. Do not leave cash in your hotel room—it is safer to deposit it in the hotel's safe-deposit box immediately upon arrival at the hotel. Do not wear expensive jewelry or display other symbols of affluence.

Never let a stranger inside your car. Be careful even when you stop at an intersection; drivers nationwide are being carjacked in broad daylight. If you become so victimized, you may be forced out and the thief will drive off to possibly sell your car for its parts.

Never drink anything that could be contaminated while you look away, not even if offered by a seductive woman, who might slip something into your glass before or after you take her to your room. If you are lucky, she may only rob you. Try to be part of a group whenever possible after dark, even if you make-believe that you are a straggler from a group of strangers in front of you.

Mostly for Women

Women should choose the most expensive hotel they can afford, even if they stay in the cheapest room. Generally, the better the class of the hotel, the less harassment you may likely endure if you are traveling alone. Fortunately, some Fort Worth hotels have floors where only guests with electronic keys may enter and women should feel quite safe. Ask about safety before you arrive and again before you register.

Among the more unsafe areas in downtown Fort Worth, according to the residents, is that area south of Ninth Street, around the Fort Worth Convention Center and Water Gardens, where homeless and other assorted characters tend to congregate.

It really is not a good idea for a single woman in Fort Worth to walk around alone almost anywhere else beyond the Sundance Square downtown after dark. If you plan to have dinner alone outside your hotel, decide on your restaurant, then take a taxi. Return the same way, unless you are absolutely convinced the risk of walking is worth taking.

OTHER MATTERS

Automobile Rentals

The rental companies in the Metroplex abound; not only will you find all the national firms, but also a few local companies. They require a valid international driver's license and at least your passport. Unless you have made arrangements through your local travel agent abroad, you will need an internationally accepted credit card as additional identification and to pay for your rental. Cash payments are not welcome. The driver's minimum age requirement may vary from one company to the next. Tax on car rentals is 10 percent and if you pick up your car at D/FW airport, you will pay another 10 percent surcharge for that location. Insurance coverage is recommended. You can never ask too many questions when renting an automobile.

For names and telephone numbers of the rental companies, please see the TRANSPORTATION chapter.

Bank Hours

The banking hours in Fort Worth are generally from 9-10 am to 3:30 pm, with some banks open until 5 or 6 pm on Fridays and until noon on Saturdays. Some also have drive-in branches that are also open weekdays and Saturdays.

No bank downtown exchanges foreign currencies, unless you make prior arrangements or have time to wait for clearance. Please see listing of such facilities at the Dallas-Fort Worth International Airport in the TRANSPORTATION chapter. American Express also exchanges foreign currencies at Ridgmar Mall (see entry).

Consulates

These are the consulates located in Dallas:

Belgium . . . . (214) 987-4391
Belize . . . . (972) 579-0070
Bolivia . . . . (214) 571-6131
Canada . . . . (214) 922-9806
Chile . . . . (214) 528-2731
Czech Republic . . . . (214) 350-6871
Denmark . . . . (214) 863-4221
Dominican Republic . . . . . . (214) 826-5231
El Salvador . . . . (214) 637-1018
Finland . . . . (214) 855-4715
France . . . . (214) 855-5495
Germany . . . . (972) 239-0707
Great Britain . . . . (214) 521-4090
Greece . . . . (214) 526-7504
Honduras . . . . (214) 979-0020
Iceland . . . . (972) 699-5417
Italy . . . . (214) 368-4113
Japan . . . . (214) 979-7730

```
Korea . . . . . . . . . . . . . . . . .(972) 644-8010
Luxembourg . . . . . . . . . . . .(817) 878-8102
Malta . . . . . . . . . . . . . . . . .(214) 969-0010
Mexico . . . . . . . . . . . . . . . .(214) 630-7341
Monaco . . . . . . . . . . . . . . .(214) 521-1058
Norway  . . . . . . . . . . . . . . .(214) 826-5231
Spain . . . . . . . . . . . . . . . . .(214) 373-1200
Sweden  . . . . . . . . . . . . . . .(214) 630-9112
Switzerland  . . . . . . . . . . . .(214) 871-0871
Taiwan . . . . . . . . . . . . . . . .(972) 436-4242
Thailand  . . . . . . . . . . . . . .(214) 740-1498
```

The **Mexican Consulate** in Fort Worth is located downtown across the street from the Tarrant County Courthouse, at 108 North Commerce St., (817) 870-2270.

Credit Cards and Traveler's Checks ———

Guard your credit card as you would your cash because in the wrong hands your card becomes a potent criminal tool that can go through thousands of dollars in an hour or less.

There are about a dozen automatic teller machines at the Dallas-Fort Worth International Airport, operated by NationsBank, which merged into Bank of America in 1998.

To report lost or stolen credit cards, call one of these numbers:

```
American Express  . . . . . . . . . .(800) 992-3404
AT&T Universal Card . . . . . . .(800) 423-4343
Carte Blanche  . . . . . . . . . . . .(800) 234-6377
Diners Club  . . . . . . . . . . . . . .(800) 234-6377
Discover Card  . . . . . . . . . . . .(800) 347-2683
MasterCard  . . . . . . . . . . . . . .(800) 826-2181
VISA . . . . . . . . . . . . . . . . . . .(800) 336-8472
```

While in one respect they are even better than cash because when they are lost or stolen you can have them replaced, traveler's checks have a drawback: they cost you money when you purchase them. Some merchants in the Metroplex are just a bit reluctant to accept them because they are not widely used. They might ask for your passport or driver's license to verify your identity and your counter-signature. Never agree to pay any fee to cash traveler's checks.

To report lost or stolen *traveler's checks*, call one of these numbers:

```
American Express. . . . . . . . . . (800) 221-7282
Citicorp . . . . . . . . . . . . . . . . . (800) 645-6556
Thomas Cook/MasterCard . . . . (800) 223-7373
VISA . . . . . . . . . . . . . . . . . . . . (800) 227-6811
```

Foreign currencies can be exchanged at Thomas Cook Dallas-Fort Worth International Airport locations or at Ridgmar Mall (see individual entries), at the northeast corner of Interstate 30 and State Highway 183.

Customs Allowances

Foreign nationals may bring into the U.S. one liter of alcoholic beverages for each adult nonresident, 200 cigarettes, 50 cigars, and gifts valued up to $100. Your personal exemption is $400. Gifts mailed to the U.S. up to $25 are duty free.

Driving

Driving in the U.S. is in the right lane of a two-way, two-lane roadway. You need a valid international driver's license. Most gasoline stations are open 24 hours a day and you have the option of pumping your own gas or paying a little extra to have an attendant do it for you.

Texas has a seat belt law that states that all front-seat passengers must wear a safety belt or risk a $200 fine. In Fort Worth, you may turn right on a red light after you have stopped and looked in both directions to make sure the way is clear.

In 1996, the Texas transportation commission raised the speed limit from 55 to 60 miles per hour on most highways inside the Fort Worth city limits, except for short stretches of a few select roads, which remain at 55 mph.

The changes took place after the U.S. Congress overturned mandatory federal speed limits. Many interstate and state highways now have 70-mph limit outside cities. Highway traffic has the right of way and is not required to yield to entering traffic; exiting traffic has the right of way on access roads. The speed limit on most residential streets is 30 miles, and 20 miles in school zones with flashing yellow lights.

Speeding is a major problem in the Metroplex and could quickly get you a $100-plus ticket. Statistically, the most dangerous four-hour period to drive in Fort Worth is 4-8 pm. A 24-hour hot line—(817) 392-SAFE—is aimed at building a database of problem spots in the city and cracking down on aggressive drivers.

Electricity

110 volts 60 cycles A.C. You will need a plug adapter and a voltage converter for foreign electrical appliances. They can perhaps be found at Voyagers, The Travel Store, at 1600 South University Dr. in University Park Village mall (see entry), or at select other stores.

Hospital Emergencies

In an emergency call 911. Most Metroplex hospitals have 24-hour emergency care.

All Saints Episcopal Hospital, 1400 Eighth Ave.; (817) 926-2544; 24-hour emergency, 922-7070.

Cook Children's Medical Center, 801 Seventh Ave.; (817) 885-4000; 24-hour emergency, (817) 885-4093.

Harris Methodist Fort Worth, 1301 Pennsylvania Ave., (817) 882-2000; 24-hour emergency, 882-3333.

Harris Methodist H.E.B., 1600 Hospital Pkwy., Bedford; (817) 685-4000; 24-hour emergency, 685-4611.

Huguley Memorial Hospital, 11801 South Fwy.; (817) 293-9110; 24-hour emergency, 551-2462.

John Peter Smith Hospital, 1500 South Main St.; (817) 921-3431; 24-hour emergency, (817) 927-1110 or 927-1222.

Medical Center of Arlington, 3301 Matlock Rd., Arlington; (817) 457-3241; 24-hour emergency, (817) 472-4868.

Osteopathic Medical Center of Texas, 1000 Montgomery St.; (817) 731-4311; 24-hour emergency, 735-3100.

Medical Insurance

Medical insurance should be secured prior to your arrival. There is no national health service system in the U.S., although you will receive emergency medical care regardless of who you are and where you come from. Health care is costly and payment is usually required at the time of treatment for foreign visitors.

Money

The U.S. dollar is divided into 100 cents. The coins are the penny, worth 1 cent (copper-colored); nickel, worth 5 cents; dime, worth 10 cents; quarter, worth 25 cents; half-dollar, worth 50 cents (all silver-colored); and occasionally you will run across a dollar coin. The bills or notes are, unlike in other countries, all of the same size and predominantly printed in green and black ink on white paper. Denominations are one dollar—the note that has carried George Washington's portrait since 1869—five dollars, ten dollars, twenty dollars, fifty dollars, and one hundred dollars.

Since the unsuccessful launching of the Susan B. Anthony dollar coin in 1979, the U.S. Mint is coming out with another in the year 2000. It will feature Sacagawea, the Shoshone Indian slave woman who accompanied the 1803-05 Lewis and Clark expedition while carrying a baby on her back.

Pharmacies

Pharmacies are scattered throughout Tarrant County. Eckerd's 24-hour pharmacies are listed in the Fort Worth MATTERS OF FACT chapter and the ARLINGTON chapter, under the Matters of Fact section.

For other pharmacies, including those located in the supermarkets, please see the white or yellow telephone directories of Fort Worth or Arlington.

Postal Service

First-class letters inside the U.S. are usually delivered within two to four days, provided they contain the recipient's zip code and proper postage.

Various other classes of mail are also available, including express and priority mail, at charges corresponding to how fast the letter or package arrives. Air-mail envelopes, used elsewhere worldwide, are not in common usage in the U.S. because most first-class mail is automatically transported by air.

The most recent addition to the U.S. Postal Service is Global Priority Mail, an international service comparable to express mail, but at a lower price. It is available for delivery in 27 countries in Canada, Western Europe, and the Pacific Rim in flat-rate envelopes or packages of up to four pounds, starting for as little as $3.75 for a 6" x 10" envelope to Canada or Western Europe.

For general postal information, weekdays 8 am-5 pm, call (817) 543-8400 or (214) 741-5508; for express or global priority mail pickup, (800) 222-1811 or (214) 760-4640; and for zip code information weekdays 8:30 am-5 pm, (972) 647-2996.

Among the two downtown post offices, one is located in the Federal Building at 819 Taylor and West Tenth streets, (817) 332-7477, another on the lower level at the Fort Worth Outlet Square (see entry), 401 One Tandy Center, near the ice rink. Advertised as the nation's first environmentally friendly post office—built with recycled materials and utilizing energy-efficient systems—that the U.S. Postal Service said would be a model for similar facilities opened at 2600 Eighth Avenue, between West Robert and Cantey streets, in southwest Fort Worth.

A majestic U.S. Post Office towers at 251 West Lancaster Ave. and Jennings St., (817) 870-8102/8103, next to Texas & Pacific Terminal and southwest from the Fort Worth Water Gardens (see individual entries). However, being situated on the southern edge of downtown in a somewhat unappetizing section of the city, we advise elderly and women on foot against wandering around here alone.

There is a postal facility at the Dallas-Fort Worth International

Airport (see entry), 2300 West 32nd Street, off International Parkway; (972) 456-2060. It is open 24 hours a day, 365 days a year, and also provides passport and notary services.

Public Holidays and Notable Dates in Texas History

Days marked in **bold** are recognized Federal holidays, when most government offices, banks, and other institutions are closed.

The two most widely observed holidays are Thanksgiving and Christmas. Practically all businesses, even supermarkets and most restaurants, are closed on those two days, as are the stock and commodity exchanges, schools, city, county, state, and federal offices. The post office at Interstate 30 and Sylvan Avenue in Dallas is open, as is the one at the Dallas-Fort Worth International Airport (see entry). If you are not staying at a hotel, the Seven-Eleven convenience shops may be one of the few places to get beverages, food, newspapers, and cigarettes. Compared with how enthusiastically it is celebrated in Europe, New Year's Day is not as major a holiday in the U.S.

January 1:	**New Year's Day.**
January 7, 1905:	First large oil strike is made in Harris County.
Third Monday in January:	**Martin Luther King's (1929-1968) birthday** (Assassinated Black Civil Rights Leader).
January 20, 1925:	Mrs. Miriam "Ma" Ferguson (1875-1961) (Inaugurated first woman governor of Texas).
February 14:	Valentine's Day.
Third Monday in February:	**President's Day** (Celebrates Lincoln's birthday on February 12 and Washington's on February 22).
March 2, 1836:	Declaration of Independence of the Republic of Texas; now Texas Independence Day.
March 2, 1793:	Birthday of Sam Houston, President of the Republic of Texas, (Born in Rockbridge County, Virginia; died 1863).
March 6, 1836:	Most defenders of the Alamo are killed as it falls to the forces of General Santa Anna.

March 17:	St. Patrick's Day.
March 26, 1918:	Texas Governor William P. Hobby gives women the right to vote.
March 30, 1846:	Dallas County is created.
First Sunday in April:	Daylight Savings Time begins (Clocks should be set one hour forward at 2 am Fort Worth time).
April 21, 1836:	Slaughter of 610 Mexicans at San Jacinto leads to Texas independence.
Second Sunday in May:	Mother's Day.
Last Monday in May:	**Memorial Day** (in remembrance of war dead).
June 6, 1849:	City of Fort Worth is established.
Third Sunday in June:	Father's Day.
June 19, 1865:	Texas Emancipation Day (Juneteenth), when General Granger arrived at Galveston proclaiming U.S. authority over Texas, at the end of the Civil War, declaring slaves free.
July 4:	**Independence Day** (Commemorates the adoption of the Declaration of Independence in 1776).
August 27, 1908:	Pres. Lyndon Baines Johnson's birthday; the 36th president died in 1973.
First Monday in September:	**Labor Day** (Recognizes American workers).
Second Monday in October:	**Columbus Day** (Originally commemorated landing of Columbus in the Bahamas in 1492; now an increasingly controversial holiday).
October 14, 1890:	Pres. Dwight D. Eisenhower's birthday; the 34th president died in 1969.
October 16, 1836:	Soldier and politician Sam Houston (1793-1863) becomes president of the Republic of Texas.
Last Sunday in October:	Daylight Savings Time ends (Clocks get set back one hour).
October 31:	Halloween.
November 3, 1793:	Birthday of Stephen F. Austin, "Father of Texas."
November 11:	**Veterans Day** (Commemorates the end of wars in 1918 and 1945, and honors veterans of both, as well as of Vietnam War).

November 22, 1963:	Pres. John F. Kennedy assassinated in downtown Dallas.
November 24, 1963:	Kennedy's alleged assassin Lee H. Oswald shot.
Fourth Thursday in November:	**Thanksgiving Day** (Since 1674, a day for giving thanks for Divine goodness).
December 25:	**Christmas Day.**
December 29, 1845:	Texas becomes the 28th state of the U.S.

Shopping

The largest shopping centers in Fort Worth, including **Fort Worth Outlet Square, Hulen Mall, Ridgmar Mall, University Park Village,** and **The Parks at Arlington Mall** in Arlington, have limited capabilities to cater to foreign shoppers.

There is an **American Express Travel Agency,** with foreign currency exchange, one block north of Ridgmar Mall. See the SHOPPING chapter for more details. Except for the Dallas-Fort Worth International Airport (see entry), there are no other retail foreign currency exchange facilities in Fort Worth or Arlington.

Taxes

Texas has no state personal income tax.

There is an 8.25 percent state sales tax on all purchases, except non-restaurant food and prescription medications.

Fort Worth hotel-room tax is 15 percent, six percent of which is returned to the state. Of the remaining nine percent, seven percent is earmarked to promote local culture and tourism. Since 1998, an additional 2 percent on the bed tax has raised money earmarked for renovation of the Fort Worth Convention Center (see entry).

Telephone and Telegrams

The Southwestern Bell's **Fort Worth White Pages** directory combines residential and business numbers in one volume. The residential and business sections are divided by blue-rimmed pages of helpful numbers, as well as city, county, state, and federal government listings.

The 1,224-page Bell's **Greater Fort Worth Yellow Pages** directory, which is arranged alphabetically, according to the subject, will come in handy when you try to find listings in a variety of categories, such as churches or mortgage companies. The red-rimmed alphabetical index is at the beginning of the directory. A full-page listing in the yellow pages does not mean that an establishment is preferable to one that only identifies itself with one line, it just means the first one can afford to pay for a full page.

Both white and yellow pages for Arlington are combined in one 360-page residential, 90-page business, and 954 yellow-page Southwestern Bell directory.

Calling inside Fort Worth and Arlington—within area code 817, which covers Tarrant County and some surrounding territory—is a local call, which at some hotels may be free, while others can charge you practically any amount. The explosion of fax machines, cellular telephones, pagers, and Internet lines has consumed most numbers in the 817 area code. As a result, the State Public Utility Commission has authorized a second telephone area code, 682, for the area. Beginning in mid-2000, callers are required to dial 10 digits to place local telephone calls.

When the area code system began in 1947, Texas only had four area codes. Now there are 21. If you call a Dallas number, preceded by area code 214 or 972, from Tarrant County, this is always a long-distance call. To avoid misunderstandings, ask your hotel for details before you make such calls.

Public pay phones in 1999 required mostly a 35-cent deposit. Simply lift the receiver, listen for the dial tone, deposit the coin, and dial the number. If the line is busy, the coin will be returned when you hang up. When calling long distance, first dial 1, followed by the area code, then the telephone number.

Numbers preceded by (800) are toll-free and can be made nationwide. Dial first 1, then (800), followed by the seven-digit number. If there is a local equivalent, use the local number. You can dial toll-free (800)—and sometimes (888) and (877) numbers—anywhere in the U.S. or Canada.

Area codes for a few other Texas cities: **Abilene, El Paso,** and **San Angelo**—915; **Amarillo** and **Lubbock**—806; **Austin** and **Corpus Christi**—512; **Beaumont** and **Galveston**—409; **Houston**—713 or 281; **San Antonio** and **McAllen**—210; **Midland** and **Odessa**—915; **Tyler**—903; **Waco**—817.

Incidentally, telephone solicitors may not call a residence before 9 am or after 9 pm on weekdays and Saturdays, or before noon and after 9 pm on Sundays. Texas law also requires them to identify themselves by name, identify the business they represent, the purpose of the call, and the organization's telephone number at which they can be reached.

To place an international call directly, dial **011,** then the country code, followed by the city's code, and finally the telephone number.

Tipping

Do not tip flight attendants or pilots, maitre d's, busboys, pool and sauna helpers, and hospital staff.

Dining: Waiters and waitresses, 10-15 percent, unless the service is exceptional or lacking; if lacking, you should contact the restaurant manager. Bartender and wine steward, about 15 percent. Checkroom, $1 per coat. Washroom attendant, $1-$2. Musicians, $2-$5 for a special request. Valet parking, $1-$2, when the car is returned to you.

Hotels: Bellman, $2 if you have only one or two bags, otherwise $1 for each. Concierge, 10-20 percent for hard-to-get tickets, $5-$10 for not-easy-to-get dinner reservations, $2 for earnest try, even if unsuccessful. Doorman, $1-$2 for unloading your luggage on arrival or loading your luggage on departure. Maid, $1-$2 a night, depending on the class.

Personal Care: Barbers, manicure, and massage, 10-20 percent, but not less than $1.

Transportation: Cabbies, not less than a dollar, unless he expects you to load and unload your own bags, drives you insane with idle talk, has a radio blaring, or climate controls adjusted to suit him. Charters, $1-$5 for bus drivers acting as tour guides, depending on their competence. Limousine driver, at least 10 percent, if you are satisfied with the service. Airport skycaps, $1 per bag.

Tours

The largest tour operator in the Metroplex is Gray Line. In the Metroplex, the Gray Line contractor, **Kerrville Bus Co.,** located at 710 East Davis St. in Grand Prairie, offers tours daily. Call (800) 256-4723 anywhere in the U.S. or (972) 263-0294, Fax 262-2761, between 8 am and 6 pm.

Another tour operator that will take you around is **Texas Trails Tours,** located in Garland; (800) 785-8302 or (972) 487-9406, Fax 487-5880.

THE SPECIAL TRAVELER

SENIOR CITIZENS

Many organizations offer special discounts to citizens age 55 or older. Regardless of what the regular posted price is, always ask whether there is a discount for seniors and at what age.

Texas Department on Aging can be reached in Austin at (800) 252-9240 or (512) 424-6840, Internet www.texas.gov/agency.

Senior Citizen Services of Greater Tarrant County is located at 1000 Macon St.; (817) 338-4433. Its Arlington Senior Center is at 2015 Craig Hanking Dr.; (817) 460-5009.

The regional office of the **American Association of Retired Persons (AARP)** is at 8144 Walnut Hill Ln., Suite 700-LB-39, (214) 265-4060, in north Dallas. AARP members enjoy discounts and special services everywhere, from hotels to car rentals.

Meals on Wheels, 320 South Freeway; (817) 336-0912, Internet http://mealsonwheels.org, was founded in 1973 by a group of Fort Worth churches. Monday through Friday, its volunteers prepare hot meals for 1,600 homebound elderly residents of Tarrant County. Volunteers are always sought.

The elderly can attract swindlers of every stripe and age and of both sexes. Follow the old adage that if a deal, any deal, seems too good to be true, it probably is and someone might be trying to take advantage of you.

See also the MATTERS OF FACT chapter for additional information.

HANDICAPPED PERSONS

The Dallas-Fort Worth International Airport has signs posted prominently for wheelchair accessibility so the handicapped can get around.

Many area hotels and restaurants, especially newer ones, have facilities to make it possible for the handicapped to reach their destinations. Always call ahead to find out what exactly is available.

Consider also these resources: Adult Abuse Hotline, (800) 252-5400; American Cancer Society, (817) 737-9990; American Council of the Blind, (817) 561-1800; American Red Cross, (817) 335-9137; Braille Rallye Association for the Blind, (817) 468-7597; Disability Services of the Southwest, (817) 531-7474; Disabled American Veterans, (817) 336-1881; Goodrich Center for the Deaf TDD & Voice, (817) 926-5305; Goodwill Industries, (817) 332-7866; National Mental Health Institute on Deafness, (817) 640-8083; New Life Deaf Fellowship, (817) 457-5587; United Way, (817) 258-8000.

CHILDREN

There is plenty to see and do for children in Fort Worth and Arlington. Here are just a few attractions, many of which are described in more detail elsewhere:

The **Fort Worth Museum of Natural History,** the **Science Place** with the **Planetarium,** and for kids of all ages the **Fort Worth Zoo** or the **State Fair of Texas** in Dallas.

Lone Star Park horse races are held in Grand Prairie, **Championship Rodeo** takes place in Mesquite, the **Movie Studios at Las Colinas** are located in Irving.

And there is, of course, that children's paradise, the **Six Flags Over Texas,** or, for the water afficionados, **Hurricane Harbor,** both in Arlington and separated only by Interstate 30. There is also **Ripley's Believe It or Not/Wax Museum,** a few minutes away in Grand Prairie.

The Clubhouse for Kids Only, at 2200 Airport Fwy. in Bedford, (817) 868-1800, is for children age 12 and under. It is open Tue-Thu 10 am-8 pm, Fri-Sat 10 am-9 pm, Sun noon-6 pm. Admission for kids 2-12 years is $7, adults are free. Offers birthday parties and group rates.

Steven Spielberg's **Sega Gameworks,** at **Grapevine Mills** shopping center, 3000 Grapevine Mills Pwy., Suite 525, in Grapevine, (972) 539-6757, is a 32,000-square-foot mall entertainment complex that houses "almost any computer game you could want to play" for kids age six and older. It is open Sun-Thu 11 am-1 am, Fri 11 am-2 am, Sat

10 am-2 am. Games are up to $3 each. Midnight Madness starts two hours before closing time. **Grapevine Mills 30,** a huge movie megaplex seating 6,000, is nearby, as is the mall's food court that seats 1,000.

Laser Quest, at 7601 Grapevine Hwy. in North Richland Hills, (817) 281-0360, **Mountasia Family Funcenter,** at 8851 Grapevine Hwy., (817) 498-4488, and **NRH$_2$O Family Water Park,** two blocks away, are described under NRH$_2$O in the SIGHTS chapter.

Laser Storm, at 201 Harwood Rd. in Bedford, (817) 498-3777, is open Tue-Thu 4:30-9 pm, Fri 4:30-10 pm, Sat 11 am-10 pm, and Sun 1-9 pm. **Putt Putt Golf & Games,** at 609 N.E. Loop 820 in Hurst, (817) 589-0523, is open Sun-Thu 10 am-midnight, Fri 10 am-2 am, and Sat 9 am-2 am.

For those interested in sports, there are the **Dallas Cowboys** football games at Texas Stadium in Irving, **Texas Rangers** baseball at the Ballpark in Arlington, **Dallas Mavericks** basketball, hockey, and soccer in Fort Worth or Dallas.

Culturally inclined children just might enjoy a performance at the **Bass Performance Hall** or **Jubilee Theatre,** both downtown.

Kids will also enjoy hiking in one of these areas that are covered in more detail in the SIGHTS chapter, except for River Legacy. Have them bring plenty of water, sunscreen, a hat, and light-colored, loose clothing because temperatures often hit the eighties by midmorning. They should wear hiking boots or sneakers and socks, not sandals.

• **Fort Worth Botanic Garden,** 3220 Botanic Garden Blvd.; (817) 871-7686. CH. Its nature trail skirts the perimeter of the wooded area.

• **Fort Worth Nature Center & Refuge,** 9601 Fossil Ridge Rd.; (817) 237-1111. CH. Hikes are usually held on weekend mornings and groups are limited to 20.

• **Fossil Rim Wildlife Center** in Glen Rose, southwest of Fort Worth; (254) 897-2960. CH. Guided and self-guided tours on two nature trails.

• **River Legacy Living Science Center,** 703 N.W. Green Oaks Blvd., Arlington; (817) 860-6752. CH. Hikes usually start at 10 am Fridays and Saturdays, all year long.

STUDENTS

Fort Worth Universities

Please see the NEW RESIDENTS chapter.

Popular Student Hangouts

Among the most popular college hangouts in Arlington and Fort Worth, listed alphabetically, are

8.0, 111 East Third St.; (817) 336-0880. A downtown cafe diagonally across from Barnes & Noble Booksellers and a block from the Bass Performance Hall (see individual entries). More details are available in the DINING chapter.

The Aardvark, 2905 West Berry St.; (817) 926-7814. (See NIGHTLIFE chapter for more details.)

A Bar, 2308 West Seventh St.; (817) 336-1410. An upscale cocktail lounge particularly crowded on weekends.

Ale House, 3024 Merida Ave.; (817) 921-6006. Has more varieties of beer than most.

Barnes & Noble Bookstore, 1612 South University Dr.; (817) 557-1171. You will always find students here and at **Starbucks** next door.

The Black Dog Tavern, 903 Throckmorton St.; (817) 332-8190. Solid jazz.

Bowling & Billiards, University Center, University of Texas at Arlington; (817) 272-2674.

Coffee Haus, 314 Lincoln Sq., Arlington; (817) 274-0006. A North Arlington cafe that has an Internet outlet and board games. For students at Texas Christian University, there is a Coffee Haus at 404 Houston St. in downtown Fort Worth; (817) 336-5282.

Coogan's, 2526 South Cooper St., Arlington; (817) 795-6712. Coffeehouse that now and then welcomes live bands.

Flying Saucer, 411 East Fourth St.; (817) 336-7468. Beers galore, bottled and on tap. (See listing in the DINING chapter.)

Four Star Coffee Bar, 3324 West Seventh St.; (817) 336-5555. A popular west Fort Worth joint.

Greek House, 3013 South University Dr.; (817) 921-1473. Mediterranean eatery across the street from Texas Christian University.

Hi-Hat, 873 East Jessamine St.; (817) 927-9970. Quite popular with Texas Christian crowd.

J. Gilligan's, 407 East South at Abram streets, Arlington; (817) 274-8561. A second home to University of Texas at Arlington students with good food and local bands.

Jons Grille, 3009 South University Dr.; (817) 923-1909. Enjoy a hamburger while you check out the graffiti on the walls.

J.R. Bentley's, 406 West Abram St., Arlington; (817) 261-7351. An English pub located next to University of Texas at Arlington campus.

Longhorn Saloon, 121 West Exchange Ave.; (817) 626-1161. Watch out for Thursday student nights and bikini contests.

Maverick's Bar & Grill, 1304 South Cooper St., Arlington; (817) 861-5439. A place to meet friends and do nothing but shoot the breeze.

Ol' South Pancake House, 1507 South University Dr.; (817) 336-0311. For those who cannot make up their minds when to call it quits. (Also see listing in the DINING chapter.)

Pig & Whistle Pub, 210 East Eighth St.; (817) 882-9966. Across the street from Radisson Plaza Hotel and next door to the bus depot downtown. (See NIGHTLIFE chapter.)

The Pour House, 209 West Fifth St.; (817) 335-2575. A downtown sports bar.

University Pub, 3019 South University Dr.; (817) 921-3332. A Texas Christian University territory.

Wreck Room, 3208 West Seventh St.; (817) 870-4900. Live music venue and neighborhood bar.

Zombies Coffee Bar, 1307 South Cooper St., Arlington; (817) 461-6388. Live music venue near University of Texas at Arlington.

NEW RESIDENTS

If Fort Worth is your new home, welcome. Like with any other city, you will like some things about Cowtown and perhaps be frustrated with others. As you try to locate housing, place your children in school, and open a bank account, we will assist you with some basics that will make that transition easier. Please refer also to other parts of this guide, which contains much handy information.

AN INTRODUCTION TO FORT WORTH LIVING

Dallas likes to think of itself as a sophisticated world citizen next to Cowtown and calls itself the Big D just to make sure that Fort Worth will listen. It is refreshing to come to Fort Worth after Dallasites have been telling you for days how big their homes are, how many cellular phones they possess, and that they are a "world-class" city. Cowtown, not beyond a little boasting itself, does it on a more bearable scale. While Dallas would be ashamed to have a cow patty spotted by a visitor, Fort Worthians are proud of them, even if the only places you will ever find them are the barns in Will Rogers Memorial Center or at the Stockyards rodeo.

Fort Worth and Dallas no longer seem to have as openly contentious a relationship as they once did, according to author Jerry Flemmons. "Fort Worth became a comfortably ambitious town with a high society always one generation removed from flour-sack underwear. Dallas was skyscraper banks and Neiman-Marcus, Fort Worth, stockyards and Leonard Brothers Department Store, where one spat tobacco juice on the floor and shopped for day-old bread and Big Mack overalls."

But most of these differences seem to disappear when the Metroplex residents talk sports. Like Dallas, Fort Worth, too, is obsessed by sports and not only football. The Arlington-based Texas Rangers baseball team, which, unfortunately, does not have much to show for its efforts, and the Dallas Mavericks basketball franchise seem to draw almost as many fans as the five-time champions, the Dallas Cowboys. Initiate a conversation about one of these teams and citizens who otherwise may not get along will chatter contentedly like children.

Fort Worth is also a favorite with those who cannot tolerate Minnesota winters or Chicago's winds. Spring and fall, even stretches during the winter, are quite enjoyable. Summers, of course, are something else, unless you have good air-conditioning.

Geographical Profile

Fort Worth is located 600 feet above sea level. It is less than an hour's driving time west of Dallas, and about three and a half hours north of Austin, the capital.

While Dallas suffered the indignity of falling to the ninth largest city in the U.S. in 1998 and, much to its chagrin, had even been surpassed by San Antonio as the second largest city in Texas and the eighth nationwide, Cowtown seems not to get excited about such rankings. It currently numbers about 500,000 residents and holds the 27th or 28th place nationwide and sixth in Texas.

Fort Worth is part of the Metroplex, a community of more than four and a half million that includes Dallas and such fast-growing cities as Arlington, Colleyville, Euless, Keller, Mansfield, River Oaks, and Southlake.

Cowtown, like Dallas, has about 100 days with 90-degree-plus heat. Summers can be oppressive and seem to drag on forever, but spring and fall are quite pleasant if somewhat brief and not defined like in the northeast or northwest. The average annual humidity is 69 percent, but it can be worse than that and air-conditioning is taken for granted. For other weather-related information, please see the chapter FORT WORTH TODAY.

The time zone in Fort Worth is Central Daylight Standard Time. Noon in Fort Worth is 1 pm in Toronto and New York; 6 pm in London; 7 pm in Paris, Berlin, and Rome; 8 pm in Helsinki; 9 pm in Moscow; 3 am in Adelaide, Australia; 4 am in Sydney; and 6 am in Auckland, New Zealand.

People Profile

Fort Worth is not as much of a melting pot as Dallas, but still spiced with various races of the world, even if, just like in Dallas, at the end of the day each one goes its separate way and to an area where other settlers of like cultural background congregate. About 56 percent of the population is white, 21 percent black, and 20 percent Hispanic.

Fort Worthians, while among the friendliest people you will find anywhere in the nation, are not quite as clannish as Dallasites. But do not expect to find them crowding the sidewalks of downtown Fort Worth, except on certain days and times in Sundance Square. If you should come from one of the great European cities, whether London, Paris, or Moscow, you will be startled at how empty the city seems most of the time. People just are not milling around, not even like in New York City's Manhattan. The oppressive heat in the summer may account for part of it. For another, Fort Worthians, again like Dallasites, have lots of entertainment options in their homes and see no pressing need to go out, except when going to work, to shop, to be entertained, or to eat. Particularly on weekends, they love to watch sports on television, surrounded by their favorite friends and snacks. Instead of walking outdoors to exercise, they are just as likely do the same on equipment installed at home.

While generous hosts and friendly when on foot, some Fort Worthians change their appearance when behind the wheel. Beware especially of those who will may tailgate or cut ahead of you, just as you might find in any city.

Fort Worth Insight

Fort Worth is not a major finance center, does not have the second largest telecommunications industry in the nation, or the largest wholesale merchandise mart in the world—all the things that Dallas advertises loudly. You may live in the Metroplex for twenty years and you will seldom hear Fort Worthians pushing theirs as a "world-class" city, something that Dallasites just cannot forego.

Cowtown promotional literature will tell you, however, that "Fort Worth is like three cities in one. The most obvious city to business travelers is the downtown one. But just north on Main Street a few short miles is another Fort Worth. Called the Stockyards National Historic District, it also seems like a complete city, particularly along Exchange Avenue," says the Official Visitor's Guide. "This Fort Worth is an experience in time travel back to the Old West." But what Fort Worth may be proudest of is its cultural district, where the city's public relations machine does succumb to promoting its "world-class museums," the Kimbell, Modern, and Amon Carter. We are not convinced about their "world-class," but heartily recommend them as among the best smaller such institutions in the nation.

The one thing that probably does give Fort Worth world spotlight is its quadrennial Van Cliburn piano competition. Now carried out from the handsome, newly built Bass Performance Hall, it has probably done more to spread Fort Worth's name abroad than all of Cowtown's museums put together.

FORT WORTH FACTS

Automobiles ─────────────────────

Auto Insurance

Texas law requires that all drivers carry minimum liability insurance or otherwise meet legal requirements for financial responsibility. If you do not, you could be fined up to $1,000, have your driver's license suspended, and have your car impounded for up to 180 days. Your insurance company will issue a liability insurance card, which you must show in case of an accident or if a policeman asks for it. This card or a copy of your insurance policy must also be shown when you apply for or renew your car registration, your driver's license, and inspection sticker. If New Jersey and New York motorists pay on average more than $1,100 yearly for each vehicle, while Iowa's and North Dakota's pay only a little over $500 in insurance, Texas is somewhere in the middle.

Auto Registration

Your vehicle must be registered within 30 days of your Texas residence and must pass inspection at a licensed station once a year. To register your car or truck with the County Tax Assessor-Collector's Office, you must submit vehicle inspection certificate from an authorized car dealer, service station, or auto service center, along with your out-of-state title, and proof of liability insurance to the Tarrant County tax office, at 100 East Weatherford Street downtown; (817) 884-1100/1101.

The minimum insurance required in Texas is $15,000 bodily injury per person, $30,000 per person for each accident, and $15,000 for property damage. You will also need your social security number and the serial number of your vehicle.

Your car may also be registered at these sub-courthouses, which are open Mon-Fri 8 am-4:30 pm:

• Northwest Sub-Courthouse, 6713 Telephone Rd., Lake Worth; (817) 238-4435.

• Southwest Sub-Courthouse, 6551 Granbury Rd.; (817) 370-4535.

• Northeast Sub-Courthouse, 645 Grapevine Hwy., Hurst; (817) 581-3635.

• Polytechnic Area Sub-Courthouse, 3210 Miller Ave.; (817) 531-5635.
• Grapevine Branch Office, 630 Main St., Grapevine; (817) 488-8565.
• Arlington Sub-Courthouse, 724 East Border St.; (917) 548-3935.

You can also renew your vehicle registration at 25 Albertson's, 23 Minyards, and 13 Tom Thumb stores throughout Tarrant County.

You will pay a $15 new resident tax, $13 for the title, and for vehicle registration, the amount of which depends on the year your car was manufactured. Boats and motor homes must also be registered with the state. Boats must be registered with the Texas Parks and Wildlife Department, 5400 Airport Freeway, Suite E; (817) 831-3128. For more information, see also Internet site http://www.dot.state.tx.us.

Driver's License

Once a vehicle is registered, the newcomer must apply for a Texas driver's license. To obtain it, you must either be 18 years old, or must be at least 16 and have completed a certified driver's education program. You can take the driver's license test at the Fort Worth locations of the Texas Department of Public Safety.

Texas driver's licenses are now being renewed every six years. For more information call (817) 590-3204. To renew yours, call one of these Department of Public Safety offices, which are open Mon-Fri 8 am-5 pm and until 7 pm on Thursdays:
• 6316 Lake Worth Blvd.; (817) 238-9197.
• 6413 Woodway Dr.; (817) 294-1075.
• 2536 Jacksboro Highway, or State Highway 199; (817) 294-1075.
• 624 N.E. Loop 820, Hurst; (817) 284-1490. This is the DPS district office, where highway patrol and related offices will also be found.
• 3901 West Arkansas Ln., Arlington; (817) 274-1818.

If you are a new resident and hold a driver's license from another state, Texas law requires you to obtain a Texas license within 30 days of establishing your residency. When applying for your driver's license, bring with you a certified copy of your birth certificate or a valid out-of-state driver's license. You will have to pass both a visual test and a written examination. If you do not have a current driver's license, you will have to take a driving test.

Vehicle Inspection

Texas law requires most vehicles to carry a safety inspection sticker. Inspections can be performed at certified garages and auto dealerships. Cost of the inspection sticker is based on the year of the vehicle. The sticker is valid for one year, except for new cars, which have two-year stickers. The sticker is displayed in the lower lefthand corner of the windshield. It shows the month and year in which the inspection expires.

Reporting of Automobile Accidents

From the national perspective, Texas has a high percentage of intoxicated drivers on the road. The "road rage" is also widely documented here so use your horn sparingly and do not tailgate. Local media suggests that you not make eye contact with the other driver as that could be construed a provocation. Carjackings are not at all uncommon, even during the day, so do not let anyone willingly into your vehicle and lock your doors and keep your windows rolled up.

In an accident with another vehicle, you might consider moving your car out of the way and exchange insurance information with the other driver. However, if you have reason to believe that the other driver may try to avoid taking the responsibility for his or her actions, try to leave the car on the spot of the accident until the police or fire truck arrives. It can only help if you carry in your car a disposable camera and document the exact position of your vehicle.

You must report the accident within 24 hours. Most insurance companies suggest that you write down names, telephone numbers, and license numbers of persons involved, as well as those of witnesses. They suggest that you notify them promptly and that you do not discuss the accident with anyone, except them or the police.

Banking

The largest Fort Worth banks and savings and loans in 1999 included:

Summit Community Bank, Assets $330 million; 3859 Camp Bowie Blvd.; (817) 735-8866.

Summit National Bank, Assets $230 million; 1300 Summit Ave.; (817) 336-8383.

Southwest Bank, Assets $210 million; 3737 S.W. Loop 820; (817) 292-4820.

First Command Bank, Assets $145 million; 4100 South Hulen St.; (817) 763-0000.

Mercantile Bank, Assets $100 million; 2550 Meacham Blvd.; (817) 831-2211.

Chambers of Commerce

American Indian Chamber of Commerce, has 300 member firms; (817) 429-2323.

Arlington Chamber of Commerce, has 2,000 member firms; (817) 275-2613.

Benbrook Chamber of Commerce, has 320 member firms; (817) 249-4451.

Burleson Chamber of Commerce, has 500 member firms; (817) 295-6121.

Fort Worth Chamber of Commerce, has 3,700 member firms; (817) 336-2491.

Fort Worth Black Chamber of Commerce, has 600 member firms; (817) 531-8510.

Fort Worth Hispanic Chamber of Commerce, has 520 member firms; (817) 625-5411.

Grapevine Chamber of Commerce, has 615 member firms; (817) 481-1522.

Hurst/Euless/Bedford Chamber of Commerce, has 1,000 member firms; (817) 283-1521.

Mansfield Chamber of Commerce, has 350 member firms; (817) 473-0507.

Northeast Tarrant County Chamber of Commerce, has 720 member firms; (817) 281-9376.

North Fort Worth Business Association, has 190 member firms; (817) 626-7921.

Tarrant County Asian Chamber of Commerce, has 195 member firms; (817) 732-7426.

Tarrant County Texas Business Association, has 300 member firms; (817) 640-3301.

Churches

There are 13 pages of churches, synagogues, temples, and mosques listed in the Fort Worth Yellow Pages directory. Here are a few.

African Methodist Episcopal, ... (214) 333-2632.
Ahavath Sholom,
 Conservative Synagogue, ...(817) 731-4721.
Baptist General Convention of Texas, . . .(817) 927-1911.
Catholic Diocese of Fort Worth, ...(817) 560-3300.
Churches of Christ, ...(817) 834-7355
 . . . . .or 246-8000.
Church of God in Christ, ...(817) 451-5493
 . . . . .or 534-2601.
Church of Jesus Christ
 of Latter-Day Saints, ...(817) 354-7444.
Congregation Beth-El,
 Reform Congregation, ...(817) 332-7141.
Eastern Orthodox Church
 of North Texas, ...(000) 753-1926.

Episcopal Diocese of Fort Worth, ...(817) 738-9952.
Evangelical Lutheran Church, ...(214) 637-6865, Dallas.
First Christian Science
    Church of Fort Worth, ...(817) 731-6891.
Fort Worth Huong Dao
    Buddhist Temple, ...(817) 531-7144.
Foursquare Gospel Church, ...(817) 536-8992.
Full Gospel Arlington Faith Chapel, ...(817) 265-6308.
Hindu Temple, ...(972) 445-3111, Irving.
Islamic Association of Tarrant County, . .(817) 737-8104.
Jehovah's Witnesses, ...(817) 496-9124;
. . . . .Arlington, (817) 277-2535.
Macedonia Ministries, ...(817) 540-2770, Bedford.
Presbyterian Church in America, ...(817) 731-3300.
Seventh-Day Adventists, ...(817) 295-0476, Burleson.
Tarrant Area Community of Churches, . .(817) 922-9446.
United Methodist Church, ...(817) 877-5222.
United Pentecostal Calvary, ...(817) 293-7103.
World Baptist Fellowship, ... (817) 274-7161.
Young Israel of Fort Worth,
    Orthodox Congregation, ...(817) 294-2505.

Concealed Arms

Texas is one among 41 states that allow residents to carry concealed handguns. Legal residents of Texas, at least 21 years old, not convicted of a felony, not addicted to drugs, of sound mind, and meeting ten other eligibility requirements, can apply for a license to carry a concealed handgun. They must undergo at least ten hours of classroom instruction on gun law and safety and pay a $140 fee.

There were nearly 200,000 such permit holders in Texas—about one percent of the state residents—in mid-1998, more than 90 percent of them were white and the vast majority men. More than 1,600 of them have been accused of crimes, 402 on felony charges.

Texas, Arkansas, and Oklahoma permit holders can carry their firearms in all three states.

About one-half of Texans own some type of gun. About a third have one handgun, and more than a quarter have two to five.

Corporate Metroplex

The following are the largest publicly-owned companies headquartered in the Metroplex, all with revenues exceeding $2 billion. Only the number of local employees is shown here.

The 100 largest companies in the Metroplex all have revenues above $200 million. The next 50 largest publicly-owned companies have revenues of at least $75 million.

Fort Worth's largest employers are American Airlines with 37,000 employees, Lockheed Martin with 13,000, Bell Helicopter-Textron with 6,300, followed by Harris Methodist Hospital, Burlington Northern & Santa Fe Railway, Alcon Laboratories, Tandy Corporation, and Southwestern Bell.

Exxon Corporation, Sales $140 billion, 380 Metroplex employees. Integrated oil company. 5959 Las Colinas Blvd., Irving; (972) 444-1000, Internet www.exxon.com.

J.C. Penney Company, Sales $33 billion, 10,000 Metroplex employees. Department store chain, Eckerd drug stores. 6501 Legacy Dr., Plano; (972) 431-1000, Internet www.jcpenney.com.

GTE Corporation, Sales $26 billion, 14,000 Metroplex employees. Telecommunications. 1255 Corporate Drive, Irving; (972) 507-5000, Internet www.gte.com.

AMR Corporation, Sales $20 billion, 30,000 Metroplex employees. Owns American and American Eagle airlines, 4333 Amon Carter Blvd., Fort Worth; (817) 963-1234, Internet www.amrcorp.com.

Halliburton, Sales $18 billion, 2,200 Metroplex employees. Oilfield services, construction, and engineering. 500 North Akard, Dallas; (214) 978-2600, Internet www.halliburton.com.

Electronic Data Systems, Sales $17 billion, 12,000 Metroplex employees. Information services. 5400 Legacy Dr., Plano; (972) 604-6000, Internet www.eds.com.

Texas Utilities Co., Sales $15 billion, 2,900 Metroplex employees. Utility holding company. 1601 Bryan St., Dallas; (214) 812-4600, Internet www.TU.com.

Kimberly-Clark, Sales $13 billion, 1,000 Metroplex employees. Household and personal care products. 351 Phelps Dr., Irving; (972) 281-1200, Internet www.kimberly-clark.com.

Union Pacific, Sales $11 billion, 1,700 Metroplex employees. Operates railroads. 1717 Main St., Dallas; (214) 743-5600, Internet www.unionpacific.com.

Associates First Capital Corp., Sales $10 billion, 7,500 Metroplex employees. Financial services. 250 East John Carpenter Fwy., Irving; (972) 652-7569, Internet www.theassociates.com.

Texas Instruments, Sales $10 billion, 9,000 Metroplex employees. Manufactures semiconductors. 8505 Forest Ln., Dallas; (972) 995-2011, Internet www.ti.com.

Burlington Northern Santa Fe, Sales $9 billion, 3,200 Metroplex employees. Railroad and transportation company. 2650 Lou Menk Dr., Fort Worth; (817) 333-2000, Internet www.bnsf.com.

7-Eleven, Inc., Sales $7.5 billion, 3,000 Metroplex employees.

Operates 7-Eleven stores. 2711 North Haskell Ave., Dallas; (214) 828-7011, Internet www.7-eleven.com.

Central & Southwest Corp., Sales $6 billion, 550 Metroplex employees. Electric utility holding company. 1616 Woodall Rodgers Fwy., Dallas; (214) 777-1000, Internet www.csw.com.

CompUSA, Sales $5 billion, 2,800 Metroplex employees. Computer retail store chain. 14951 North Dallas Pkwy., Dallas; (972) 982-4000, Internet www.compusa.com.

Tandy Corporation, Sales $5 billion, 6,000 Metroplex employees; Consumer electronics retailer, 100 Throckmorton St., Suite 1800, Fort Worth; (817) 415-3011, Internet www.tandy.com.

Southwest Airlines, Sales $4 billion, 4,900 Metroplex employees. Airline. 2702 Love Field Dr., Dallas; (214) 792-4000, Internet www.iflyswa.com.

Centex Corp, Sales $4 billion, 1,950 Metroplex employees. Home building, real estate, and banking. 2728 North Harwood St., Dallas; (214) 981-5000, Internet www.centex.com.

Suiza Foods, Sales $3 billion, 300 Metroplex employees. Produces and distributes dairy products. 3811 Turtle Creek Blvd., Suite 1300, Dallas; (214) 303-3400, Internet www.suizafoods.com.

Trinity Industries, Sales $2.5 billion, 3,700 Metroplex employees. Rail cars, marine products, and shipping containers manufacturer, 2525 Stemmons Fwy., Dallas; (214) 631-4420, Internet www.trin.net.

Commercial Metals, Sales $2.5 billion, 450 Metroplex employees; Steel and metal products manufacturer. 7800 Stemmons Fwy., Dallas; (214) 689-4300, Internet www.commercialmetals.com.

Compucom Systems, Sales $2.5 billion, 1,400 Metroplex employees. Computer reseller. 7171 Forest Ln., Dallas; (972) 865-3600, Internet www.compucom.com.

Union Pacific Resources Group, Sales $2.5 billion, 1,100 Metroplex employees. Oil and gas exploration and production. 801 Cherry St., Fort Worth; (817) 877-6000, Internet www.upr.com.

Sabre Group Holdings, Sales $2.5 billion, 5,400 Metroplex employees. Travel services. 4255 Amon Carter Blvd., Fort Worth; (817) 967-1000, Internet www.sabre.com.

D. R. Horton, Sales $2.2 billion, 200 Metroplex employees. Builds single-family homes. 1901 Ascension Blvd., Arlington; (817) 856-8200, Internet www.drhorton.com.

Cell Star Corp., Sales $2 billion, 300 Metroplex employees. Wholesale distributor of cellular phones. 1730 Briercroft Court, Carrollton; (972) 466-5000, Internet www.cellstar.com.

The largest privately-owned company in Tarrant County is the Arlington-based **Onex Food Services,** providing in-flight catering, with sales well in access of $1.7 billion. It is followed by men's and women's apparel manufacturer **Williamson-Dickie Manufacturing** and food and beverage distributor **Ben E. Keith Co.,** both with sales in excess of $700 million. The largest woman-owned business in Fort Worth is **Lucky Lady Oil Co.,** a wholesaler of motor fuel, with annual revenues of $120 million. It is run by former State Representative Sue Palmer in Fort Worth's District 89. The company was started in 1976 with a desk and a phone. It employs 125 people. The company was in the process of being renamed Continental Fuels and going public.

Among the 200 largest Metroplex companies, 104 are located in Dallas, 26 in Fort Worth, 25 in Irving, and 3 in Arlington.

EDUCATION

Childcare Facilities

Although there are nearly five pages of childcare facilities for preschoolers listed in the Fort Worth Yellow Pages telephone directory, not many are what most parents would desire. Do your homework and visit as many as possible before you decide which one is best suited for your child.

Among the resources to help you make an educated decision about your child's care, consider: **Fort Worth Child Care Reference Center,** (800) 635-4116; **Child Care Group,** (214) 630-7911; **Child Care Locators of America,** (817) 572-7664; **Child Care Referral Services,** (817) 572-7664; **Tarrant County Community Churches,** (817) 335-9341; **YMCA of Fort Worth,** (817) 332-3281/6191.

An important criterion to judge suitability of a daycare center is accreditation by the National Association for the Education of Young Children. The following Fort Worth centers were recently accredited by NAEYC:

All Saints Hospital Child Care Facility, 1709 North Enderly Place; (817) 927-6249. Open 5:30 am-6:30 pm. Has enrollment of about 160.

Camp Fires Family Centers Child Care, 2700 Meacham Blvd.; (817) 831-5050.

Children's Ministries/First United Methodist Church, 800 West Fifth St.; (817) 870-9174.

First Presbyterian Church Day School, 1000 Penn St.; (817) 335-6315.

Fort Worth Museum of Science & History Preschool, 1501 Montgomery; (817) 255-9337.

Juniors Junction, 2249 East Loop 820; (817) 284-1221.

Kinder Care Learning Center Council of Camp Fire, 3700 Basswood; (817) 232-9474.

Kinder Care #100, 6017 Westcreek Dr.; (817) 292-7281.

Montessori Children's House, 3420 Clayton Rd. East; (817) 732-0252.

Sid Richardson Child Development Center, 931 South Lake St.; (817) 882-2076.

Smithfield United Methodist Discovery School, Smithfield Rd.; (817) 281-2669.

University Christian Church Weekday School, 2720 South University Dr.; (817) 926-6631.

University United Methodist Child Development, 2416 West Berry St.; (817) 926-8706.

Westcliff Methodist Preschool, 4833 Selkirk Dr.; (817) 924-4580.

YMCA, A Child's Place, 501 Felix, Bldg. 24, Federal Center; (817) 334-5228.

YWCA Creative Enrichment Child Care Center, 512 West Fourth St.; (817) 332-6191.

YWCA Polytechnic Child Care Center, 3401 Avenue I; (817) 536-1731.

In Arlington, these centers were accredited by NAEYC:

Children's Courtyard, 2501 Ballpark Way; (817) 633-1458. Open 6:30 am-6:30 pm. With 15 locations and enrollment of about 3,150, this is the largest daycare chain in Arlington.

Children's World Learning Center, 2301 West Arkansas Ln.; (817) 261-6541.

Children's World Learning Center, 4019 Woodland Park; (817) 274-7361.

Children's World Learning Center #018, 1305 Arbrook West; (817) 465-3777.

First Presbyterian Preschool, 1200 South Collins St.; (817) 274-4051. With enrollment of about 190, this is one of the largest such facilities in Arlington.

Gateway Learning Center, 1009 Magnolia St.; (817) 277-7132.

River Legacy Nature School, 703 N.W. Green Oak Blvd.; (817) 860-2073.

Rocking Horse Academy, 1401 Caplin Dr.; (817) 557-0400.

The Children's Courtyard, 4400 West Pleasant Ridge Rd.; (817) 478-7733.

The Children's Courtyard, 1505 West Arkansas Ln.; (817) 861-9712.

The Children's Courtyard, 1825 Wimbeldon Dr.; (817) 784-5030.

The Children's Courtyard, 1865 Wimbeldon Dr.; (817) 468-5030.

Primary and Secondary Schools ————

With 78,000 students—almost 40 percent Hispanic, 33 percent

African-American, and 25 percent white—in 111 schools, the **Fort Worth Independent School District** (FWISD) is the ninth largest school district in the nation. Its offices are located at 100 North University Dr.; (817) 871-2000, Internet http://ftworth.isd.tenet.edu. It employs 4,262 teachers with eleven years of experience on average and a teacher-pupil ratio of 18.7. FWISD had an operating budget of $362 million in 1998 for its 69 elementary, 21 middle, 12 high schools, and other facilities. Spending per pupil in that year was $4,737. Fifty-seven percent of students passed all TAAS tests in grades 3-8 and ten, while the state average was 73.2 percent passing. The average SAT college entrance score was 952 in 1998, while the state score was 995.

Arlington ISD, (817) 459-7342, Internet www.dmin-dom.arlington.k12.tx.us, has about 55,000 students, with almost 59 percent being white, 17 percent Hispanic, 17 percent African-American, and 2.7 percent Asian and Native American. The Arlington Independent School District employs about 3,225 teachers with almost eleven years of experience on average and a teacher-pupil ratio of 16.5. AISD had an operating budget of $230 million in 1998 for its 63 facilities, 43 of them elementary, eleven junior high, and five high schools. Spending per pupil in that year was $3,701. Seventy-five percent of the students passed all TAAS tests in grades 3-8 and ten, while the state average was 73.2 percent passing. The average SAT college entrance score was 1,042, while the state score was 995.

The Fort Worth district enjoys a better reputation nationally among educators than it does among local residents, according to one source. Although it is not considered an "outstanding" big-city public school system—such as Seattle's and Omaha's—the Fort Worth school district is "very strong" and in league with those in El Paso, Pittsburgh, and Minneapolis. The city's Tanglewood area, for example, has a neighborhood elementary school where students boast a 97 percent passing rate on the TAAS tests and almost a third of them are in gifted and talented programs.

About 3,100 of the district's students attend 13 of the so-called magnet schools, which offer more rigorous academic instruction than most of their regular programs. Each magnet emphasizes a discipline, such as engineering and medicine. Fort Worth's first magnet program was established in 1981 to attract white students to predominantly black schools as a means of voluntary racial integration.

"About 20,000 students, or 25 percent of the student population, and 915 teachers are housed in 451 portable buildings, some a block from the principal's office and nearest restroom," said the *Fort Worth Star-Telegram* in 1999.

In 1998, Texas had more than 2.5 million high school dropouts, the second highest number in the nation.

SAT Scores

These are the 1998 scores for the verbal and math sections of the SAT test. The Texas-wide average SAT scores, in comparison, were 494 and 501, the national 505 and 512. A perfect score in each section is 800.

	Verbal	Math
Arlington	519	523
Azle	511	500
Birdville	504	517
Carroll	554	549
Dallas	438	444
Eagle Mount-Saginaw	515	506
Fort Worth	476	476
Grand Prairie	499	507
Grapevine-Colleyville	526	526
Hurst-Euless-Bedford	511	521
Keller	520	520
Kennedale	465	455
Mansfield	513	512
Northwest	513	517
White Settlement	481	471

Education is free in Texas for children from kindergarten through the 12th grade.

To enroll in the FWISD, your child must have a birth certificate, proof of immunizations, and, sometimes, proof of residence and a transcript from the previous school. For more details, please call (817) 871-2000.

Private Prep Schools

There are almost 100 secular and church-related private schools in Tarrant County. They cost up to $10,000 a year, often require a uniform, accept fewer than half of the applicants, and prepare their graduates for Cornell, Columbia, Harvard, MIT, Princeton, Stanford, and Yale.

All Saints Episcopal School, 8200 Tumbleweed Trail; (817) 246-2413, E-mail dwandel@aseschool.com. Established in 1951, it has enrollment of 760. Kindergarten-to-fifth grade lower school tuition starts at $5,700; grades six-to-eight middle school at $6,100; and grades nine-to-12 upper school at $6,500. All have a student-teacher ratio of 12:1. Students must have a minimum of 85 hours of community service to graduate, as well as be computer-literate.

Bethesda Christian School, 4700 North Beach St.; (817) 281-6446, E-mail bethesda@integrityonline2.com. Established in 1980, it has enrollment of 600. Student-teacher ratio is 11:1, with maximum class size of 18 students. Tuition starts at $1,900 for kindergarten and goes to $3,500 in tenth grade. "Provides Biblical principles and character development with challenging curricula to train young people in the highest principles of self-discipline, individual responsibility, and personal integrity," according to their promotional information.

Burton Adventist Academy, 4611 Kelly Elliott, Arlington; (817) 572-0081. Established in 1961, it has enrollment of almost 400 in grades kindergarten through 12th grade, a student-teacher ratio of 22:1, and a starting tuition of $2,200.

Cassata Learning Center, 1400 Hemphill; (817) 926-1745, E-mail cassata@hotmail.com. Established in 1975, it has enrollment of 450 in grades nine through 12, a student-teacher ratio of 15:1, and fees based on a sliding scale.

Calvary Academy, 1600 West Fifth St.; (817) 332-3351, E-mail clibrary@flash.net. Established in 1979, it has enrollment of 470, kindergarten to 12th grade. Student-teacher ratio is 20:1. Varsity sports include volleyball, basketball, football, baseball, and track & field. Tuition starts at $3,000.

Fort Worth Christian School, 7517 Bogart Dr., North Richland Hills; (817) 281-6504, Internet www.fwc.org, E-mail info@fwc.org. Established in 1958, it has enrollment of 750. The elementary through fifth grade school has a student-teacher ratio of 12:1 and tuition starting at $3,700. Middle school, grades six through eight, has a student-teacher ratio of 18:1 and tuition starting at $4,200. High school, grades nine through 12, has a student-teacher ratio of 17:1 and tuition starting at $5,000. Before- and after-school care is available.

Fort Worth Country Day School, 4200 Country Day Ln.; (817) 732-7718, Internet www.fwcds.pvt.tenet.edu. One of the largest private schools in Tarrant County. Has enrollment of 1,050, grades kindergarten through 12th grade, tuition starts at $8,200, student-teacher ratio is 9:1. Eleven percent receive financial aid and busing is provided. Co-ed school, established in 1962, with academically-advanced liberal arts curriculum.

In 1998, Country Day was one of two Tarrant County schools that were named among the nation's best by the U.S. Department of Education for their overall excellence. The other was Heritage Middle School of Colleyville, a town that is named for pioneer physician Lilburn Howard Colley.

Glenview Christian School, 4805 N.E. Loop 820; (817) 281-5155, E-mail gcschool@flash.net. Established in 1972, Glenview has enrollment of 300, a student-teacher ratio of 20:1, and a starting tuition of $1,600 for pre-kindergarten and $2,800 in sixth grade.

Grace Lutheran School, 308 West Park Row, Arlington; (817) 274-1654, Internet www.flash.net/argrace. Established in 1982, it has enrollment of 330, a student-teacher ratio of 18:1, and a starting tuition of $2,600 in its pre-kindergarten through eighth grade program.

Lake Country Christian School, 7050 Lake Country Dr.; (817) 236-8703, Internet www.lccs.org. Established in 1980, it has enrollment of 450 in kindergarten through 12th grade, a student-teacher ratio of 18:1, and a starting tuition of $3,500 in kindergarten.

Nolan Catholic High School, 4501 Bridge St.; (817) 457-2920, Internet www.azone.net/nolan, E-mail meyerpet@tenet.edu. Established in 1961. With an enrollment of more than 1,100 in grades seven through 12, it is the largest private school in Tarrant County. Student-teacher ratio is 14:1 and starting tuition $4,100.

The Oakridge School, 5900 West Pioneer Parkway, Arlington; (817) 451-4994, E-mail info@oakridge.pvt.kl2.tx.us. Has enrollment of 800 in grades pre-kindergarten through 12th, with tuition starting at $2,200. Student-teacher ratio is 10:1 and 14 percent receive financial aid. Co-ed school, established in 1979, has enrichment and art programs, college preparatory curriculum, foreign language.

Pantego Christian Academy, 2201 West Park Row, Arlington; (817) 460-3315. Established in 1962, it has enrollment of 700 in grades pre-kindergarten through 12 in a 111,000-square-foot facility, a student-teacher ratio of 15:1, and tuition starting at $1,000.

Saint Alban's Episcopal School, 911 South Davis, Arlington; (817) 460-6071. Established in 1958, it has an enrollment of 350 in pre-kindergarten through eighth grade, a student-teacher ratio of 18:1, and a starting tuition of $1,200.

Saint Andrew Catholic School, 3304 Dryden Rd.; (817) 924-8917, Internet www.standrewsch.org. Established in 1954, it has enrollment of 700 in grades kindergarten through eighth grade. Its student-teacher ratio is 18:1 and starting tuition $1,000.

Saint John the Apostle Catholic School, 7421 Glenview Dr., North Richland Hills; (817) 284-2228, Internet www.stjs.org. Established in 1965, it has enrollment of 630 in kindergarten through eighth grade, a student-teacher ratio of 22:1, and starting tuition of $950.

Saint Maria Goretti Catholic School, 1200 South Davis Dr., Arlington; (817) 275-5081, E-mail dstarkovich@smgschool.org. Established in 1954, it has enrollment of 465 in grades kindergarten through eighth grade, student teacher ratio of 25:1, and a starting tuition of $2,200.

Southwest Christian School, 4600-B Altamesa Blvd.; (817) 294-9596, Internet www.flash.net/~scs. Established in 1969, it has enrollment of 500 in grades pre-kindergarten through 12th grade, with a student-teacher ratio of 18:1, and a starting tuition of about $850.

Temple Christian School, 6824 Randol Mill Rd.; (817) 457-0770, E-mail tcsfw@flash.net. Established in 1972, it has enrollment of about

600 in kindergarten through 12th grade, a student-teacher ratio of 11:1, and a starting tuition of $1,700.

Texas Christian Academy, 915 Web St., Arlington; (817) 274-5201, E-mail tcalibrary@juno.com. Established in 1972, it has enrollment of 360 in kindergarten through 12th grade, a student-teacher ratio of 15:1, and a starting tuition of $1,900.

Trinity Valley School, 7500 Dutch Branch and Bryant Irvin Rd.; (817) 292-6060, Internet www.trinityvalleyschool.org. It has enrollment of 870 in kindergarten through 12th grade, student-teacher ratio of 10:1, with tuition starting at $7,700; 14 percent receive financial aid. The co-ed, classical-education, $29-million school, now located on a 75-acre campus, was established in 1959. It has comprehensive sports and outdoor programs, senior internships, and travel abroad. Chemistry, world history, art, Latin, and Spanish are mandatory in some grades. Ethnic makeup is 85 percent white and 8 percent Asian.

Westridge Christian Academy, 9001 Highway 80 West; (817) 244-1136, Internet startext.net/np/wca. Established in 1969, it has enrollment of 325 in kindergarten through eighth grade, a student-teacher ratio of 15:1, and a starting tuition of $250 a month.

Specialized Schools

The Tarrant Educational Coalition of Specialized Schools, which includes the schools below, has enrollment of more than 1,000 students and addresses the needs of children with learning disabilities. The primary characteristic of these schools is that instead of requiring students to adjust to their environment, teachers adapt their teaching styles so that students can succeed. These schools address dyslexia, attention deficit disorder, dyscalculia, or dysgraphia. Tuition ranges from $8,000 to $13,000 a year. For more details about the schools, call the National Center for Learning Disabilities, at (888) 575-7373.

Child Study Center, (817) 336-8611, grades pre-K through 12, average class size 12.

Fourth Street School, Arlington, (817) 265-9438, grades one through eight, class size 12.

Gateway School, Arlington, (817) 226-6222, grades seven through 12, average class size 10.

Hill School, (817) 923-9482, grades two to eight, average class size 11. Est. 1974.

Key School, (817) 446-3738, grades one through 12, average class size four. Est. 1966.

Starpoint, (817) 921-7141, TCU campus, kindergarten to fourth grade, class size ten.

Treetop International, Euless, (817) 283-1771, kindergarten to 12th grade, class size 12.

Wedgewood Academy, (817) 263-2976, grades four through 11, average class size ten.

West Academy, (817) 924-3535, grades nine through 12, average class size eight.

Tarrant County Public Colleges and Universities

Tarrant County Junior College, 1500 Houston St.; (817) 921-7810, Internet www.tcjc.cc.tx.us. A junior college, established in 1965, with enrollment of 22,000 at four campuses in Fort Worth, Arlington, and Hurst.

Texas Woman's University, Denton; (817) 898-3021. Established in 1901, it has enrollment of 9,000 and operating budget of about $83 million. The median student age is 27 years and the undergraduate student-to-faculty ratio 13:1. "A comprehensive public university, primarily for women, offering bachelor's, master's and doctoral degrees in more than 100 career programs."

University of North Texas, Denton; (800) UNT-8211 or (940) 565-2681, Internet www.unt.edu. Located 35 miles north of Fort Worth. Established in 1890, it has enrollment of 19,000 undergraduates and 6,000 graduate students, and operating budget of about $275 million. It offers 91 bachelor's, 121 master's, and 47 doctoral degree programs. This is the largest university in the greater Metroplex and the state's fourth largest. The median student age is 22.5 years and the undergraduate student-to-faculty ratio 17:1.

University of North Texas Health Science Center, 3500 Camp Bowie Blvd.; (817) 735-2000. Established in 1970, it has enrollment of 600 on a 15-acre campus in the cultural district. It includes Texas College of Osteopathic Medicine (TCOM), which has about 450 students, a faculty of 190, and a staff of 900.

The University of Texas at Arlington, 800 South Cooper St., Arlington; (817) 272-2011/8821, Internet www.uta.edu. Established in 1895, it has a budget of $200 million, enrollment of 20,000 students, 70 percent of them white. This is the sixth largest university in Texas and second in the Metroplex. The 390-acre campus lies along a creek in central Arlington and has a student population representing more than 80 nations. The median student age is 24 years and the undergraduate student-to-faculty ratio 18:1. UTA offers 58 bachelor's, 60 master's, and 22 doctoral degrees within nine units and a graduate school.

FW Weekly notes that "The UTA student is fiercely independent, forward in thinking, technically inclined, dresses casually cool (some-

where between trendy and thrift chic), self reliant, motivated to succeed yet bored by nature and politically apathetic—an urban samurai
on a quest for self discovery."

Private Colleges and Universities

Southwestern Baptist Theological Seminary, 2001 West Seminary
Dr.; (817) 923-1921, Internet www.swbts.edu. Affiliated with the
Southern Baptists, it was established in 1908 and has enrollment of
about 4,000 students whose median age is 32 years. The student-to-faculty ratio is 21:1. Southwestern is the largest theology school in the
nation.

Charles D. Tandy Archeological Museum at Southwestern Baptist,
which features the cultural artifacts of archeological excavations at the
biblical site of Tel Batash-Timnah in Israel, is located in A. Webb
Roberts Library. Open Mon-Sat 8 am-5 pm.

Texas Christian University, 2800 South University Dr.; (800)
TCU-FROG or (817) 921-7000, Internet www.tcu.edu. Originally
established in Fort Worth in 1873, and now having about 7,400 students, a full-time faculty of 350, and an operating budget of $140 mil-
lion. It was reestablished here in 1910 after its removal from Waco
because of a fire in the main building. It boasts 60 buildings on a 243-
acre campus. The median student age is 23 years, the undergraduate
student-to-faculty ratio 15:1.

The story of TCU library's namesake, **Mary Couts Burnett,** concerns one of the five daughters of Col. James Robertson Couts, a prominent banker and rancher in Parker County. Raised in Weatherford,
Texas, Mary first married Claude Barradel and was widowed. After
Barradel's untimely death she was wooed and won by wealthy cattleman, Samuel Burk Burnett, himself a widower, according to author
Joan Hewett Swaim. The one child born to the couple, Tom L. Burnett,
died in 1938 and left his holdings to his only daughter, Anne V.
Burnett. By 1920, the relationship between Mary and Samuel had
grown tense and Mrs. Burnett expressed fears that her husband was trying to kill her. Burnett claimed in court that his wife was suffering from
"hallucinations" and won sanity judgment against her. He committed
her to a limited asylum in a private Weatherford home where she was
kept virtually a prisoner until she engineered her own release on the
very day, on June 27, 1922, of her husband's death. Set free, she
obtained her "widow's half" of the estate, which Burnett had willed
almost entirely to his granddaughter, Anne Burnett. In 1923, she
shocked TCU by giving the university nearly her entire estate in trust,
more than $3 million, which today would be worth about $40 million.
(For more details about Samuel B. Burnett, "a notoriously rough-edged

character," please see entries Burk Burnett Building, Burnett Park, and Burnett Plaza in the SIGHTS chapter.)

The university's 1,200-seat Ed Landreth Auditorium gained recognition from the quadrennial Van Cliburn International Piano Competitions, which have now been moved to the Bass Performance Hall (see individual entries). In 1998, a $12-million Walsh Center for the Performing Arts was inaugurated behind the Landreth hall. It includes a 325-seat Pepsico Recital Hall and a 233-seat Hays Theatre. It is named after the Fort Worth oilman F. Howard Walsh, who "bought mink coats for his domestic help and gave millions to hospitals, churches, arts groups and schools."

The Fort Worth Transportation Authority provides free shuttle bus service around the campus for students and staff.

Texas Wesleyan University, 1201 Wesleyan St.; (800) 580-8980 or (817) 531-4444, Internet www.txwesleyan.edu. Texas Wesleyan sprawls across 60 acres atop Polytechnic Hill, one of the highest points in Fort Worth. Located five miles east of downtown, it is the oldest university in Tarrant County. It is a private United Methodist Church college, established in 1890, with a full-time faculty of 130 and enrollment of 3,200. Student-teacher ratio is 17:1. It has five schools and 46 degree offerings.

Texas Wesleyan University School of Law is located downtown at 1515 Commerce St.; (817) 212-4000.

GOVERNMENT

For an abundance of information about the city, county, and state governments and their elected officials, please check also the state's Internet site www.texas.gov.

City Government

Fort Worth has a council-city manager form of municipal government. The mayor heads an eight-member elected city council, which functions like a corporate board of directors, deciding policy and charting the city's future. Each council member represents a city district, while the mayor is elected at large. The council employs a professional manager who is responsible for the daily operations of all city departments, somewhat like the president of a company.

One councilwoman described the diverse, independent-minded city council in 1998 as "eight completely different, egotistical individuals," according to the *Fort Worth Star-Telegram*.

A city councilman since 1993, Kenneth Barr (b. 1942), has been Fort Worth's $75-a-week mayor since 1996, when his predecessor resigned to run for the U.S. Congress. The mayor, who is said to "habitually put in 60-hour weeks" easily won reelection the following year. He heads a family-owned printing business. His father, former city mayor in the 1960s, Willard Barr, "an advocate of desegregation," died in 1998 at age 90.

Bob Terrell (b. 1944) has been a civil servant for 20 years and is the city manager.

The Arlington city council operates as the city government's legislative body. It is made up of the mayor and eight council members. The mayor and three of the council members are elected "at-large" by voters citywide. The remaining five members are elected by voters in districts representing specific areas of the city. Council members serve two-year staggered terms and elections are held every May. You can reach the Arlington council members or the mayor at (817) 459-6122.

County Government

Tarrant County is one of 254 counties in Texas that were originally set up by the state to serve as decentralized administrative divisions providing state services and collecting state taxes. With a population of about 1.3 million, it is the fourth largest county in Texas and 26th nationwide. The county's main telephone is (817) 884-1111 and its Internet address www.tarrantcounty.com.

Tarrant County is served by four county commissioners in four precincts and a county judge. The judge and the commissioners form the Commissioners Court. Despite its name, this court is the governing body for Tarrant County, not a judicial court.

The Commissioners Court meets every Tuesday at 10 am on the fifth floor of the county administration building in the commissioners courtroom. The meetings are open to the public.

State Government

The 76th session of the Texas Legislature convened in 1999 with 150 House members, of whom 78 were Democrats, 121 men, and 25 new members. In the Senate, 16 of the 31 members were Republicans, 28 men, and two new members. The major issue facing the legislators was how to spend a record $5.6 billion budget surplus. The lawmakers worked "under the klieg lights of the 2000 national presidential sweepstakes," as speculation grew that Gov. George Bush was to announce his bid for the White House. Rick Perry became the first Republican lieutenant governor since Reconstruction.

U.S. Senators from Texas

Sen. Kay Bailey Hutchison, Republican, has an office in Dallas at 10440 North Central Expwy. #1160; (214) 361-3500, and in Washington, D.C., (202) 224-5922, Internet http://www.senate.gov/~hutchison.

Sen. Phil Gramm, Republican, has an office here at 2323 Bryan St. #1500, in downtown Dallas; (214) 767-3000, and in Washington, D.C., (202) 224-2934, Internet http://www.senate.gov/senator/gramm.html.

HEALTH AND DENTAL CARE

Whatever health or dental emergencies you may have, none should be too challenging for the facilities available. Fort Worth has a dozen hospitals with close to 3,000 beds and more than 6,000 doctors.

For emergencies, consider one of these Tarrant County hospitals, where most of your minor ailments could be taken care of at the out-patient or emergency clinic. The cost, however, could be higher than if you sought an individual doctor. Unless a state resident, you will prob-ably have to pay cash or use a universally recognized credit card, such as American Express, MasterCard, or VISA.

All Saints Episcopal Hospital, 1400 Eighth Ave., Fort Worth; (817) 926-2544; 24-hour emergency, 922-7070; Fax 927-6226; Internet www.allsaints.org. Established in 1906, the nonprofit All Saints has 520 beds, staffs 870 physicians and 425 nurses. Daily rate for semi-pri-vate room is $415.

Arlington Memorial Hospital, 800 West Randol Mill Rd., Arlington; (817) 548-6100, Internet www.arlingtonmemorial.org. A full-service hospital established in 1958 and owned by a private foun-dation, it has 380 beds, staffs 450 physicians and 700 nurses. Daily rate for semi-private room is $360.

Cook Children's Medical Center, 801 Seventh Ave., south of downtown Fort Worth; (817) 885-4000; 24-hour emergency, (817) 885-4093; Internet www.cookchildrens.org. Established in 1918, this private nonprofit hospital also includes 13 specialty clinics throughout the county, has 208 beds, staffs 145 physicians and 575 nurses. The six-story, castlelike hospital in the city's medical district "is the result of an ambitious, and some thought undoable, merger of the city's two pedi-atric hospitals," according to the *Fort Worth Star-Telegram*. It is "one of the nation's most respected pediatric medical centers and a rare exam-ple of locally owned and controlled hospital." Daily rate for private room is $430; no semi-private rooms are available.

Cook Children's Community Clinics are located at 780 N.W. 21st St. in north Fort Worth, (817) 624-1770; at 1131 Fifth Ave. in south

Fort Worth, (817) 810-0262; at 2803 Miller Ave. in southeast Fort Worth, (817) 534-7110; and at 210 West South St. in Arlington, (817) 460-4447.

Robert Muse and Anne Bass, members of the Fort Worth billionaire clan, served on the medical center's board for several years. While they gave millions of dollars to Yale and Stanford universities, "it is Cook Children's that they have considered their highest philanthropic priority."

Harris Methodist Fort Worth, 1301 Pennsylvania Ave., (817) 882-2000; Emergency room, 882-3333; Fax 882-2553; Internet www.hmhs.com/hmfw. Along with JPS (see below), one of the busiest hospitals in Fort Worth. Established in 1930, the nonprofit Harris Methodist has 525 beds, 875 physicians, 868 nurses, and 3,800 employees. Daily rate for semi-private room is $335.

Harris Methodist ranked for six straight years as one of the top 100 hospitals in the country, according to surveys that measure clinical quality, operations, and financial management.

Harris Methodist H.E.B., 1600 Hospital Pkwy., Bedford; (817) 685-4000; 24-hour emergency, 685-4611; Fax 685-4890; Internet www.texashealth.org. Established in 1973, the nonprofit Harris Methodist H.E.B. has 251 beds, staffs 380 physicians and 438 nurses. Daily rate for semi-private room is $350.

Huguley Memorial Hospital, 11801 South Fwy. (Interstate 35 West), in far-south Fort Worth, north of East Rendon-Crawley Rd.; (817) 293-9110; Emergency room, 551-2462; Fax 568-1296. Established in 1977 and owned by Adventist Health System of Orlando, Florida, it has 213 rooms, staffs 320 physicians and 400 nurses. Daily rate for semi-private room is $367.

For its 24-hour Huguley Fitness Center, next door, (817) 568-3131, please see listing.

John Peter Smith Hospital, 1500 South Main St. at Allen in Fort Worth; (817) 921-3431; 24-hour emergency, (817) 927-1110 or 927-1222; Internet www.jpshealthnet.org. JPS, a nonprofit facility, admits about 20,000 yearly, more than 300,000 as outpatients, and 60,000 emergency cases. It has 429 beds, staffs 560 physicians and 1,000 nurses. Daily rate for semi-private room is $300.

John Peter Smith Hospital opened in 1906. It is named after the man who opened Fort Worth's first school in 1853 and served two terms as that city's mayor. He was born in Kentucky in 1831, studied Greek, Latin, and literary classics, and came to Dallas in 1854. He saw Dallas as "a muddy village"; he moved to Fort Worth and loved it. After his teaching career, Smith worked as a surveyor, attorney, and even as a Texas Ranger. In 1901, aged 70, Smith went to see a friend off at the railway station in St. Louis and was beaten and robbed while returning to his hotel. He died six days later. His marble bust can be seen at 1100

Jennings St., just west of the Fort Worth Convention Center (see entry).

JPS Health Network also includes several other locations in Fort Worth, Azle, and Bedford, as well as JPS Health Center Arlington, located at 601 West Sanford; (817) 920-6300.

Medical Center of Arlington, 3301 Matlock Rd.; (817) 457-3241; 24-hour emergency, (817) 472-4868; Internet www.medicalcenterarlington.com. A full-service, acute care medical and surgical hospital, with 24-hour emergency service, outpatient surgery center. Established in 1969, it has 287 beds, staffs 450 physicians and 255 nurses. It is part of Columbia/HCA Healthcare Corp., like Plaza Medical Center of Fort Worth (below).

North Hills Hospital, 4401 Booth Calloway Rd., North Richland Hills; (817) 590-1000, Fax 284-4817, Internet www.northhillshospital.com. Established in 1961, it has 144 beds, 427 physicians, and 310 nurses. Daily rate for semi-private room is $510. Like Plaza Medical Center of Fort Worth and Medical Center of Arlington (see below), it is part of the 16-hospital Columbia Health Network of North Texas.

Osteopathic Medical Center of Texas, 1000 Montgomery St. at Modlin Ave.; (817) 731-4311; 24-hour emergency, 735-3100; Fax 735-3338; Internet www.ohst.com. Established in 1946, this nonprofit organization has 265 beds, staffs 300 physicians and 240 nurses. Daily rate for semi-private room is $380.

Plaza Medical Center of Fort Worth, 900 Eighth Ave.; (817) 336-2100, Fax 347-5796. Established in 1976, it is part of the 16-hospital Columbia Health Network of North Texas. Has 320 beds, staffs 900 physicians and 300 nurses. Daily rate for semi-private room is $425.

Inoculations

The International Travel Clinic of the Tarrant County Health Department, (817) 871-7360, is located at 1800 University Dr. Visits to the clinic are $25 and follow-ups $15. Counseling and information about the countries you visit are available.

The Texas College of Osteopathic Medicine has an International Travel Medicine Clinic, (817) 735-2608, Internet www.hsc.unt.edu/clinics/itmc/travel.htm, located at 1500 Camp Bowie Blvd.

JURY DUTY

The selection for jury duty is made from voter registration and driver's license lists. If an American citizen, you could be called for jury duty on weekdays, Monday through Thursday, for civil and criminal cases in city, county, and federal cases once every six months. Not many are exempt from jury duty, but they include parents who have children under ten years of age or those who are incapacitated due to illness. "Willful disobedience of your summons is subject to contempt action punishable by a fine of $100 to $1,000."

For more details, please call the Tarrant County Jury Services Department, 401 West Belknap St., 8 am-4 pm, at (817) 884-2968.

LAWYERS

Texas lawyers are prohibited by State Bar disciplinary rules to contact potential clients either in person or by telephone to solicit business stemming from a specific incident like a death, an arrest, or a lawsuit. They may solicit their existing clients. The punishment for breaking the rule can be a reprimand, license suspension, or disbarment.

Texas criminal statute also bars them from soliciting any for-profit business in person or by telephone, and they may not institute a lawsuit without authorization. This statute also applies to chiropractors, physicians, surgeons, and private investigators. The punishment for this third-degree felony is up to ten years in prison and a $10,000 fine.

LIBRARIES

See the Fort Worth Public Library entry in the SIGHTS chapter.

LOCAL LAWS

In one week's time in 1998, the Fort Worth Police Department issued 1,953 traffic tickets to drivers who ran signal lights, exceeded the 30 mph speed limit, turned from a non-designated lane, drove continuously in a bus lane, and committed other violations that could cause a traffic accident. In addition, 12 jaywalking tickets had been issued to pedestrians.

Tickets for these traffic offenses ranged from $10, plus court costs, to $99.25. Speeding ten miles over the posted speed limit could result in a $99.25 fine, while running a red light could cost $89.25.

For more information about Texas laws, see also the state's Internet site www.texas.gov.

Liquor and Smoking Laws

More than six decades after the federal repeal of Prohibition, 53 of Texas's 254 counties are considered "completely dry" by law. Everything about the wet-dry situation in Texas is complicated. Since 1992, only one county went from "dry" to "wet," joining 185 counties where sale of distilled spirits is legal, although many have "dry" zones. Liquor by the drink was not permitted in Texas until 1971, although "every country club in the state was already doing it—illegally," said a state senator at the time. Even in "dry" domains, legislation since the 1950s has permitted drinking in "private clubs" whose members may pay dues.

"The remarkable proliferation of restaurants, resort hotels, and clubs offering every sort of entertainment is because of liquor by the drink, since such establishments make most of their money from selling drinks," says *Texas Monthly*. "Without liquor by the drink, Texas would have been doomed as a backwater, an also-ran, defeated by our own pride and obstinacy." The magazine points out that it's important to remember that this measure was only approved statewide by 1 percent.

No business may be selling alcoholic beverages on Sundays until after noon. While most bars can remain open until 2 am, those not having the late-hour permit cannot sell alcohol after midnight on weeknights and after 1 am on weekends.

The minimum legal age to buy, possess, or consume alcoholic beverages in the state is 21 years. Under the "zero tolerance" legislation, which became effective on September 1, 1997, anyone younger than age 21 caught driving with even a trace of alcohol in their system will lose their driver's license; 60 days for the first offense, 120 days for the second, and 180 for any subsequent offenses. Minors also face criminal sanctions, which include fines, community service, and the possibility of jail time for the third offense.

Senate Bill 55, in force since the beginning of 1998, prohibits persons younger than 18 years from buying, using, or possessing tobacco products, unless they are in the presence of their parent, guardian, or spouse. It subjects violators to a fine of up to $250 and attendance in a tobacco awareness program. It also allows the state to suspend or deny a driver's license for minors who violate the law. Retailers must ask for identification from anyone who appears to be 27 or younger wishing to buy a tobacco product. The law also prohibits cigarette vending machines in businesses that are accessible to minors.

Pets

Pets must be licensed and vaccinated against rabies every year by the time they are four months old. Any veterinarian can vaccinate your animal and provide the proper tags. For more details, call the city Animal Control Division, at (817) 871-7290. All dogs must be kept in fenced yards or on a leash.

The city's $2.5-million, 18,068-square-foot **Animal Control Center,** which picks up stray and injured animals, is located seven miles southeast of downtown, at 4900 Martin St., (817) 561-3737, and is open weekdays 8 am-4:30 pm and weekends 8 am-3 pm. It has 50 kennels for small dogs and 93 cat cages.

The **Humane Society of North Texas** is located at 1840 East Lancaster Ave.; (817) 332-5367; 24-hour emergency rescue, (817) 332-4768. In 1997, the nonprofit animal welfare organization took in almost 47,000 animals; more than three-quarters of them were destroyed.

The animal control facility in Arlington can be reached at (817) 451-3436.

PRESS, RADIO, AND TV

The *Fort Worth Star-Telegram* (Internet www.star-telegram.com)—with a daily circulation of about 245,000 and 340,000 on Sundays—is the third largest daily in Texas and recipient of two Pulitzer Prizes. A former Amon Carter soapbox and cash cow, it was sold to The Walt Disney Company, and in 1970 to the Knight-Ridder chain. The *Star-Telegram*, like the *Dallas Morning News*, has a Friday tabloid insert, "Star Times," which is not as clearly organized as the News' "Guide," but carries reviews of Fort Worth, Arlington, Northeast Tarrant County, and Dallas restaurants and clubs, as well as cultural events. One of the *Star-Telegram's* unique features are the telephone numbers and E-mail addresses of reporters at the end of their articles.

In the Metroplex, the most read newspaper is the **Dallas Morning News** (Internet www.dallasnews.com), even if it does carry three pages of comics every day. Circulation-wise, it is one of the top ten dailies in the country, printing daily more than 500,000 copies and nearly 800,000 on Sundays. "Newest major-league player," called it *Time* magazine, adding, "After killing off the Times Herald, its afternoon competitor, the Morning News didn't get complacent; it got better." It has a good sports section and Friday's tabloid insert, "Guide," which covers Metroplex events and restaurants. Established in 1885, the *News* is the oldest daily in the state and part of A. H. Belo Corp., which also owns **Channel 8,** an ABC-TV affiliate, as well as other properties, such as the statewide **Texas Cable News,** which in most of the Metroplex can be seen as Channel 38. Belo owns 17 network-affiliated television stations nationwide.

The Business Press (Internet www.bizpress.com) is Tarrant County's weekly business journal that also publishes a helpful annual Book of Lists, which includes everything from the county's largest private schools to the county's most prestigious zip codes.

FW Weekly (Internet www.ftweekly.com) is a free 40-page news, arts, and entertainment gazette covering Tarrant County, with an occasional biting feature.

The national editions of the **New York Times** and the **Wall Street Journal** are widely available on the newsstands and a welcome relief from the somewhat provincial outlook of the state dailies. International dailies, such as the London's **Financial Times** or the **International Herald Tribune,** will only be found in large bookstores.

The monthly **D Magazine** (Internet www.dmagazine.com) was resurrected in 1995, after ceasing publication for several years. It has interesting, even provocative feature articles and extensive coverage of local events, in addition to listings of the Metroplex restaurants and entertainment. While the sleek magazine, which carries enough ads for plastic and laser surgeons to remove every wrinkle in the state, has the word Fort Worth on its masthead, it is struggling for recognition outside of Dallas; when Arlington landed in 39th place among *D Magazine*'s "best area places to live" in 1998, one Arlington councilwoman dismissed the survey as "stupid."

In December 1998, a sleek **Fort Worth, Texas,** monthly made its debut to memorialize "the people, places and events that make our area one of the greatest in the world." Regretfully, it takes time to find a worthwhile feature here and there, buried among advertising for every plastic surgeon in the state.

The out-of-state visitor will not want to ignore **Texas Highways** (Internet www.texashighways.com, www.traveltex.com, www.dot.state.tx.us), a 45-year-old monthly travel magazine of Texas. Published by the Texas Department of Transportation and free of advertising, it often features breathtaking photos and informative articles on sights well known and not. There is also the ad-free monthly **Texas Parks & Wildlife,** Internet www.tpwl.state.tx.us.

And, finally, look for **Texas Monthly** (Internet www.texasmonthly.com), headquartered in Austin and published since 1973. It covers events of the entire state. Like *D Magazine,* it carries restaurant and cultural reviews, but for the entire state.

There is a radio station for every lifestyle, either on AM or FM band. Among the most popular ones on the FM band are **KHKS-FM 106.1,** known as Kiss FM, which plays contemporary hits; **KKDA-FM 104.5,** which plays contemporary urban music; the perennial top-three member, the 30-year-old **KVIL-FM 103.7,** which bills itself as a light rock station and "remains a veritable money-making machine: it ranked eighth nationwide in 1997 in revenue," according to the *Dallas Morning News;* and the Arlington-based **KSCS-FM 96.3,** which plays country-Western style music. Each of these four stations has about five percent of the market.

On the AM band, **KRLD-AM 1080** is an all-news and talk Arlington-based CBS station, as is the Dallas-based **KLIF-AM 570,** which is an ABC affiliate. In 1922, **WBAP-AM**—which now broadcasts out of Arlington and is the most popular news-and-talk station in the Metroplex—became the first radio station in the country to transmit cotton and grain exchange reports. WBAP-TV is now KXAS-TV, Channel 5, which, like the radio station, was also founded by the publisher Amon Carter.

KERA-FM 90.1 is the non-commercial National Public Radio station, broadcasting classical and jazz music and featuring news. **KNTU-FM 88.1, KTCU-FM 88.7,** and **KOAI-FM 107.5** all feature lots of jazz. You can listen to at least half a dozen Spanish-speaking radio stations in the Metroplex, in addition to two Hispanic television channels.

The city's oldest radio station is **WRR-FM,** at 101.1, which is the only municipal radio station in the U.S. It is also the only full-time classical music station in the area.

There are Dallas/Fort Worth ABC, CBS, and NBC affiliates of the television networks based in New York. **WFAA-TV** (Internet www.wfaa.com), Channel 8, seems to have the most credibility with viewers; for more details visit their Internet site. There is also the **Fox** group, locally known as **KDFW-TV,** Channel 4, which is a Rupert Murdock network. All four have nightly news reports at 10 o'clock, with Fox starting at 9 pm. **Texas Cable News,** providing 30-minute news segments 24 hours a day, started operation in 1999, as did **KDAF-TV,** Channel 33, owned by the *Chicago Tribune,* with nightly local news starting at 9 pm.

NBC-owned affiliate, **KXAS-TV** (Internet www.kxas.com or www.nbc5dfwfw.com), Channel 5, aired its first program in 1948, featuring a public appearance by Pres. Harry Truman. Today it has the most respected weather broadcasters and can be browsed on the Internet, where you will find local news, weather, road conditions, as well as news about the Dallas Cowboys football and the Texas Rangers baseball teams. KXAS's forecasting reputation was built by the legendary weathercaster Harold Taft, who joined the station in 1948 and stuck with it until 1991, when he died of cancer. This was also the station, when still known as WBAP, that broadcast the shooting of the accused assassin Lee Harvey Oswald by Jack Ruby in the basement of the old city hall in downtown Dallas.

Local educational and commercial-free channels are **KDTN's** Channel 2 and **KERA's** Channel 13 (Internet www.kera.org), **KDFI,**

Channel 27, and **KXTX** (Internet www.kxtx.com), Channel 39, are independent channels.

To find out what is on television, buy the Sunday *Fort Worth Star-Telegram* or *Dallas Morning News*, which carry weekly television magazines, or look up the programs in the daily papers.

PUBLIC SERVICES

Electricity is supplied by **TXU Electric;** (800) 242-9113 or (972) 791-2888. For emergency service, call (800) 233-2133.

You can reach the gas supplier, **TXU Gas,** at (800) 460-3030 or (817) 921-6400 for new service or billing inquiries; for emergencies call (800) 817-8090.

If you need residential service from the **Southwestern Bell Telephone Co.,** call (800) 464-7928, (800) 585-7928 for billing inquiries, and (800) 246-8464 for 24-hour service. GTE Southwest can be reached at (800) 483-4400 or (800) 772-6250.

The **Water Department** is accessible at (817) 871-8210, Mon-Fri 8 am-5 pm. For after-hours emergency assistance, call (817) 871-8300. New residents can apply for water service in Arlington by calling (817) 275-5931.

For newcomers, deposits are usually required for public services, but might be refunded after a year with interest. Give as much advance notice as possible for the required services.

Garbage pickup is provided twice weekly, either on Monday and Thursday, Tuesday and Friday, or Wednesday and Saturday. Recycling is in effect once weekly. For more details, call (817) 871-5150, or 871-8900 for litter control.

Arlington has twice-weekly curbside pickup. Call (817) 275-5931 for information.

To request cable service, call (817) 509-6272, in Arlington (817) 265-7766.

If you have a question, Fort Worth's **Action Center** probably has an answer, just call (817) 871-8888. Established in 1980, Action Center serves as the city's switchboard, as its information and referral center, and as its resolution center. Action Center's hours are Mon-Fri 8 am-5 pm. It is located on the ground level of the City Hall, at 1000 Throckmorton St. downtown. After 5 pm and on weekends and holidays, emergency numbers are given through the city's switchboard at (817) 871-8900. Action Center also provides assistance in Spanish, as well as to the hearing-impaired. Animal Control, (817) 871-7345; Code Compliance, (817) 871-6320; Potholes & Street Conditions,

(817) 871-8100; and Zoning, (817) 871-8028, are the most commonly requested numbers.

TAXES

Texas is one of the few remaining states that has no state, county, or city income tax.

Sales tax, however, is 8.25 percent, but excludes most prescription drugs and foods. One percent of the sales tax goes to the city's transit, 1 percent to the city, and the remaining 6.25 percent to the state. For more information call (800) 252-5555.

The Tarrant County property tax rate on land and real estate is 0.56 per $100 value, with the owner paying 100 percent of the assessed valuation. There are four tax exemptions:

General Homestead Exemption is a 20 percent reduction off appraised value. **Over 65 Exemption** is an additional $40,000 off appraised value. **Disabled Persons Exemption** reduces the appraised value by an additional $40,000. **State Mandated Disabled Veterans Exemption** ranges $5,000-$15,000.

To qualify for any of these exemptions, you must own your home and you must use the home as your principal residence. If you own more than one home, you only get exemptions for the home that is your main residence. Homeowners 65 years and older must reapply every ten years for the over-65 exemption. Disabled homeowners are required to reapply every five years. Filing is simple. Call the **Tarrant County Appraisal District,** (817) 284-0024/4063, and ask that the appraisal forms be mailed to you. Include a copy of your Social Security card, Texas driver's license, or a Texas personal identification certificate. Return the form to the district between January 1 and April 30.

The appraisal district, located at 2500 Handley-Ederville Rd., is open Mon-Fri 8 am-5 pm and maintains an Internet page at www.tad.org.

VOTING

To be eligible to vote, you must be an American citizen, must fill out an application, and register 30 days before voting. Applications are available at libraries and post offices. You can get more details from the **Tarrant County Election Administrator,** at 100 West Weatherford St. Call (817) 884-1115 Mon-Fri 8 am-4:30 pm.

A new certificate is issued automatically every couple of years as long as you report all changes of address. The **League of Women Voters of Tarrant County,** located at 1401 Ballinger St., can also assist you; (817) 336-1333. In Arlington, such voter information by the League is available at 7400 Business Pl.; (817) 472-5982.

TARRANT COUNTY REAL ESTATE

Fort Worth and Arlington have housing available for every budget, be it a $100 a month room over the garage or a $5-million house in Colleyville. Do not even look at a house or apartment without working air-conditioning because it is indispensable between June and September. Rare is the home or apartment in the Metroplex that measures less than 1,000 square feet.

A median price of a home in the Dallas/Fort Worth area was $119,900 in 1997, with an average down payment being about 17 percent and the average monthly payment of about $987. Forty-four percent of the buyers were first-time purchasers, 34 percent bought new homes, and 77 percent were married.

Among the Internet sites to consider if you are looking for a house or an apartment in Fort Worth/Arlington area are **http://www.realtor.com,** which is the official Web site of the National Association of Realtors; **http://www.homes.com,** which includes a mortgage calculator and a guide to banking services; **http://www.xmission.com/~realtor1,** which links to hundreds of related sites; **http://www.treb.com,** which offers sales analysis of comparable homes and relocation information; and **http://www.homeweb.com,** which has a map showing a home's proximity to schools, shopping, banks, and other services.

Tarrant County's largest residential real estate agencies—with anywhere from 45 to 300 Tarrant County agents and one to eight offices—include:

Re/Max of Texas, P.O. Box 64980, Dallas; (800) 950-2181, Internet www.remax-texas.com.

Coldwell Banker, 6115 Camp Bowie Blvd., Suite 160; (817) 732-8833, Internet www.cbdfw.com. Coldwell Banker Paula Stringer and William Rigg Realtors merged into Coldwell Banker.

Ebby Halliday, 4455 Sigma Rd., Dallas; (972) 991-9142, Internet www.ebbyhaliday.com.

Henry S. Miller, 331 South Bowen Rd., Arlington; (817) 861-9955, Fax 548-2990.

Century 21 Mike Bowman, 150 Westpark Way, Euless; (817) 354-7653, Fax 354-4836.

Century 21 Herman Boswell, 1708 South Cooper St., Arlington; (817) 274-2521, Fax 274-3719.

Prudential Sutherland, 4200 South Cooper St., Arlington; (817) 468-4200, E-mail billsuth@worldnet.att.net.

Brants Realtors, 4541 Bellaire Dr. South; (817) 731-8466, Fax 731-1573.

Art Cooper & Associates, 6616 Meadowbrook Dr.; (817) 457-3666, Fax 451-8989.

Tarrant County's
Most Prestigious Zip Codes

Fort Worth houses range from the $3,000 rural shacks to mansions that are valued at $6.6 million. Property values in Southlake, Keller, and Colleyville—all part of the fast-growing northeast Tarrant County—now surpass those in west and southwest Fort Worth, which once dominated the Cowtown wealth index.

Tarrant County boasts about 500 homes with a median taxable value of $737,000. About 155 of these mansions are located in Mira Vista, a 1990s gated community near Benbrook Lake. Homes here range in price from $400,000 to $2 million. A golf course, wooded hills, and man-made lakes are just some among its amenities. Another 75 such homes will be found in Westover Hills and Montclair Park.

The costliest Fort Worth mansion, hidden behind a nine-foot masonry wall near River Crest Country Club, a few blocks west of the cultural district, sits on a 25-acre property and is owned by billionaire Sid Bass. It measures more than 18,000 square feet, has five bedrooms and an eight-car garage, and is valued at $6.6 million.

The next most valuable home is owned by video producer Michael Brown and his wife, novelist Sandra Brown, and located on the opposite end of town from the Basses, in far east Fort Worth. The 12,000-square-foot, four-bedroom mansion on a 17-acre piece of land is valued at $3.7 million. The couple built the residence on the site of an existing house that actor Chuck Norris blew up, an event that became part of the television show, *Walker, Texas Ranger.* They at least had enough sense to donate some of the staff from the old house to a Fort Worth women's shelter.

Computer software entrepreneur Kenneth Hill has what may be the third most expensive house, valued at $3.2 million, located in

Westover Hills, west of downtown. It commands six bedrooms and baths with a four-car garage on a 1.6-acre parcel of land.

Westover Hills, incidentally, is a village of about 700 persons living in 260 residences that measures 450 acres and has fewer than eight miles of paved roads. The *Fort Worth Star-Telegram* once called it "one of the smallest, richest, safest and most unusual and secretive islands of affluence in all of America." *Worth* magazine ranked it among the nation's 20 richest towns and the wealthiest in Texas. The median annual income in Westover Hills is about $300,000, as compared to $39,000 in Fort Worth. Median home value is $500,000, while it is $81,000 in Cowtown. There are no cafes, churches, or schools in Westover Hills. Among its residents, you will find Perry and Nancy Bass of the Bass Performance Hall fame, and talking about the downtown concert hall, Van Cliburn also lives next door to the Basses on an 18-acre spread atop a bluff and overlooking a nature preserve. Supposedly, eleven Steinway pianos are also part of his household.

If you visit, tread cautiously, for the Westover Hills police know all residents on a first-name basis, as well as their relatives, maids, gardeners, pets, and their cars. When these folks are out of town, the Westover Hills police obediently fetch their mail and promptly deliver it upon their return. Oilman Kay Kimbell also lived here, as did the former governor of Texas, John Connally, and Amon Carter's son.

About fifteen homes in Arlington are valued at more than $1 million. Two of those are modeled after historic houses: the White House, near Lake Arlington, is valued at about $2.5 million and claims 16,000 square feet. Andrew Jackson's home, called the Hermitage, is located near Park Spring Boulevard and Arkansas Lane on the west side. Having 10,000 square feet of space, it is valued at $1.3 million.

According to Fort Worth's *Business Press*, these are among the most prestigious zip codes in the county:

Zip Code	City	Average New Home	Maximum/ Minimum New Home
76013	Pantego	$350,000	$350,000
76092	Southlake	$338,852	$705,000-$117,000
76034	Colleyville	$324,780	$975,000-$196,500
76132	Fort Worth	$273,495	$1,250,000-$129,700
76051	Grapevine	$220,796	$329,900-$100,000
76020	Azle	$210,000	$750,000-$60,000
76006	Arlington	$206,045	$569,900-$159,990
76054	Hurst	$196,283	$220,000-$149,900
76248	Keller	$176,568	$299,900-$108,490
76021	Bedford	$172,535	$232,990-$96,000

More than 290,000 out of 5.8 million Texas households had incomes of at least $100,000 a year in 1998. Almost 33 percent of households in Colleyville earned $100,000, followed by 23 percent in Southlake, 17.3 percent in the Hulen area of Fort Worth, 13.2 percent in northwest Arlington, and 11.8 percent in Keller.

Apartment Rentals

Fort Worth has more than 270 apartment complexes with a total of more than 42,500 units. Arlington has some 280 complexes with more than 40,600 units. See also the apartment section in the LODGING chapter.

These are among the largest apartment communities in Tarrant County. They all provide one- and two-bedroom apartments.

- **Westdale Hills** (2,139 units), 1401 Sotogrande Blvd., Euless; (817) 267-7171.
- **Equestrian Pointe** (835 units), 8435 Thousand Oaks Dr., North Richland Hills; (817) 498-0580.
- **Gateways at Centreport** (726 units), 14300 Statler Blvd., Fort Worth; (817) 540-1173.
- **Forest Ridge** (660 units), 2508 Forest Point Dr., Arlington; (817) 988-3505.
- **Pear Tree/Plum Tree** (616 units), 2216 Plum Ln., Arlington; (817) 265-2073.
- **Ivory Canyon** (602 units), 4701 American Blvd., Euless; (817) 540-3222.
- **Park Ridge** (565 units), 2501 Park Ridge Court, Fort Worth; (817) 921-6111.
- **Amli at Verandah** (538) units), 1705 N.E. Green Oaks Blvd., Arlington; (817) 588-2777.
- **Highland Park** (500 units), 5836 Highland Park Dr., Fort Worth; (817) 731-0216.
- **The Pavilion** (500 units), 3500 Willowood Circle, Arlington; (817) 472-9685.
- **L'Atriums on the Creek** (484 units), 1676 Carter Dr., Arlington; (817) 261-7797.
- **Collins Pointe** (476 units), 2601 Furrs St., Arlington; (817) 261-3138.

Information and Referrals

Among the sources of information about the Metroplex housing consider these:

Better Business Bureau—(817) 332-7585.

Chambers of Commerce—Please see MATTERS OF FACT chapter.

Tarrant County Apartment Association—(817) 284-1121.

Fort Worth Convention & Visitors Bureau—(817) 336-8791.

Air Pollution Control—(214) 948-4435.

Greater Fort Worth Association of Realtors—(817) 336-5165.

Housing Counseling for Homebuyers & Renters/U.S. Department of Housing & Urban Development—(800) 569-4287.

Texas Attorney General/Consumer Protection Division—(214) 742-8944.

Metroplex Tax Rates per $100 Valuation of Market Value
            Dallas County .0.44
            Tarrant County 0.56

	City Tax	School Tax
Arlington	0.64	1.44
Bedford	0.344	1.61
Cedar Hill	0.6613	1.76
Colleyville	0.347	1.54
The Colony	0.79500	1.43700
Fort Worth	0.8975	1.485
Grand Prairie	0.695599	1.4678
Grapevine	0.385	1.54
Hurst	0.524	1.54
North Richland Hills	0.57	1.50
Southlake	0.422	1.74

ARLINGTON

ARLINGTON PAST

Where Arlington stands today, Gen. Edward H. Tarrant (1796-1858) authorized in 1841 Jonathan Bird to establish a fort, called Bird's Fort (near present Euless in Tarrant County), so that the settlers would have protection from the Indians. Friction between the tribes and Anglo settlers resulted in the 1841 Battle of Village Creek, when Tarrant led 69 volunteers against the Caddo tribal villages, burning 225 of their lodges, and forced them to start their permanent retreat. More than 20,000 Caddos once lived in the area, farming, hunting, and trading with the French, Spaniards, and Mexicans. The area became even more attractive with the Santa Fe Trail running through the region.

In 1842, Texas Ranger Middleton Tate Johnson (1810-1866), a member of the Alabama state legislature, arrived and began a settlement called Johnson Station, which was later renamed Arlington, after Arlington, Virginia, Confederate general Robert E. Lee's hometown. The following year, the Republic of Texas signed its first peace treaty here with nine tribes. In 1857, a grist mill was built on the Trinity River and later bought by R. A. Randol to be operated as Randol's Mill. "The mill was necessary for the early settlers of the area; they could take their corn and grains to the mill to be ground and their trees to be planed into boards," says *Arlington Morning News'* guide to the city. "The original mill burned in 1862 and the new mill survived from 1880 until 1933, when it burned."

During the Civil War, the non-Indian population dropped severely. When the Texas & Pacific Railroad was building a line from Dallas to Fort Worth, it decided on Johnson Station as the stop between the two towns. When the owner of the right of way refused it access through his property, the railroad chose a site three miles north—about where the intersection of Collins and Abram streets is located today. The new station was named Arlington. The first train came through Arlington in the summer of 1876. Less than eight years later, Arlington was incorporated as a city. In 1890 it had 664 residents.

What is today University of Texas at Arlington (see entry) was founded in 1895 as Arlington College. The Interurban, an electric trolley system linking Arlington with Fort Worth and Dallas, started operation in 1902; the city's first house with running water was built in 1904; and the natural gas line arrived five years later. The worldwide influenza epidemic of 1918 decimated Arlington. Already weakened by World War I, when it had fewer than 3,000 inhabitants, it lost still more of them to the flu. In the 1920s, the first public library and the first city park were established. Cattleman W. T. Waggoner, who built the Fort Worth's mansion Thistle Hill (see entry) for his daughter, opened the famous Arlington Downs racetrack in 1933, but had to shut it down three years later when the state outlawed pari-mutuel betting.

As recently as 1951, the city had a population of 7,800 and measured no more than four square miles; ten years later, when the Six Flags Over Texas (see entry) entertainment center opened, it skyrocketed to 45,000. General Motors built a $35-million assembly plant in Arlington in 1954 that now builds about 500 trucks a day and employs 2,400. By the end of 2000, a $500-million expansion and retooling were to increase the plant's production capacity to 200,000 trucks a year and the employment of another 500. Arlington Stadium became home to the Texas Rangers baseball team, until then known as the Washington Senators, in 1972. The following year, the Dallas-Fort Worth International Airport opened. By the mid-1980s, Arlington's population soared past the one-quarter-million mark.

ARLINGTON TODAY

Arlington (pop. 300,000), the seventh largest city in Texas and the 56 largest in America, now measures almost 100 square miles. In 1890, the city had only 664 inhabitants and even in 1950 there were only 7,692 residents. Arlington is located at an altitude of 484-864 feet. More than 40 percent of its population is between 25 and 44 years old and the median age is 31.7 years. Caucasians make up 82 percent of the residents.

Arlington is located between Dallas and Fort Worth, but shares its western border with the latter. Texas Pulitzer Prize-winning author Larry McMurtry—who now runs a 200,000-volume used bookstore in Archer City, a town of 1,918 northwest of Cowtown—dismissed Arlington by calling it a giant amusement park encircled by a "vast labyrinth of cul-de-sacs." Even today, many will undoubtedly agree

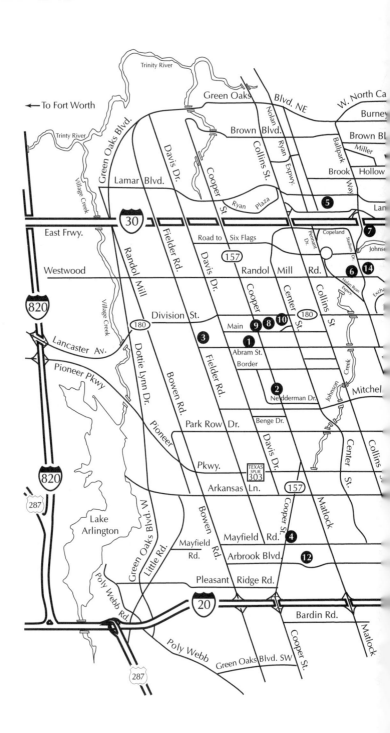

1 Antique Sewing Machine
Museum
2 University of Texas at
Arlington
3 Fielder House Museum
4 M.T. Johnson Plantation
Cemetery and Historic Park
5 Hurricane Harbour
6 The Ballpark in Arlington
7 Six Flags Over Texas
8 Arlington Museum of Art
9 Theatre Arlington
10 Johnnie High's Country
Music Revue
11 Festival Marketplace
12 The Parks at Arlington
13 Six Flags Mall
14 Visitor Information Center

with his observation. Looking for downtown in Arlington is like looking for a regular bookstore in downtown Dallas; just when you think
you have found it, you realize it does not exist. To some, Arlington is
just a nondescript suburb of Dallas and Fort Worth.

But don't tell that to the Arlingtonians. In 1998, Dallas's *D
Magazine's* survey of "the best area places to live" rated Arlington as
39th, just above Grand Prairie, next door. The data in 21 categories was
analyzed and weighted according to seven variables. Both cities scored
well below average in the categories of education and safety. One
Arlington councilwoman said the survey was "stupid." The president of
the Arlington Chamber of Commerce noted that the education results
were "absolutely ludicrous. Arlington schools are clearly very good.
You're talking about comparing a neighborhood like Highland Park (a
wealthy Dallas enclave, which ranked first) to a city like Arlington,
and it's not an apples-to-apples comparison."

But the city boasts more than six million visitors a year, most of
them paying good money to get scared at one of the Six Flags Over
Texas rides, to cool off at Hurricane Harbor water theme park, or to
catch a Texas Rangers baseball game at its ballpark. They spend more
than $400 million a year. The average summer temperature in
Arlington is 95 degrees, and the average in the winter is 57 degrees.
Average annual rainfall is about 31 inches.

Public transportation—to the dismay of many first-time visitors—is
practically non-existent in the city, although a poll in 1997 disclosed
that almost half of all residents want more tax dollars going for public
transportation. However, twice, in 1985 and 1997, Arlington voters
had rejected proposals for public transportation systems. There is a free
trolley service for tourists staying at the entertainment district hotels,
which participate in the program. As a guest at one of them, you can
receive free trolley passes. The service is available between hotels and
the city's most popular attractions, from about 9:30 am to 11:30 pm.

There are 48 parks, 26 lighted tennis courts, four recreation centers,
and three municipal golf courses in the city.

Arlington is perhaps best known for its new Ballpark stadium (see
entry), home of the Texas Rangers baseball team, with its museum, and
recreation spots that include Six Flags Over Texas and Hurricane
Harbor, both of which are described in the Sights section in this chapter. Arlington has its own Museum of Art, Antique Sewing Machine
Museum, Theatre Arlington, and Le Theatre de Marionette, which are
also described here.

Other attractions to consider include:

Air Combat School, at 921 Six Flags Drive, (817) 640-1886, makes
it possible for you to strap into a real jet fighter flight simulator made

from an actual jet cockpit and engage in hour-long air combat maneuvers against various types of threats. You must be at least 4'10" tall to participate.

You might also enjoy the **Family Golf Center,** located at 1301 Green Oaks Blvd., east of Collins St., (817) 261-6312, with two 18-hole miniature golf courses.

The 958-acre **River Legacy Park & Science Center** is a city-run forest flood plain on the West Fork of the Trinity River. It has 26 miles of trails that follow the Trinity's steep southern banks and picnic areas—located one-and-a-half miles north of Interstate 30—that are also worthy of your consideration if outdoors is what you desire. The Science Center is located at 703 N.W. Green Oaks Blvd.; (817) 860-6752, Internet www.riverlegacy.com. It is open Tue-Sat 9 am-5 pm, Sun 1-5 pm.

The **General Motors** assembly plant, at 2525 East Abram Street, which now employs some 1,800 assembly, trade, and maintenance workers on three shifts, produces about 550 vehicles a day. After 1960, write Victoria and Walter Buenger in their 1998 history of Leonard Brothers Department Store (see entry), "More Oldsmobiles, Buicks, and Pontiacs rolled off the nearby General Motors assembly line than were produced by all the rest of GM's American Olds-Buick-Pontiac plants combined." Although tours are occasionally available at the plant by calling (817) 652-2085, it is located in a depressingly plain area that has little else to offer.

You will find more than 40 hotels and 80 restaurants in Arlington and a few among them are described in the Lodging and Dining sections of this chapter.

The telephone area code for Arlington, just like for Fort Worth, is 817. The **Chamber of Commerce** can be reached at 275-2613, **City Hall** at 277-2292, **Convention Center** at 459-5000, **Arlington Memorial Hospital** at 548-6100, **Columbia Medical Center** at 467-7486, Time and Temperature at 277-4000.

Arlington Convention & Visitors Bureau is located at 1250 East Copeland Rd., Suite 650; (800) 433-5374 or (817) 265-7721, Internet www.arlington.org. Its **Visitor Information Center** and gift shop at 1905 East Randol Mill Rd.; (800) 342-4305 or (817) 461-3888, E-mail visitinfo@acvb.org, Internet www.acvb.org/welcome/.

The towns of **Dalworthington Gardens** and **Pantego** are completely surrounded by Arlington. Dalworthington was started by Pres. Franklin Roosevelt as a subsistence homestead in 1933 and today has a population of about 2,200. Pantego was originally inhabited by the Caddo Indians and it is named after a Native American friend of Frederick Forney Foscue, who began purchasing its land before the Civil War. Today, Pantego has a population of about 2,400.

ARLINGTON
MATTERS OF FACT

Here is a short list of useful Arlington telephone numbers.

Some of these and related numbers might also be listed in chapters THE INTERNATIONAL VISITOR, NEW RESIDENTS, TRANS-PORTATION, etc., and particularly in the Fort Worth MATTERS OF FACT chapter.

See also Arlington's Internet site www.ci.arlington.tx.us.

Airport—5000 Collins St., (817) 465-2615.

Ambulance—Emergency, 911; Non-emergency, (817) 861-5555.

Animal Shelter—(817) 451-3436.

Arlington Morning News—Editorial Department, (817) 461-6397.

Arlington Night Shelter—(817) 548-9885.

Arlington Police Department Victim Assistance—(817) 459-5340.

Central Library—101 East Abram St., (817) 459-6900.

City Government—Information, (817) 277-2292, or TDD Deaf Phone, 459-6156.

City Hall—Municipal Building, 101 West Abram St., (817) 275-3271.
City Manager's Office, (817) 459-6100.
Mayor and City Council, (817) 459-6122.

Convention & Visitors Bureau—1905 East Randol Mill Rd., (817) 265-7721.

Convention Center—1200 Ballpark Way, (817) 459-5000.

Courts—Municipal Court, (817) 275-5970.
Fine Information, (817) 275-5970.

Fire Reports—(817) 459-5535.

Handitran—(817) 459-5390.

Hospitals—JPS Health Center, 601 West Sanford St., (817) 861-0095.

Licenses—Driver's License, (817) 274-1818.

Municipal Court—200 West Abram St.
Administration, (817) 459-6950.
Fine Information, (817) 275-5970.

Parks & Recreation Department—717 West Main St., (817) 459-5474.

Pharmacies—Eckerd Drugs Stores Open 24 Hours:
903 East Park Row Dr. at South Collins St., (817) 274-5531.
5715 West Interstate 20 at West Green Oaks Blvd., (817) 483-4995.

Police—620 West Division St.
Auto Pound, (817) 265-1336; Desk Officer, (817) 459-5667; Narcotics, (817) 459-5748; Service Desk/24 Hours, (817) 459-5700.

Population—About 300,000.

Postal Service—General Information, (817) 543-8400.
  Customer Service, 300 East South St., (817) 795-5830.
Six Flags Over Texas—I-30 at State Highway 360, (817) 640-8900.
  Hurricane Harbor, 1800 East Lamar Blvd., (817) 265-3356.
Tax Office—101 West Abram St., (817) 459-6260.
Tennis Center—500 West Mayfield Rd., (817) 557-5683.
Transportation—Airport, (817) 465-7831; Handitran, (817) 459-5390.
Visitor's Information Center—1905 East Randol Mill Rd., (800) 342-4305 or (817) 461-3888.
Water Service—101 West Abram St., (817) 275-5931.
Women's Shelter—24-hour Hot Line, (817) 460-5566.
YMCA—2200 South Davis Dr., (817) 274-9622.

LODGING

International visitors should be aware that outside of Dallas-Fort Worth International Airport and the American Express office, located just north of the Ridgmar Mall (see individual entries) in southwest Fort Worth, there is no retailer in Arlington or Fort Worth to exchange foreign currencies.

Hotel tax in Arlington is 13 percent. Tax on Arlington automobile rentals is 10 percent.

All hotels below are grouped into one of these approximate price categories:

I   Inexpensive, up to $50 for a single room
M   Moderate, $50-$100 for a single room
E   Expensive, more than $100 for a single room

Amenities available are noted with these abbreviations:

C tells there is a concierge available on the premises.

CF designation means that there is no charge for children who occupy the same room as the adult that accompanies them. The minimum age limit varies.

CM indicates cable television and movies are available in your room.

FT means that the hotel provides free shuttle to and from the airport, or complimentary transportation within a few miles, such as to the nearest shopping center, or both.

HC indicates there are health club facilities available, although sometimes there may be a charge for the use of equipment.

HR will alert you to hotels that provide rooms for the handicapped and which are handicapped-accessible.

MF indicates that meeting facilities are available.

PA designation is included if pets are allowed.

PT abbreviation indicates the hotel is near public transportation, such as city bus route.

RS tells that room service is available.

ARLINGTON HILTON, 2401 East Lamar Blvd.; (800) HILTONS or (817) 640-3322, Fax 652-0234, Internet www.hilton.com. E. Has 309 rooms and suites, more than half of them on floors for non-smokers, priced at $100-$165 a night. Located in the heart of the entertainment district, nine miles from Dallas-Fort Worth International Airport, north of Six Flags Over Texas theme park (see individual entries), north of Interstate 30, which connects Dallas with Fort Worth, and west of State Highway 360.

Amenities: Concierge floor with private lounge, restaurant & cocktail lounge with dancing nightly, business center, two-line phones with dataports, in-room coffeemakers & hair dryers, heated indoor/outdoor swimming pool, guest laundry, gift shop. Sofa beds and wet bar available in suites. Also C, CF, CM, HC, HR, MF, RS.

You will need a car to get around, but Trail Dust Steak House is within walking distance. The 16-story hotel is also close to the Hurricane Harbor water park and the Ballpark in Arlington, home of the Texas Rangers (see individual entries). Tennis, racquetball, and golf are available nearby. Transportation to the area attractions within five miles of the hotel is complimentary, airport shuttle to D/FW Airport is available 7 am-11 pm at a nominal charge. Hotel guests without their own transportation can use free trolley service to and from Six Flags and The Ballpark daily, roughly 9:30 am-6:30 pm.

ARLINGTON HOWARD JOHNSON, 117 South Watson Rd. at Abram St.; (817) 633-4000, Fax 633-4931. M. Has 192 smoking and non-smoking rooms and suites priced at $55-$120 a night. Located in east Arlington, east of State Highway 360 (also known as Watson Road), and south of Interstate 30, which connects Dallas with Fort Worth.

Amenities: Restaurant & cocktail lounge, complimentary breakfast, swimming pool. Also CF, CM, FT, HC, MF.

Unless you have deep pockets for taxi or a rental car, there is not much to do in the immediate vicinity. Hotel does provide complimentary transportation to D/FW Airport, Ballpark in Arlington, Six Flags Over Texas, and Hurricane Harbor theme parks (see individual entries). "If the van is not busy," you might be able to talk the hotel driver into taking you to the Six Flags Shopping Mall (see entry), located on the other side of Division Street at State Highway 360; it includes stores such as Dillard's, Foley's, and Sears.

BALLPARK INN, 903 North Collins St. at Randol Mill Rd.; (817) 261-3621, Fax 274-7420. M. Has 186 rooms and suites priced at $70-$90 a night. Located southwest from the Ballpark in Arlington, roughly between the entertainment district and the downtown area, west of State Highway 360 and south of Interstate 30, which connects Dallas with Fort Worth.

Amenities: Complimentary breakfast, cocktail lounge with entertainment, outdoor swimming pool, laundry room. Also CF, CM, HC, MF, PA, RS.

No hotel transportation to and from the D/FW Airport is available and the city trolley does not stop here. The hotel van will take you to Six Flags Over Texas and Hurricane Harbor theme parks, as well as to the Ballpark. Arlington Museum of Art and Theatre Arlington are not far away (see individual entries).

COMFORT INN, 1601 East Division St. at Chapel Dr.; (817) 261-2300, Fax 861-8679. M. Has 250 smoking and non-smoking rooms and suites priced at $50-$140 a night. Located south of Interstate 30, which connects Dallas with Fort Worth, and south of the Ballpark in Arlington (see entry).

Amenities: Complimentary breakfast, cocktail lounge, outdoor swimming pool, laundry room. Also CF, CM, HC, HR, MF, PA.

A large, but tired old hotel in the middle of nowhere that has seen better days, and where some rooms surround a small outdoor swimming pool. When calling the main number be prepared for the phone to ring for minutes before anyone will pick it up. There is no restaurant on the premise, but the Bodacious Bar-B-Q (see listing) is within walking distance and open Mon-Sat 11 am-9 pm.

ATM is in the lobby at a $2 charge. No airport shuttle, but the city trolley will take you to and from the Ballpark and Six Flags theme park (see entry). Enterprise car rental is farther west, at 1112 East Division, and barely within walking distance.

If you have bored elementary or middle-school kids, Putt-Putt Golf & Games, (817) 277-6501, nearby will keep them busy for a day; they can eat here, too. For the adults, there is Studer's Sports Bar, next door to it.

HAWTHORN SUITES, 2401 Brookhollow Plaza Dr. at Lamar Blvd.; (800) 527-1133 or (817) 640-1188, Fax 640-1188, ext. 4001, Internet www.hawthorn.com. M. Has 129 suites priced at $95-$110. Located about seven miles southwest from D/FW Airport, north of Interstate 30 and west of State Highway 360, behind Hilton Hotel. Trail Dust Steak House is nearby (see individual entries).

Amenities: Complimentary breakfast buffet and hors d'oeuvres Mon-Thu 5-7 pm, outdoor swimming pool, sports court, coin-operated washers & dryers, valet service. Also CF, CM, HC, HR, MF, PA.

A "home away from home"-atmosphere hotel with a large living area and fireplace, fully equipped kitchens with coffeemakers, stoves, microwaves, dishwashers, refrigerators, dishes, and cooking utensils. The master bedroom has a king-size bed, remote-controlled TV, and walk-in closet with iron and ironing board.

No airport shuttle is available, the hotel does not provide any transportation, and the trolley does not stop at Hawthorn Suites; taxi and car rental are the only options. All reservations must be guaranteed by credit card or advance deposit.

HOLIDAY INN ARLINGTON, 1507 North Watson Rd.; (888) 255-3352 or (817) 640-7712, Fax 640-3174, Internet www.holidayinnarl.com. M. Has 237 smoking and non-smoking rooms priced at $95-$105 a night. Located in north Arlington, north of Interstate 30, and west of State Highway 360, whose frontage road is known as Watson Road.

Amenities: Restaurant & cocktail lounge with entertainment, heated indoor & outdoor swimming pool, in-room coffeemakers & hair dryers, laundry room. Also CF, CM, HC, HR, MF, RS.

There is no public transportation in Arlington, except for the trolley service to and from the Six Flags theme park and the Ballpark in Arlington. Hotel provides free transportation to and from the D/FW Airport and within the five miles of the inn, which would include the Arlington Museum of Art or Theatre Arlington (see individual entries). There are a couple of fast-food restaurants within walking distance.

LA QUINTA CONFERENCE CENTER, State Hwy. 360 at Six Flags Dr.; (800) 453-7909 or (817) 640-4142, Fax 649-7864. E. Has 340 rooms and suites in a complex of six buildings priced at $85-$140 a night. Located in the entertainment center across the street from Six Flags theme park (see entry), south of Interstate 30 that connects Dallas with Fort Worth and west of Highway 360. In 1999, this was the largest Arlington hotel.

Amenities: Complimentary breakfast, cocktail lounge, kitchenettes or in-room coffeemakers, outdoor swimming pool, laundry room & dry cleaning service, gift shop. Also C, CF, CM, HC, HR, MF, PA, RS.

There is no restaurant on the premises, but Bennigan's and Owens are located on North Watson Road, which is the service road of Highway 360, and Steak and Ale on Six Flags Drive, all within walking distance.

There is no public transportation available, although the hotel van will take you to the D/FW Airport free of charge, as well as within a five-mile radius of the hotel, which includes the Hurricane Harbor, the Ballpark in Arlington, or Ripley's Believe It or Not/The Palace of Wax in nearby Grand Prairie (see individual entries). If you decide to go to The Parks at Arlington Mall (see entry), the city's largest shopping center, which is located at Interstate 20 and Cooper Street, you will need a car or will have to take a taxi.

RADISSON SUITE HOTEL, 700 Avenue H East, near Six Flags Drive Exit; (800) 333-3333 or (817) 640-0440, Fax 649-2480, Internet www.radisson.com. *E.* Has 203 smoking and non-smoking suites priced at $115-$160 a night. Located in northeast Arlington, north of Interstate 30, which connects Dallas with Fort Worth, and east of State Highway 360.

Amenities: Atrium restaurant & cocktail lounge, complimentary breakfast & evening beverages, indoor swimming pool. Also CF, CM, HC, HR, MF, RS.

No other eating or entertainment facilities are within walking distance, but the hotel van will take you eating and shopping inside a five-mile radius. Since no public transportation is available, hotel guests can ride a complimentary trolley to and from Six Flags and Ballpark at Arlington, home of the Texas Rangers (see individual entries).

RESIDENCE INN BY MARRIOTT, 1050 Brookhollow Plaza Dr. and Lamar Blvd.; (800) 331-3131 or (817) 649-7300, Fax 649-7600. *E.* Studio, one-, and two-bedroom smoking and non-smoking suites are priced at $110-$150 a night. Located about seven miles southwest from D/FW Airport, north of Interstate 30 and west of State Highway 360.

Amenities: Complimentary breakfast & newspaper, kitchens with microwaves & refrigerators, social hour with barbecue Mon-Thu, swimming pool, sports court for racquetball, basketball & volleyball, laundry room. Also CF, CM, HC, HR, MF.

"The next best thing to home," Residence Inn by Marriott is "for people who travel for a living," according to Marriott's own advertising. Arlington has no public transportation, except for a trolley that will take you to Six Flags Over Texas and Ballpark in Arlington stadium (see individual entries). Complimentary transportation to restaurants and other sites within a five-mile radius is provided. The nearest restaurant that you might conceivably walk to is Trail Dust Steak House (see entry).

WYNDHAM ARLINGTON, 1500 East Convention Center Dr.; (800) 442-7275 or (817) 261-8200, Guest Fax (817) 548-2873. Internet www.wyndham.com. *E.* Has 310 smoking and non-smoking rooms and suites in a 19-story building priced at $150-$185 a night. Located in the heart of the Arlington entertainment district, at Copeland Road and Ball Park Way, south of Interstate 30 and next door to the 110,000-square-foot Arlington Convention Center. There are ten restaurants, cafes, and bars within one-half mile.

Opened in 1985 as a Sheraton, this hotel was known from 1993 until 1998 as Arlington Marriott, then underwent a multimillion-dollar renovation to make it "the showpiece hospitality property in Arlington and a very luxurious four-star hotel," according to a company spokesperson. As many as 200 additional rooms were planned, which would make it the third largest Tarrant County hotel. It has 21,200 square feet of meeting space and the largest meeting room can accommodate 700 persons.

Amenities: Safe-deposit boxes, restaurant & sports bar, in-room coffeemakers and complimentary coffee, irons & ironing boards, hair dryers, dataports, business center, outdoor swimming pool, indoor fitness center, jogging trail, laundry and valet service, notary public, airline desk, gift shop. Also C, CF, CM, HC, HR, RS.

East of here is Six Flags Over Texas entertainment park and across Interstate 30 the Hurricane Harbor, formerly a Wet & Wild water theme park. This is the closest hotel to the Ballpark in Arlington (see individual entries), home of the Texas Rangers baseball team. Golf and tennis are available nearby. No airport shuttle is available, but the hotel van will take you within a radius of three miles at no charge. There is free daily trolley service to and from the Ballpark and Six Flags, roughly 9:30 am-6:30 pm.

Bed and Breakfasts ─────────────────

In Arlington, a bed and breakfast option would be **Sanford House, Ltd.,** a French country-style frame house at 506 North Center St., (817) 861-2129, southwest of Six Flags (see entry). It has seven rooms, each with its private bath and different decor. There is a library at the top of the spiral staircase and fireplace in the parlor. You can also enjoy the outdoor swimming pool and a garden with a gazebo.

DINING

Arlington bans smoking in public places, with some exceptions. Restaurants with smoking designations must have a ventilation system that removes air from the building, or a separate ventilation system with a physical barrier.

Barbecue ──────────────────────────

Bodacious Bar-B-Q, 1206 East Division St.; (817) 860-4248. *I*. Open Mon-Sat 11 am-9 pm, closed Sundays. Located in northeast Arlington, east of Collins Street (also known as FM 157) and a few blocks from Comfort Inn (see listing). Once part of Dixie Overland Highway, which connected Savannah, Georgia, and San Diego 2,700 miles to the west, this stretch of the two-lane road was named Division Street in 1914. By 1930, Division was paved and widened to four lanes as it remains today. At the intersection with Collins, Arlington erected its first traffic light in 1923.

"No beefing about the brisket here, whether you get the combo plate or a chopped beef sandwich," says the *Fort Worth Star-Telegram* reviewer. The most popular are barbecue and rib plates, all around $10 each. There are also beef, turkey, and ham sandwiches. All items can also be sold by the pound for take-outs. Desserts include pecan pie, banana pudding, and lemon ice-box pie.

Brazilian

Rodizio Grill, 4040 South Cooper St.; (817) 417-7600. M. Open Sun-Thu 11 am-11 pm, Fri-Sat 11 am-midnight. Has a full bar. Smoking on patio. Adults pay $11 for all-you-can-eat lunch and $16 for dinner. Children under 6 years eat free, 7-12 years $5 for lunch, $7 for dinner. Located one block north of Interstate 20, across the street from The Parks at Arlington Mall (see entry) and next door to Bennigan's.

A Brazilian-style steakhouse with 15 kinds of steak and a 35-item salad bar that includes romaine, potato, and Caesar's. Salmon and Brazilian sausage are also served. The servers, dressed as southern Brazilian gauchos, are armed with two-foot skewers of meat that they carve for the patrons. Each table has a wooden signal—green at one end and red the other—which you display if you want more meat or want it to stop coming.

"Four cuts of beef are offered, of which we preferred the fraldinha, which are tender tips," notes the *Fort Worth Star-Telegram*. The reviewer noted, however, that the two sirloin offerings were "mundane," and the lamb seemed to be "a little dumbed-down," as if the steakhouse feared diners wouldn't care for "true lamb flavor."

Caribbean

Rosy's Caribbean Restaurant & Sports Bar, 1004 East Division St.; (817) 267-3434. M. Open Mon-Thu 11 am-9:30 pm, Fri 11 am-10:30 pm, Sat noon-9:30 pm. Located in northeast Arlington, east of Collins Street (also known as FM 157), and next door to Fiesta Motor Inn and Caravan Motor Hotel, not the two most pleasant hostelries.

A Cuban-Dominican-Mexican restaurant that also serves seafood, such as lobster and shrimp. "Plan to order six hours ahead if you want paella," advises the *Fort Worth Star-Telegram* reviewer. Appetizers include shrimp cocktail and beef empanadas. There are several soups and salads, including cow tripe soup Caribbean style. Among seafood dishes, you can try the above-mentioned paella—the costliest dish at Rosy's—which includes rice, shrimp, chicken, clams, and lobster. It is followed, in descending price order, by lobster stuffed with seafood, lobster in Caribbean sauce, and several varieties of shrimp entrees. Steaks, pork chops, and beef stew are also on the menu. Or you can try several kinds of chicken prepared Caribbean style. Among Mexican dishes, the most expensive entrees are chicken and beef fajitas.

Chinese

Arc-en-Ciel, 2208 New York Ave. at Pioneer Pkwy. (Spur 303); (817) 469-9999. M. Open Mon-Thu 11 am-10 pm, Fri 11 am-11 pm, Sat 10 am-11 pm, Sun 10 am-10 pm. Dim sum appetizer dishes are served daily until 3 pm. Wheelchair-accessible, no smoking area. Banquet facilities next door can accommodate 1,600. Located in east Arlington, west of Watson Road (also known as State Highway 360) and south of Interstate 30.

"With an encyclopedic Chinese and Vietnamese menu of 281 items and a gigantic dining room that looks like a hotel ballroom and packs in the crowds, Arc-en-Ciel makes a big impression," says the *Dallas Morning News,* adding that the food is prepared with the same attentiveness one will find in a small, family-run restaurant. Arc-en-Ciel (French for "rainbow") boasts mouth-watering appetizer dishes known as "dim sum," which loosely translates as "hot delights." The *Fort Worth Star-Telegram* notes, "Standouts are hot and sour soup, rare beef with lime sauce, and charcoal-broiled pork over vermicelli. While the Vietnamese dishes will knock you over, the Szechuan, Hunan and Cantonese meals are also worth trying." You can bring your own alcoholic beverages.

There are several other fine restaurants along the Asian "restaurant row" on Pioneer Parkway.

French

Cacharel, 2221 East Lamar Blvd., Suite 910; (817) 640-9981. *E.* Open for lunch Mon-Fri 11 am-2 pm, for dinner Mon-Fri 5:30-9:30 pm. Full service bar. No smoking. Wheelchair-accessible. Located on the ninth floor of the office building that also houses WBAP radio station, a couple of blocks from the Hilton Hotel (see entry) and within the sight of the Six Flags rollercoasters. "That's the Six Flags oil derrick, not the Eiffel Tower you see out the ninth-story window," says the *Fort Worth Star-Telegram,* "but Cacharel's atmosphere is as close to France as you're likely to get locally."

"With country French decor, this fixed-price refuge easily tops

Arlington's dining scene," says the *D Magazine* restaurant reviewer, while *Texas Monthly* declares: "We were delighted with our salads of Belgian endive, apples, walnuts, and Roquefort, and crab cakes on a rich cream sauce were both artistic and tasty." Notes the *Dallas Morning News*: "Service suave and assured."

The fixed-price menu, which changes daily, might include escargot Cacharel and Caesar salad. It also showcases grilled swordfish steak, Maryland crab cakes, roasted breast of duck, or center-cut pork rib chop. A la carte selections include the $50 steak and lobster combination and financially a bit more bearable lobster tail. Twenty-ounce T-bone steak, 16-ounce bone-in ribeye, 14-ounce New York strip, and 8-ounce filet mignon round up the grill selections, which also includes grilled filet of Texas ostrich. New York-style cheesecake and chocolate mousse, which "evaporates on contact with your palate," are two among the desserts in this costly but elegant eatery with pink table linen.

Hamburgers

Al's Hamburgers, 1001 Green Oaks Blvd., N.E.; (817) 275-8918. *I*. Open Mon-Thu 11 am-10 pm, Fri-Sat 11 am-11 pm. Located in north Arlington, north of Interstate 30 and east of Collins Street, also known as FM 157.

Probably the most famous burger joint in Arlington. "The '50's are gone but the benchmark burger lives on, courtesy of Al, who has kept the griddle going for a whole new generation of fans," says the *Fort Worth Star-Telegram*, adding that Al's fries and grilled chicken are also worth sampling.

Observes the *New York Times*: "When the lease ran out on Al's in the early 1980's and a shopping-mall developer took over the sacred space that Al's had become (4,000 people attended Al's farewell party), Mr. Mathews took his grill with him, stored it and brought it out again when he opened a new place in 1987."

Al's burgers used to be only 80 percent lean, but in trying to serve more health-conscious customers, the establishment changed to using leaner meat—chuck, at 89 to 92 percent lean. Mrs. Mathews told the reporter that what might appear to be grease on the hamburger was really condensation.

Italian

Italy, 2221 Browning Dr.; (817) 276-8687/3200. *I*. Open for lunch and dinner Mon-Fri 11 am-10 pm, Sat-Sun noon-10 pm. Located in southeast Arlington, west of New York Avenue, between Arkansas Lane and Pioneer Parkway.

The owner was born in Sicily to Albanian parents. He arrived in the U.S. in 1990 and worked at pizzerias in New York City and several restaurants in Dallas before opening this eatery in 1996. The *Fort Worth Star-Telegram* describes it modestly as an "Authentic New York-style neighborhood Italian restaurant with pizza, pasta and Italian entrees, plus the best stromboli and calzone on the planet." On another occasion, the *Star-Telegram* declares that "You'd have to go to Italy—the country, that is—to get better calzone." Chef's and antipasto are two among the salads. Chicken and veal entrees are offered as marsala, francese, cacciatore, picata, and parmigiana. Seafood dishes are the most expensive. New York-style pastas, such as fettucine, lasagna, manicotti, canelloni, and ravioli are also offered. There are Italian sausage, chicken, and veal parmigiana sandwiches. Pizzas are available with numerous toppings. For dessert try the Italian cheesecake.

Pasta Oggi, 5743 Southwest Green Oaks Blvd.; (817) 561-7500/7501. M. Open for lunch and dinner Mon-Sat 10 am-10 pm, Sun noon-9 pm. Located in southwest Arlington, south of Interstate 20, in Lincoln Plaza shopping center.

"Today's Pasta," as the restaurant's name translates from Italian, was opened in 1996 by transplanted New Yorkers. "Excellent appetizers, pasta, pizza, chicken and veal dishes in pleasantly unfussy setting," says the *Dallas Morning News* reviewer. Minestrone soup, mozzarella sticks, baked mushrooms, and fried calamari are some of the soups and appetizers. The veal selections include parmigiana, Siciliana, and with peppers; those with chicken include marsala, cacciatore, and lemon-sauteed picata. Among the dozen pastas, you can select from fettucini, cavatelli, rigatoni, tortellini, linguine, and, yes, spaghetti. Neapolitan pizzas are also featured. For those on the run there are hot and cold sandwiches. The menu notes to "please feel free to bring in your own wine."

Piccolo Mondo, 829 East Lamar Blvd. at North Collins Rd.; (817) 265-9174, Internet www.piccolomondo.com. M. Open for lunch Mon-Fri 11:30 am-2:30 pm, for dinner Mon-Thu 5:30-10:30 pm, Fri-Sat 5:30-11 pm, Sun 5-10 pm. Wheelchair-accessible. Has a smoking area. Located in the Parkway Center in north Arlington.

One of the more popular Arlington dineries that on its Internet page quotes *D Magazine* as rating it one of the "best restaurants in America" and the *Fort Worth Star-Telegram* as saying that it serves "appealing and satisfying Italian continental fare featuring shellfish, salmon, veal, gnocchi and pasta."

Appetizers include prosciutto e melone and escargot alla Romana. The costliest seafood entree is lobster tail with angel hair pasta, followed by two versions of shrimp. Lobster tail with broiled medallion of beef tenderloin and broiled New York strip steak are also for those with deep pockets. Gnocchi al pomodoro, penne con broccoli, and eggplant parmigiana are three among the house specialties. Chicken and vegetarian dishes are also on the menu. Pastas include spaghetti, linguini, fettucine, tortellini, and baked manicotti. If you dare, add a dessert, such as cheesecake, cannoli, or tiramisu.

Mexican

Casa Jose, 2030 South Cooper St.; (817) 265-5423. *I*. Open for breakfast and lunch Mon 7 am-2 pm, for breakfast, lunch and dinner Tue-Thu 7 am-8:30 pm, Fri-Sat 8 am-9:30 pm, Sun for breakfast and lunch 8 am-3 pm. Located in south Arlington, at South Cooper and Spur 303, also known as Pioneer Parkway, between Matlock Road and Davis Drive, across from Auto Zone discount auto parts store.

Casa Jose, approaching the end of its second decade, has split dining areas, with one section actually an enclosed patio, which is open during the warm weather, the other decorated with posters and a painting of Selena, the Texas singing phenomenon who was murdered in 1995. "It doesn't get any more down-home than this when it comes to Mexican cooking," says the *Fort Worth Star-Telegram*, while *D Magazine* notes, "The best Tex-Mex cafe in Arlington offers all the regular Tex-Mex dishes but specializes in soft flour tortilla tacos." Breakfast is served most of the day.

Excluding shrimp plates, few dishes at Casa Jose are over $10. You can consider beef and chicken fajitas, club steak ranchero or grilled steak strips, crispy or soft beef or chicken tacos, tamales, enchiladas, chicken flautas, beef tostadas, and grilled catfish. There are no desserts available, but you can treat yourself to fried flour tortillas dusted with cinnamon sugar and served with honey.

Cozymel's, 1300 East Copeland Rd.; (817) 469-9595. *M*. Open for lunch and dinner Sun-Thu 11 am-10 pm, Fri-Sat 11 am-11 pm. Reservations are suggested on weekends. Has Sunday brunch. Located in north Arlington. Cajun-cuisine Pappadeaux Seafood Kitchen, at 1304 East Copeland, is also nearby.

The restaurant, which opened in 1996, is one of about a dozen nationwide and named after Cozumel Mexican beaches. The history on the menu traces its name to a small Mexican grocery and cafe, where a freshly painted sign for Mercado Cozumel was caught in a rainstorm, causing the letter "u" to run into a "y". "Confounding low chain-restaurant expectations, Cozymel's taking the 'yuck' out of Yucatan cuisine and innovating with such items as lamb fajitas and succulent seafood," says the *Fort Worth Star-Telegram* reviewer.

Appetizers include shrimp and bay scallops, crab cakes, Mexican fondue, and quesadillas. There are a couple of soups and salads. Traditional favorites include a variety of chicken and cheese enchiladas. Burritos come charbroiled, with shredded pork, beef, or chicken. Shrimp, sword-fish, grilled salmon, and Yucatan sea bass are a few examples of the coastal fare, served with Yucatan rice, Mexican vegetables, and black beans. Fajitas come in a variety of flavors and sizes, including the one-pound beef or chicken special for two for less than $20. There is also grilled chicken breast, roasted beef, and tenderloin medallions. You have nine varieties of sauces and five kinds of Mexican peppers to cus-tomize your meal.

Mercado Juarez, 125 Interstate 20 East; (817) 557-9776. M. Open for lunch and dinner Sun-Thu 11 am-10 pm, Fri-Sat 11:30 am-11 pm. Located in south Arlington, about one-half mile east of The Parks at Arlington Mall and one block east of Matlock Road. It is situated next door to Hampton Inn hotel and near Iron Skillet, a 24-hour restaurant.

Open in 1996, Mercado sports terra-cotta walls, wrought iron, vault-ed ceilings, and heavy carved chairs. "Festive digs and quick service plus excellent fare make this spots to return to," says the *Dallas Morning News*. "Our picks include Juarez special platter, fajita adobada, and cabrito al pastor." There are nachos, fajita salad, and quesadillas for starters, and tortilla or bean soup. Most dinner entrees are below $15, including mesquite-roasted goat, mentioned by the *News,* shrimp and vegetables, charbroiled pork ribs, half of a marinated chicken, and a variety of fajitas. For about $40, four diners can have a Fajita Blast, with beef, chicken, and pork fajitas served with grilled shrimp. You can also enjoy orange roughy fish and shrimp stuffed with white or Monterrey cheese. There are steaks and chicken dishes. If adventurous, you can try such Mexican plates as chimichangas, chili, cheese, beef, or chicken rellenos, or cheddar cheese enchiladas.

Ninfa's, 923 Six Flags Dr.; (817) 640-6462. M. Open for lunch and dinner Sun-Thu 11 am-10 pm, Fri-Sat 11 am-11 pm. Located at Interstate 30 and Highway 360, near Six Flags Over Texas (see entry), where thousands of out-of-town tourists always outnumber the locals.

Ninfa's parent corporation owns some 35 Italian, Cajun, and Mexican restaurants in Texas and Louisiana. Appetizers take half a page on the menu, from the bean and cheese nachos to the fiesta plat-ter; in-between you will find chili con queso, pork and chicken fajitas, jalapenos stuffed with shrimp and cheese, and spicy ground beef nachos. Among the soups and salads, there is caldo xochitl (chicken breast in broth) with Mexican rice, as well as taco, fajita, and gua-camole salads. Chalupas and tacos are mostly under $10 each and served with Mexican rice and beans. Except for Tejas Combo—with beef taco and cheese enchilada, also beef, chicken, or pork fajitas—and El Rancho, which run higher, most combo platters are around $10. Mariscos (seafood), served with rice, beans, pico de gallo, guacamole, and chili con queso, are the most expensive entrees, followed by jumbo shrimp, and beef, chicken, or pork tenderloin fajitas platters. The *Fort Worth Star-Telegram* calls attention to Ninfa's "Lethal margaritas in festive patio setting with attentive, pleasant service."

Middle-Eastern

Queen of Egypt, 423 Fielder North Pl.; (817) 276-3232. *I.* Open for lunch Mon-Sat 11 am-2 pm, for dinner Mon-Thu 5-9 pm, Fri-Sat 5-10 pm, closed Sundays. Located inside Fielder Plaza shopping center at Fielder and Randol Mill roads, a couple of miles west of the Ballpark in Arlington (see entry).

The owner grew up in Egypt and owned an Egyptian restaurant in New York City before moving to the Metroplex in the mid-1980s. This is a modest eatery with good food and friendly service. Appetizers include dolma (grape leaves stuffed with rice), sambosa (phyllo pastries filled with ground beef), and falafel (deep-fried meat balls). Among the soups, you can try harira, a traditional cream of tomato soup; among salads feta (lettuce, tomato, cucumber, feta cheese) or tabbuli (parsley, wheat, onion, and tomato).

There are several kebabs, including shish kebab and lamb kebab of marinated cubes of lamb. Mossaca (grilled eggplant stuffed with beef sirloin), gyros (strips of lamb and beef), and baked Egyptian lasagna with ground beef sirloin are but three traditional dishes available. You can also try beef, chicken, or lamb shwarma, or strips of such meats. Yes, Queen of Egypt does have baklava dessert and kahwa Turkish coffee.

Sports Bars

Humperdink's Bar & Grill, 700 Six Flags Dr.; (817) 640-8553. *M.* Open daily 11 am-2 am. Located across the street from Six Flags Over Texas and across Interstate 30 from Hurricane Harbor entertainment parks (see individual entries). Amerisuites and Sleep Inn hotels are nearby. The Big Horn Brewery, Arlington's first brewpub, is situated across the street.

Open in 1996, this is probably the largest Humperdink's in the Metroplex. Having the outside resemblance of the red-bricked Arlington Ballpark up the street, it contains a two-story bar and a large game room. You can see from here the wooden curves of Six Flags' Judge Roy Scream roller coaster across the street.

Starters include nachos, fried mozzarella, armadillo eggs, and potato skins. Among the salads, you can pick from Caesar's, spicy sirloin, and chicken almond. A variety of burgers and several sandwiches, such as blackened tuna and Philly, are also on the menu. Grilled steaks, Texas or Italian style, are the most expensive items, particularly the 20-ounce porterhouse. There are several pastas, as well as house features, such as chicken fried steak.

Steaks

Trail Dust Steak House, 2300 East Lamar Blvd.; (817) 640-6411. E. Open for dinner from 5 pm daily and from noon Sundays. Live bands every night. Located across Interstate 30 from Six Flags Over Texas (see entry).

"Don't wear a tie; they cut them off," says the *Fort Worth Star-Telegram*. "Huge, mesquite-grilled steaks, Old West atmosphere." The *Dallas Morning News* cautions about the "killer pecan pie, cobblers."

You can pick from among the starters, such as chilled shrimp, cheese sticks, and fried zucchini. It is the steaks, however, that rule at Trail Dust: the costliest is the 50-ounce porterhouse and it may take you the whole evening to finish it, pardner. Other selections, in descending price order, include the 32-ounce porterhouse or T-bone, 12-ounce tenderloin, 12-ounce New York strip, and 12-ounce sirloin. You might also find it hard to resist babyback pork ribs, mesquite-broiled swordfish, fried catfish, fried shrimp, or chicken. Desserts include cheesecake and chocolate fudge cake.

Other Trail Dust Steak Houses are located in northwest Dallas and at 21717 Lyndon B. Johnson Freeway in Mesquite, next to the Mesquite Championship Rodeo (see entry).

THE PERFORMING ARTS

Ballet Arlington, 1303 West Abram St.; (817) 465-2268, Fax (817) 465-5636, Internet www.balletarlington.org.

A nonprofit company formed in 1997 by the Russian-born Svetlana Stanova and her husband Nikolay Semikov, a former principal dancer with the Moscow's Bolshoy Ballet and Kirov Ballet. "We are a very young company, and it takes a long time to develop dancers," Stanova told the *Dallas Morning News*. "I think Arlington is ready for a classical ballet company." Semikov stood out at Fort Worth Dallas Ballet (see entry) for his immensely authoritative interpretation of prince roles, a testament to the years of intensive schooling in style and character that Russians are noted for, observed the *News'* dance critic.

Stanova was accepted at the official school of the Bolshoy Ballet at the age of ten. Upon graduation, she joined the Moscow Classical Ballet and toured Europe. Before coming to the U.S. in 1988, Stanova taught at the State Ballet School in Krasnogorsk, near Moscow. She has danced for the Berkshire Ballet and taught at the New Jersey Ballet School.

Her husband, Nikolay Semikov, also began his ballet training at the age of ten, at the renowned Kirov Ballet in St. Petersburg. He was a principal dancer with both the Bolshoy Ballet Theatre and the Moscow Classical Ballet Theatre.

Paul Mejia, former artistic director of the Fort Worth Dallas Ballet, joined the company in 1998. His staging of *Romeo and Juliet*, based on Tchaikovsky's score, brought to Arlington two principal dancers with the Bolshoy Ballet: Anna Antonicheva and Dmitry Belogolovtsev, winners of the gold and silver medals respectively in the 1998 USA International Ballet competition.

The 1999-2000 season featured *The Nutcracker, Apollo*, based on music by Stravinsky, and *Hamlet* by Tchaikovsky. All performances are held at the Texas Hall of the University of Texas at Arlington, 701 South Nederman Drive.

CATS (Creative Arts Theatre & School), 1100 West Randol Mill Rd.; (817) 861-CATS. Located near the Arlington Ballpark and Six Flags entertainment complex (see individual entries).

CATS was established in 1977 as a nonprofit cultural art institute to draw on the talents of young people in drama, musical, ballet, and modern dance. CATS has staged more than 230 productions since its founding by a husband-and-wife team. It is the only youth theater in North Texas and one of only about 60 in the U.S. The cast of *Pecos Bill*, a 2000 production, numbered 215, ranging in age from 8 to 18.

Among its recent theatrical productions were *The Secret Garden, Winnie the Pooh, Beauty and the Beast*, and *Little Women*, a dramatization of Louisa May Alcott's novel of the same name.

Le Theatre de Marionette, 207 North Elm St.; (817) 275-1516. Le Theatre is a children's theater dedicated to the revival of the puppetry arts through its presentation of classic children's stories and dramatic scores.

Theatre Arlington, 305 West Main St.; (817) 275-7661. Located one block west of the Arlington Museum of Art, on the city's only street that might pass for downtown. Johnnie High's Country Music Revue (see entry) and Arlington City Hall are about a block away.

A quarter-century old, Jimmy Kier Memorial Theatre, as it is formally known, presents award-winning plays and musicals in a theater that seats 200.

Among its recent performances the theater staged Neil Simon's *Laughter on the 23rd Floor*, about a roomful of gag writers for a television show of the 1950s.

NIGHTLIFE

Cowboys Arlington, 2540 East Abram St.; (817) 265-1535. Open Wed-Thu & Sat 7 pm-2 am, Fri 5 pm-2 am, Sun 4 pm-2 am. Cover charge. Wednesdays are ladies' nights and Fridays they pay no cover charge 7-9 pm, Saturdays until 8 pm. Live music nightly. Located in a former Kmart store, east of Watson Road, also known as State Highway 360. A rugged and authentic country honky-tonk joint that opened in 1994. It is mobbed on Wednesdays and Fridays, when the large parking lot is often filled by the early evening. "Most come to dance rather than listen," says *D Magazine*. Once inside and if you like shufflin' and two-steppin', you'll have a real ball on the 3,500-square-foot dance floor—of course "the largest in Texas." The *Dallas Morning News* says, "There's plenty of boy-meets-girl action going on here and a variety of dance music that brings in a crossover crowd."

Dance lessons could be had for free Thu-Fri 7-8 pm, and Sundays 4:30-8 pm. For those wanting to show off their dexterity there is a mechanical bull, which never gets tired, as well as pool and craps tables.

Another country place in Arlington is **John B's,** at 2005 West Arkansas Ln.; (817) 265-3702. It is open daily 4 pm-2 am. There is no cover charge. Has recorded music.

Daddy Rocks, 428 East Lamar St.; (817) 461-2583. Open Mon 1-7 pm, Tue-Fri 4 pm-2 am, Sat 6 pm-2 am. Located in northeastern Arlington, north of Interstate 30.

A blues joint. Live music Mon-Sat, starting at 9 pm. Karaoke Tuesdays, rock jam Wednesdays. "Nothing fancy neighborhood spot once known as Fatso's, where college kids and 20- and 30-something mingle, shoot pool and dance to blues and rock stuff," says the *Fort Worth Star-Telegram*.

J. Gilligan's Bar & Grill, 407 East South St.; (817) 274-8561. Open Sun-Wed 11 am-1 am, Thu-Sat 11 am-2 am. Live entertainment Thu-Sat, starting at 10 pm; also local rock acts. No cover charge. Located in central Arlington, east of University of Texas at Arlington and south of Abram Street.

"Big ol' friendly Gilligan's sets the standard for college bars in the area: a good menu of standard bar food and decent local bands playing on a postage-stamp stage," says the *Fort Worth Star-Telegram*. Gilligan's Drafthouse, with pool table and 35 beers on tap, is nearby.

Johnnie High's Country Musical Review, Arlington Music Hall, 224 North Center St.; (817) 226-4400 or (800) 540-5127, Internet www.mid-cities.com/cmr. A live country music stage show featuring a cast of 20 singers, dancers, and musicians Fri-Sat at 7:30 pm.

The tall, lanky native Texan, who was born in 1929, is known for "his boundless energy and upbeat, driven personality. High was a nomad with his show for 20 years," says the *Fort Worth Star-Telegram*, "bouncing from Grapevine to Fort Worth, but he found a home in 1995. Loyal fans, friends and musicians contributed money and labor to remodel the old movie theater at North Center Street."

SIGHTS

Antique Sewing Machine Museum, 804 West Abram St.; (817) 275-0971. CH. Open Mon-Sat 10 am-5 pm. Located north of University of Texas at Arlington (see entry), a few blocks west of what might pass for downtown, in a house built in 1905.

The first *practical* sewing machine was invented in 1846 by American Elias Howe, not Isaac Singer as is commonly thought. A two-thread, lock-stitch machine, it put to use a technology that has never been bettered for garment making. Today's machines still operate on Howe's principle; even computerized machines make no better stitches than Howe's. A German mechanic living in London, Charles Weisenthal was granted a British patent in 1755 for a two-pointed needle with an eye near one of the points that passed through fabric. This needle, however, was attached to an embroidery, not garment-making, machine.

At Frank Smith's four-room Sewing Machine Museum, you can see on exhibit some 155 machines from his collection of more than 200. They date from 1852 (he thinks) to the 1950s. The earliest Howe machine on exhibit dates from 1869. The Civil War-era Folsom Globe machine, brought west into Minnesota by its owner, reputedly was the first sewing machine to cross the Mississippi River. The museum started as a small exhibit for the 1976 Bicentennial celebration at the old Leonards Department Store (see entry) in downtown Fort Worth and traveled around until it opened as the permanent museum here in 1988. Other memorabilia, such as machine tools, patterns, and buttons line the shelves.

In 1996, Smith—who has been in the business of selling and repairing them his entire adult life—built what is supposedly the world's largest working sewing machine, 16 feet long and 10 feet high, with a needle that looks like a dagger and small rope for thread. Taking a year to build and get it to sew, it is now on display in front of the museum.

The Fielder House Museum, including Johnson Plantation Cemetery & Park, 1616 West Abram St.; (817) 460-4001. CH. Open Wed-Fri 10 am-2 pm, Sun 1:30-4:30 pm. Located in central Arlington on the corner of West Abram and Fielder streets.

The two-story red-brick building that houses the Fielder Museum was built as a prairie-style home by the prominent local landowner and community leader James Park Fielder (d. 1948) and his wife in 1914 and was occupied until 1978. The Fielders at one time owned more than 10,000 acres of land and this residence was for many years a popular gathering place and a landmark. The museum, which is the oldest brick residence in Arlington, has two Texas State Historic markers and it opened its doors to the public in 1980.

The City of Arlington purchased and leased the building to the newly-formed Fielder Foundation, which, in addition to this museum, comprises the **M. T. Johnson Plantation Cemetery and Historic Park,** just east of Matlock Road and on the north side of Arkansas Lane, about three miles south of the Fielder House.

The area was once part of large land holdings of Col. Middleton Tate Johnson (1810-1866), a noted Texas Ranger who is buried here. Johnson founded the site for Fort Worth, gave the land for its courthouse, and is known as the father of Tarrant County. Johnson County was named after him.

Johnson and his wife came from Tennessee in 1839. Their plantation was like a town with buildings and houses and streets, according to one source. Houses were in rows facing the streets, which cut through the slave quarters. There was a shoe shop, blacksmith, gin mill, spinning mill, and a store. The slaves learned they were freed in 1865, but all of those on the Johnson plantation chose to remain as paid workers, says Fort Worth historian Bill Fairley.

Several log structures that predate Arlington have been moved to the Johnson Plantation Cemetery and Park. They include two log cabins, a one-room schoolhouse, and a farm equipment barn. One of them, the Watson cabin, is a dogtrot, or two-room cabin, built in 1855 by J. B. Watson, who was son of the founder of Watson Community, a site north of the Pioneer Trail. The structures are open by appointment only.

Near **Founders Park,** actually at Marrow Bone Springs—east of Matlock Road and just south of Arkansas Lane—the first Grand Council of Indians was held, starting on September 29, 1843. Some 400 Indian chiefs and warriors met with generals Edward H. Tarrant and G. W. Terrell, representing Texas president Sam Houston, smoked the peace pipe, and signed the first treaty that was ratified by the Republic of Texas on January 31, 1844.

It was not well known that more than 150 years earlier, French explorer Rene Robert Cavelier, Sieur de la Salle, was murdered here by his own men. After exploring along the Mississippi River, La Salle claimed everything west of the river for France. He made his way to what was then a small water source from which he planned to continue his explorations. The Gallic adventurer was murdered at Marrow

Bone Springs in 1687 in a dispute over animal marrow bones, which at the time were valuable nourishment.

South of the Fielder House, at Mayfield Road and east of Cooper Street, Colonel Johnson's plantation included a large, two-story house that became Johnson Station, a stagecoach stop for three forks of the Overland Stage route to Dallas, Fort Worth, and Austin. Buried at the Johnson Station Cemetery here are settlers who obtained their land from the Peters Emigration & Land Company of Louisville, Kentucky, which was given a grant to colonize Texas in 1841.

Northwest of Johnson Station and Cemetery, a granite marker, just west of the Village Creek bridge on Pioneer Parkway, commemorates the last Indian raid in Tarrant County on May 24, 1841. On that day, General Tarrant led the attack on the village of the Caddo tribe, which was located along Village Creek, and his militia burned 225 Indian dwellings. Much of the battle site is now under water. The Indian tribes who had long inhabited this valley permanently abandoned their settlements here after this raid.

Hurricane Harbor/Formerly Wet & Wild, 1800 East Lamar Blvd. at Ballpark Way; (817) 265-3356. Open daily 10 am-9 pm May 22-August 16, and weekends only until the middle of September. Admission depends on height, CH for parking. Season passes are available. Located across Interstate 30 from the Arlington Ballpark and Six Flags Over Texas (see individual entries).

Whatever Six Flags does on the ground and in the air, Hurricane Harbor does in the water. Opened in 1983, this is the most popular water theme park in the Metroplex, especially in July and August, when the asphalt melts in the scorching sun. More than 600,000 visitors come every summer to this park, one of the ten largest in the nation. It bore the Wet & Wild moniker for 14 years and was renamed Hurricane Harbor in 1997.

The 47-acre park has pools, 21 twisting and plunging slides, and other thrilling rides from heights of up to six stories. The 60-foot-high and 500-foot-long **Black Hole** slide, resembling "a flying saucer with tentacles," twists and turns in complete darkness and usually has the longest lines. **Der Stuka,** named after the German dive bomber, is a seven-story climb to the top of the tower, after which you lie down and drop 72 feet. There is **Caribbean Swing** sky coaster, **Bubba Tub** tube ride, **Geronimo** serpentine flume, and two enclosed serpentine flumes, **Blue Niagara** and **Hydra Maniac.**

The 830-foot-high **Sea Wolf** water raft ride forces visitors to maneuver a four-person bobsled at speeds up to 50 miles an hour; toboggans are powered by water blasting at the rate of 4,000 gallons per minute. In **Blue Raider,** two-passenger inner tubes zip 530 feet down a twisting slide that ends with a huge splash. Four separate slides, side-by-side, blast riders with 1,000 gallons of water per minute through each slide barrel in what is called **Shotgun Falls.** There is also a 231-foot-long open flume **Atlantic Panic,** where sliders are pushed by the flow of 1,500 gallons of water per minute, and 244-foot-long **Caribbean Chaos,** which are both hurricane inspired.

In 1999, the park inaugurated a $3-million, 40,000-square-foot family-oriented **Hook's Lagoon** with a five-story "treehouse," a pirate ship, and three pools. It includes dozens of effects, such as squirt guns, water drops, slides, and waterfalls. Hook's Lagoon is located on the east side of the park, in an area occupied by miniature golf and basketball courts. The location allows families to have their own place, away from the thrill rides, which are concentrated on the west side of the park.

More than three million gallons of water are pumped through Hurricane Harbor. Water for rides on the east side is heated in early and late season. Recirculating daily, it is filtered and treated. There is also a two-acre water playground for small children, with waterfalls and slides, and a shallow pool. Lifeguards are on duty throughout the park. Seven more acres of the former FunSphere, an entertainment park that closed in 1995, were also incorporated into Hurricane Harbor. It includes a four-court sand beach volleyball area and two volleyball courts.

Six Flags Over Texas, 2201 Road to Six Flags at State Hwy. 360; Ticket Information, Special Events Information, and Parking Information, (817) 530-6000; Internet www.sixflags.com/Texas. The park is open daily 10 am-10 pm during the summer; on weekends, in spring and fall closing times vary. Admission is $36 for adults and $18 for children under 48 inches plus tax, although discounts are available. Some rides have height requirements. Admission fee includes most of the rides and shows. Parking fee. An ATM machine is outside the front gate. Ice chests and picnic baskets are not permitted in the park. No smoking. A booklet is available about services for the handicapped. Rental strollers and air-conditioned kennels are available at a charge. Hurricane Harbor (see entry) water amusement park is across Interstate 30.

If coming from Fort Worth, you will likely be heading east on Interstate 30, or the Old Dallas/Fort Worth Turnpike. It should not take you more than 20 minutes from downtown Cowtown. Coming from Dallas, you will be going west on Interstate 30.

Employing 2,700, this is probably the most popular entertainment park in the Metroplex. Conceived in the late 1950s by a Dallas businessman, Angus G. Wynne, it opened in the summer of 1961. With about three million visitors a year, it is the second most popular tourist attraction in Fort Worth or Arlington, just behind the Texas Rangers Baseball Club. Arlington's Six Flags is among the 20 largest theme parks in the U.S. and is larger than Disneyland.

The six flags—Spanish, French, Mexican, Republic of Texas, Confederate, and American—that have flown over Texas between 1519 and 1865 are commemorated in the name of this amusement park, one of the earliest American theme parks. Started on 65 acres of empty prairie land, it has since been enlarged to 205 acres and encompasses eleven themed areas.

You will enjoy roller coaster rides, like the 14-story 1990 **Texas Giant,** whose 143-foot climb is followed by a 62-mile-an-hour ride; it is believed to be one of the best wooden roller coasters in the country. There is a 1976 17-story parachute drop, called **Texas Chute-Out, G-Force,** with gondolas dropping like falling elevators, and the 1978 **Shock Wave** double-loop roller coaster, the world's first vertical back-to-back looping roller coaster. The **Flashback** is another ride that drops from a 125-foot tower and careens through three loops at speeds of 55 miles an hour—and again, but backwards. **The Right Stuff,** a supersonic aviation jet fighter race challenging the sound barrier, was replaced in 1999 with **Escape from Dino Island 3-D,** an animated thrill ride.

Also in 1999, Gotham City Park was developed, with **Batman The Ride,** the park's first inverted roller coaster. The 50-mile-per-hour ride features spiral S curves, two vertical loops, two corkscrews, and six inversions. The 2,700-foot-long Batman coaster is called an inverted coaster because riders' feet dangle as in a ski lift. Batman The Ride and Mr. Freeze are both located in the new Gotham City Park.

Mr. Freeze is billed as the state's tallest, fastest, most technologically advanced roller coaster and is 236 feet high. It is built with a technology that uses linear induction motors, which give the trains enough momentum to top steep hills alone, as opposed to traditional coasters, which require chains and cables to pull the trains uphill before gravity takes over. Linear induction launches the trains from a standstill to more than 70 miles per hour in less than four seconds. After boarding, you will experience a launch through a 190-foot tunnel, unexpectedly corkscrew straight up in the air, then careen straight down backward. There is just one problem: you may have to wait for up to two hours, first in the boiling sun and then in the dark corridors, for a ride that lasts about 45 seconds.

Considering its high admission and parking fees, *FW Weekly* staff named this park the "best tourist trap."

There are Western shows at the **Crazy Horse Saloon** and pop concerts at the 10,000-seat **Music Mill Amphitheater,** but at an additional charge. **Looney Tunes Land** is for younger children. Food and drinks are plentiful, but expensive. Facilities are clean.

There are several restaurants near Six Flags, most within walking distance of several hotels. Among the nearest hotels are La Quinta

Conference Center, some of whose rooms actually overlook the park, as do the small suites at the Ranger Inn Suites. Sleep Inn, with an ATM in the lobby, AmeriSuites, Budgetel, and Rodeway Inn are also nearby.

VISUAL ARTS

Arlington Museum of Art, 201 West Main St.; (817) 275-4600. *NCH.* Open Wed-Sat 10 am-5 pm. Wheelchair accessible. There is a small gift shop on the ground floor. Located in a whitewashed 1950s restored J.C. Penney department store, north of Abram and east of Cooper streets, across the street from the City Hall, on what is perhaps the only Arlington street that comes even close to resembling downtown in a city without downtown. Theatre Arlington is on the same block and Johnnie High's Country Music Revue (see individual entries) is across the railroad tracks.

Begun 40 years ago as an art association, this is the oldest art organization in Arlington and has a two-story open gallery. It became a museum in 1989 and it is a museum without a permanent collection, a "relentless showcase for homegrown contemporary art." AMA, with an annual operating budget of about $300,000, claims to be the only museum in Texas "dedicated to celebrating and showcasing Texas contemporary art." It is located "in a small, conservative community where the general public often scratches its collective head at edgy contemporary art," according to the *Dallas Observer* weekly.

Eight to ten exhibitions are mounted yearly in the 20,000-square-foot facility with tall ceilings and plenty of natural light. Its director since 1991, native New Yorker Joan Davidow is a former art critic for Dallas's public radio and an assistant curator at the Dallas Museum of Art.

Arlington Galleries ————————————————

Kevin Curry Exhibitions, 2514 White Oak Ln.; (817) 265-4585. Open by appointment. Exhibits mostly works by contemporary Texas artists. **Artists:** David Lamb, Rob Erdle, Robin Germany, Dan Havel, Mary Iron Eyes, Gloria Kenyon, Heather Marcus, Mark Monroe, Eddy Rawlinson, Pehr Smith, Hills Snyder, Mary Vernon.

Rainone Gallery, 1212 West Park Row; (817) 461-5666. Open Mon-Fri 10 am-6 pm. Established 1955. Showcases 19th- and 20th-century American and European art, with emphasis on early Texas and Taos, New Mexico, artists. **Artists:** Albert Bierstadt, William Merritt Chase, Edouard Cortes, E. I. Couse, W. H. Buck Dunton, William Lester, Robert Onderdonk, Norman Rockwell, Charles Russell, and Olin Travis.

The 20,000-square-foot Arlington Museum of Art, located in a 1950s restored department store, across the street from the City Hall, was initiated in 1989. It claims to be the only museum in Texas dedicated to showcasing Texas contemporary art and it is a museum without a permanent collection. (Photo by Yves Gerem)

Upstairs Gallery, 1038 West Abram St., between Cooper St. and Davis Dr.; (817) 277-6961 or 261-0061. Open Tue-Sat 10 am-5 pm. Established 1967. Focuses on paintings, sculpture, pottery, and graphics of mostly Texas artists. **Artists:** Alvis Ballew, Al Brouillette, Larry Harris, Darnell Jones, former UTA professor and 80-plus-year-old Arlington resident Dr. Jess Lord who creates pottery, Judy Mason, Martha Sue Meek, Jessica Neary, Sandy Rabbitt, and Douglas Walton.

SHOPPING

Festival Marketplace, 2900 East Pioneer Pkwy.; (817) 649-8065. Located in east Arlington, at State Highway 360 (also known as Watson Rd.) and Spur 303, a couple of miles south of Six Flags Mall (see entry).

Until 1998 known as Forum Value Mall, the 28-year-old shopping center claims 795,000 square feet of space, with only 20 permanent tenants, but more than 500 booths, kiosks, and carts selling brand-name merchandise at discount prices. Described as "an upscale flea market," it is modeled after a similar mall in Pompano Beach, Florida.

The Parks at Arlington mall, 3811 South Cooper St.; (817) 467-2757 or 467-0200, Internet www.mallibu.com. Located in central Arlington, just north of Interstate 20.

Having 1.2 million square feet of leasable space, this is the second largest mall in Tarrant County and the largest in Arlington. Built in 1988, it has some 170 tenants, including anchor stores, such as **Dillard's, J.C. Penney's, Sears, Foley's,** and **Mervyn's.**

Other shops include **Waldenbooks, Eddie Bauer, Foot Locker, Frederick's of Hollywood, Gadzooks, The Gap, LensCrafters, Merle Norman Cosmetics, Naturalizer Shoes, Radio Shack, Stride Rite Bootery,** and **Whitehall Jewelers,** as well as eateries, such as **Chic-Fill-A, Frullati Cafe, Sbarro Cafe, Steak Place,** and **Wendy's Old Fashioned Hamburgers.**

Six Flags Mall, 2911 East Division St.; (817) 640-1641, Fax (817) 649-1825. Located in northeast Arlington, just east of Watson Road, also known as State Highway 360. Six Flags (see entry) theme park is located less than two miles northwest of here.

Opened in 1970, this is the second largest shopping center in Arlington. It has 1.05 million square feet of leasable space and some 75 tenants, including such anchor stores as **Dillard's, Sears,** and **Foley's.** Also in the mall are shops, such as **Bag 'N Baggage, Foot Locker, Radio Shack,** and **Waldenbooks.**

A nine-screen **Cinemark Theaters,** a marionette theater, and a miniature golf course are also located here.

BITS AND PIECES

Aggie: Graduate of Texas A & M University at College Station. Watch out for thousands of the so-called Aggie jokes.

Ah: Texan for I.

All: Oil, petroleum.

Beggar: Bigger, larger.

Bidness: Business.

Big D: Dallas.

Blue Norther: A strong cold wind from the north; temperatures can drop 30 or 40 degrees in just a few hours.

Buffalo chip: A dropping of cow manure.

Burritos: Large flour tortillas stuffed with rice, beans, meat, or cheese.

Chalupas: Deep-fried corn tortillas.

Chicken-fried steak: An inexpensive piece of steak or cutlet coated with egg batter and fried in fat like chicken, then smothered with thick white gravy.

Chili: Since 1977, the official state dish, whose origins have been debated for a hundred years.

Corny dog: Frankfurter on a stick (most Americans know it as a corn dog), dipped in cornmeal batter that clings to the dog, then deep-fried. First offered at the 1942 State Fair of Texas.

Cowboys: Dallas Cowboys football team.

Cowtown: Fort Worth.

Da boys: Dallas Cowboys.

Enchiladas: Tortillas rolled around cheese, chicken, or beef in chili gravy, with beans and rice.

Fajita: The Tex-Mex specialty made of marinated, grilled meat, flour tortillas, tomatoes, chili peppers, and avocados that calls Dallas home.

Fixin': Getting ready to.

Guacamole: Cold, uncooked dip of mashed avocado and seasonings.

Hog heaven: A state of utter happiness.

Hush puppies: Deep-fried cornmeal and egg ball-shaped Southern side dish.

Longneck: A tall bottle of beer.

Ma'am: Address to woman of almost any age; from "madame."

Margarita: Dallas is the birthplace of this frozen cocktail made of tequila, lime juice, sugar, and salt.

Nacho: Fried tortilla chip appetizer, sprinkled with cheese and jalapeno, invented in Mexico and introduced at Arlington stadium in 1977.

Plumb tuckered out: Tired.

Prickly heat: Hot Texas weather.

Sun Belt: California, Florida, and Texas collectively.

Taco: Soft or crisp tortilla filled with pork or beef.

Tortilla: Thin unleavened cornmeal or wheat bread.

Y'all: You all, one syllable.

INDEX